Rock *and* Popular Music

York University
Department of Music

 KENDALL/HUNT PUBLISHING COMPANY
4050 Westmark Drive Dubuque, Iowa 52002

Credits:

Chapters 1, 6, and 9 from *From Woodstock to the Moon: The Cultural Evolution of Rock Music, Second Edition* by Chas Smith. Copyright © 2003 by Kendall/Hunt Publishing Company. Reprinted by permission.

Chapters 4, 5, and 7 from *Rock and Roll Essentials: A Comprehensive Guide through the Best of Rock and Roll's First Thirty Years* by John R. Turk. Copyright © 2002 by Kendall/Hunt Publishing Company. Reprinted by permission.

Chapters 2, 3, 8, 10 and 11 from *A History of Rock Music* by Stephen Valdez. Copyright © 2004 by Stephen Valdez. Reprinted by permission of Kendall/Hunt Publishing Company.

Cover credits: Guitar images © PhotoDisc, background © Digital Juice

Copyright © 2005 by Kendall/Hunt Publishing Company

ISBN 0-7575-2268-8

All rights reserved. No part of this publication may be reproduced, stored in a retrieval system, or transmitted, in any form or by any means, electronic, mechanical, photocopying, recording, or otherwise, without the prior written permission of the copyright owner.

Printed in the United States of America
10 9 8 7 6 5 4 3 2 1

Contents

Chapter 1
20th-Century America
The Landscape of Possibilities 1

Chapter 2
The Blues 37

Chapter 3
Country and Western Influences 57

Chapter 4
Searching for Masterpieces from the 1950s 67

Chapter 5
The Lean Years 81

Chapter 6
The Early Sixties 87

Chapter 7
The Beatles and the Stones 111

Chapter 8
Folk and Related Styles 143

Chapter 9
The 1970s—Out with the Old—In with the New 175

Chapter 10
Heavy Metal 199

Chapter 11
Fusions 219

1 20th-Century America
The Landscape of Possibilities

The Many Voices of the New World

As the people of America merged together, regardless of the circumstances that brought them there, it was inevitable that their cultures, art, music, and beliefs would merge together to form a wholly new culture. The results of this mass merging, sometimes referred to as the melting pot, climaxed in the late 1960s as America exploded with new ideas about civil rights (free speech, black rights, and women's liberation), technology (space, communications, and computers), politics and international policy (Vietnam), and renewed spirituality (neo-paganism, Eastern mysticism). Rock music united all of these ideas into a new view of the world and the possibilities of the human race and gave voice to the concerns of a generation that was prepared to question all authority.

But taken a step or two back, the ideas of rebelling against dominating authority seem part of the American landscape. The underdogs and their struggles and concerns are exactly what makes rock music so endearing. It is the music of the lower and middle classes of America—the underdogs. And when we root out the evolution of the music, we find countless stories in every era of its development of the music giving voice to their concerns.

The Story of the Delta

The story of the Africans brought to America as slaves is indeed a sad chapter in U.S. history. It is the story of a collective people who endured hundreds of years of denial of property, family, mind, and self. They could own no property. Their families were torn apart, with children torn from mothers' arms and sold off. The slaves were severely whipped, beaten and murdered on a daily basis. They were kept uneducated and ignorant of the world they came from. Most horrific of all, their sense of community and self, of who they were as a people and individually, that they even were human, was systematically removed from their awareness. Or so the slave masters thought.

The Oral Tradition

The American bound slaves from Africa, like native America and all tribal cultures, came from what is known as an oral tradition. Meaning that the history and varied stories and beliefs of the tribes were handed down orally. One generation to the next, the collective memory of tribal culture is passed down via storytelling and song. Nothing is written down, as western and Asian civilizations had been doing for hundreds, even thousands, of years. Every bit of information in the collective knowledge of a tribe must be protected and transmitted around fires at night and in the fields at day. There were no books, no magazines, no encyclopedias, no documents, not even glyphs chiselled into stone. There are transitional tribes, who painted picture stories on cave walls or created visual earthworks indicating some sense of mythos and spirituality (a good example is the earthwork of the Adena Serpent Mound in Ohio, which is the image of a snake with mouth open and either swallowing or producing from its mouth a large egg), but by and large the tribes passed the detailed majority of their history through oral transmission. When coming into contact with a culture with a written tradition this puts the oral based tribal culture at a grave disadvantage.

One of the most striking examples of the awareness of this disadvantage and the clash of culture can be heard in the song *The Talking Leaves* by Johnny Cash, off of his *Bitter Tears* album *(Columbia Rec. 66507)*. It is the true story of Saquoia of the Cherokee nation.

Listen

THE TALKING LEAVES
JOHNNY CASH

This song illustrates the strong conflict of culture between societies based on oral tradition versus those based on written tradition. The written tradition culture stands at a strong advantage over the oral tradition culture, and this advantage was exploited to great affect by American slave masters and the Indian killers alike. The oral tradition, however, facilitates a storytelling, song singing culture that actually was the only means by which the African slaves in America had to hang on to their sense of self, culture, and society.

Griots

The most important people to a tribe are the ones that keep that tradition alive. **Griots** are just that to Africans' tribal culture. The griot of any tribe is usually also the shaman (or medicine man) of the tribe. Griots are the living journals and encyclopedias of tribal culture. They are the keepers and transmitters of the tribe's history, beliefs, customs, mythology, and folklore; and they ply their craft, for the most part, through storytelling in song form. The topics of the griots songs may be anything having to do with that tribe, but usually with a focus on important events like hunting, planting, harvesting, births, deaths, and celebrations. The griot is important to the tribe not only sitting around the fires at night, but also in their day-to-day struggles to feed and care for themselves. Thus the griot might preside over celebrations and rituals, but also keep the field workers happy as they toiled the land during the day with rhythmically upbeat worksongs.

The one thing that the griot is not is a scribe. Griots must, before they die, pass their knowledge and craft to the next generation. The songs are not written down, and remain alive only as long as they remain in the tribal memory. If there is only one griot in a tribe, and he or she dies before passing on the comprehensive body of information they hold, then the tribal continuity is in trouble. They immediately lose the vast majority of their history. Fortunately, tribal culture is aware of this danger, and there is usually a small school of apprentices whom the griot teaches over very extended periods of time. In fact, once taken as an apprentice, the future griot will spend their life in the trade.

In addition to their voices, the primary tool of the griot, and shamans in general, regardless of tribal geography on this planet, is the drum. The drum, and thus rhythm, is utilized by shamans on all occasions, but most particularly when they are involved in spiritual quests and healing.

As America was being built on the backs of the slaves, the slave masters found that the griots could keep the slaves working through those rhythmically upbeat work songs. Thus griots and their work songs became quite important to the goals of the slave masters in keeping the slaves working. The slave masters, at first, were not even concerned with what words were being used in the work songs. Frequently the griot was allowed to sing in their own language, or it was the case that, to the slave masters, the English spoken by the slaves was so bastardized and mixed with their own languages, and in many cases, Native American languages as well, that the slave masters permitted whatever words the singers wanted to use, as long as the slaves kept working. This labor management technique would conspire against the slave masters.

Listen

AKIWOWO
OLATUNJI

Brush Arbor

In order to hold on to their traditions and culture, the American slaves would frequently hold secret night time meetings in the deep forests surrounding the plantations. **Brush Arbor**, as these gatherings were called, was a time (the only time) for the slaves to get together, share news and each others company, sing songs and dance together around the fires, and sometimes, to plot rebellion against their slave masters. The slaves were simply trying to hold on and maintain continuity to their collective sense of self, community, and culture through these meetings. Brush Arbor usually went late into the night, and it was the only time they had to catch up on news from neighboring plantations. But Brush Arbor was anything but a party in the woods. The slaves held a strong sense of anger against their slave masters and unjust bondage. Rebellions and escapes were plotted at Brush Arbors as well, and the details of these plots were spread from plantation to plantation, right under the noses of the slave masters, via work songs. To the slave master, the slaves were simply working and singing songs to keep their work rhythm going. But to the slaves, the words of the work songs held the information—the where, when, how, and other details they needed for rebellion.

One such rebellion, plotted at a Brush Arbor, was the Nat Turner Rebellion of 1831 in Virginia. Seventy-three people died in the rebellion, creating a desperate sense of fear of blacks by their white slave masters. When it was found out that the rebellion was planned at a Brush Arbor, the meetings were outlawed and the slave masters' oppression increased.

The Sacred versus Secular Conflict

Sacred music, like spirituals and gospel songs, are songs with religious and spiritual topics, while **secular** music, like the blues, is any music not about religious topics. By the mid-1800s the blues and spirituals coexisted and emanated from the same people. The primary difference between the two is that the blues burns deep with straight truth, with lyrical topics of everyday struggles and the burden and repression of life in a slave society, while gospel and spirituals focused on the promised land, heaven, and the non-earthly rewards awaiting the faithful.

Although in most cases it was sung and played by the same people who sang and played sacred gospel music, blues musicians were frequently derided in their own communities for singing secular music. Most blues singers grew up learning music in the church. When they shifted to the secular blues forms, they found that even in their own families they were derided for singing "the devil's music." The conflict arises from the idea that God gave you this gift to sing and play and how dare you *not* use your talents for that sacred purpose. This sacred versus secular conflict has been a concern in American culture, for both black and white musicians, especially those from southern states and the Mississippi delta region into the 1950s and 1960s. Little Richard and Aretha Franklin had to deal with this conflict just as much as Bessie Smith and Son House did.

Early Gospel

Black gospel music was strongly associated with certain musical techniques. Though gospel did not originate these ideas, it was strongly responsible for its popularization in American music. **Call and response** refers to the technique of one person "calling" alone, then having the rest of the people in the congregation respond to that call. The call and response technique comes right from the pulpit, where a preacher might call for the congregation to witness to something just said. Almost every church service has moments where the preacher says a prayer, then the people say "amen" (meaning I agree).

We can find examples of call and response in every style of music on this planet. Literally, everyone does it, whether gospel, blues, hillbilly, cowboy, jazz, classical, Native American, or Indian. All forms of music created by humans have some elements of call and response. No matter what music you listen to, no matter what culture you come from, call and response is woven into the music of all cultures. Call and response is certainly woven into the fabric of our being far beyond a human level. We hear it being used in the majority of species of the animal world, from monkeys, to wolves, to whales, to frogs, to crickets.

Another aspect of early gospel forms that plays a large role in the emergence of rock and roll is the use of strong vocal harmony. So much vocal music from the 20th-century, including the complete genre of doo wop, is heavily influenced by the vocal harmony styles set down by early gospel harmony. Another very important aspect of gospel vocal music is that it was the first music from black America to cross over to white American audiences. Traveling shows featuring gospel singers and choirs, known as **Jubilees**, were the first popular exposure that most of America had to black music and culture. The Jubilee shows also provided black musicians with a respectable means of support, as opposed to the hard road life of the blues singer. Jubilees performed in large theaters in big cities for white audiences; a far cry from the crossroad honky tonks and chitlin houses of the south.

 **Listen**

MY SOUL IS A WITNESS
AUSTIN COLEMAN
circa 1925

I GOT A HIDING PLACE
THE CHURCH OF GOD IN CHRIST
circa 1930

Work Songs and Gandy Dancers

Gandies and **gandy dancers** were, and actually still are, railroad track laborers whose work songs were once heard along the railroad tracks that crisscross the South. The gandy dancer's job is to straighten the miles of railroad tracks after heavy use by heavy trains shift and warp the path of the track. The gandy is the caller, while the gandy dancers answer his call (sound familiar?). A very rhythmic vocal line, much like a military cadence, is sung by the gandy, while the gandy dancers, armed with long steel crow bars, grunt, groan, and wedge their bars under the track, slowly loosening the track with small but forceful shimmies of the bar. Then when the call cycles to the next 8, 12, or 16 bars, the dancers reel back and give one combined strong lift on their bars and the train track moves. All of this work is done to the rhythm of the gandy, and when the moment comes for the heavy move of the track, the dancers all grunt in unison to the downbeat. The gandy technique of using strongly rhythmic music was utilized in other aspects of building the nation's railroad system as well. Driving the steel spikes that secures the track to the thick wooden ties, and carving tunnels out of mountains using pickaxes and shovels were all done to the rhythm of the gandy's song.

The vital aspect of this technique of straightening railroad track is that all of the workers need to be in perfect rhythm with each other in order to shift the heavy track. The constant, repetitive vocal songs of the gandy, and the downbeat grunts of the gandy dancers supplies that rhythm. Their songs traveled with them throughout the south, heard by anyone who wished to watch this seeming miracle of a handful of men moving what seems to be the immovable. Today, gandy dancing is a performed art at folk festivals. At these festivals the music must be placed in context in order to authentically perform it. Fifty to 100 feet of real railroad track (with ties) are set down at the festival, and a handful of men, frequently retired railroad workers, actually perform the art of moving that track using nothing more than their muscles, a six-foot steel-bar, and a song. The fact that gandy dancing is still done today, transformed from a hard, thankless job into a highly respected performed art, is a tribute to the rhythmic vitality of the work song form and its role in transforming the American landscape of possibilities.

Delta Blues

A primary difference in the previously mentioned sacred versus secular conflict is that sacred music was sung in community, meaning that it was performed with, and including, other people of the congregation. It is a music for the people to share in to create a sense of fellowship. Blues music, on the other hand, was performed mostly by one man and his guitar, roaming the country and living a more solitary, transient lifestyle. Blues musicians traveled the south and performed and stayed wherever they could, from chitlin houses to backwoods honky tonks, all the while laboring in the day. They worked wherever someone would hire them, frequently working for a few weeks on a farm, plantation, or herding cattle, then moving on to the next adventure. Many times the pay for this work was simply a place to stay and meals to eat. Many times they were locked up in jails or imprisoned on chain gangs on trumped-up charges by a white sheriff who feared this roaming freed slave. And in some cases the blues singer just got tired of the delta region and traveled to western states to herd cattle and work as a cowboy. (This mix of culture—the black and white cowboys working together and sharing musical styles—creates its own style of music that we will discuss later.)

But for all the drawbacks to this lifestyle, this adventurous calling and the experiences they had traveling the land and constantly meeting new people provided the blues singer with a vast variety of stories and song topics, as well as expanded the scope of their musical influences. The classic picture of the traveling blues singer is a young black man with absolutely no alternative than to travel the land and sing about the good times and the bad. As Leadbelly said, "When you got the blues, you wear out your shoes." That says it all.

Early blues music from the south, also called **Delta Blues** or **Country Blues**, has a vital ingredient that gives the music a gritty edge . . . *truth*. The blues singer sang mostly about the truth of an all too prevalent racist society that was at the core of American culture. This truth was frequently not welcome. Blues music, and even its primary instrument, the guitar, were, in some circles, considered decadent and unsavory, sometimes even among the black community from which it came.

But in order to understand where the blues comes from, we must understand that blues music tells a story: the story of Africans in America. Blues music and spirituals project the collective voice of the people who endured the horrors of slavery: of being forcibly removed from their homeland, shipped across the Atlantic Ocean like packed cargo, and placed into a completely unfamiliar environment thousands of miles and an ocean away from everything they knew. The family separations, the hard labor, the whippings, the beatings, and the unjust murder of so many. In order to keep the slaves ignorant and docile, the slave masters were quite successful at removing from the slaves a sense of self. They could own no property, their family structures were torn apart, and their minds were kept in the darkness of ignorance. For what, you may ask?! To pick cotton and tobacco. It is certain that if they could have enslaved the Native American into forced labor, we would be studying the roots of rock music through very different musical channels. But America was the natives' home turf. In the eyes of the people in charge of the new American agricultural system, the Native American was too savage and independent to enslave in cotton fields. The only choice seemed to be to wipe them out of the picture completely, which came pretty close to happening.

But the slave masters' strategy never worked. As seen in Brush Arbor, the slaves did retain, frequently at great personal risk, a sense of community and self; of themselves as a people. And they did it through their music. Given this historic scenario, and the fact that the most popular forms of music around the planet today, namely rock and roll and its musical descendants, evolved primarily from the blues, it seems the question of "Who really won the battle for self?" can still be hotly debated. Now we find ourselves in the 21st-century, and the game, as it were, is still being played out.

As the 20th-century bore on, emancipated slaves and their children spread the sound of the blues throughout the country. From its home in New Orleans and the Mississippi delta region, the blues spread around the southern states first, then slowly moved west into Arkansas and Texas, and up into St. Louis and Memphis. But soon the call of the industrial northern states led black Americans and their families to more lucrative jobs in cities like Chicago, New York, Detroit, Cleveland, and Pittsburgh.

A new version of the blues started to evolve out of these urban environments, primarily centered in Chicago, called **electric blues**. Electric guitars and amplifiers replaced the acoustic guitar, but the emotion, 12-

bar form, and lyric content remained. The essence of the blues singer, one person with a guitar standing up against the world, also remained. It is really this essence that drives the spirit of true rock and roll. The underdogs, with no other options than to stand up and let their voices be heard, is a hallmark of the American experiment. Whether that experience comes from emancipated black America or immigrant white America, the very essence of what it is to be American is defined by this music. The hard-working family struggling to create a life for themselves is, in fact, what is sometimes called the American way. It's even on the Statue of Liberty: "Give me your tired, your hungry, your huddled masses yearning to be free . . ." Blues music resonates that yearning like no other, as so many 20th-century Americans were legally free, but institutionally bound in cultural slavery, racial stereotypes, and discrimination.

In this way, the blues, and rock and roll, are the logical musical results of the toil, the hardships, the insecurities, and uncertainties of the future; the personal tragedies and triumphs, and the melting pot of cultures found in the history of this young nation. Sadly, the only voice that seems to be missing from this cultural fugue, with few exceptions, is the voice of the people who settled America long before the Europeans. The Native American is, by and large, left out of this picture. Their voice, all too often, stands alone, removed from the cultural fugue called America.

Early Pioneers of the Blues

There were few opportunities for early blues men to record their music. The music of black America was woefully neglected until the 1920s when Mamie Smith recorded *Crazy Blues*. However, the first blues recordings were more on the jazz side of the blues. The real grit and dirt of authentic delta blues took some getting used to. The blues men wandered throughout the delta regions, working, performing, and just trying to get by. For most blues singers, only on rare occasion would there be an opportunity to travel to the big cities where the recording studios were. Even then, there was no profit or fame in it for the musician. Many of the names we now associate with early blues masters were virtually unknown in their time, and only in the blues revivals of the 1960s did some of them find a more appreciative audience in mainstream American culture.

Charley Patton (1887–1934)

Charley Patton broke ground for all country blues musicians by being one of the first to record authentic delta blues. Patton was the mold into which so many blues musicians poured themselves. He richly embodied the lifestyle previously described of the traveling blues man, constantly on the road, performing in crossroad shacks and chitlin houses, and only on a few occasions traveling to the big cities to record. His musical style had a strong feel of grassroots authenticity. His worn, raspy voice, heavy southern black dialect, and heavy-handed guitar playing style became the standard for authentic blues. His recording of his song, *High Sheriff Blues*, illustrates the gruff, authentic qualities and spirit of the blues, and is truly our point of embarkment into the evolution of rock and roll. His soulful interpretation of the blues heavily influenced later blues men that came along. One of his students in the blues was Robert Johnson, the King of the Blues Guitar.

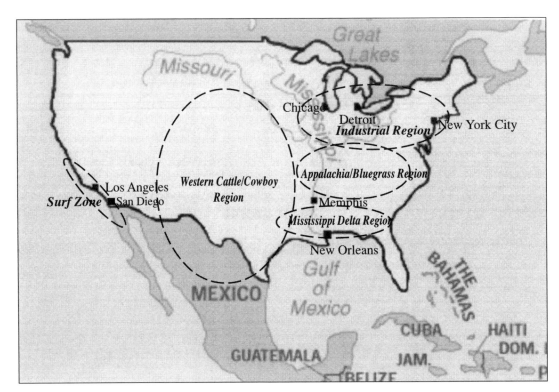

Dominant regional influences in 20th-century American music.

Robert Johnson (1911–1938)

Known as the "King of the Blues Guitar," Robert Johnson cut a name for himself as the best and most controversial blues guitarist of all time, and he did it in just 27 years of life. His influence on the musical and mythopoeic essence of the blues is prodigious, and still growing. He may, in fact, have perpetrated one of the first sensational publicity stunts in the history of rock music, convincing the public that he had sold his soul to the devil in exchange for his talent and seven years with which to take his place in history. His song, *Crossroad Blues*, recorded in 1936 in a Texas hotel room, details how you go about selling your soul to the devil. This song certainly did not hinder the Johnson mythos. In fact, Robert Johnson, aside from the sensationalism, possessed extraordinary natural talent and the good fortune to have been taught the blues by some heavy names in the genre, like Charlie Patton and Son House. However, Johnson loved the attention and fed into the myth, which seems to grow stronger as the years pass. Even though he recorded a total of only 29 songs, the CD boxed set of those songs is one of the top selling box sets today in any genre. Through those few recordings, he is still teaching those who want to play the blues. Johnson also lived the life of the classic blues man, constantly traveling and performing the juke-joint and chitlin house circuit throughout the delta region. Like a self-fulfilling prophesy, Johnson died at the age of twenty-seven after he drank whiskey poisoned by the jealous husband of a woman he had an affair with. In that short twenty-seven years, Johnson created a name for himself that still holds true as one of the best blues men to ever live.

Huddie Ledbetter aka. Leadbelly (1888–1949)

Huddie Ledbetter, better known as Leadbelly, didn't fit into any of the blues men molds. Though he did travel extensively in his youth, he truly was his own person, and is heralded in blues and folk music circles alike. He is, in fact, the most griot-like personality of all the blues men in his early years. After traveling and performing all over the southern United States gaining great popularity in grassroots circles, he then spent the last fifteen years of his life in New York City recording all of the rich music of the land he had learned for the Smithsonian archives. His voice was clear, his diction meticulously precise, and his 12-string guitar playing created a rich bodied fullness of sound to accompany that voice, creating a style all his own. He sang the blues, folk legend songs, gospel songs, and worksongs. He even sang cowboy songs, and was one of the first blues men to use the walking bass type accompaniment known as boogie woogie. Because he sang all genres of folk music, his voice resonates from the people of the land stronger than any other, and his passion was for the people as a whole, not black, not white, but for the common folk and folk heroes of America.

Eddie James "Son" House Jr. (1902–1988)

Eddie James House Jr., better known as Son House, is certainly one of the most intense musical figures to come out of the blues. In his guitar playing style he utilized the power chord long before Link Wray's *Rumble* or Dick Dale's *Miselou*. He played a strong, hard-hitting attack at the instrument, combined with jabbing bottleneck slides, and his voice was extremely powerful, raspy, gruff, and soaked in deep southern black dialect. Along with Willie Brown and his mentor, Charlie Patton, Son House is one of the major figures in the development of the delta blues style and maintained a lifelong commitment to preserving the authenticity of that style. In the music of Son House, you can almost taste the mud of the Mississippi delta.

Son House actually came to the blues in his 20s, after he had already begun a life as a preacher. If there was ever a good example of the sacred versus secular conflict of the blues singer, this is it. He even chronicles the tempestuous nature of this conflict in his song *Preachin' Blues*.

Son House moved to Rochester, New York in the early 1940s and disappeared from the blues scene until the blues revival of the mid-1960s, when his music was rediscovered by the blues revivalists. He returned to the recording studio and left us a legacy of what it means to play authentic blues.

Big Bill Broonzy (1893–1958)

William Lee Conley Jr., better known as Big Bill Broonzy, represents *THE* classic example of the transplantation and transformation of southern country blues to big-city Chicago electric blues. His musical stylings on the guitar helped to steer blues music into new directions in the 1930s as electric blues gradually replaced the country blues style. He moved from Arkansas to Chicago in the 1920s and eventually became one of the biggest names in the emerging Chicago blues scene of the 1930s and 1940s. Broonzy's work on the guitar and the blues form represents a bridge between country blues and electric blues. He would end up being shadowed in the electric blues realm by names like Muddy Waters and T. Bone Walker, but his impact on the transformation from one style to another is still highly regarded among blues fans.

Early Country and Rockabilly Roots

The picture of the American folk landscape that rock and roll emerges from is certainly not a study of black America alone. The rich musical traditions of poor and working class white America also played heavily into the mixture, and most particularly, the folk music from Appalachia, commonly called country or hillbilly music. Not to be confused with the polished stylings of what is today called country music, the most direct descendent of hillbilly music today is bluegrass. Again, just like the blues, this is the music of the poor and working class of America that spent most of their lives toiling in farm fields, mines, shipyards, railroads, and factories that helped build the nation, celebrated from their own heritage and traditions. Ethnically, hillbilly music descends predominantly from English, Irish, Scottish, and western and some central European 19th and early 20th-century immigrants to America, bringing with them Celtic and European instruments and song styles.

Just as the southern blues men had good reason to sing the blues, hillbilly and bluegrass music stems from the lifestyle of the people who created it. It also expresses the concerns, trials and tribulations, failures and triumphs, loves gained and lost, the happiness and sorrows, the love of the land, and everyday existence of the people whose sweat and labor built America. Centered in the Appalachian mountain mid-regions of America east of the Mississippi, country and hillbilly music is the voice of a people who have endured the hard work of eking out an existence in the rugged, isolated, and frequently hostile mountain life.

The spirit of grassroots America is not easily foiled by ruggedness of life. Frequently, that rugged life became the inspiration for art. One way for the mountain folk to bear the hard work and uncertainty of mountain life was to celebrate it. The Saturday night **Barn Dance** was nearly as sacred to the hillbillies as was Sunday morning church service. There are many slow and sad country songs, but there is no slow mournful crooning at the barn dance. Tempos in barn dance music are lightning fast, songs are upbeat and danceable, and the whole point is to have fun in a community social setting after laboring so hard all week long. Another reason for partying so hard on Saturday might also be to get the week's sins out of the way before Sunday morning service.

Bluegrass music today maintains the up tempo spirit of authentic hillbilly music. The instruments used by bluegrass musicians today are the same as the hillbilly musician of years past, though authentic hillbilly music is frequently performed on homemade instruments. The washtub bass (eventually replaced by the stand-up bass in western and rockabilly music), washboard percussion, along with fiddles, guitars, harmonicas (aka. mouth organ) and banjos were common tools for these musicians. How the banjo ended up in hillbilly music is a unique story all its own, considering that the instrument has African origins and was introduced to America by the slaves.

Another aspect of hillbilly music, bluegrass culture, and mountain life in general, is that in any household everyone works and everyone plays. Ability on some instrument or another was common for all family members, and in fact, many bands were made up of complete families. The extended family structure of mountain culture facilitates the passing of musical ability, traditions, beliefs, culture, and folklore from one generation to the next. Mountain communities are close knit social structures where everyone knows each other and are strongly tied together by a shared sense of attachment to the land and each other as a people of that land.

Calling

Calling is a specific vocal style used on fast songs at the barn dances, commonly called contra dances today. The person who sings the lyrics is known as the **caller**. Extremely fast and rhythmically precise song lyrics contain the instructions for the dance. In this traditional "*swing your partner*" call, every one of the lines below are delivered in a single breath. Breaths are indicated by ^.

> ^All join your hands and circle to the south and little bit o' moonshine in your mouth.
> ^Lose your hold with a grand lean back and the lady in the lead.
> ^All men turn left turn right your partner go right and left and hurry up boys and don't be slow and shift your heel 'n meet your doe 'n meet your partner walk slow.
> ^Take her home.
> ^First couple out to the right and around that couple go through and swing.
> ^Back through that couple go 'round and swing and lead 'em up to circle a ring.
> ^Change a right hand lady with a left hand 'round and point her to the right as she comes 'round through your hole and take a little natural and swing your honey and watch her plant.

All of these lyrics are delivered within 50 seconds of the song *Round that Couple Go Through and Swing* on a recording by Roy Rogers in 1940. The song then continues on for another two minutes of nonstop lyric delivery. Today the tradition is kept alive at contra dance halls, where the advertised main attraction of the night isn't the bands or who may be playing, but the caller. Barn dances go late into the night, and the dancers are just as fanatical about learning their steps for the dance as the musicians are about virtuosity on their instruments. It's not just a group of couples dancing together, but an entire group of people interwoven together into the dance, which makes for a wonderful analogy to their way of life.

Hillbilly Boogie and Western Swing

Arising out of Tennessee, Oklahoma, Texas, and the southwest, hillbilly boogie, and western swing came about in the 1930s and flowered in the 1940s as musicians merged heavy doses of boogie woogie and rhythm and blues with the country feel and instruments of bluegrass—fiddles, mandolins, banjos, guitars, accordions, and steel slide guitars (an offshoot of the Hawaiian slide guitar), mixed also with the popular stylings of swing jazz and the romantic image of the singing cowboy.

Bands like Spade Cooley and His Orchestra, Leon McAuliffe and His Western Swing Band, Bob Wills and His Texas Playboys, and Tex Williams and His Western Caravan thrilled radio audiences throughout the 1940s and into the 1950s with their lively, foot stomping songs; breakneck speed slide guitar; fiddle, mandolin, and accordion solos; and precise vocal harmony. This is music that you literally can *not* sit still through. It is made for cheerful times and dancing through and through and is performed with big smiles, wide brim cowboy hats, polished boots, white shirts, and an enthusiasm for virtuosity and speed that has no equal in western music. Western swing and hillbilly boogie and the musicians who played it were, in fact, some of the most popular styles of music and well known band names in mainstream America before the explosion of rock and roll in the early to mid-1950s.

Listen

SMOKE, SMOKE, SMOKE THAT CIGARETTE
TEX WILLIAMS AND HIS WESTERN CARAVAN

TAKE IT AWAY, LEON
LEON McAULIFFE AND HIS WESTERN SWING BAND

OKLAHOMA STOMP
SPADE COOLEY AND HIS ORCHESTRA

COWBOY STOMP
BOB WILLS AND HIS TEXAS PLAYBOYS

To the cowboy swingsters, virtuosity and speed were everything. Extraordinary ability at extraordinary tempos is the hallmark of the guitar and slide guitar legends of country music and is certainly the element that still attracts so many to the rockabilly and bluegrass sound. The heavy emphasis on the back beat—the two guitars, one electric and one steel slide—dueling it out, first one solos while the other plays rhythm, then reversing roles, and the **breakdown** tempos conspire against the listener to bring them to their feet. If you ever meet anyone who says, "Oh . . . I don't dance," then you've certainly met someone who has never heard this music.

Like the blues, the impact and influence of cowboy swing and hillbilly boogie on the emergence of rock and roll cannot be overstated. In fact, Elvis Presley introduced America to rock and roll using what is now seen as a standard rockabilly band and sound. But once Elvis opened the door to mainstream America, everybody else came through as well, whether from the country-rockabilly realm, the New Orleans rhythm and blues realm, the Chicago electric blues realm, or the gospel and doo wop realm. Every one of these genres are like the separate cars of a train, a little different but linked together. As the rock and roll train gained momentum, regardless of whether it was rhythm and blues, blues, doo wop, or country rooted, more and more people fell in line to the diversity of sounds and the infectious dance rhythms and tempos. At the front of the rock and roll train was a locomotive engine called rockabilly.

Listen

HURRICANE
LARRY COLLINS AND JOE MAPHIS
(Rhino, Legends of Guitar Vol. 1 Country)

Would rock and roll have emerged without this impetus? Yes, it certainly would have. The times were changing, and whether his name was Elvis or not, whether he came from Memphis, New Orleans, or Chicago, sooner or later someone would have come along to blow the doors open for all of the rich regional flavors of music evolving in America. Rock and roll was already firmly in place and growing before Elvis ever met Sam Phillips. The advent of electric instruments and amplification and the fact that there was room for all (*except the Native American*) of the many and varied voices and music found in America insured that the rock and roll train could not be derailed.

The Singing Cowboy and the American Balladeer

The romantic image of the American cowboy played heavily into the image of America itself in the first half of the 20th-century. The cowboy was independent, brave, bold, daring, rustic, and strong, and shared a binding sense of camaraderie honed through many years and many hard miles of driving cattle over vast territories of the country. Though this romantic image captured the public's fancy around the turn of the 20th-century through traveling cowboy shows and silent film and was used as costume for the western swing bands later on, it was in the new age of *talky* movies and radio theatre that the cowboy would rise to mythological grandeur. In the movies and on radio the singing cowboy was born and soon dominated American culture.

The singing cowboy was not, however, something made up by Hollywood directors. The technology simply caught up with what the cowboy was good at besides herding and driving cattle. Then that image was fed to the public, who loved it and elevated the singing cowboy to star status. Once the formula was proven to work with the public, cowboy stars were cultivated by Hollywood and radio, and soon everyone was wearing a Stetson and cowboy boots and having portraits taken of their children sitting on ponies and dressed in leather chaps and cowboy hats, but the essence of where the singing cowboy came from was real.

Cowboys were truly on their own out in the wilderness of western America. If they wanted a meal, they had to cook it. If something broke, they had to fix it. If they wanted to be entertained at night, they had to do the entertaining. Singing songs and storytelling around the campfire and under the stars was a staple of cowboy night life on the prairies. But the functionality of the cowboy being able to sing soothing ballads and strum a guitar went beyond their own entertainment and chronicling their exploits. The phrase "music calms the savage beast" was not just a phrase to the cowboy.

Circle herding is a technique used by the cowboys to bed the cattle down for the night. After a long day of driving them non-stop through the great plains of the West, the cattle were often reluctant to lie down and sleep. The cowboys would herd them into a circle until there was no front of the line, and slowed their pace until the cattle stopped their march. Once the cowboys achieved this, the next step was getting a few of them to lie down. Once one laid down, the rest would follow suit and the cowboy could finally set up camp, eat, and relax for the night. But getting them to bed down was not easy, as the cattle were always restless from the day's drive and the sounds of the wilderness around them. Until the cattle were down, there was the danger of stampede; the cowboy's worst fear. The cowboys found that if they sang to the cattle, it calmed them. They would slowly ride around the circled herd strumming and singing soft and low ballads. This verse of the traditional *Circle Herding Song* perfectly captures the cowboys sentiment. *"Oh slow up doggies, quit roaming around. And stop this forever a shifting around. Lie still, little doggies and drown the wild sound—that'll leave when the day rolls around. Lie still, little doggies, lie still."*

Cowboy songs give us a tremendously clear picture of early 20th-century life in America west of the Mississippi. The repertoire of cowboy songs provide very colorful interpretations of how those people viewed themselves, their lives, and the land they worked. Cowboy song forms are also the mold into which so many American ballads were poured. Songs like *Tumbling Tumbleweeds, Red River Valley, The Streets of Laredo, Back In the Saddle, High Noon, Riders in the Sky*, and the many odes to Texas, Arizona, and Montana are detailed storytelling songs reflecting the lives of the American cowboy.

The one song most associated with cowboys, *Home On the Range*, wasn't a cowboy song at first at all, but the cowboys knew a good ballad when they heard it and changed a few key words to fit their need, a very common practice among the cowboys. Songs would change in time as cowboys added their own lyrics to already established songs. *Home On the Range* was originally composed by a homesteader in Kansas, and the change in one word transformed the song. The line "I would not exchange my home on the range," was originally penned "I would not exchange my home *here* to range." The old English implication of the original is that the singer would not exchange his freedom to roam the land and to keep moving from valley to valley. The cowboys changed the lyric to "home on the range" to reflect their feeling that the range itself was home to them.

The American cowboys captured the imagination of the country, and the spirit of freedom that they represented gave many of the people of America a sense of identity and independence. Their music is associated with everything from western swing to rockabilly to American ballads. Their crooning style was emulated by many musicians, and their image, like the blues men of the south, of a lone man and his guitar exploring and traveling the land, plays into the sense of liberty, freedom, and hope for the common man that became the hallmark image for rock and roll.

BACK IN THE SADDLE AGAIN
GENE AUTRY

Roots Americana

Uncle Dave Macon

Uncle Dave Macon, beginning his professional musical career after the age of fifty, brought musical and performance traditions of the 19th-century South to the radio shows and the recording catalogues of the early country music industry. In 1925, he became one of two charter members of the Grand Ole Opry, then called the WSM Barn Dance. A consummate showman on the banjo and a one-man repository of countless old songs and comic routines, Macon remained a well-loved icon of country music until and beyond his death in 1952.

Born David Harrison Macon in Smartt Station in middle Tennessee's Warren County, he was the son of a Confederate officer who owned a large farm. Macon heard the folk music of the area when he was young, but he was also a product of the urban South: after the family moved to Nashville and began operating a hotel, Macon hobnobbed with traveling vaudeville musicians who performed there. After his father was stabbed near the hotel, Macon left Nashville with the rest of his family. He worked on a farm and later operated a wagon freight line, performing music only at local parties and dances. Macon's return to music was due partly to the advent of motorized trucks, for his wagon line fell on hard times in the early 1920s after a competitor invested in the horseless novelties. In 1923, he struck up a few tunes in a Nashville barbershop with fiddler Sid Harkreader, and an agent from the Loew's theater chain happened to stop in. Soon Macon and Harkreader were touring as far afield as New England, and when George D. Hay began bringing together performers two years later for what would become the Opry, Macon was a natural choice. The tour also brought Macon the first of his many recording dates, held in New York for the Vocalion label in 1924. Macon would record prolifically through the 1930s (and occasionally up to 1950) for various labels, accompanied at different times by Harkreader, the brother duo of Sam and Kirk McGee, the Delmore Brothers, the young Roy Acuff, and other string players including a then-unknown Bill Monroe.

Macon's recordings are richly enjoyable in themselves and are priceless historical documents, both for the large variety of banjo styles they preserve and for the window they afford on American songs of the late 19th century. Macon performed musical-comic routines such as the *Uncle Dave's Travels* series, topical songs, often of his own composition (*Governor Al Smith*), playful folk songs (*I'll Tickle Nancy*), gospel with his Dixie Sacred Singers, blackface minstrel songs, unique proto-blues pieces that Macon learned from African-American freight workers (*Keep My Skillet Good and Greasy*), and songs of many other types. Yet "the Dixie Dewdrop" was loved most of all for his presence as a live musician, captured not only on the weekly Opry broadcasts (which were broadcast nationally for a time in the 1930s) but also in the 1940 film *Grand Ole Opry*.

Macon delivered what an 1880s southern vaudeville audience would have demanded for its hard-earned dollar: showmanship (he handled the banjo with Harlem Globetrotters-like trick dexterity), humor, political commentary (often of the incorrect variety by modern standards), and unflagging energy. Macon continued to appear on the Opry almost until his death, gradually taking on the status of a great-hearted living link to country music's origins. He became the tenth member of the Country Music Hall of Fame in 1966, and the revival of old-time music that flourished as part of the folk movement focused the attention of younger listeners on his music. Yet Macon remains less well understood, and less present in the musical minds of country listeners, than Jimmie Rodgers or the Carter Family, even though he was nearly as well known in his own day. Perhaps that's because he represents an older layer of American music-making than almost any other performer known to country audiences. Modern hearers can easily connect with Rodgers' blues or the Carters' homespun sentiment, but Macon may require greater effort. Such effort, in any case, is well repaid by an acquaintance with his musical legacy. Probably the most significant aspect of Uncle Dave Macon is that he opened the gates for all performers and musicians to be characters.

Deford Bailey

Deford Bailey was another early Opry regular. Known as "The Harmonica Wizard," Bailey played what he liked to call "black hillbilly music." His solo performance of *Pan American Blues*, named after a train that passed near his house, soon became an Opry favorite, garnering Bailey more Opry appearances than any other performer in 1928. Bailey was for a time a familiar act at the Grand Ole Opry. That is, until a tiff with Opry founder George Hay led to his dismissal.

Bailey was a professional musician from the age of fourteen, by which time he was already supporting himself around Smith County, Tenn., by playing the harmonica. He had also picked up a few other instruments that were required items in country music from his dad and uncle. The music that was being passed around was something Bailey described as black hillbilly, half country and half blues. And nobody listening cared if a particular song had a bit more country than blues and vice versa. Bailey was given a chance and went on to become the Opry's first solo star as well as its first black artist. Historians lobbying for Bailey's importance go on to point out that in 1928, the Opry's first year, the harmonica player did his thing on 49 of the 52 programs. No other artist even came close to that record of appearances. A symbolically more important event was the fact that immediately after the audience heard the phrase Grand Ole Opry announced for the very first time, on came Bailey blowing his train imitation on the harp.

He remained secure in this contract with the Opry for about fifteen years. He recorded in the late 1920s on labels such as Columbia, Brunswick, and Victor. His sessions were the first decently recorded examples of harmonica playing and were incredibly influential. His effect on the history of the instrument itself is measurable, because his success led to opportunities for many other harmonica players to record and perform.

Bailey also helped establish several performers by appearing as a solo artist in front of their bands, including Roy Acuff. Venues at this time included tent shows and county fairs as well as theatres. Wherever the tour might lead, Bailey always had to be back in Nashville for the Saturday night Opry show.

Even after his death, the fight between Bailey and the Nashville establishment continues, with Roy Acuff bristling at the idea of honoring the man with a membership in the Country Music Hall of Fame, although many other old-time performers of Bailey's generation have already been inducted. After all, it was these original old-time performers who, with their personality and unique music, had managed to launch what would become an unstoppable institution in country music.

Jimmie Rodgers

His brass plaque in the Country Music Hall of Fame reads, "Jimmie Rodgers' name stands foremost in the country music field as *the man who started it all.*" This is a fair assessment. The "Singing Brakeman" and the "Mississippi Blue Yodeler," whose six-year career was cut short by tuberculosis, became the first nationally known star of country music and the direct influence of many later performers—from Hank Snow, Ernest Tubb, and Hank Williams to Lefty Frizzell and Merle Haggard. Rodgers sang about rounders and gamblers, bounders and ramblers—and he knew what he sang about. At age fourteen he went to work as a railroad brakeman, and on the rails he stayed until a pulmonary hemorrhage sidetracked him to the medicine show circuit in 1925. The years with the trains harmed his health but helped his music.

In an era when Rodgers' contemporaries were singing only mountain and mountain/folk music, he fused hillbilly country, gospel, jazz, blues, pop, cowboy, and folk; and many of his best songs were his compositions, including *TB Blues*, *Waiting for a Train*, *Travelin' Blues*, *Train Whistle Blues*, and his thirteen blue yodels. Although Rodgers wasn't the first to yodel on records, his style was distinct from all the others. His yodel wasn't merely sugar-coating on the song, it was as important as the lyric, mournful and plaintive or happy and carefree, depending on a song's emotional content. His instrumental accompaniment consisted sometimes of his guitar only, while at other times a full jazz band (horns and all) backed him up.

Country fans could have asked for no better hero/star—someone who thought what they thought, felt what they felt, and sang about the common person honestly and beautifully. In his last recording session, Rodgers was so racked and ravaged by tuberculosis that a cot had to be set up in the studio, so he could rest before attempting that one song more. No wonder Rodgers is to this day loved by country music fans.

The youngest son of a railroad man, Rodgers was born and raised in Meridian, Miss. Following his mother's death in 1904, he and his older brother went to live with their mother's sister, where he first became interested in music. Rodgers' aunt was a former teacher who held degrees in music and English, and she exposed him to a number of different styles of music, including vaudeville, pop, and dancehall. Though he was attracted to music, he was a mischievous boy and often got into trouble. When he returned to his father's care in 1911, Rodgers ran wild, hanging out in pool halls and dives, yet he never got into any serious trouble. When he was twelve, he experienced his first taste of fame when he sang *Steamboat Bill* at a local talent contest. Rodgers won the concert and, inspired by his success, decided to head out on the road in his own traveling tent show. His father immediately tracked him down and brought him back home, yet he ran away again, this time joining a medicine show. The romance of performing with the show wore off by the time his father hunted him down. Given the choice of school or the railroad, Rodgers chose to join his father on the tracks.

For the next ten years, Rodgers worked on the railroad, performing a variety of jobs along the South and West Coasts. In May of 1917, he married Sandra Kelly after knowing her for only a handful of weeks; by the fall, they had separated, even though she was pregnant (their daughter died in 1938). Two years later, they officially divorced, and around the same time, he met Carrie Williamson, a preacher's daughter. Rodgers married Carrie in April of 1920 while she was still in high school. Shortly after their marriage, Rodgers was laid off by the New Orleans and Northeastern Railroad, and he began performing various blue-collar jobs, looking for opportunities to sing. Over the next three years, the couple was plagued with problems, ranging from financial to health—the second of their two daughters died of diphtheria six months after her birth in 1923. By that time, Rodgers had begun to regularly play in traveling shows, and he was on the road at the time of her death. Though these years were difficult, they were important in the development of Rodgers' musical style as he began to develop his distinctive blue yodel and worked on his guitar skills.

In 1924, Rodgers was diagnosed with tuberculosis (TB), but instead of heeding the doctor's warning about the seriousness of the disease, he discharged himself from the hospital to form a trio with fiddler Slim Rozell and his sister-in-law Elsie McWilliams. Rodgers continued to work on the railroad and perform blackface comedy with medicine shows while he sang. Two years after being diagnosed with TB, he moved his family out to Tucson, Ariz., believing the change in location would improve his health. In Tucson, he continued to sing at local clubs and events. The railroad believed these extracurricular activities interfered with his work and fired him. Moving back to Meridian, Rodgers and Carrie lived with her parents before he moved away to Asheville, N.C., in 1927. Rodgers was going to work on the railroad, but his health was so poor he couldn't handle the labor; he would never work the rails again. Instead, he began working as a janitor and a cab driver, singing on a local radio station and events as well. Soon, he moved to Johnson City, Tenn., where he began singing with the string band the Tenneva Ramblers. Prior to Rodgers, the group had existed as a trio, but he persuaded the members to become his backing band because he had a regular show in Asheville. The Ramblers relented, and the group's name took second billing to Rodgers, and the group began playing various concerts in addition to the radio show. Eventually, Rodgers heard that Ralph Peer, an RCA talent scout, was recording hillbilly and string bands in Bristol, Tenn. Rodgers convinced the band to travel to Bristol, but on the eve of the audition, they had a huge argument about the proper way they should be billed, resulting in the Tenneva Ramblers breaking away from Rodgers. He went to the audition as a solo artist, and Peer recorded two songs—the old standards *The Soldier's Sweetheart* and *Sleep, Baby, Sleep*—after rejecting Rodgers' signature song, *T for Texas*.

Released in October of 1927, the record was not a hit, but Victor Records did agree to record Rodgers again, this time as a solo artist. In November of 1927, he cut four songs, including *T for Texas*. Retitled *Blue Yodel* upon its release, the song became a huge hit and one of only a handful of early country records to sell a million copies. Shortly after its release, Rodgers and Carrie moved to Washington, where he began appearing on a weekly local radio show billed as the Singing Brakeman.

Though *Blue Yodel* was a success, its sales grew steadily throughout early 1928, which meant that the couple wasn't able to reap the financial benefits until the end of the year. By that time, Rodgers had recorded several more singles, including the hits *Way Out on the Mountain*, *Blue Yodel No. 4*, *Waiting for a Train*, and *In the Jailhouse Now*. On various sessions, Peer experimented with Rodgers' backing band, occasionally recording him with two other string instrumentalists and recording his solo as well. Over the next two years, Peer and Rodgers tried out a number of different backing bands, including a jazz group featuring Louis Armstrong, orchestras, and a Hawaiian combo.

By 1929, Rodgers had become an official star, as his concerts became major attractions and his records consistently sold well. During 1929, he made a small film called *The Singing Brakeman*, recorded many songs, and toured throughout the country. Though his activity kept his star shining and the money rolling in, his health began to decline under all the stress. Nevertheless, he continued to plow forward, recording numerous songs and building a large home in Kerrville, Tex., as well as working with Will Rogers on several fundraising tours for the Red Cross that were designed to help those suffering from the Depression. By the middle of 1931, the Depression was beginning to affect Rodgers as well, as his concert bookings decreased dramatically and his records stopped selling. Despite the financial hardships, Rodgers continued to record.

Not only did the Great Depression cut into Rodgers' career, but so did his poor health. He had to decrease the number of concerts he performed in both 1931 and 1932, and by 1933, his health affected his recording and forced him to cancel plans for several films. Despite his condition, he refused to stop performing, telling his wife that "I want to die with my shoes on." By early 1933, the family was running short on money, and he had to perform anywhere he could—including vaudeville shows and nickelodeons—to make ends meet. For a while, he performed on a radio show in San Antonio, but in February he collapsed and was sent to the hospital. Realizing that he was close to death, he convinced Peer to schedule a recording session in May. Rodgers used that session to provide needed financial support for his family. At that session, Rodgers was accompanied by a nurse and rested on a cot in between songs. Two days after the sessions were completed, he died of a lung hemorrhage on May 26, 1933. Following his death, his body was taken to Meridian by train, riding in a converted baggage car. Hundreds of country fans awaited the body's arrival in Meridian, and the train blew its whistle consistently throughout its journey. For several days after the body arrived in Rodgers' hometown, it lay in state as hundreds, if not thousands, of people paid tribute to the departed musician.

The massive display of affection at Rodgers' funeral services indicated what a popular and beloved star he was during his time. His influence wasn't limited to the 1930s, however. Throughout country music's history, echoes of Rodgers can be heard, from Hank Williams to Merle Haggard. In 1961, Rodgers became the first artist inducted into the Country Music Hall of Fame; 25 years later, he was inducted as a founding father at the Rock and Roll Hall of Fame. Though both honors are impressive, they only give a small indication of what Rodgers accomplished—and how he affected the history of country music by making it a viable, commercially popular medium—during his lifetime.

The Carter Family

The most influential group in country music history, the Carter Family, switched the emphasis from hillbilly instrumentals to vocals, made scores of their songs part of the standard country music canon, and made a style of guitar playing, "Carter picking," the dominant technique for decades. Along with Jimmie Rodgers, the Carter Family were among the first country music stars. Comprised of a gaunt, shy gospel quartet member named Alvin P. Carter and two reserved country girls—his wife, Sara, and their sister-in-law, Maybelle—the Carter Family sang a pure, simple harmony that influenced not only the numerous other family groups of the 1930s and the 1940s, but folk, bluegrass, and rock musicians like Woody Guthrie, Bill Monroe, the Kingston Trio, Doc Watson, Bob Dylan, and Emmylou Harris, to mention just a few.

It's unlikely that bluegrass music would have existed without the Carter Family. A.P., the family patriarch, collected hundreds of British/Appalachian folk songs and, in arranging these for recording, enhanced the pure beauty of these "facts-of-life tunes" and at the same time saved them for future generations. Those hundreds of songs the trio members found around their Virginia and Tennessee homes, after being sung by A.P., Sara, and Maybelle, became *Carter* songs, even though these were folk songs and in the public domain. Among the more than 300 sides they recorded are *Worried Man Blues*, *Wabash Cannonball*, *Will the Circle Be Unbroken*, *Wildwood Flower*, and *Keep on the Sunny Side*.

The Carter Family's instrumental backup, like their vocals, was unique. On her Gibson L-5 guitar, Maybelle played a bass-strings lead (the guitar being tuned down from the standard pitch) that is the mainstay of bluegrass guitarists to the present. Sara accompanied her on the autoharp or on a second guitar, while A.P. devoted his talent to singing in a haunting though idiosyncratic bass or baritone. Although the original Carter Family disbanded in 1943, enough of their recordings remained in the vaults to keep the group current through the '40s. Furthermore, their influence was evident through further generations of musicians, in all forms of popular music, through the end of the century.

Initially, the Carter Family consisted of just A.P. and Sara. Born and raised in the Clinch Mountains of Virginia, A.P. (b. Alvin Pleasant Delaney Carter, April 15, 1891; d. November 7, 1960) learned to play fiddle as a child, with his mother teaching him several traditional and old-time songs; his father had played violin as a young man but abandoned the instrument once he married. Once he became an adult, he began singing with two uncles and his older sister in a gospel quartet, but he became restless and soon moved to Indiana where he worked on the railroad. By 1911, he had returned to Virginia, where he sold fruit trees and wrote songs in his spare time.

While he was traveling and selling trees, he met Sara (b. Sara Dougherty, July 21, 1898; d. January 8, 1979). According to legend, she was on her porch playing the autoharp and singing *Engine 143* when he met her. Like A.P., Sara learned how to sing and play through her family. As a child, she learned a variety of instruments, including autoharp, guitar, and banjo, and she played with her friends and cousins.

A.P. and Sara fell in love and married on June 18, 1915, settling in Maces Springs, where he worked various jobs while the two of them sang at local parties, socials, and gatherings. For the next eleven years, they played locally. During that time, the duo auditioned for Brunswick Records, but the label was only willing to sign A.P., and only if he recorded fiddle dance songs under the name Fiddlin' Doc; he rejected their offer, believing that it was against his parents' religious beliefs.

Eventually, Maybelle Carter (b. Maybelle Addington, May 10, 1909; d. October 23, 1978)—who had married A.P.'s brother Ezra—began singing and playing guitar with Sara and A.P. Following Maybelle's addition to the Carter Family in 1926, the group began auditioning at labels in earnest. In 1927, the group auditioned for Ralph Peer, a New York-based A&R man for Victor Records who was scouting for local talent in Bristol, Tenn. The Carters recorded six tracks, including *The Wandering Boy* and *Single Girl, Married Girl*. Victor released several of the songs as singles, and when the records sold well, the label offered the group a long-range contract.

The Carter Family signed with Victor in 1928, and over the next seven years the group recorded most of its most famous songs, including *Wabash Cannonball*, *I'm Thinking Tonight of My Blue Eyes*, *John Hardy Was a Desperate Little Man*, *Wildwood Flower*, and *Keep on the Sunny Side*, which became the Carters' signature song. By the end of the '20s, the group had become a well-known national act, but its income was hurt considerably by the Great Depression. Because of the financial crisis, the Carters were unable to play concerts in cities across the United States and were stuck playing schoolhouses in Virginia. Eventually, all of the members became so strapped for cash they had to move away from home to find work. In 1929, A.P. moved to Detroit temporarily while Maybelle and her husband relocated to Washington, D.C.

In addition to the stress of the Great Depression, A.P. and Sara's marriage began to fray, and the couple separated in 1932. For the next few years, the Carters only saw each other at recording sessions, partially because the Depression had cut into the country audience and partially because the women were raising their families. In 1935, the Carters left Victor for ARC, where they re-recorded their most famous songs. The following year, they signed to Decca.

Eventually, the group signed a lucrative radio contract with XERF in Del Rio, Texas, which led to contracts at a few other stations along the Mexican and Texas border. Because of their locations, these stations could broadcast at levels that were far stronger than other American radio stations, so the Carters' radio performances could be heard throughout the nation, either in their live form or as radio transcriptions. As a result, the band's popularity increased dramatically, and their Decca records became extremely popular.

Just as their career was back in full swing, Sara and A.P.'s marriage fell apart, with the couple divorcing in 1939. Nevertheless, the Carter Family continued to perform, remaining in Texas until 1941, when they moved to a radio station in Charlotte, N.C. During the early 1940s, the band briefly recorded for Columbia before re-signing with Victor in 1941. Two years later, Sara decided to retire and move out to California with her new husband, Coy Bayes (who was A.P.'s cousin), while A.P. moved back to Virginia, where he ran a country store. Maybelle Carter began recording and touring with her daughters, Helen, June, and Anita.

A.P. and Sara re-formed the Carter Family with their grown children in 1952, performing a concert in Maces Spring. Following the successful concert, the Kentucky-based Acme signed A.P., Sara, and their daughter Janette to a contract, and over the next four years they recorded nearly 100 songs that didn't gain much attention at the time. In 1956, the Carter Family disbanded for the second time. Four years later, A.P. died at his Maces Spring home. Following his death, the Carter Family's original recordings began to be reissued. In 1966, Maybelle persuaded Sara to reunite to play a number of folk festivals and record an album for Columbia. In 1970, the Carter Family became the first group to be elected into the Country Music Hall of Fame, which is a fitting tribute to their immense influence and legacy.

Grand Ole Opry

Perhaps no other institution is more synonymous with country music than WSM Radio's Grand Ole Opry in Nashville, Tenn. Since 1925, it has featured country music acts on its stage for live Saturday night broadcasts. This program has introduced the nation to most, if not all, of the greats of country music. To this day, membership on the Opry remains one of the greatest ambitions of a country music artist.

The Opry began as a show with primarily part-time artists who used the show to promote their live appearances throughout the South and Midwest, but with the help of Roy Acuff, the professionalism of country music became established at the Opry.

The King of Country Music could well have become another Lou Gehrig or Babe Ruth. Born in Maynardville, Tenn., Roy Claxton Acuff seemed destined to become an athlete. Following a move to Fountain City (near Knoxville), Acuff gained thirteen varsity letters in high school, eventually playing minor league ball and being considered for the New York Yankees. Severe sunstroke in 1929 put an end to that career.

By 1933, Acuff formed a group, the Tennessee Crackerjacks, in which Clell Summey played dobro, thus providing the distinctive sound that came to be associated with Acuff (and later provided by Pete 'Bashful Brother Oswald' Kirby). Acuff married Mildred Douglas in 1936, that same year recording two sessions for ARC (a company controlling a host of labels that later merged with Columbia). Tracks from these sessions included two of his greatest hits: *Wabash Cannonball* (featuring vocals by Dynamite Hatcher) and *The Great Speckle Bird*.

Making his first appearance on the Grand Ole Opry in 1938, Acuff soon became a regular on the show, changing the name of the band once more to the Smoky Mountain Boys. He won many friends with his sincere, mountain-boy vocal style and his dobro-flavored band sound, and eventually became as popular as Uncle Dave Macon, who was the Opry's main attraction at the time.

During the 1940s, Acuff's recordings became so popular that he headed Frank Sinatra in some major music polls and reportedly caused Japanese troops to yell 'To hell with Roosevelt, to hell with Babe Ruth, to hell with Roy Acuff' as they banzai-charged at Okinawa. These years also saw some of his biggest hits, including *Wreck on the Highway* (1942), *Fireball Mail* (1942), *Night Train to Memphis* (1943), *Tied Down, That's What Makes the Jukebox Play*, and his classic *The Precious Jewel*.

Acuff's tremendous contribution to country music was recognized in November 1962, when he became the first living musician to be honored as a member of the Country Music Hall of Fame. He guested on the Nitty Gritty Dirt Band's triple album set *Will The Circle Be Unbroken?* in 1972, lending credence to contemporary and country-rock music. He continued to appear regularly on the Grand Ole Opry throughout the '70s and '80s, but cut down on his previously extensive touring schedule, until by the early '90s his only appearances were infrequent guest spots at Opryland. He died on November 23, 1992, following a short illness.

Bob Wills & His Texas Playboys

Bob Wills' name will forever be associated with Western swing. Although he did not invent the genre single-handedly, he did popularize the genre and changed its rules. In the process, he reinvented the rules of popular music. Bob Wills & His Texas Playboys were a dance band with a country string section that played pop songs as if they were jazz numbers. Their music expanded and erased boundaries between genres. It was also some of the most popular music of its era. Throughout the 1940s, the band was one of the most popular groups in the country and the musicians in the Playboys were among the finest of their era. As the popularity of Western swing declined, so did Wills' popularity, but his influence is immeasurable. From the first honky tonkers to Western swing revivalists, generations of country artists owe him a significant debt, as do certain rock and jazz musicians. Bob Wills was a maverick and his spirit infused American popular music of the 20th-century with a renegade, virtuosic flair.

Bob Wills was born outside of Kosse, Tex., in 1905. From his father and grandfather, Wills learned how to play mandolin, guitar, and eventually fiddle, and he regularly played local dances in his teens. In 1929, he joined a medicine show in Fort Worth, where he played fiddle and did blackface comedy. At one performance, he met guitarist Herman Arnspiger and the duo formed the Wills Fiddle Band. Within a year, they were playing dances and radio stations around Fort Worth. During one of the performances, the pair met a vocalist called Milton Brown who joined the band. Soon, Brown's guitarist brother Durwood joined the group, as did Clifton "Sleepy" Johnson, a tenor banjo player.

In early 1931, the band landed their own radio show, which was sponsored by the Burris Mill and Elevator company, the manufacturers of Light Crust Flour. The group re-christened themselves the Light Crust Doughboys and their show was being broadcast throughout Texas, hosted and organized by W. Lee O'Daniel, the manager of Burris Mill. By 1932, the band was famous in Texas but there was some trouble behind the scenes; O'Daniel wasn't allowing the band to play anything but the radio show. This situation led to the departure of Milton Brown; Wills eventually replaced Brown with Tommy Duncan, who he would work with for the next sixteen years. By late summer 1933, Wills, aggravated by a series of fights with O'Daniel, left the Light Crust Doughboys and Duncan left with him.

Wills and Duncan relocated to Waco, Texas, and formed the Playboys, which featured Wills on fiddle, Duncan on piano and vocals, rhythm guitarist June Whalin, tenor banjoist Johnnie Lee Wills, and Kermit Whalin, who played steel guitar and bass. For the next year, the Playboys moved through a number of radio stations, as O'Daniel tried to force them off the air. Finally, the group settled in Tulsa, where they had a job at KVOO.

Tulsa is where Bob Wills & His Texas Playboys began to refine their sound. Wills added an eighteen-year-old electric steel guitarist called Leon McAuliffe, pianist Al Stricklin, drummer Smokey Dacus, and a horn section to the band's lineup. Soon, the Texas Playboys were the most popular band in Oklahoma and Texas. The band made their first record in 1935 for the American Recording Company, which would later become part of Columbia Records. At ARC, they were produced by Uncle Art Satherley, who would wind up as Wills' producer for the next twelve years.

The bandleader had his way and they cut a number of tracks that were released on a series of 78s. The singles were successful enough that Wills could demand that steel guitarist Leon McAuliffe—who wasn't on the first sessions due to ARC's abundance of steel players under contract—was featured on the Playboys' next record, 1936's *Steel Guitar Rag*. The song became a standard for steel guitar. Also released from that session was *Right or Wrong*, which featured Tommy Duncan on lead vocals.

Toward the end of the decade, big bands were dominating popular music and Wills wanted a band capable of playing complex, jazz-inspired arrangements. To help him achieve his sound, he hired arranger and guitarist Eldon Shamblin, who wrote charts that fused country with big band music for the Texas Playboys. By 1940, he had replaced some of the weaker musicians in the lineup, winding up with a full eighteen-piece band. The Texas Playboys were breaking concert attendance records across the country, filling out venues from Tulsa to California; and they also had their first genuine national hit with *New San Antonio Rose*, which climbed to number eleven in 1940.

Throughout 1941 and 1942, Bob Wills & His Texas Playboys continued to record and perform, and they were one of the most popular bands in the country. However, their popularity was quickly derailed by the arrival of World War II. Tommy Duncan enlisted in the Army after Pearl Harbor and Al Stricklin became a defense plant worker. Late in 1942, Leon McAuliffe and Eldon Shamblin both left the group. Bob Wills enlisted in the Army late in 1942, but he was discharged as being unfit for service in the summer of 1943, primarily because he was out of shape and disagreeable. Duncan was discharged around the same time and the pair moved to California by the end of 1943. Wills revamped the sound of the Texas Playboys after World War II, cutting out the horn section and relying on amplified string instruments.

During the 1940s, Art Satherley had moved from ARC to OKeh Records and Wills followed him to the new label. His first single for OKeh was a new version of *New San Antonio Rose* and it became a Top Ten hit early in 1944, crossing over into the Top Twenty on the pop charts. Wills stayed with OKeh for about a year, having several Top Ten hits, as well as the number ones, *Smoke on the Water* and *Stars and Stripes on Iwo Jima*. After he left OKeh, he signed with Columbia Records, releasing his first single for the label, *Texas Playboy Rag*, toward the end of 1945.

In 1946, the Texas Playboys began recording a series of transcriptions for Oakland, Calif.'s Tiffany Music Corporation. Tiffany's plan was to syndicate the transcriptions throughout the Southwest, but their goal was never fulfilled. Nevertheless, the Texas Playboys made a number of transcriptions in 1946 and 1947, and these are the only recordings of the band playing extended jams. Consequently, they are close approximations of the group's live sound. Though the Tiffany transcriptions would turn out to be important historical items, the recordings that kept Wills & The Texas Playboys in the charts were their singles for Columbia, which were consistently reaching the Top Five between 1945 and 1948; in the summer of 1946, they had their biggest hit, *New Spanish Two Step*, which spent sixteen weeks at number one.

Guitarist Eldon Shamblin returned to the Playboys in 1947, the final year Wills recorded for Columbia Records. Beginning in late 1947, Wills was signed to MGM. His first single for the label, *Bubbles in My Beer*, was a Top Ten hit early in 1948, as was its follow-up, *Keeper of My Heart*. Though the Texas Playboys were one of the most popular bands in the nation, they were beginning to fight internally, mainly because Wills had developed a drinking problem that caused him to behave erratically. Furthermore, Wills came to believe Tommy Duncan was demanding too much attention and asking for too much money. By the end of 1948, he had fired the singer.

Duncan's departure couldn't have come at a worse time. Western swing was beginning to fall out of public favor, and Wills' recordings weren't as consistently successful as they had been before; he had no hits at all in 1949. That year, he relocated to Oklahoma, beginning a fifteen-year stretch of frequent moves, all designed to find a thriving market for the band. In 1950, he had two Top Ten hits: *Ida Red Likes the Boogie* and *Faded Love*, which would become a country standard; they would be his last hits for a decade. Throughout the 1950s, he struggled with poor health and poor finances, but he continued to perform frequently. However, his audience continued to shrink, despite his attempts to hold on to it. Wills moved throughout the Southwest during the decade, without ever finding a new home base. Audiences at dance halls plummeted with the advent of television and rock and roll. The Texas Playboys made some records for Decca that went unnoticed in the mid-1950s. In 1959, Wills signed with Liberty Records, where he was produced by Tommy Allsup, a former Playboy. Before recording his first sessions with Liberty, Wills expanded the lineup of the band again and reunited with Tommy Duncan. The results were a success, with *Heart to Heart Talk* climbing into the Top Ten during the summer of 1960. Again, the Texas Playboys were drawing sizable crowds and selling a respectable amount of records.

In 1962, Wills had a heart attack that temporarily debilitated him, but by 1963, he was making an album for Kapp Records. The following year, he had a second heart attack that forced him to disband the Playboys. After the second heart attack, he performed and recorded as a solo performer. His solo recordings for Kapp were made in Nashville with studio musicians and were generally ignored, though he continued to be successful in concert.

In 1968, the Country Music Hall of Fame inducted Bob Wills, and the following year the Texas State Legislature honored him for his contribution to American music. The day after he appeared in both houses of the Texas state government, Wills suffered a massive stroke, which paralyzed his right side. During his recovery, Merle Haggard—the most popular country singer of the late '60s—recorded an album dedicated to Bob Wills, *A Tribute to the Best Damn Fiddle Player*, which helped return Wills to public consciousness and spark a wide-spread Western swing revival. In 1972, Wills was well enough to accept a citation from ASCAP in Nashville, as well as appear at several Texas Playboy reunions, which were all very popular. In the fall of 1973, Wills and Haggard began planning a Texas Playboys reunion album, featuring Leon McAuliffe, Al Stricklin, Eldon Shamblin, and Smokey Dacus, among others. The first session was held on December 3, 1973, with Wills leading the band from his wheelchair. That night, he suffered another massive stroke in his sleep; the stroke left him comatose. The Texas Playboys finished the album without him. Bob Wills never regained consciousness and he died on May 15, 1975, in a nursing home. Wills was buried in Tulsa, the place where his legend began.

Hank Williams

Hank Williams is the father of contemporary country music. Williams was a superstar by the age of twenty-five; he was dead at the age of twenty-nine. In those four short years, he established the rules for all the country performers that followed him and, in the process, much of popular music. Williams wrote a body of songs that became popular classics, and his direct, emotional lyrics and vocals became the standard for most popular performers. Williams lived a life as troubled and reckless as that depicted in his songs.

Hank Williams was born in Mount Olive, Al., on September 17, 1923. When he was eight years old, Williams was given a guitar by his mother. His musical education was provided by a local blues street singer, Rufus Payne, who was called Tee Tot. From Tee Tot, Williams learned how to play the guitar and sing the blues, which would come to provide a strong undercurrent in his songwriting. Williams began performing around the Georgiana and Greenville areas of Alabama in his early teens. His mother moved the family to Montgomery, Al., in 1937, where she opened a boarding house. In Montgomery, he formed a band called the Drifting Cowboys and landed a regular spot on a local radio station, WSFA, in 1941. During his shows, Williams would sing songs from his idol, Roy Acuff, as well as several other country hits of the day. WSFA dubbed him "the Singing Kid" and Williams stayed with the station for the rest of the decade.

Williams met Audrey Mae Sheppard, a farm girl from Banks, Ala., in 1943, while he was playing a medicine show. The following year, the couple married and moved into Lilly's boarding house. Audrey became Williams' manager just before the marriage. By 1946, he was a local celebrity, but he was unable to make much headway nationally. That year, Hank Williams and Audrey visited Nashville with the intent of meeting songwriter/music publisher Fred Rose, one of the heads of Acuff-Rose Publishing. Rose liked Williams' songs and asked him to record two sessions for Sterling Records, which resulted in two singles. Both of the singles—*Never Again* in December 1946 and *Honky Tonkin'* in February 1947—were successful and Williams signed a contract with MGM Records early in 1947. Rose became the singer's manager and record producer.

Move It On Over, released later in 1947, became Hank Williams' first single for MGM. It was an immediate hit, climbing into the country Top Five. By the summer of 1948, he had joined the Louisiana Hayride, appearing both on its tours and radio programs. *Honky Tonkin'* was released in 1948, followed by *I'm a Long Gone Daddy*. While neither song was as successful as *Move It On Over*, they were popular, with the latter peaking in the Top Ten. Early in 1949, he recorded *Lovesick Blues*, a Tin Pan Alley song initially recorded by Emmett Miller and made popular by Rex Griffin. The single became a huge hit upon its release in the spring of 1949, staying at number one for sixteen weeks and crossing over into the pop Top Twenty-five. Williams sang the song at the Grand Ole Opry, where he performed an unprecedented six encores. He had become a star.

Hank and Audrey Williams had their first child, Randall Hank, in the spring of 1949. Also in the spring, Hank Williams assembled the most famous edition of the Drifting Cowboys, featuring guitarist Bob McNett, bassist Hillous Butrum, fiddler Jerry Rivers, and steel guitarist Don Helms. Soon, he and the band were earning $1,000 per concert and were selling out shows across the country. Williams had no fewer than seven hits in 1949 after *Lovesick Blues*, including the Top Fives *Wedding Bells*, *Mind Your Own Business*, *You're Gonna Change (Or I'm Gonna Leave)*, and *My Bucket's Got a Hole in It*; in addition to having a string of hit singles in 1950 including the number ones *Long Gone Lonesome Blues*, *Why Don't You Love Me*, and *Moanin' the Blues*; as well as the Top Tens *I Just Don't Like This Kind of Livin'*, *My Son Calls Another Man Daddy*, *They'll Never Take Her Love From Me*, *Why Should We Try*, and *Nobody's Lonesome for Me*. That same year, Williams began recording a series of spiritual records under the name Luke the Drifter.

Williams continued to rack up hits in 1951, beginning with the Top Ten hit *Dear John* and its number one flip-side *Cold, Cold Heart*. That same year, pop vocalist Tony Bennett recorded *Cold, Cold Heart* and had a hit, leading to a stream of covers from such mainstream artists as Jo Stafford, Guy Mitchell, Frankie Laine, Teresa Brewer, and several others. Williams had also begun to experience the fruits of crossover success, appearing on the Perry Como television show and being part of a package tour that also featured Bob Hope, Jack Benny, and Minnie Pearl. In addition to *Dear John* and *Cold, Cold Heart*, Williams had several other hits in

1951, including the number one *Hey, Good Lookin'* and *Howlin' at the Moon*, *I Can't Help It (If I'm Still in Love With You)*, *Crazy Heart*, *Lonesome Whistle*, and *Baby, We're Really in Love*, which all charted in the Top Ten.

Though his professional career was soaring, Hank Williams' personal life was beginning to spin out of control. Before he became a star, he had a mild drinking problem, but it had been more or less controlled during his first few years of fame. However, as he began to earn large amounts of money and spend long times away from home, he began to drink frequently. Furthermore, Hank's marriage to Audrey was deteriorating. Not only were they fighting, resulting in occasional separations, but Audrey was trying to create her own recording career without any success. In the fall of 1951, Hank was on a hunting trip on his Tennessee farm when he tripped and fell, re-activating a dormant back injury. Williams began taking morphine and other pain killers for his back and quickly became addicted.

In January of 1952, Hank and Audrey separated for a final time and he headed back to Montgomery to live with his mother. The hits were still coming fast for Williams, with *Honky Tonk Blues* hitting number two in the spring. In fact, he released five more singles in 1952—*Half As Much*, *Jambalaya*, *Settin' the Woods on Fire*, *You Win Again*, and *I'll Never Get Out of This World Alive*—which all went Top Ten. In spite of all of his success, Hank turned completely reckless in 1952, spending nearly all of his waking hours drunk and taking drugs, while he was frequently destroying property and playing with guns.

Williams left his mother in early spring, moving in with Ray Price in Nashville. In May, Audrey and Hank were officially divorced. She was awarded the house and their child, as well as half of his future royalties. Williams continued to play a large number of concerts, but he was always drunk during the show, or he missed the gig altogether. In August, the Grand Ole Opry fired Williams for that very reason. He was told that he could return once he was sober. Instead of heeding the Opry's warning, he just sank deeper into his self-destructive behavior. Soon, his friends were leaving him, as the Drifting Cowboys began working with Ray Price and Fred Rose no longer supported him. Williams was still playing the Louisiana Hayride, but he was performing with local pickup bands and was earning reduced wages. That fall, he met Billie Jean Jones Eshlimar, the nineteen-year-old daughter of a Louisiana policeman. By October, they were married. Hank also signed an agreement to support the baby—who had yet to be delivered—of one of his other girlfriends, Bobbie Jett, in October. By the end of the year, Williams was having heart problems, and Toby Marshall, a con-man doctor, was giving him various prescription drugs to help soothe the pain.

Hank Williams was scheduled to play a concert in Canton, Ohio, on January 1, 1953. He was scheduled to fly out of Knoxville, Tenn., on New Year's Eve, but the weather was so bad he had to hire a chauffeur to drive him to Ohio in his new Cadillac. Before they left for Ohio, Williams was injected with two shots of the vitamin B-12 and morphine by a doctor. Williams got into the backseat of the Cadillac with a bottle of whiskey and the teenage chauffeur headed out for Canton. The driver was stopped for speeding when the policeman noticed that Williams looked like a dead man. Williams was taken to a West Virginia hospital and he was officially declared dead at 7:00 A.M. on January 1, 1953. Hank Williams had died in the back of the Cadillac, on his way to a concert. The last single released in his lifetime was *I'll Never Get Out of This World Alive.*

Hank Williams was buried in Montgomery, Al., three days later. His funeral drew a record crowd, larger than any crowd since Jefferson Davis was inaugurated as the President of the Confederacy in 1861. Dozens of country music stars attended, as did Audrey Williams, Billie Jean Jones, and Bobbie Jett, who happened to give birth to a daughter three days later. *I'll Never Get Out of This World Alive* reached number one immediately after his death and it was followed by a number of hit records throughout 1953, including the number ones *Your Cheatin' Heart, Kaw-Liga,* and *Take These Chains From My Heart.*

After his death, MGM wanted to keep issuing Hank Williams records, so they took some of his original demos and overdubbed bands onto the original recording. The first of these, *Weary Blues from Waitin',* was a hit but the others weren't quite as successful. In 1961, Hank Williams was one of the first inductees to the Country Music Hall of Fame. Throughout the 1960s, Williams' records were released in overdubbed versions featuring heavy strings, as well as reprocessed stereo. For years, these bastardized versions were the only records in print and only in the 1980s, when his music was released on compact disc, was his catalog restored to its original form. Even during those years when only overdubbed versions of his hits existed, Hank Williams' impact never diminished. His songs have become classics, his recordings have stood the test of time, and his life story is legendary. It's easy to see why Hank Williams is considered by many as the defining figure of country music.

Johnny Cash: The Man in Black

Johnny Cash was one of the most imposing and influential figures in post-World War II country music. He is one of those few people whose tremendous impact on American music grows deeper as the years progress. With his deep, resonant baritone and spare, percussive guitar, he had a basic, distinctive sound. Cash didn't sound like Nashville, nor did he sound like honky tonk or rock and roll. He created his own sub-genre, falling halfway between the blunt emotional honesty of folk, the rebelliousness of rock and roll, and the world weariness of country. Cash's career coincided with the birth of rock and roll, and his rebellious attitude and simple, direct musical attack shared a lot of similarities with rock. However, there was a deep sense of history—as he would later illustrate with his series of historical albums, particularly on the album *Bitter Tears*—that kept him forever tied with country. And he was one of country music's biggest stars of the 1950s and 1960s, scoring well over 100 hit singles.

Johnny Cash was born and raised in Arkansas, moving to Dyess when he was three. By the time he was twelve years old, Cash had begun writing his own songs. Johnny was inspired by the country songs he had heard on the radio. While he was in high school, he sang on the Arkansas radio station KLCN. Johnny Cash graduated from college in 1950, moving to Detroit to work in an auto factory for a brief while. With the outbreak of the Korean War, he enlisted in the Air Force. While he was in the Air Force, Cash bought his first guitar and taught himself to play. He began writing songs in earnest, including *Folsom Prison Blues.* Cash left the Air Force in 1954, married a Texas woman named Vivian Leberto, and moved to Memphis, where he took a radio announcing course at a broadcasting school on the GI Bill. During the evenings, he played country music in a trio that also consisted of guitarist Luther Perkins and bassist Marshall Grant. The trio occasionally played for free on a local radio station, KWEM, and tried to secure gigs and an audition at Sun Records.

Cash finally landed an audition with Sun Records and its founder, Sam Phillips, in 1955. Initially, Cash presented himself as a gospel singer, but Phillips turned him down. Phillips asked him to come back with something more commercial. Cash returned with *Hey Porter*, which immediately caught Phillips' ear. Soon, Cash released *Cry Cry Cry/Hey Porter* as his debut single for Sun. On the single, Phillips billed Cash as "Johnny," which upset the singer, because he felt it sounded too young; the record producer also dubbed Perkins and Grant the Tennessee Two. *Cry Cry Cry* became a success upon its release in 1955, entering the country charts at number fourteen and leading to a spot on the Louisiana Hayride, where he stayed for nearly a year. A second single, *Folsom Prison Blues*, reached the country Top Five in early 1956 and its follow-up, *I Walk the Line*, was number one for six weeks and crossed over into the pop Top Twenty.

Johnny Cash had an equally successful year in 1957, scoring several Top Ten country hits including the Top Fifteen *Give My Love to Rose*. Cash also made his Grand Ole Opry debut that year, appearing all in black where the other performers were decked out in flamboyant, rhinestone-studded outfits. Eventually, he earned the nickname of *The Man in Black*. Cash became the first Sun artist to release a long-playing album in November of 1957, when *Johnny Cash With His Hot and Blue Guitar* hit the stores. Cash's success continued to roll throughout 1958, as he earned his biggest hit, *Ballad of a Teenage Queen* (number one for ten weeks), as well as another number one single, *Guess Things Happen That Way*. For most of 1958, Cash attempted to record a gospel album, but Sun refused to allow him to record one. Sun also was unwilling to increase Cash's record royalties. Both of these were deciding factors in the vocalist's decision to sign with Columbia Records in 1958. By the end of the year, he had released his first single for the label, *All Over Again*, which became another Top Five success. Sun continued to release singles and albums of unissued Cash material into the 1960s.

Don't Take Your Guns to Town, Cash's second single for Columbia, was one of his biggest hits, reaching the top of the country charts and crossing over into the pop charts in the beginning of 1959. Throughout that year, Columbia and Sun singles vied for the top of the charts. Generally, the Columbia releases—*Frankie's Man Johnny*, *I Got Stripes*, and *Five Feet High and Rising*—fared better than the Sun singles, but *Luther Played the Boogie* did climb into the Top Ten. That same year, Cash had the chance to make his gospel record—*Hymns by Johnny Cash*—which kicked off a series of thematic albums that ran into the 1970s.

The Tennessee Two became the Tennessee Three in 1960 with the addition of drummer W.S. Holland. Though he was continuing to have hits, the relentless pace of his career was beginning to take a toll on Cash. In 1959, he had begun taking amphetamines to help him get through his schedule of nearly 300 shows a year. By 1961, his drug intake had increased dramatically and his work was affected, which was reflected by a declining number of hit singles and albums. By 1963, he had moved to New York, leaving his family behind. He was running into trouble with the law, most notably for starting a forest fire out West.

June Carter—who was the wife of one of Cash's drinking buddies, Carl Smith—would provide Cash with his return to the top of the charts with *Ring of Fire*, which she co-wrote with Merle Kilgore. *Ring of Fire* spent seven weeks on the top of the charts and was a Top Twenty pop hit. Cash continued his success in 1964, as *Understand Your Man* became a number one hit. However, Cash's comeback was short-lived, as he sank further into addiction and his hit singles arrived sporadically. Cash was arrested in El Paso for attempting to smuggle amphetamines into the country through his guitar case in 1965. That same year, the Grand Ole Opry refused to have him perform and he wrecked the establishment's footlights. In 1966, his wife Vivian filed for divorce. After the divorce, Cash moved to Nashville. At first, he was as destructive as he ever had been, but he became close friends with June Carter, who had divorced Carl Smith. With Carter's help, he was able to shake his addictions; she also converted Cash to fundamentalist Christianity. His career began to bounce back as *Jackson* and *Rosanna's Going Wild* became Top Ten hits. Early in 1968, Cash proposed marriage to Carter during a concert; the pair were married in the spring of 1968.

In 1968, Johnny Cash recorded and released his most popular album, *Johnny Cash at Folsom Prison*. Recorded during a prison concert, the album spawned the number one country hit *Folsom Prison Blues*, which also crossed over into the pop charts. By the end of the year, the record had gone gold. The following year, he released a sequel, *Johnny Cash at San Quentin*, which had his only Top Ten pop single, *A Boy Named Sue*, which peaked at number three; it also hit number one on the country charts. Johnny Cash guested on Bob Dylan's 1969 country-rock album, *Nashville Skyline*. Dylan returned the favor by appearing on the first episode of *The Johnny Cash Show*, the singer's television program for ABC. *The Johnny Cash Show* ran for two years, between 1969 and 1971.

Johnny Cash was reaching a second peak of popularity in 1970. In addition to his television show, he performed for President Richard Nixon at the White House, acted with Kirk Douglas in *The Gunfight*, sang with John Williams and the Boston Pops Orchestra, and he was the subject of a documentary film. His record sales were equally healthy, as *Sunday Morning Coming Down* and *Flesh and Blood* were number one hits. Throughout 1971, Cash continued to have hits, including the Top Three *Man in Black*. Both Cash and Carter became more socially active in the early 1970s, campaigning for the civil rights of Native-Americans and prisoners, as well as frequently working with Billy Graham.

In the mid-1970s, Cash's presence on the country charts began to decline, but he continued to have a series of minor hits and the occasional chart topper like 1976's *One Piece at a Time*, or Top Ten hits like the Waylon Jennings duet *There Ain't No Good Chain Gang* and *(Ghost) Riders in the Sky*. *Man in Black*, Johnny Cash's autobiography, was published in 1975. In 1980, Johnny Cash became the youngest inductee to the Country Music Hall of Fame. However, the 1980s were a rough time for Cash, as his record sales continued to decline and he ran into trouble with Columbia. Cash, Carl Perkins, and Jerry Lee Lewis teamed up to record *The Survivors* in 1982, which was a mild success. The Highwaymen—a band featuring Cash, Waylon Jennings, Willie Nelson, and Kris Kristofferson—

released their first album in 1985, which was also moderately successful. The following year, Cash and Columbia Records ended their relationship and he signed with Mercury Nashville. The new label didn't prove to be a success, as the company and the singer fought over stylistic direction. Furthermore, country radio had begun to favor more contemporary artists and pop formulaic formats for their musical direction, and Cash soon found himself shut out of the charts.

Johnny Cash was the embodiment of the life he sang about. A true American icon right on up to today. His legacy will undoubtedly carry on for many years as an American musical institution. He had never been afraid to evolve musically, constantly reinvented himself while maintaining that unique sound that was Cash.

Bill Monroe: the Birth of Breakdown Bluegrass

The person responsible for popularizing the bluegrass sound and regarded as a heavy influence on rockabilly styles is singer, band leader, and mandolinist **Bill Monroe**. Monroe grew up on a family farm in Kentucky where he learned the styles and forms of fast hillbilly (breakdowns), country blues (soulful ballad), and church music (spirituals). Monroe formed his band, Bill Monroe and his Blue Grass Boys, in 1939 and was invited to join the Grand Ole Opry radio show. With faster tempos and thin, high vocals in the music, The Blue Grass Boys redefined the spirit of how country music should be played. Monroe was a master of reshaping older styles like country blues to fit his new, spirited model of bluegrass. In his book, *Bluegrass: A History*, Neil Rosenburg illustrates a curious irony. *"Monroe had done to 'Mule Skinner Blues' what Elvis Presley would later do to his 'Blue Moon Of Kentucky' in 1954."* An even bigger irony is that Presley completely transforms *Blue Moon Of Kentucky* on his very first record for Sun Records using his own style of rockabilly, the direct rock descendent of hillbilly and bluegrass music.

Bill Monroe is the father of bluegrass. He invented the style, invented the name, and for the great majority of the twentieth-century, embodied the art form. Beginning with his Blue Grass Boys in the 1940s, Monroe defined a hard-edged style of country that emphasized instrumental virtuosity, close vocal harmonies, and a fast, driving tempo. The musical genre took its name from the Blue Grass Boys, and Monroe's music forever has defined the sound of classical bluegrass—a five-piece acoustic string band, playing precisely and rapidly, switching solos and singing in a plaintive, high lonesome voice. Not only did he invent the very sound of the music, Monroe was the mentor for several generations of musicians. Over the years, Monroe's band hosted all of the major bluegrass artists of the 1950s and 1960s, including Flatt & Scruggs, Reno & Smiley, Vassar Clements, Carter Stanley, and Mac Wiseman. Though the lineup of the Blue Grass Boys changed over the years, Monroe always remained devoted to bluegrass in its purest form.

Monroe was born into a musical family. His father had been known around their hometown of Rosine, Ky., as a step-dancer, while his mother played a variety of instruments and sang. His uncle, Pendelton Vanderver, was a locally renowned fiddler. Both of his older brothers, Harry and Birch, played fiddle, while his brother Charlie and sister Bertha played guitar. Bill himself became involved with music as a child, learning the

 **Listen**

BLUE MOON OF KENTUCKY
BILL MONROE AND HIS BLUE GRASS BOYS

BLUE MOON OF KENTUCKY
ELVIS PRESLEY

KATY HILL
BILL MONROE AND HIS BLUE GRASS BOYS

GOIN' TO THE BARN DANCE TONIGHT
CARSON ROBINSON AND HIS PIONEERS

mandolin at the age of ten. Following the death of his parents while he was a pre-adolescent, Monroe went to live with his Uncle Pen. Soon, he was playing in his uncle's band at local dances, playing guitar instead of mandolin. During this time, Monroe met a local blues guitarist called Arnold Shultz, who became a major influence on the budding musician.

When Monroe turned eighteen, he moved to East Chicago, Ind., where his brothers Birch and Charlie were working at an oil refinery. Monroe also got a job at the Sinclair oil refinery and began playing with his brothers in a country string band at night. Within a few years, they performed on the Barn Dance on WLS Chicago, which led to the brothers' appearance in a square dance revue called the WLS Jamboree in 1932. The Monroes continued to perform at night, but Birch left the band in 1934. Ironically, it was just before the group landed a sponsorship of the Texas Crystals Company, which made laxatives. Charlie and Bill decided to continue performing as the Monroe Brothers.

The Monroe Brothers began playing in other states, including radio shows in Nebraska, Iowa, and both North and South Carolina. Such exposure led to record label interest, but the Monroe Brothers were initially reluctant to sign a recording contract. After some persuasion, they inked a deal with RCA-Victor's Bluebird division and recorded their first session in February of 1936. One of the songs from the sessions, *What Would You Give in Exchange*, became a minor hit and the duo recorded another sixty tracks for Bluebird over the next two years.

In the beginning of 1938, Bill and Charlie parted ways, with Charlie forming the Kentucky Pardners. Bill assembled his own band with the intention of creating a new form of country that melded old-time string bands with blues and challenged the instrumental abilities of the musicians. Initially, he moved to Little Rock, where he formed the Kentuckians, but that band was short-lived. He then relocated to Atlanta, where he formed the Blue Grass Boys and began appearing on the Crossroad Rollies radio program. Monroe debuted on the Grand Ole Opry in October of 1939, singing *New Mule Skinner Blues*. It was a performance that made Monroe's career as well as established the new genre of bluegrass.

In the early 1940s, Monroe & the Blue Grass Boys spent some time developing their style, often sounding similar to other contemporary string bands. The most notable element of the band's sound was Monroe's high, piercing tenor voice and his driving mandolin. The Blue Grass Boys toured with the Grand Ole Opry's road shows and appeared weekly on the radio. Between 1940 and 1941, he cut a number of songs for RCA-Victor, but wartime restrictions prevented him from recording for several years. The classic lineup of the Blue Grass Boys fell into place in 1944, when guitarist/vocalist Lester Flatt and banjoist Earl Scruggs joined a lineup that already included Monroe, fiddler Chubby Wise, and bassist Howard Watts. This is the group that supported Monroe when he returned to the studio in 1945, recording a number of songs for Columbia. Early in 1946, he had his first charting hit with *Kentucky Waltz*, which climbed to number three; it was followed by the number five hit *Footprints in the Snow*.

Throughout 1946, the Blue Grass Boys were one of the most popular acts in country music, scoring hits and touring to large crowds across America. At each town they played, the band would perform underneath a large circus tent they set up themselves; the tent would also host a variety of other attractions, including Monroe's baseball team, which would play local teams before the concert began. During the late 1940s, the Blue Grass Boys remained a popular act, landing five additional Top Twenty singles. Numerous other acts began imitating Monroe's sound, most notably the Stanley Brothers.

Flatt & Scruggs left the Blue Grass Boys in 1948 to form their own band. Their departure ushered in an era of stagnation for Monroe. After Flatt & Scruggs parted ways from his band, he left Columbia Records in 1949 because they had signed the Stanley Brothers, who he felt were simply imitating his style. The following year, he signed with Decca Records, who tried to persuade Monroe to attempt some mainstream-oriented productions. He went as far as cutting a few songs with an electric guitar, but he soon returned to his pure bluegrass sound. At these sessions, he did meet Jimmy Martin, who became his supporting vocalist in the early 1950s.

Throughout the 1950s—indeed, throughout the rest of his career—Monroe toured relentlessly, performing hundreds of shows a year. In 1951, Monroe opened a country music park at Bean Blossom, Ind.; over the years, the venue featured performances from a number of bluegrass acts. Monroe suffered a serious car accident in January of 1953, which sidelined his career for several months. The following year, Elvis Presley performed Monroe's *Blue Moon of Kentucky* at his one and only Grand Ole Opry appearance, radically reworking the arrangement; Presley apologized for his adaptation, but Monroe would later perform the same arrangement at his concerts.

Monroe released his first album, *Knee Deep in Bluegrass*, in 1958, the same year he appeared on the country singles chart with *Scotland*; the number twenty-seven single was his first hit in over a decade. However, by the late 1950s, his stardom was eclipsed by Flatt & Scruggs. Monroe was not helped by his legendary stubbornness. Numerous musicians passed through his band because of his temperament and his quest for detail. He rarely granted press interviews and would rarely perform on television; he even canceled a concert at Carnegie Hall because he believed the promoter, Alan Lomax, was a communist. In the 1960s, Monroe received a great career boost from the folk music revival, which made him popular with a new generation of listeners. Thanks to his new manager, ex-Greenbriar Boys member Ralph Rinzler, Monroe played bluegrass festivals across the United States, frequently on college campuses. In 1967, he founded his own bluegrass festival, the Bill Monroe Bean Blossom Festival, at his country music park, which continued to run into the 1990s.

In 1970, he was inducted into the Country Music Hall of Fame. The following year, he was inducted into the Nashville Songwriters Association International Hall of Fame. Throughout the 1970s, he toured constantly. In 1981, Monroe was diagnosed with cancer and underwent treatment for the disease successfully. After his recovery, he resumed his busy touring schedule, which he kept into the 1990s. In 1991, he had surgery for a double coronary bypass, but he quickly recovered and continued performing and hosting weekly at the Grand Ole Opry. In 1993, the Grammys gave Monroe a Lifetime Achievement Award. After suffering a stroke in early 1996, Monroe died on September 9, 1996, four days short of his eighty-fifth birthday.

Flatt & Scuggs

Probably the most famous bluegrass band of all time was Flatt & Scruggs and the Foggy Mountain Boys. They made the genre famous in ways that not even Bill Monroe, who pretty much invented the sound, ever could. Because of a guitar player and vocalist from Tennessee named Lester Flatt and an extraordinary banjo player from North Carolina named Earl Scruggs, bluegrass music has become popular the world over and has entered the mainstream in the world of music.

Like so many other bluegrass legends, Flatt & Scruggs were graduates of Bill Monroe's Blue Grass Boys. Because of the unique sound they added ("overdrive," one critic called it), Monroe felt let down after Flatt's quality vocals and Scruggs's banjo leads left in 1948. Quickly, the two assembled a band that in the opinion of many was among the best ever, with Chubby Wise on fiddle and Jody Rainwater on bass; a later band, with Paul Warren on fiddle and Josh Graves on dobro, was equally superb. With so many extraordinary musicians and the solid, controlled vocals of Flatt, it's no wonder the Foggy Mountain Boys were the band that brought bluegrass to international prominence. From 1948 until 1969, when Flatt & Scruggs split up to pursue different musical directions, they were *the* bluegrass band, due to their Martha White Flour segment at the Opry and, especially, their tremendous exposure from TV and movies.

Flatt & Scruggs were originally brought together by Monroe in 1945, when they joined a band that also featured fiddler Chubby Wise and bassist Cedric Rainwater. This quintet created the sound of bluegrass and helped bring it to national recognition through radio shows, records, and concerts. After three years with Monroe, Flatt left the mandolinist behind in 1948, and Scruggs followed his lead shortly afterward. The duo formed their own band, the Foggy Mountain Boys. Within a few months, they recruited ex-Blue Grass Boy Rainwater, fiddler Jim Shumate, and guitarist/vocalist Mac Wiseman. Initially, the band played on radio stations across the South, landing a record contract with Mercury Records in late 1948. Over the next two years, they toured the United States constantly, played many radio shows, and recorded several sessions for Mercury. One of the sessions produced the original version of *Foggy Mountain Breakdown*, which would become a bluegrass standard.

In 1951, Flatt & Scruggs switched record labels, signing with Columbia Records. By this point, the band now featured mandolinst/vocalist Curly Seckler, fiddler Paul Warren, and bassist Jake Tullock. Where the careers of other bluegrass and hard country acts stalled in the early and mid-1950s, the Foggy Mountain Boys flourished. One of their first singles for Columbia, *'Tis Sweet to Be Remembered*, reached the Top Ten in 1952, and in 1953, the Martha White Flour company sponsored a regular radio show for the group on WSM in Nashville. In 1955, the band joined the Grand Ole Opry. The following year, they added a dobro player called Buck Graves to the lineup.

Flatt & Scruggs reached a new audience in the late 1950s, when the folk music revival sparked the interest of a younger generation of listeners. The duo played a number of festivals targeted at the new breed of bluegrass and folk fans. At the same time, country music television programs went into syndication, and the duo became regulars on these shows. In the summer of 1959, Flatt & Scruggs began a streak of Top

Forty country singles that ran into 1968—their chart performance was directly tied to their increased exposure. The duo's popularity peaked in 1962, when they recorded the theme song to the television sitcom *The Beverly Hillbillies*. The theme, called *The Ballad of Jed Clampett*, became the first number one bluegrass single in early 1963, and the duo made a number of cameos on the show.

The Beverly Hillbillies began a streak of cameo appearances and soundtrack work for Flatt & Scruggs in television and film, most notably with the appearance of *Foggy Mountain Breakdown* in Arthur Penn's 1968 film *Bonnie and Clyde*. With all of their TV, film, and festival appearances, Flatt & Scruggs popularized bluegrass music more than any artist, even Monroe. Ironically, that popularity helped drive the duo apart. Scruggs wanted to expand their sound and pushed Flatt to cover Bob Dylan's *Like a Rolling Stone* in 1968 as well as land concert appearances in venues that normally booked rock and roll acts. Flatt wanted to continue in a traditional bluegrass vein. Inevitably, the opposing forces came to a head in 1969, and the duo parted ways. Appropriately, Flatt formed a traditional bluegrass band, the Nashville Grass, while Scruggs assembled a more progressive outfit, the Earl Scruggs Revue.

Throughout the 1970s, both Flatt and Scruggs enjoyed successful solo careers. In 1979, the duo began ironing out the details of a proposed reunion album, but they were scrapped upon Flatt's death on May 11, 1979. Scruggs retired in the 1980s. In 1985, Flatt & Scruggs were inducted into the Country Music Hall of Fame.

Poised to Shake, Rattle and Roll

This was the landscape of possibilities in America in the first half of the twentieth-century. Black music descended from slavery—through worksongs and gospel, then the blues, and rhythm and blues. White music descended from poor, working class immigrants to America from Ireland, Scotland, England, Spain, Germany, and other western European countries—through barn dances, ballads, polkas and breakdowns, then to western swing, hillbilly boogie, and rockabilly. As the people of America mixed, the music mixed as well, and soon this combination would shake up the realms of music and culture with unprecedented force. The status quo structure of popular music and idols in America, that of the squeaky clean, well bred, cabaret suave yet homespun image, would soon be annihilated in the years following World War II. A new music and image reflecting the changing times would emerge with the post-war generation, different enough to cause confusion and misunderstanding in their parents, yet completely evolved out of the music and culture that came before.

It's been said that rock and roll is a great mongrel. There are so many different ethnic and regional influences to be found in the study of rock and roll; from the musicians, the independent record labels who produced it, the disc jockeys that played it, the people who danced to it—all came from diverse backgrounds, and all sought to graft a little bit of themselves onto the tree of music. Looking at the evolution of this true folk music gives us a clear picture of American culture at its grassroots.

2 The Blues

Introduction

Rock music developed from several different sources including **country & western, jazz, Cajun music, Broadway** and **Tin Pan Alley** popular songs, and the **blues**. Of all these sources, it is the blues that has contributed most to the development of rock music. From the blues, rock has inherited form in the strophic structure, melody through the use of blue notes, harmony in the chordal structure of the 12-bar blues progression, and style or expression in the manner in which the music is performed. The characteristic features that distinguish the blues include:

- Call and response performance
- Descending melodic line
- Use of blue notes
- Simple harmonic structure
- Strophic song form

The musical elements that characterize the blues are thought to have come from many different sources. An understanding of these characteristics in the blues will help illustrate the influence of the blues on the development of rock music.

Call and Response

The style of performance called **call and response** (also known as **antiphonal singing**, particularly in the Western art music tradition) came from the work songs of slaves (pre-Civil War), field hands (post-Civil War), and prison work gangs. In doing hard, tedious labor in the fields or on the docks, the work-gang leader would often begin singing a melody (the call) which the other workers would repeat back to him (the response) either as a refrain to the leader's song or as the next line of the song. The call and response style of performance is found not only in the blues, but also in Gospel music, jazz, country & western, and rock music.

Descending Melodic Line

The melody of the blues song is thought to have been derived from another type of work song called the **field holler**. In a field holler, which is performed by a single worker in a field, a melody is shouted out loud and long. As with any type of speech that is yelled or shouted, the field holler has a tendency to fall in pitch from high-pitched notes at the outset to lower-pitched notes at the end of the holler as the singer runs out of breath. The field holler originated in the savannas of western Africa, from where most of the slaves brought to the United States were taken in the seventeenth through the nineteenth centuries. It has been speculated that the field holler was a means of communication from one large field to the next during the Reconstruction period that followed the Civil War.[1] Like the melody of the field holler, the typical blues line begins on a high pitch and descends, usually reaching the lower tonic note by the end of the line (example 2-1).

Example 2-1

Descending blues melody, Bessie Smith *Reckless Blues* (1925), line 1

Blue Notes

Blues melodies are full of slightly altered pitches called **blue notes**. Microtonally altered pitches are common in many cultures of the world including those found in west Africa. In the western European musical system the smallest interval in common usage is the semitone, or half-step **(see Chapter 1)**; the blue note, or any other type of microtone, is an even smaller interval for which western notation cannot accommodate. Compared with the major scale, the altered notes of the blues scale are typically the third and seventh scale degrees:

major scale: C D E F G A B C
blues scale: C D **E** F G A **B** C **(bold = blue note)**

These pitches are slightly lowered, or blued, in performance, but not to the point of making the note a minor third or a minor seventh. This melodic feature is also present in some rock performances, particularly by those rock singers imitating blues singers. Technically, every note in a scale or key can be blued, however, the standard performance practice is to blue the third and seventh scale degrees, and sometimes the fifth scale degree.

Harmony

The simple harmonic structure of the blues, which will be thoroughly discussed below, is thought by some blues authorities to have been inspired by the chord structures of simple Anglo/Scottish/Irish church hymns. These hymns were brought over by European settlers and learned by the African slaves, who eventually assimilated them into their music.

Form

Finally, the strophic song form of the blues, that is, a series of verses in which the melody is repeated with new words, was adapted from Anglo/

Scotch/Irish folk songs of the mid- to late-nineteenth century. Many of these folk songs were learned by the African American workers, who often changed the words to fit a black folk hero, as in the case of *John Henry*. The narrative style of text that was used in these folk songs, telling a story throughout the song, was also adapted into the blues song.

History and Structure

The blues as a genre developed in the latter part of the nineteenth century. Authorities are unsure of how exactly the blues developed since it existed for a long time as an aural/oral tradition. It is thought to have developed in part from the tribal songs of the slaves who were brought over to America from west Africa. It was from the ethnic groups the Wolofs from Senegal and Gambia, and the Ashanti from Ghana that much of the slave populations were taken. Since most of the slave population was located in the southern United States, especially in the Atlantic port cities (Savannah, Charleston) and metropolitan areas (Atlanta), and along the Mississippi River, it is no surprise that the blues first developed in these parts of the country.

The African musicians who correspond most closely to the blues singers are the **jali** (plural **jalolu**), historian/musicians from northwest Africa. The jalolu are sometimes referred to as **griots** (pronounced gree-oh), a term given to these historian/musicians by the French colonists of western Africa. Jalolu play a handmade plucked-string instrument called a **kora**, a type of lute-harp. A kora is constructed from a hollowed, dried gourd. Twenty-one strings are stretched over a goatskin that covers an opening in the gourd. The jali plucks the strings as he keeps time by tapping two sticks attached to the gourd near the neck of the instrument. Some elements of the blues are found in the jali songs, such as the vocal performance style, the use of blue notes, and the cross-rhythms that are heard between the voice and the instrument. But jali songs differ from the blues in that the vocal part is usually a long, unstressed or unmetered pattern that follows the rhythm of the text (unlike the more regularly metered blues) and the text content is often about the wars between empires or the history of a specific ethnic group (rather than the unfaithful partners or drinking themes in the blues).

When the blues were first documented in the 1880s there was no specific form for either the text or the harmonic progression to follow. There was no set number of measures, no set chord progression, and no set meter that composers/performers followed. The words and the melody were usually improvised according to the mood of the singer at that specific time. By the 1910s, composers who had had some formal musical training began to notate the blues, which previously had been passed on by oral tradition. The most famous composer of the blues in the 1910s was William Christopher Handy (1873–1958), who is often referred to as "the Father of the Blues." Handy is most often credited with stylizing the blues form that has remained more or less constant to the present day. Some of the blues songs that Handy wrote and published include *Memphis Blues* (1912), *Beale Street Blues* (1916), and the extremely popular and often covered *St. Louis Blues* (1914). Handy did not invent the blues; his text and harmonic structures are based on what he heard street musicians in

Memphis playing. He is one of the first composers, however, to use "blues" as a part of the title of a publication.[2] The music publishing industry in the 1910s and the recording industry of the 1920s, when the blues and other popular songs were recorded and widely distributed, helped to codify the form of the blues into what has become known as the **classic twelve-bar blues form**.

The twelve-bar blues form is so-called because each verse is twelve bars (or **measures**) long. No matter what the tempo of the song, there is a basic pulse that is counted in groups of four, with four pulses (beats) to each bar. The twelve bars are arranged into three groups of four measures: 4 + 4 + 4 = 12 bars.

The poetic structure of the blues song is a rhymed couplet: one line of the text (a) is sung to the first four measures, that same line of text (or a varied repetition of it) is sung to the second group of four measures, and a different, rhyming line of text (b), in which the thought presented in the first line is completed, is sung to the third group of four measures:

Example 2-2

Bessie Smith, *Reckless Blues* (1925), first verse

a When I was nothing but a child
a When I was nothing but a child
b All you men try to drive me wild.

The "a a b" rhyme scheme is not constant in all blues, although it is by far the most common pattern. Some blues singers might sing the same line of text for one verse resulting in an "a a a" rhyme scheme,

a When I was nothing but a child
a When I was nothing but a child
a When I was nothing but a child

and then answer that line in the next verse:

(Verse 2) a All you men try to drive me wild
           a Yes you men just try to drive me wild
           a I said you men just drive me wild

Another singer might change the rhyme scheme to "a b b," still a rhymed couplet but emphasizing the outcome:

a When I was nothing but a child
b All you men try to drive me wild
b All you men try to drive me wild

Still another singer might change the rhyme scheme to "a b c" by adding a new, improvised line to the text:

a When I was nothing but a child
b All you men try to drive me wild
c So stay with me just for a little while

But again, let me emphasize that by far the most common form of the blues verse is the "a a b" rhymed couplet.

Each verse of the song is sung in the same pattern to the same melody and with the same harmonic accompaniment, resulting in a strophic song form. (Most blues songs are strophic song forms with no recurring **refrain** or **chorus**, while most rock songs are strophic forms that include a recurring chorus.)

The basic harmony that is played in the accompaniment is as follows: the four bars of the first line is accompanied by the tonic chord; on the second line of text, the first two bars (measures 5 and 6) are accompanied by the subdominant chord and the last two bars (measures 7 and 8) return to the tonic chord; on the last line, the first two measures (measures 9 and 10) are accompanied by the dominant chord and the last two bars (measures 11 and 12) return again to the tonic chord. There are of course many variations on this basic chord progression possible, running a gamut from a simple monochordal accompaniment by a rural blues performer (an accompaniment using only the tonic chord as a drone) to the complex blues progressions of bebop jazz performers such as Charlie Parker or Thelonious Monk, in which a different chord is played on every single beat of the twelve measures. Very often on the last measure of the progression (measure 12), the dominant chord is played to set up the return of the tonic chord at the beginning of the next verse; this device is called a **turnaround**. The above verse from Smith's *Reckless Blues* might be diagrammed in the following way:

Example 2-3

Bessie Smith, *Reckless Blues*, first verse, harmonic structure

```
     |III            |III            |III      |III
a    When I was      nothing but a   child (instrumental fill)
     Tonic ----------------------------------------------------

     |III            |III            |III      |III
a    When I was      nothing but a   child (instrumental fill)
     Subdominant ---------------------- Tonic ----------

     |III            |III            |III  |III
b    All you men     try to drive me wild. (Turnaround)
     Dominant ------------------------- Tonic (Dominant)
```

In this diagram, the longer lines indicate the downbeat, or beat one, of every measure while the three shorter lines indicate the remaining beats of each measure. The last two measures of each sung line are an improvised instrumental passage called a **fill**, an instrumental response to the sung call. Fills are used to lead the singer to the next line of text and are played over the harmonically stable tonic chord. The turnaround in measure twelve is harmonically a stronger formula than the fill because it is on the dominant chord and is therefore harmonically unstable; the resolution of the turnaround demands a tonic chord, either the tonic chord of the first bar of the next verse, or a final tonic chord **(full cadence)** to end the song.

In the structure and performance of a blues song, the concept of call and response occurs on the following levels:

+ Between the singer (text) and the instrument (fills)
+ Between the first line of the couplet (a) and the ending line (b)
+ Between the fills and the turnaround

Blues Styles

There are two general types of blues: **rural** (or **country**) blues and **urban** (or **city**) blues. This section will deal with the rural blues first because it is from this genre that the urban blues developed.

Rural Blues

Rural blues developed in the 1920s and 1930s, primarily in the southeast (Georgia and the Carolinas), in the region known as the Mississippi delta, and in the southwest (Kansas City, St. Louis, Oklahoma City, and Dallas). Although these different styles of rural blues are defined principally by the regional characteristics of each style and in the individual performance traditions of the singers, there are some musical features that all have in common:

+ They are performed primarily by solo male singers.
+ The singers accompany themselves on acoustic instruments.
+ Words and melodies are frequently improvised.
+ Meters are irregular as needed in order to fit in all the words according to the feelings of the performer; some measures may consist of four beats, some of three beats, others of two beats within the same song and even within the same verse.
+ Performers do not always use the twelve-bar blues progression; many recorded blues (for instance by Blind Willie McTell) are based on ragtime styles.

While all the above-mentioned blues styles are interesting for their own specific characteristics, the rural blues styles that have been most influential on the development of rock music are those that developed in the Mississippi delta region and, particularly for guitarists, the Texas style that originated in Dallas.

Texas Rural Blues

The Texas rural blues style developed as a hybrid of many musical traditions that include rural white folk and dance music, Mexican folk music, Cajun and Creole music, and Eastern and Central European folk music as well as black folk music and work songs.[3] While many of the notable characteristics of the Texas rural blues style pertain to the vocal performance, the guitar accompaniment is quite noticeably different in comparison with other blues guitar styles. In general, the Texas rural blues can be characterized by (in contrast to the delta blues style):

+ Lyrics are sung more clearly.
+ Singing is in a higher register.

- Guitar lines are not as thick in texture (not chordal), but are more linear and melodic.
- Guitar accompaniment is less percussive, more smoothly picked.
- The guitar fills frequently alternate between the high and the low string of the guitar.
- Melodic fills at the end of sung lines are usually performed on single strings with little dependence on full, six-string chords.
- There is a tendency to play repeated melodic figures, or **riffs**, on the lower strings.
- Accompaniment sometimes utilizes arpeggiated chords, meaning the notes of a chord are sounded one after another rather than simultaneously.

The Texas blues is a tradition that stems from rural bluesmen Blind Lemon Jefferson, Henry "Texas" Thomas, and Texas Alexander and develops to include urban performers Aaron "T-Bone" Walker, Lowell Fulson, and Sam "Lightnin'" Hopkins to the rock/blues guitarists Johnny Winter, Billy Gibbons (from ZZ Top), and Stevie Ray Vaughan. The Texas guitar style, particularly through the works of T-Bone Walker, influenced a number of contemporary delta and Chicago blues guitarists such as B.B. King, Albert King, Albert Collins, and John Lee Hooker. The foremost figure in the Texas rural blues style was Blind Lemon Jefferson.

Blind Lemon Jefferson (c. 1893–1929)

Blind Lemon Jefferson was born in east Texas and made his way to Dallas in the 1910s. He was a street musician whose voice was said to have been able to carry well above the noise of downtown Dallas.[4] Much of Jefferson's history is speculative; blues historians have estimated that he was born around 1883, perhaps as early as 1880. It has been suggested that the name "Lemon" came from the supposition that he had a fairly light, somewhat yellowish, complexion although this is unsubstantiated.[5] Many sources indicate that Lemon was his given name, though some sources state that his real name was Clarence. Although legally blind, he had very weak eyesight that is generally attributed to some childhood disease; he was not born blind as some sources state.

Jefferson frequently traveled with a young protégé who served as his "eyes," that is, the person who guided him through the city especially when he had to play in unfamiliar surroundings. His "eyes" were also responsible for keeping track of Lemon's money, making sure that no one stole from the hat or put counterfeit money into it. For a time Jefferson's "eyes" was young Aaron Walker who later came into his own as guitarist T-Bone Walker.

Jefferson was discovered playing on street corners in the mid-1920s by a recording scout for Paramount Records who signed him to a recording contract. Jefferson recorded several songs between 1926 and 1929 for the Paramount label and for a small independent competitor, Okeh. One of his most frequently covered songs is *Matchbox Blues* (recorded in 1927), which was also recorded by Larry Hensley (1934), Huddie Ledbetter (better known as Leadbelly; 1935), Carl Perkins (1957), the Beatles (1964), and Doc and Merle Watson (1973), to name a few.

Listening Chart 1

MATCHBOX BLUES
BLIND LEMON JEFFERSON
from *King of the Country Blues*, Yazoo 1069 (1990). Originally released as Paramount 1274, 1927. Blind Lemon Jefferson, vocal and guitar.

Sound: Solo male voice self-accompanied on an acoustic guitar; tenor range; homophonic texture.

Form: Strophic song form with an eight-measure introduction. Six verses.

Harmony: The twelve-bar blues progression in A throughout (except the introduction).

Rhythm: The basic pulse at the beginning of the song is between 104 and 108 beats per minute. By the third verse, Jefferson has gradually increased the tempo (**accelerando**) to about 132 beats per minute; the tempo at the end of the song is about 168 beats per minute. The song is basically in quadruple meter (4/4), yet this meter is highly irregular, with Jefferson deleting and adding beats to various measures resulting in some measures of 3/4 and some in 5/4 as well as the basic 4/4. The surface rhythms in the vocal and in the guitar fills are evenly paced.

Melody: A small melodic range in the voice, well within an octave; the range of the guitar is very wide, accentuated by fills played alternately on the low strings and on the high strings. There are many single-note runs on the bass strings and the fills at the end of the sung lines are also mostly single-string runs. The vocal melody has a definite descending shape reminiscent of the field holler. There are also many repeated melodic riffs in the bass strings.

Text: The poetic form of the text is the standard blues aab form. As with most blues, *Matchbox Blues* relates a story of a love gone bad, although the verses do not necessarily relate to each other thematically. It was standard practice for a blues singer to improvise lyrics as well as the melodies and fills in a performance.

Because of the large quantity of recordings he turned out between 1926 and 1929, Jefferson became the first successful "down home" (rural) blues artist according to blues authority Stephen Calt. The success of Jefferson's records transformed the **race** record industry from its dependence on female blues singers such as Ma Rainey and Bessie Smith (often referred to as "classic blues singers"), to the male blues singer self-accompanied on acoustic instruments. Jefferson's relationship with the young T-Bone Walker provides a link between the rural Texas blues and the urban Texas blues, and ultimately on rock 'n' roll. Information concerning Jefferson's death is as conflicting as that of his life in general. He died in December 1929 and sources have stated variously that he froze to death, died of drinking too much, died in a car accident, and even that he was murdered. The most plausible story is that he died of a heart attack; sources close to Jefferson recalled that his heart attack occurred during a snow storm and this is likely the source of the claim that Jefferson froze to death.[6]

Mississippi Delta Blues

The Mississippi delta blues is considered by most rock historians to have had the strongest influence on the development of rock music. This is due to the fact that the delta rural blues style was such a strong influence on the Chicago style of urban blues, from which many rock performers took inspiration. The Mississippi delta blues developed in a triangular (delta-shaped) area of land along the Mississippi River bordering the states of Mississippi, Arkansas, and Tennessee; it is not referring to the delta of the Mississippi River, i.e., the mouth of the river as it flows into the Gulf of Mexico. The general characteristics of the delta blues include:

+ Frequent sliding from note to note (both in the guitar accompaniment and in the singing).
+ Frequent use of a metal sleeve or small glass bottle on the chording hand (slide guitar).
+ A hard, percussive picking style.
+ A forlorn, wailing type of singing.
+ A small melodic range, sometimes spanning only three or four different pitches.
+ Intricate polyrhythms between the vocal part and the guitar accompaniment.
+ Guitar fills are more typically chordal and rhythmic rather than single note melodies.

There were many figures in the rural delta region who were important in developing the Mississippi delta blues in the 1920s and 1930s, including Son House (b. Eddie James Jr.; 1902–1988), Tommy Johnson (c. 1896–1956), Willie Brown (c. 1900–1952), and especially Charley Patton (1891–1934), who is often referred to as "the father of the delta blues style." Patton's raw vocal style and his percussive guitar accompaniment, often performed with a slide, were an immense influence on his contemporaries and on the next generation of rural delta blues players, which included Robert Johnson and Nehemiah "Skip" James (1902–1969). In the late 1930s the Mississippi delta rural blues was transplanted from the farms and fields of the south to the industrial centers of the northern and midwestern United States, developing into the urban or city blues. The delta blues became the electric Chicago urban blues style practiced by Muddy Waters, Howlin' Wolf, James Cotton, B.B. King, and many others and as such exerted a great influence on the development of rock music. The rural delta bluesman who is most frequently cited as an important influence on rock performers is Robert Johnson.

Robert Johnson (1911–1938)

Robert Johnson was born in Hazlehurst, Mississippi. As with Blind Lemon Jefferson, many of the details of Johnson's life are speculative, perhaps due to the confusion surrounding his parentage. He was the illegitimate son of Julia Major Dodds, wife of a Hazlehurst furniture builder, and Noah Johnson, an itinerant plantation worker. In the course of his short life, Johnson was known variously as Robert Dodds, Robert Spencer, Robert Dusty, and, after he had learned who his father was, Robert Johnson.[7] He learned the rudiments of the blues from his brother, Charles Dodds, and Johnson's first instrument was the harmonica or mouth harp. He also learned the basics of blues guitar from Dodds.

When Johnson was a young man just learning to play the blues (c. 1925–1930), he learned the blues style by observing various traveling blues musicians including Charley Patton, Son House, and Willie Brown. At first the older bluesmen regarded Johnson as little more than a nuisance, bothering them at Saturday night dances, always wanting to play their guitars while the singers were on break. Later interviews with Brown and House state that early on Johnson was not very good and several times was chased away and booed by the audience.[8] Johnson reportedly disappeared for some time, most probably traveling around the area and learning as much as he could about playing the blues. When he returned to his old neighborhood and friends, Johnson reportedly had improved considerably both as a singer and as a guitarist. He had in fact become so good on the guitar that it was believed that he had sold his soul to the Devil in order to learn to play well and become famous. Three of Johnson's twenty-nine recorded songs deal with his supposed pact with the Devil: *Me and the Devil Blues, Hell Hound on my Trail,* and his most famous blues, *Cross Road Blues.*

Cross Road Blues illustrates both Johnson's personal style and the rural delta blues style in general. Notice the liberties that he takes with the meter, especially when he changes the accompaniment chords, his anguished style of singing, as if the Devil is after him, and his use of slide guitar. All of these characteristics influenced many of the urban blues artists in the 1940s and 1950s, some of the rock 'n' roll artists of the 1950s, and the blues rockers of the 1960s.

Listening Chart 2

CROSS ROAD BLUES (Take 2)
ROBERT JOHNSON
from *The Complete Recordings,* Columbia C2K 46222 (1990).
Originally recorded 1936.
Robert Johnson, vocal and guitar.

Sound:	Solo male vocal, self-accompanied on an acoustic guitar. The guitar is played with a slide and the strings are struck in a very strong, percussive manner. The voice has a pained, wailing quality to it that expresses the emotion of the text. The texture is homophonic.
Form:	Strophic song form with a three-bar introduction and a one-bar coda. Four verses.
Harmony:	The twelve-bar blues progression in B-flat, freely applied.
Rhythm:	The basic pulse is between 84–88 beats per minute performed in what classical music performers refer to as a **rubato** style of playing, meaning that there is a constant pushing ahead and pulling back on the basic pulse. The meter is primarily in duple (4/4) time, but it is highly irregular; Johnson adds and deletes beats in various measures according to the feeling of the words and how the performer responds to the words. The surface rhythm of the vocal part is mostly even, although the rhythm of the sung melody does not necessarily coincide with the basic pulse. The surface rhythm of guitar accompaniment subdivides the basic pulse into a triple pattern (i.e., three shorter beats to each pulse), resulting in a bouncy, uneven rhythm. This rhythm is sometimes called a **barrelhouse rhythm** and is derived from boogie woogie piano blues (see below). There are also some interesting **polyrhythms** between the voice and the guitar. Note the register changes of the guitar accompaniment, first playing a chordal rhythm in the low

	range and then suddenly sliding up the strings to the high range of the instrument.
Melody:	The vocal melody is almost static with a slight descent at the end of each sung line. An interesting trait of Johnson's playing is the melodic introduction of the song, particularly the descending figure on the bass strings. This descending bass-line introduction is used in almost every song recorded by Johnson and has since been used as a standard blues introduction by practically every blues player to the point that this introductory figure has become a cliché.
Text:	The poetic form of the text is the standard blues aab structure. The text, which at the outset takes place in the past but leads up to the present, relates a narrative of how Johnson went to the cross road looking for something. The last verse offers a warning to his friend Willie Brown not make the same mistake that Johnson did in going to the cross road to seek a favor that carries a high cost.

Johnson's *Cross Road Blues* contributes to the legends that surround the blues in general and Johnson in particular. One of the most well-known legends of the blues is the idea of selling one's soul to the Devil for the high life. Certainly not a new legend in history, it is the basis of the Faust legend, about a 16th century alchemist who supposedly sold his soul to the Devil for riches and fame, and is perhaps best known from the 19th century play entitled *Faust* by the German poet Johann Wolfgang von Goethe. The 19th century musician Niccoló Paganini, one of the greatest violin virtuosi ever, played in such a technically complex manner that his rivals also claimed that Paganini had made a pact with the Devil (it is also interesting to note that Paganini was also a virtuoso and flamboyant guitarist). In blues mythology, legend has it that if one wants to learn to play the best blues then one must go stand at a cross road at midnight on a Saturday and wait. Eventually a man will come up and tune your guitar (or fiddle), play a song on the instrument, and hand it back to you. If you take it back the deal is set: you will attain fame and fortune with your instrument, but when you die (usually at a tragically young age, often under mysterious circumstances, and always at the peak of your career), your soul belongs to Satan.[9] Supposedly, Johnson had his guitar tuned by Mr. Legba (or Old Man Scratch in other tellings) during the time that he was absent from his home town because when he returned and played for his mentors Willie Brown and Son House he reportedly astounded them with the vast improvement in his playing.[10]

Johnson died at a young age (27 years old) and under mysterious circumstances: in the past his death was variously attributed to stabbing, gunshot, and poisoning, all done by either a jealous girlfriend or the boyfriend or husband of some woman whom Johnson was bedding. It was also said that Johnson died insane and howling at the moon. Recent research by Peter Guralnick and Stephen La Vere has confirmed that on the evening of Saturday, August 13, 1938 Johnson played a dance at a juke joint in Three Forks, Mississippi. He had been flirting with the bar owner's wife that night and during a break was given an opened bottle of whiskey, which the bar owner had spiked with strychnine. After drinking the whiskey, Johnson became very sick but showed signs of improvement by Monday, August 15. Unfortunately, the poison had weakened his system and he died of pneumonia on Tuesday, August 16, 1938.[11]

Johnson was certainly at the peak of his career when he died: he had recently returned to his home town area and was beginning to make a name for himself as an important and talented blues performer. He had successfully recorded several songs in late November 1936 and mid-June 1937, and supposedly had other recording dates scheduled. Record executive and talent scout John Hammond was about to offer Johnson a chance to perform on a major black music concert that Hammond was organizing in New York City, called "From Spirituals to Swing," thereby introducing Johnson to a new (white) audience, when Hammond heard of Johnson's death. Johnson would likely have gained a recording contract from Hammond, who was responsible for discovering and promoting for Columbia Records such talent as Bessie Smith, Charlie Christian, Aretha Franklin, Bob Dylan, and Bruce Springsteen.

Robert Johnson remains an important figure in American music. He was a strong influence on the generation of Chicago blues singers who followed him, including Muddy Waters, B.B. King, Howlin' Wolf, Robert Jr. Lockwood, and Johnny Shines. Johnson was also a major influence on such rock performers as Eric Clapton, Jimi Hendrix, Mick Jagger and Brian Jones, Jimmy Page, and several others. Many of his songs have been covered by rock performers, for example *Cross Road Blues* (Cream, 1968) and *Love In Vain* (the Rolling Stones, 1969).

Urban Blues

Urban, or city, blues developed in the late 1930s in the large cities of the United States such as New York City, St. Louis, Dallas, and Kansas City, and remained popular into the 1940s and 1950s. However, the place that is most often associated with the urban blues style is Chicago. One important phenomenon that led to the development of the urban blues was the migration of African-Americans in the 1920s and 1930s from the rural areas of the south to the industrial areas of the north. Another element that contributed to the development of the urban blues was the invention of the electric guitar in the 1930s.

Like rural blues, there are many different styles of urban blues that are identified by the region or city in which they developed. And, like rural blues, there are general style characteristics that are common to all urban blues styles:

+ A male singer typically accompanied by a small group.
+ Instrumentation typically consists of electric guitars, acoustic bass, drums, piano, and harmonica. Some groups, particularly from the southwest (Kansas City, Dallas) and from Los Angeles may also include a horn section. In the Chicago blues style, the principal soloists are the harmonica and the guitar.
+ Because of amplification and extra personnel, the volume is very loud.
+ The music is more regularly metered than in rural blues because of the increased number of musicians who have to play together and because they primarily played in bars for dancing.
+ The twelve-bar blues progression is used almost exclusively.

Like the rural blues, there are specific regional characteristics that identify the various urban styles of blues. The urban styles that are most important in regard to the development of rock music are the Texas blues style, represented by Aaron "T-Bone" Walker, and the Chicago style represented by Muddy Waters.

Texas Urban Blues

Generally speaking, the Texas blues of the 1940s and 1950s had a stronger influence on other blues styles, some jazz styles, and southwestern rhythm and blues than it did on the development of rock music. The influence of the Texas urban blues style is reflected in the playing of many blues-based rock guitarists—Johnny Winter and Stevie Ray Vaughan for example. It was an extremely popular style of African American music in the years after World War II and is closely related to jazz styles of the same time, so much so that many jazz and blues musicians felt equally at home playing either style of music. The guitar stylings are typically jazz-influenced, using fast, evenly-spaced notes that are sometimes highlighted by "ghost" notes (notes that are fingered on the fretboard but are lightly picked or dampened).

The Texas urban blues style of guitar is based largely on the Texas rural blues style discussed above with two important differences: a full-sized band backs up the solo vocalist and the guitar is amplified. With the exception of Lowell Fulson and T-Bone Walker, the saxophone is often the solo instrument and brass are used in the backup band. This is reminiscent of the rhythm and blues or jump bands that were forming in the southwest (St. Louis and Kansas City) at the same time. It should also be stated that although the principal players of the Texas urban blues style, T-Bone Walker and Lowell Fulson, originally were based in Texas, after the War these performers' bases of operation transferred out to California, especially Los Angeles. However, they developed their style in east Texas, and based their style on the works of Blind Lemon Jefferson. The Texas urban blues is mentioned as a contributor to rock music primarily because of the influence of T-Bone Walker on other blues guitarists, such as B. B. King, Albert King, and Buddy Guy, each of whom was an influence on later rock guitarists, including Chuck Berry, Eric Clapton, and Jimi Hendrix.

Aaron Thibeaux "T-Bone" Walker (1910–1975)

T-Bone Walker was born in Linden, Texas and moved to Dallas when he was very young. While he was growing up, Walker was strongly influenced by the blues singing and guitar playing of Blind Lemon Jefferson, to whom he frequently listened on the streets of Dallas; as a young boy, Walker served as Jefferson's "eyes" (see above). He was also influenced by the boogie woogie pianists in the area and by such classic blues singers as Gertrude "Ma" Rainey and Ida Cox.

Walker was instrumental in bringing the electric guitar into prominence in the typically piano-based Texas blues. His approach was not to use the guitar as a harmony/rhythm instrument, as Johnson and the other delta blues players did. Instead, Walker followed the lead of Jefferson and the blues saxophonists, using the guitar for single-string improvised solos and fills. In his soloing style, Walker seems to have been influenced by jazz guitarist Charlie Christian; Walker's single-line fills in turn exerted a great deal of influence on B.B. King and others.

Walker achieved some fame in the 1950s only after he had moved from the Dallas area to California, where he recorded the classic *Mean Old World* in 1952. His greatest commercial success, however, was *Call It Stormy Monday Blues* (1947).

Listening Timeline 2-1

CALL IT STORMY MONDAY BLUES (1947)
T-BONE WALKER
Strophic song form
12-bar blues progression in G
Black and White BW 122
2:37

0:00	Introduction	Full band plays.
0:07	Verse 1, "They call it stormy Monday . . ."	Sax, piano, and single-string guitar fills.
0:48	Verse 2, "The eagle flies . . ."	Muted trumpet and guitar chordal fills.
1:31	Guitar solo (Walker)	Backed by tremolo piano, sax section riff.
2:14	Verse 3, "Lord have mercy . . ."	Tenor sax fills, muted trumpet growls, full guitar chord fills.

Walker influenced virtually every important post-World War II guitarist including B.B. King, Buddy Guy, Otis Rush, Jimi Hendrix, Eric Clapton, and Stevie Ray Vaughan.[12] He is considered to be the first blues artist to record with an electric guitar and to explore the wide range of sound possibilities on the electric guitar. He was also said to have been an excellent entertainer, playing his guitar behind his back and between his legs and doing splits on stage.[13] This was no doubt an influence on the stage antics of Chuck Berry and Jimi Hendrix. Problems with ulcers and alcoholism contributed to his death of bronchial pneumonia in 1975.

Chicago Urban Blues

Stylistically, Chicago blues is related to the Mississippi delta blues. This is because many of the major figures in the Chicago blues scene were born and raised in the delta region. Chicago blues and delta blues have much in common:

+ Frequent use of slide guitar.
+ Frequent sliding between pitches before settling on a specific pitch.
+ Numerous single-string fills at the end of a sung line (a trait influenced by Texas blues guitarists rather than delta blues guitarists).
+ Frequent use of bent notes.
+ Use of intricate rhythm patterns and polyrhythms.
+ Frequent use of double-stopped strings.

(It should be pointed out that rural blues performers rarely played solo breaks on their recordings, while in the urban blues style there is plenty of room for improvisation.)

Of the many excellent Chicago blues figures, two of the most notable performers are Muddy Waters and B.B. King (b. Riley King, 1925). The important role played by the Chicago blues style in the development of rock music cannot be overestimated. It exerted a strong influence on rock 'n' roll performers such as Chuck Berry, Bo Diddley, and Buddy Holly in the 1950s; this influence is evident primarily in these performers' guitar styles, which will be examined in later chapters. The Chicago bluesmen, Muddy Waters in particular, also made an enormous impact on such rock performers as Eric Clapton, the Rolling Stones, and a host of American and British blues-based musicians in the 1960s.

Muddy Waters (1915–1983)

Born McKinley Morganfield in Rolling Fork, Mississippi, Muddy Waters was adopted by his grandmother who moved him to a plantation near Clarksdale, Mississippi, one of the focal points of the delta blues. According to Waters, his nickname was given to him by his grandmother, who called him "Muddy" because he liked to crawl around and play in the mud (and eat it) when he was a toddler; as he got older, his main farm chore was to pump water for the farm animals, and his friends gave him the name "Waters."[14] The stage name he adopted therefore firmly tied him to his roots in the Mississippi delta region.

Waters' blues style is strongly based on the rural delta blues, which he heard as he was growing up in the south. His vocal style has a raw energy that stems from the work songs he sang as a young boy. His guitar sound is likewise based in delta blues tradition and the electric whine from his slide playing is a suitable match for his powerful voice. He was influenced by the performances of Son House that he attended whenever House was in the Clarksdale area, and Waters has also stated that he was strongly influenced by the recordings of Robert Johnson.

Muddy Waters moved up to Chicago in 1943 and, with the help of bluesman Big Bill Broonzy (1893–1958), entered the lively blues scene of the period. One of his first jobs was playing acoustic guitar in the backup band of singer/harmonica player John Lee "Sonny Boy" Williamson (Sonny Boy Williamson I; 1914–1948).[15] Waters soon switched to electric guitar, which he played in the delta slide manner.

Recording at the Chess studio in Chicago, Waters and his band made several excellent blues recordings in the 1950s. Many of these songs were covered by various rock groups in the 1960s and later, including *Hoochie Coochie Man*, *I Just Wanna Make Love To You*, *Little Red Rooster*, and so on. Waters' band consisted of some of the major figures of the blues including his half-brother Otis Spann (piano), Little Walter Jacobs (harmonica), and one of the most important figures in blues and rock, Willie Dixon (bass) who, in his roles as a composer, performer, and producer, served as an important link between the Chicago blues and rock music. Other blues performers who have played with Waters include Big Walter Horton (harmonica), Earl Hooker (guitar), James Cotton (harmonica), Joe "Pinetop" Perkins (piano), Fred Below (drums), and John "Memphis Slim" Chatman (piano). The nearly endless list of musicians who have played with Waters is a virtual Who's Who of the Chicago blues scene. In the late 1960s, Waters achieved a great deal of fame in the United States and England, and toured with several rock groups of the time. Though perhaps not as well known as other songs in Water's repertoire, the song *Blow Wind Blow* is typical of Muddy Waters' blues style and the Chicago urban blues style in general at the beginning of the 1950s.

Listening Chart 3

BLOW WIND BLOW
MUDDY WATERS

from *The Chess Box*, MCA CHD3-80002 (1989). Originally released as *Chess* 1550, 1950.

Muddy Waters, vocal and guitar; Walter "Shakey" Horton, harmonica; Otis Spann, piano; Jimmy Rogers, guitar; Elgin Evans, drums.

Sound: Solo male vocal in the bass range, rhythm electric guitar, lead electric guitar (fills), harmonica, piano, and drums; homophonic texture. The recording also has a thick, murky or muddy sound quality. The principal solo instruments are the harmonica and the piano.

Form: Strophic form with a twelve-bar introduction, four verses with an instrumental solo (harmonica) between verses two and three, and a solo (piano) between verses three and four.

Harmony: The twelve-bar blues progression in G.

Rhythm: The basic pulse is between 116 and 120 beats per minute and the meter is in 4/4 duple time. The ostinato figure played by the piano left hand (bass notes) has a bounced feel to it while the lead guitar and the right hand of the piano perform a constant triplet (fast three pulses) pattern. The rhythm guitar and the drums maintain a constant even pulse. The surface rhythms of the vocal coincide with the accents of the words.

Melody: The melody has a narrow range that starts on a high pitch followed with a noticeable descent at the end of each line. Waters sometimes shouts the opening line of a verse, emphasizing blue notes. The tone quality of the harmonica is particularly interesting in the solo: Horton often bends and sometimes pinches the notes of the harmonica in his unique approach to playing the instrument.

Text: The poetic form of the text is the standard aab pattern of the blues. The singer first addresses the world at large (one to the world) that he has woken up alone and that his woman is with another man. He then addresses the wind to bring back his woman, that he is lonely but he still loves her. The last verse is sung directly to his woman (one to another) in which he tells her goodbye and to go ahead and have her own way.

Muddy Waters is considered the major figure of post-World War II Chicago blues. His influence is expansive; a brief list of artists who were influenced by Muddy Waters includes Chuck Berry, Eric Clapton, Bob Dylan, Jimi Hendrix, Jeff Beck, Johnny Winter, Stevie Ray Vaughan, Robert Cray, and the Rolling Stones. Muddy Waters is an important link from the rural Mississippi delta blues of Charley Patton, Son House, and Robert Johnson and the hard-edged Chicago urban blues, which in turn exerts a strong influence on the development of rock. His recordings of the 1950s, such as *Mannish Boy, Hoochie Coochie Man, I Just Want To Make Love To You, Little Red Rooster*, and *Got My Mojo Workin'* are the classic recordings of Muddy Waters and define the sound of Chicago electric blues. They are among the greatest blues songs ever recorded, not only in terms of representing the Chicago urban blues style, but also in their far-reaching influence on rock music. Muddy Waters was also one of the few blues performers who was able to capitalize on his own music before others could push him aside. He died in his sleep of a heart attack at age sixty-eight.

Boogie Woogie

Boogie woogie, also known as honky tonk, is a percussive piano blues style that developed in the late 1920s and remained popular well into the 1940s, dying out after World War II. The name may come from the African Mandingo word **buga**, meaning "to beat a drum." It may also stem from the English slang terms **bogy** or **boogie**, which have been used to refer to dark-skinned people, or to dark apparitions, such as the "boogie man."[16] The term "boogie woogie" originally referred to a style of dancing that was popular in honky tonks, and the piano blues that accompanied the dancing came to be known as boogie woogie by the late 1920s. The first recording that had "boogie woogie" in the title was Clarence "Pine Top" Smith's *Pine Top's Boogie Woogie*, which was released in 1928.[17] However, the characteristic bass line that is associated with boogie woogie had appeared in sheet music publications in 1915 and Texas rural blues singer Blind Lemon Jefferson had been singing songs with the words "booger rooger" in 1917 or 1918.[18] Boogie woogie developed in the southwest (Kansas City, St. Louis, Dallas, and Oklahoma City are important centers); some of the major figures in boogie woogie include Meade "Lux" Lewis (1905–1964), Albert Ammons (1907–1949), Charles "Cow Cow" Davenport (1894–1955), and Jimmy Yancy (1898–1951).

The principal feature of boogie woogie is a repeated, or **ostinato**, bass line that is usually played in a fast, eight-pulses to a measure, subdividing a standard 4/4 meter into an 8/8 feel. Sometimes the bass rhythm is a steady, even eighth-note pulse, but more often it is played in a bouncy, long note/short note rhythm called a **barrelhouse rhythm** (Ex. 2-4).

Example 2-4

Boogie Woogie barrelhouse rhythm.

This bass ostinato sometimes takes the form of a **walking bass line**, a style of bass developed by the ragtime pianists of the late 19th century:[19]

Example 2-5

Walking bass line

The harmonic structure of boogie woogie follows the twelve-bar blues progression. There are a wide variety of boogie woogie bass lines, depending on the performer. Some typical examples follow:

Example 2-6
Boogie Woogie bass lines

Against these repeated bass lines, the performer improvised various intricate rhythmic figures in the right hand, creating layers of complex polyrhythms.

Sound: Acoustic piano.
Form: Strophic form with a free-form, one-bar introduction and a four-bar coda; ten verses. As an instrumental blues, this can be seen as a variation on a chord progression, what would be called a *chaconne* in classical music, rather than as a song form.
Harmony: The twelve-bar blues progression in G is used throughout. The ostinato bass pattern is an alteration of an open fifth on the downbeat and a major sixth on the upbeat of each chord.
Rhythm: The basic pulse is a steady eighth-note pattern ("eight to the bar") that is bounced in the barrelhouse rhythm. The meter can be referred to as an 8/8 meter, though it is probably notated in 4/4. The tempo is between 168 and 176 beats per minute with no deviation in tempo until the coda, where there is an abrupt tempo change to a slower tempo followed by a slight **ritardando**. The surface rhythms of the right hand feature a constant syncopation against the left-hand ostinato. Sometimes the surface rhythms are three pulses in the right hand against two pulses in the left, producing interesting cross-rhythms.
Melody: The melodic range is wide and punctuated with repeated riffs.

 **Listening Chart 4**

HONKY TONK TRAIN BLUES (Version 3)
MEADE "LUX" LEWIS
from *The Smithsonian Collection of Classic Jazz*, Columbia Special Products PC 11891 (1973).
Originally released by RCA Victor, 1937.
Meade "Lux" Lewis, piano.

The boogie woogie bass figure can be heard in blues recordings by Blind Lemon Jefferson, Charley Patton, Skip James, Robert Johnson, and other rural blues guitarists. This piano style is a noticeable influence on the piano playing of Fats Domino, Little Richard, and Jerry Lee Lewis. The basic rock 'n' roll accompaniment heard in songs by Chuck Berry, the Rolling Stones, the Who, and countless others is clearly derived from the boogie woogie accompaniment.

Endnotes

1. Paul Oliver, *Field holler* in *The New Grove Dictionary of American Music*, edited by H. Wiley Hitchcock and Stanley Sadie (New York: Grove's Dictionaries of Music, Inc., 1986), II, p. 116.
2. Robert Santelli, *The Big Book of Blues* (New York: Penguin Books, 1993), p. 166.
3. Alan Govenar, liner notes for *Blues Masters Volume 3: Texas Blues* (Rhino R2 71123, 1992), p. 1. See also Francis Davis, *The History of the Blues* (New York: Hyperion, 1995), p. 116.
4. Paul Oliver, "Blues," in *The New Grove Gospel, Blues, and Jazz* (New York: W.W. Norton & Co., 1986), p. 60.
5. See liner notes by Stephen Calt for *Blind Lemon Jefferson: King of the Country Blues* (Yazoo 1069, 1990).
6. Calt, liner notes for *Blind Lemon Jefferson: King of the Country Blues*.
7. See Peter Guralnick, *Searching for Robert Johnson* (New York: Dutton, 1992), pp. 10–12.
8. Guralnick, *Searching for Robert Johnson*, pp. 15–17.
9. See Jon Michael Spencer, *Blues and Evil* (Knoxville, TN: University of Tennessee Press, 1993), pp. 27–29.
10. Guralnick, *Searching for Robert Johnson*, p. 17.
11. Stephen La Vere, notes to accompany *Robert Johnson: The Complete Recordings* (Columbia C2K 46222, 1990), pp. 16–18.
12. Robert Santelli, *The Big Book of Blues*, p. 424.
13. Francis Davis, *The History of the Blues* (New York: Hyperion, 1995), p. 163.
14. Robert Palmer, *Deep Blues* (New York: The Viking Press, 1981), p. 100.
15. Santelli, *Big Book of the Blues*, p. 435.
16. Robert Palmer, *Deep Blues* (New York: The Viking Press, 1981), pp. 130–131.
17. ibid., p. 131.
18. Paul Oliver, Boogie woogie in *The New Grove Dictionary of American Music* (New York: Grove's Dictionaries of Music, Inc., 1986), I, p. 257. See also Palmer, *Deep Blues*, pp. 106–107 and p. 131.
19. Oliver, *Boogie woogie*, p. 257.

3 Country and Western Influences

Country and western music is derived from the folk music brought by British, Scottish, and Irish settlers to the southern United States and the mountain regions of the eastern part of the country in the 17th and 18th centuries. This folk music, which had become widely popular throughout the southern countryside in the latter part of the nineteenth century and the early twentieth century, spread across the country in the 1920s and 1930s. Hoping to capture the nostalgia of a time before the advent of automobiles, airplanes, and world-wide war, record companies at first referred to this music as old-time music—the type of music that was played at barn dances, corn huskings, and other rural communal activities in the last century. By the late 1920s, this style of music was known, most often derogatorily by record executives and almost always distastefully by the performers, as **hillbilly music**.[1] Eventually, the record trade magazines such as *Billboard* and *Cashbox* began to call the music country and western, shortened to C&W.

In addition to recordings, another important avenue for the performance of country music in the 1920s was the radio. Two important live radio broadcasts were the National Barn Dance, which debuted on WLS in Chicago in 1924, and the Grand Ole Opry, appearing on WSM in Nashville in 1925. These radio broadcasts, both founded by radio executive George D. Hay, followed the old time barn dance format: simple, nostalgic old-time music interspersed with jokes and monologues of rustic country humor. These broadcasts were extremely popular with their respective audiences, which were largely composed of middle-aged and older farm people.[2] The Grand Ole Opry in particular has remained popular to the present and has served as a starting point for many of the current country & western personalities. The Grand Ole Opry also inspired the television version of the barn dance, *Hee Haw!*, which debuted with hosts Buck Owens and Roy Clark in 1969. Although for a while it was felt that the Opry was in danger of losing its audience, in 1999 many younger country performers began going back to performing at the Opry and the cable television station TNN (The National Network) is broadcasting a few hours of the Opry on Saturday evenings.

The earliest country groups (c. 1900–1920) were sometimes called **string bands** and consisted of a lead vocalist, backup vocalists, fiddles, acoustic guitars, banjo, and acoustic bass; some groups also included the mandolin. Notice that there is no drums or piano employed in these early bands, just string instruments. By the late 1920s, country & western had developed into three distinct but closely related styles: **Southern Country, Bluegrass,** and **Southwestern Country Swing**. For this study, southern country music is of more importance, for it is from this style that many rock 'n' roll performers, particularly the white southern artists, drew inspiration, and it is this style that was mixed with the music of African-American blues singers to create the early sounds of rock 'n' roll. Of a lesser importance for the development of rock is southwestern country swing, which was from where Bill Haley rose to become one of the first rock 'n' roll acts.

Southern Country

The southern style of country & western, also known as southern country and which is associated with the Grand Ole Opry in Nashville, had a strong influence on the development of rock 'n' roll, especially through the music of Elvis Presley, Carl Perkins, and Buddy Holly. Many southern country tunes are based on the standard blues progression and the performance style also incorporates some of the techniques used in the blues, such as sliding between pitches and using blue notes. The general characteristics of southern country can be described as:

- Simple melodies with narrow ranges and uncomplicated surface (melodic) rhythms.
- Simple harmonic structures: sometimes the tonic-subdominant-dominant patterns found in the blues and very often an even simpler tonic-dominant structure.
- Simple, straightforward rhythms in which there is a clear meter of either three or four beats per measure with little or no **subdivision** of the basic pulse. When beat subdivisions are present, they tend to be even (that is, the basic pulse divides into two equal shorter pulses) rather than uneven or bounced (as in the **barrelhouse rhythm** discussed in Chapter 2).
- The basic beat generally remains steady throughout the song and all performers play strictly on the beat.
- The use of a **two-beat bass** in which the bassist plays the root of the chord on the first beat of a 4/4 measure and the fifth of the chord on the third beat of a measure. Guitarists strum the chord on beats two and four of the measure, resulting in a constant pulse throughout the measure. (In a triple meter, the root of the chord is played on beat one of one measure and the guitar strums the chord on beats two and three, then the bass plays the fifth of the chord on beat one of the next measure with the chord strums on beats two and three.)
- Lyrics often deal with unrequited love, jilted lovers, or a love gone bad.
- The instrumental solos tend to stay close to the established melody; there is very little elaborate improvisation.
- The vocalists have a nasal quality, slide from pitch to pitch (rather than producing a clear intonation), and sometimes use **yodeling** technique.
- Some bands also use the steel guitar (or Hawaiian guitar) as part of the band, which provides a twangy sliding effect that matches the voice.

The old-timey sound of Appalachian-based country music is demonstrated by the many recordings of the Carter Family. The Carters, consisting of Alvin Pleasant (A.P.) Carter, his wife Sara, and his sister-in-law Maybelle, formed as a performing group in Virginia in the 1920s. They all sang in a close-harmony "church-style," singing about family, rural life in general, and a churchly life as well (many of their songs were gospel songs). In addition, Sara sometimes played guitar or autoharp and Maybelle played guitar. Their repertoire consisted of gospel songs, folk ballads, and 19th century popular parlor songs. A.P. collected many of the songs they sang, British-Appalachian folk ballads that he gleaned from the surrounding area (he could be considered one of the first American ethnomusicologists). These songs were then arranged for Carter performances and recordings by A.P., though many may have been arranged by Sara. The sound of the Carter Family is described as a subdued sound "a straightforward music filled with honest feeling; a template for what would be called country."[3]

Maybelle Carter developed an interesting guitar style that became the model for later country-style guitar playing. Variously referred to as "the Carter scratch" or "Carter picking," her guitar style consisted of plucking the melody with her thumb on the bass strings while simultaneously brushing her fingers downward across the treble strings for the rhythm and harmony. An example that demonstrates the sound of the Carters is the song *Wildwood Flower*. *Wildwood Flower* is based on a 19th century parlor song called *The Pale Amaranthus*. Sara's vocal line features a lack of vibrato, a nasal twang, and her Appalachian pronunciation of words, resulting in a reserved singing style that seems to hold back on expressing emotion. Maybelle's guitar playing is her Carter picking style; later country guitarists used the song as a basis of their own playing style.

Listening Timeline 3-1

WILDWOOD FLOWER (1928)
THE CARTER FAMILY
From *Wildwood Flower*
Strophic song form
Simple I, V, IV progression
ASV 5323, 2000
3:10

0:00	Introduction	Solo acoustic guitar plays main melody on bass strings and strummed guitar chords.
0:22	Verse 1	Solo female vocal (Sara) joins guitarist.
0:43	Interlude	Instrumental melody.
1:04	Verse 2	
1:25	Interlude	
1:46	Verse 3	
2:07	Interlude	
2:28	Verse 4	
2:49	Coda/Interlude	

The sound of *Wildwood Flower* is typical of the Carter Family's recordings, particularly the alternation of sung verses and instrumental interludes. The Carters were an extremely successful recording group, recording up to 1943. At this time, Sara retired from show business (she and A.P. had divorced sometime back in the 1930s), and Maybelle continued to perform with her daughters; her daughter June later married country singer Johnny Cash. The Carters were one of the important dynasties in country music.

Jimmie Rodgers (1897–1933)

An important figure in the creation of modern southern country in the 1920s was Jimmie Rodgers, who is sometimes known as the "father of country music." Jimmie Rodgers, also widely known as the "Singing Brakeman," was born in Meridian, Mississippi in 1897. Although associated with the railroad in the 1920s, it is not actually known if Rodgers ever worked as a brakeman for any railroad.[4] Growing up in Mississippi, Rodgers was strongly influenced by the blues songs he heard there. In 1927 he teamed with a string band called the Tenneva Ramblers (the band members were from Tennessee and Virginia) who specialized in old-time music, and the group made plans to record for the Victor Talking Machine Company. Because of a conflict between Rodgers and the rest of the band concerning the name of the band, the group disbanded leaving Rodgers to record as a solo act for the Victor Company.

The songs that Rodgers recorded for the Victor Company sold fairly well, enough so that record executive Ralph Peer decided to record more songs by Rodgers. The first two songs were in the old-time manner: soft, simple ballads with Rodgers accompanying himself on an acoustic guitar. The third song he recorded introduced Rodgers' unique style that combined the old-time country style with the blues structure and sentiments with which he had grown up. The song *Blue Yodel* became a national hit and led to the billing of Rodgers as "America's Blue Yodeler."[5]

Listening Timeline 3-2

BLUE YODEL (1927)
JIMMIE RODGERS
from *First Sessions: 1927–1928*
Strophic song form
12-bar blues progression in A-flat
Rounder CD 1056, 1990
3:23

Time	Section	Description
0:00	Introduction	Strummed guitar.
0:05	Verse 1 ("T for Texas . . .")	
0:28		Yodel fill.
0:35	Verse 2 ("If you don't want me mama . . .")	
1:01		Yodel fill.
1:08	Verse 3 ("I'm gonna buy me a pistol . . .")	
1:33		Yodel fill.
1:40	Verse 4 ("I'm going where the water . . .")	
2:03		Yodel fill.
2:10		Guitar fill, irregular measures.
2:18	Verse 5 ("I'm gonna buy me a shotgun . . .")	
2:43		Yodel fill.
2:49		Guitar fill, irregular measures.
2:55	Verse 6 ("Rather drink muddy water . . .")	
3:17		Yodel fill with fade.

The combination in Rodgers' music of an old-time country sound and his country approach to rhythm mixed with the harmonic, melodic, and textual structure of the blues, and the blues lyric content as well, are what led to his reference as the "father of country music." The yodeling technique that became a trademark sound for Rodgers was possibly adapted from different sources, including field hollers, street vendors' cries, train whistles, and imitations of Swiss yodeling as performed in minstrel shows or vaudeville acts.[6] The yodel is the origin of the cracked or breaking vocals of such rock 'n' roll singers as Elvis Presley, Jerry Lee Lewis, and Buddy Holly, and the technique is still used by country performers.

Jimmie Rodgers died of tuberculosis in 1933. His songs exerted a great influence on such country performers as Ernest Tubb, Bill Monroe, Hank Snow, and most notably Hank Williams Sr., who in turn influenced his contemporaries in country music and, more importantly for our study of rock, was a great influence on many of the early singers of rock 'n' roll.

Hank Williams (1923–1953)

Hiram Hank Williams was born in rural Alabama and was raised by his mother. There are many different sources of Williams' music: his maternal grandfather was a blacksmith and supposedly made up work songs that accompanied his hammering; Williams also learned southern white gospel music from his mother who was a church organist for the family Baptist church. As a youth, Williams lived for a time with relatives in a small logging community and was exposed to weekly Saturday night dances that featured some old-time string bands. He was also influenced by various string band musicians and street singers in his hometown of Georgiana, Alabama. Many sources state that perhaps the biggest influence on Hank Williams was an itinerant black street singer named Rufe Payne who went by the name of Tee-Tot. Besides learning about the blues, Williams learned from Tee-Tot the art of working his audience, of giving them what they wanted and what they paid for.[7]

While still in junior high school, Williams won a local talent show in Montgomery, Alabama and through this earned a bi-weekly, 15-minute radio program on WFSA.[8] As a result of this radio exposure, Williams began to tour the area, playing at schools and at barn dances, and in this way he gradually attracted a following. He assembled a band of his friends in Montgomery to back him on these tours. It was the format of this band—fiddle, lead electric guitar, string bass, steel guitar, and Williams on vocals and acoustic rhythm guitar—that eventually coalesced into Williams' longtime group, the Drifting Cowboys. In the early days, this band played the part of complete entertainers: they told jokes and humorous short stories, sang and played up-tempo dance music, and sang slow ballads and inspirational gospel songs; there was something for everyone in the audience, just as Tee-Tot had taught him.

In 1946, Williams went to Nashville with the hope of finding an agent/promoter and a publisher for his songs. He signed with the publishing company owned by Fred Rose and Roy Acuff, the biggest publisher of country music in Nashville. In December of that year he returned to Nashville to record some demonstration tapes and in early 1947 Williams signed a recording contract with MGM Records. One of the first songs he recorded for MGM was the humorous, and perhaps autobiographical, *Move It On Over*, which was a great success for him. Although considered a "novelty" song, because of its humorous aspect, his songs were not just novelties. As one of Williams' fiddlers, Jerry Rivers, stated "they were serious, not silly . . . *Move It On Over* hits right home, 'cause half the people he was singing to were in the doghouse with the ol' lady."[9]

Listening Chart 5

MOVE IT ON OVER
HANK WILLIAMS
from *24 of Hank Williams' Greatest Hits*, Mercury 823 293-2 (1976).

Originally released as MGM 10033, 1947.

Hank Williams, vocal and guitar; Tommy Jackson, fiddle; Zeke Turner (James Cecil Grishaw), electric guitar; Brownie Reynolds, bass; Smokey Lohman, steel guitar.

Sound: Solo male vocal, tenor-baritone range with a backing band consisting of an electric guitar, pedal steel guitar, fiddle, acoustic bass, and acoustic rhythm guitar; the backing band members also sing a response in unison to the soloist in each chorus or refrain; the method of bass playing **(slapped bass)** and the strumming of the rhythm guitar provides a percussive pulse that is very drum-like in its sound; homophonic texture. Solos are performed by the electric guitar and the pedal steel guitar; during most verses the electric guitar and the fiddle provide countermelodies behind the lead vocal.

Form: A strophic song form with a four-measure introduction. Seven verses consisting of a four-bar verse and an eight-bar chorus; an electric guitar solo is played between verses 3 and 4, and a pedal steel guitar solo is played between verse 5 and 6.

Harmony: The 12-bar blues progression in E is used throughout the song. The bass provides a two-beat bass pattern for each verse and the first four bars of each chorus and then turns to a walking bass pattern for the last four bars; the walking bass pattern is maintained behind the solo instruments.

Rhythm: The basic pulse, set by the bass and the rhythm guitars, is approximately 160 beats per minute. The meter is a very regular quadruple meter and the band stays very close to the beat. The surface rhythms are primarily even with even beat subdivisions. The electric guitar solo contains some triple subdivisions of the beat **(triplets)** and the pedal steel guitar solo begins with a syncopated feel.

Melody: The voice and the solo instruments perform in a narrow range. The vocal melody is built mainly of ascending arpeggios in the verse and descending step-wise melodies in the chorus. There are some slides in the vocal part, with a little performance of blue notes.

Text: The text is a narrative ballad style in which the story is told in the four-bar verses in the form of a rhyming couplet. Each couplet is followed by an eight-bar refrain. The sentiment of the text involves the story of a man who, after carousing at bars, returns home to find that his wife has locked him out of the house and has changed the locks so that he must sleep in the dog house. The song is directed to the man's dog.

Williams became a regular performer on the radio program Louisiana Hayride in 1948. In 1949 he had his first number one hit song with *Lovesick Blues*. In June 1949, Williams debuted on the live broadcast of the Grand Ole Opry to a rousing applause that brought him back for six encores.[10] He signed a contract with the Opry and became a regular Saturday night performer until he was fired in 1952 for missing performances and generally being undependable.

Throughout his life, Williams had been plagued by a congenital back disorder that introduced him to prescription painkillers, for which he developed an addiction. In addition, Williams was an alcoholic by the time he was fourteen and this disease ravaged him mentally and physically all his professional life. He was at the peak of his career in 1951 when he began to quickly slide downwards due to his addictions. By 1952, Williams had become completely undependable, either performing at concerts drunk or not showing up at all. Williams signed a contract to play a performance in Canton, Ohio on New Year's Eve 1952 but never made it. He died in Tennessee sometime between December 31, 1952 and January 1,

1953, either in his motel room or in his car, from complications of drinking, ingesting prescription painkillers, and from two shots of vitamin B12 that each contained a quarter grain of morphine.[11] The official autopsy stated that Williams died of a heart condition brought on by excessive drinking.

Williams' voice is described as being reedy and piercing with a natural break in it (similar to yodeling) that put a somewhat mournful cry in his voice. This strained, mournful singing style is often attributed to drug and alcohol addiction and to his troubled marriage.[12] He sang his own compositions almost exclusively and his songs were written in very plain language. In some instances, such as *Cold, Cold Heart* and *Your Cheatin' Heart*, it is thought that the songs were successful because they are autobiographical, and as such, are teeming with emotion that cannot be falsified.[13] A part of Williams' importance in the history of American popular music lies in the songs he wrote, many of which were covered by other artists from Tony Bennett to Ray Charles to Elvis Presley; his songs include *Cold, Cold Heart*, *Jambalaya*, and *Your Cheatin' Heart*. Williams' importance in the history of rock music lies in his influence on the Memphis country rock style of Elvis Presley, Jerry Lee Lewis, Carl Perkins, and Johnny Cash. The Memphis country rock style, most often referred to as **rockabilly**, was influenced by Williams' songs such as *Move It On Over*, *Honky Tonk Blues*, and *Honky Tonkin'*.

Western Swing

The southwestern country style, referred to as **western swing**, originated in the Texas string bands of the late 1920s and early 1930s. Along with the typical fiddles and acoustic guitar instrumentation, the western swing bands also added **drums, piano, steel guitar,** and in some cases a **horn section** (saxophones, clarinet, trumpet, trombone). These bands performed the usual folk song and country ballad repertoire of the southern country tradition, but they also included performances of popular blues, jazz, and pop tunes. The players in western swing groups were generally more innovative and more receptive to other musical styles than were the southern country performers, and unlike their southern country counterparts, western swing musicians were encouraged to improvise like jazz players. Western swing was influential on mainstream southern country through the use of drums, walking bass lines, and electric instruments. One of the most important figures in western swing was Bob Wills (1905–1975).

James Robert "Bob" Wills was born near Kosse, Texas. His father was a farmer and a champion fiddler. When Wills was very young he began accompanying his father on mandolin and guitar; eventually he learned to play fiddle from his father and his grandfather. Through his youth, Wills was a popular performer at local dances. He moved to Fort Worth in 1929 and worked for a short time in a medicine show. Wills met guitarist Herman Arnspiger and formed the Bob Wills Fiddle Band. The duo played at local dances and house parties and eventually added singer Milton Brown to the group.

The Wills Fiddle Band was hired to play a radio show in Dallas in 1931, sponsored by a company that made Light Crust flour. They changed their name to the Light Crust Doughboys and their popularity in east

Texas soared because of their radio exposure. However, the band ran into many difficulties with the owner of the flour company and eventually Wills quit to form a new band, the Texas Playboys. Arnspiger remained with Wills but Brown formed his own western swing group, the Musical Brownies; Wills replaced Brown with a popular local singer named Tommy Duncan. Wills relocated to Waco, Texas where the band was very popular due to their radio show performances. When Wills learned that most of his fan base was in Oklahoma, he moved the band to Oklahoma City and later to Tulsa in 1934. It was at this time that he expanded the band to include horns, drums, steel guitar, and piano. Earning a recording contract in 1935 with the American Recording Corporation, the Playboys released a number of popular recordings between 1935 and 1940 on the independent labels Vocalion and Okeh.[14]

World War II brought many changes to the band. Shortly after the attack on Pearl Harbor, singer Duncan joined the army and other band members either were drafted or moved on to work at war plants; Wills himself joined the army for a short time. After leaving the army in 1943, Wills reorganized the Playboys and moved to California where they had a huge audience of transplanted Texans and Oklahomans who were working at various defense plants. Although the band personnel continued to change throughout the 1940s, they remained extremely popular with their audiences. They continued to play throughout the southwest in the 1950s and 1960s. A typical example of the western swing style is demonstrated by Wills' song *Swing Blues No. 1*, which they recorded in 1936.

Listening Timeline 3-3

SWING BLUES NO. 1 (1936)
BOB WILLS AND HIS TEXAS PLAYBOYS
Strophic song form
12-bar blues progression in C
Old Timey OT 105, 1966
2:30

Time	Section	Performer
0:00	Introduction	Full band plays.
0:19	Instrumental verse	Fiddle (Jesse Ashlock)
0:37	Verse 1 ("Lord my baby's got something . . .")	(Tommy Duncan)
1:00	Steel guitar solo	(Leon McAuliffe)
1:20	Verse 2 ("Listen here all you rounders . . .")	(Bob Wills)
1:45	Clarinet solo	(Ray DeGreer or Zeb McNally)
2:03	Verse 3 ("Lord I walked from Dallas . . .")	(Tommy Duncan)

Wills disbanded the Playboys in the mid-1960s, continuing as a solo performer into the late 1960s. In 1969, he was crippled by a stroke and was confined to a wheel chair. He suffered another stroke and died in May 1975. Wills is easily the most important figure in the western swing style of country music. In the early 1970s, the style enjoyed a brief revival due to performers like Red Steagall and His Coleman County Cowboys and, especially popular in the mid-1970s, the band Asleep at the Wheel.

The influence of country and western music on the development of rock music is sometimes overlooked, or at least underestimated by many writers on rock music. This may be due to an attempt to deny the influence of white musicians on the development of rock, or perhaps some writers are embarrassed by the old-fashioned, "hillbilly" roots of rock 'n' roll and they therefore downplay the music's role in the formation of rock 'n' roll. However, through its contact and intermixing with African American blues, Mexican folk music, Cajun folk music, and other ethnic musical styles, country and western had a great effect on the early performers of rock 'n' roll in the 1950s: Bill Haley, Elvis Presley, Jerry Lee Lewis, Chuck Berry, and Buddy Holly are all indebted to country and western in the formation of their own personal styles. Through these artists, country and western influenced some of the major rock performers from the 1960s to the present.

Endnotes

1. Douglas B. Green, *Country Roots: The Origins of Country Music* (New York: Hawthorn Books, Inc., 1976), p. 4.
2. Douglas Green, *Country Roots*, pp. 21–25.
3. Nicholas Dawidoff, *In the Country of Country: A Journey to the Roots of American Music* (New York: Vintage Books, 1997), p. 59.
4. Nolan Porterfield, liner notes for Jimmie Rodgers, *First Sessions, 1927–1928*, Rounder CD 1056, 1990.
5. Porterfield, *First Sessions* liner notes.
6. Curtis W. Ellison, *Country Music Culture: From Hard Times To Heaven* (Jackson, MS: University Press of Mississippi, 1995), pp. 37–38.
7. George William Koon, *Hank Williams: A Bio-Bibliography* (Westport, CT: Greenwood Press, 1983), pp. 10–11.
8. Koon, *Hank Williams*, p. 13.
9. Colin Escott with George Merritt and William MacEwan, *Hank Williams: The Biography* (Boston: Little, Brown, and Company, 1994), p. 62.
10. Koon, *Hank Williams*, p. 29.
11. Koon, *Hank Williams*, p. 51.
12. Bill C. Malone, "Hank Williams" in *The New Grove Dictionary of American Music* (New York: Grove's Dictionaries of Music, Inc., 1986), IV, p. 530.
13. Malone, "Hank Williams," p. 530.
14. It is interesting to note that the labels Vocalion and Okeh were extremely important labels for African American blues recordings, releasing records by Lemon Jefferson and Robert Johnson among many other blues artists.

4 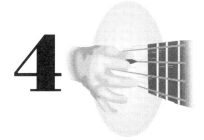 Searching for Masterpieces From the 1950s

Does this sound like someone you know? He gets up at 7:00 a.m. every weekday morning, has breakfast by 8:00 and is at work by 9:00. Noon is lunch. Work continues at 1:00 and concludes at 5:00. Dinner is at 6:00. The remainder of the evening is devoted to television. 11:30 is "lights out." The next day (and the next day) are the same. Saturday is reserved for yard/house work. Sunday is time for church and for the watching of professional sports. Sound familiar? What I'm describing is what is generally termed "the mainstream lifestyle." While throughout history this lifestyle has been pursued by many, it was especially prevalent (and pursued) during the era which many historians refer to as the 1950s. While it may be convenient to pigeonhole this time period into the ten-year span of 1950 to 1960, a more accurate duration would be 1945 to 1963. That is, the end of World War II through the assassination of John F. Kennedy.

There were three reasons why this lifestyle was so prominent (and indeed, so prized) during the 1950s. World War II and the experiences of the millions of young men who were processed by the military served to create several false impressions. While few would disagree with the United States prosecution of the war, it was easy to come away with the impression that the good guys (those on the right and just side) will always win. It taught millions to follow orders and to stifle any form of creative thinking. And, it gave the impression that a good war could pull the country out of economic difficulties.

The second influence upon the 1950s mainstream lifestyle was the Post War Baby Boom. Like the perennial pig which is swallowed by the python, this boost in the United States population eased along in a predictable manner, a manner which could not be missed by the country's economists, retailers, and advertisers. Economists knew exactly when there would be an increased need for baby carriages, for elementary schools, and for wedding rings. By 1956 there were over 13 million teenagers in America with approximately 7 billion dollars of disposable allowances and earnings. General Motors had it figured out. It produced five different grades of automobiles—each targeted at a different phase of the baby boom. Chevrolets, the cheapest, were intended for the teen buying a first new or used car. The Pontiac was for those landing a first job. Oldsmobiles were intended for those who were "moving up" and needed to transport a growing family. The Buick was for those who had reached the top of most professions and the Cadillac was reserved for attorneys, doctors, and politicians. The federal government encouraged this emphasis of the mainstream lifestyle by making the tax codes friendly to homeowners, growing families, and big business.

The third, and perhaps the most decisive influence on the mainstream lifestyle, was television. By the mid 1950s a television set in the living room was a given for middle-class families—just as a piano in the parlor had been a given for the middle-class of an earlier generation. If there was any doubt as to what the mainstream lifestyle (the goal for which to aspire) was supposed to look like, television rammed it home with weekly presentations of *Father Knows Best, The Adventures of Ozzie and Harriet, Leave it to Beaver,* and *Trouble with Father*. Here were white, middle class Americans living the ideal lifestyle in small (nondescript) towns with plenty of money, with parents who never seemed to sleep in the same bed, and with children who had no learning disabilities and no behavioral problems. In describing the hypothetical mainstream person at the outset of this chapter, I used the masculine form of the pronoun. While not exactly politically correct by the 1980s, it is perfectly accurate in describing the mainstream of the 1950s. As television clearly showed, women, many of whom had assumed factory jobs during the height of World War II and had learned to enjoy regular employment (and a regular pay check) were, once again, relegated to a supporting role. Despite Harriet Nelson's and June Cleaver's apparent joy with regular housekeeping, the resentment felt by many women during the 1950s would provide the basis for the women's movement of the 1960s.

The afterglow of World War II, the almost surreal economic growth spawned by the Post War Baby Boom and the spreading of the American "dream" through television, made it possible to ignore the excesses of forced segregation and to turn away from a war in Korea—a war which we did not win. And with personal home fallout shelters whose "three feet" of protective earth, transistor radios, stocks of canned goods, and Geiger Counters promised to protect the mainstream from possible atomic attack, it was quite possible to avoid a growing counterculture.

At the same time (although unseen and undetected by those living or striving for the mainstream dream) there was an active subculture, a culture whose "dreams" revolved around realities as well as self-indulgence, drugs, eastern mysticism, art, and homosexuality—in short, the exact opposite of the world of *Father Knows Best*. Dubbed Beats or Beatniks by the press, advocates of this subculture naturally gravitated to (and remained within the confines of) the bohemian districts of major cities, e.g. New York's Greenwich Village and San Francisco's North Beach. The counterculture occasionally came to the attention of the mainstream through the literature created by some of the culture's leaders—the so called Beat Poets.

Allen Ginsberg's poem "Howl" (1955) is a scathing indictment of the American mainstream and its effects on creativity, thought, and freedom. Jack Kerouac's novels, especially *On the Road* (1955) describe a lifestyle so far removed from the world of Ozzie and Harriet that it sounds like a different planet. Kerouac's characters lack commitment to any form of steady employment, lack what the 1990s would term family values, and a lack of anything except for living for the moment. William S. Burroughs' *The Naked Lunch* (1959) wallowed in the Beat's world of drugs and sex. Lawrence Ferlinghetti's collection of poems entitled *A Coney Island of the Mind* (1958) is a circus for the mind—an escape into the absurd. These, and other works, published in very small numbers and frequently banned from the collections of major libraries, had only a minor impact upon the mainstream culture. However, in other forms of media, some of the tenants of beat culture did sneak through.

Several films of the period featured young people who had difficulty fitting into the system. The "troubled teens" of the 1955 movie *The Blackboard Jungle* were not only anti-establishment but were associated with black styles of music—rock and roll and progressive jazz. Others including *Rebel Without a Cause* and *Streetcar Named Desire* reflected the "howling" of Allen Ginsberg and Jack Kerouac.

While it was easy enough for the mainstream to avoid such films, the aspects of beat culture which occasionally slipped past the censors and appeared on television were more difficult to dodge. Prime time television programing of the mid 1950s was dominated by the figure of Ed Sullivan. In addition to being a columnist of the *New York Daily News*, Sullivan hosted a weekly variety show which featured pop singers, comedians, and circus acts. *The Toast of the Town*, scheduled for Sunday nights at 8:00 p.m. (family time) was watched over by prim and proper (and wooden) Sullivan who endeavored to serve up wholesome entertainment which complemented the mainstream culture. Both Elvis Presley fans and students of broadcast history remember Presley's 1956 performance on Sullivan's show. Standing squarely against Presley's appearance on his wholesome show but bowing to economic realities, Sullivan insisted that the bottom half of the television screen be "blacked out"—an effort to protect the nation's teenage girls from seeing his hip gyrations and imagined obscene acts.

At the same time another variety show with essentially the same format was hosted by Steve Allen. Allen, a comedian and accomplished musician, occasionally pushed his show toward beat culture. Among the predictable appearances by comedians and pop singers, Allen (using a troupe of in-house cast, including Tom Poston and Don Knotts) poked fun at mainstream culture. Using the format known as "man on the street" interviews, Allen attempted to discuss current events with "normal looking folks"—folks who were too stressed out by their mainstream jobs to understand his questions or too high on life to care.

Another regularly occurring feature was a "band" called the "Unidentified Flying Objects." Allen always interviewed the band prior to its performances. While the band's bass, piano, and guitar players usually seemed quite normal, a fourth player (who played a different "instrument" each week) did not. On one evening's performance he played ice. As he explained during the interview, he started out with ice cubes and eventually worked his way up to blocks—played with an ice pick. On another occasion he played meat. Surrounded by various cuts of beef he explained how he had started out with hot dogs and eventually worked to "slapping real meat."

An additional aspect of the beat culture was its interest in urban black culture—especially its music. It was through several forms of this music that beat culture floated through the veneer of the mainstream culture.

Jazz, which had been invented and developed by black musicians during the opening years of the 1900s, eventually became white pop music. By 1940 swing, one of its many styles, was performed by white swing ("big") bands, was broadcast on white owned radio stations, was recorded by white owned record companies, and was danced to by whites of all ages. With the end of World War II and the emergence of the 1950s mainstream culture, dance halls closed down, thousands of talented musicians saw their lucrative jobs in big bands evaporate, and television became the primary source of American entertainment. And American pop music entered into one of its most inane periods. The vacuum created in the jazz world was filled with a new style known as bebop. Bebop, created in the jazz clubs of Harlem, was intense, complicated, and demanded too much of the average listener's attention. During the early 1950s most Americans turned to the style of popular music which was being produced by "canaries." Canaries were former featured singers with big bands. Their names e.g., Eddie Fisher, Dinah Shore, Tony Bennett, Frank Sinatra continued to be part of the American entertainment landscape well into the 1990s. They recorded "singles" which appealed to the newly emerging mainstream culture. As with the television programs of the period, they espoused antiseptic male-female relationships, good clean family fun, and wholesome humor. Number one songs of 1950 included "How Much is that Doggie in the Window," "Mona Lisa," "Tennessee Waltz," and "The Shrimp Boats are Coming." No wonder rock and roll sounded so radical!

While it is usually (and correctly) assumed that black musicians had a deep impact upon popular music in America, their role in other forms of music is often overlooked. The Colored American Opera Company, one of the first owned and operated black businesses, was founded in Washington, D.C. in 1872. With black musicians on stage, in the orchestra pit, on the conductor's podium, and in the front offices, it predated Motown Records by almost a century. Black concert pianist Louis Moreau Gottschalk made extensive concert tours of the United States and Europe. And Black Swan Records (founded in 1921) proudly printed on all its record labels, "Only Records Made Entirely by Colored People." The first time the majority of white America came face to face with this aspect of black culture was within the pages of *Ebony*, a magazine founded in 1942 which presented stories about black professionals, black social events e.g. "coming out parties," and black entertainers. Nevertheless, it was the black style known as the blues which had the biggest impact upon American popular music and which was the ancestor of rock and roll.

Despite several theories which suggest an African origin (and even a French origin), the blues appears to be a style of music which was developed in the rural south by black musicians. While hundreds of different styles of blues evolved before and after 1900 (many suggest that each blues performer creates his or her own style) they all had several elements in common. In its purest form, the blues is performed by one singer who usually accompanies himself with the guitar. The tempo is slow, the subject is "blue"—usually about a painful relationship with a member of the opposite sex, and the mood is generally one of lost hope. Holding all this together is a form which is both ingenious and simple. It is generally referred to as the "12 bar blues form." The form is divided into three phrases of identical length. Each consists of four measures of quadruple meter—16 pulses. See Fig. 4.1.

During phrase A the first of three lines of text is presented. Typically it occupies only the first two measures. The remaining two are devoted to instrumental "fill." Depending on the skill of the performer, this fill can answer, reinforce, and/or continue the mood of the words. Phrase B is an exact (or almost exact) repetition of the text from phrase A. The text in phrase C, the climaxing moment of the form, answers or comments upon

FIGURE 4.1 Standard 12-bar blues form.

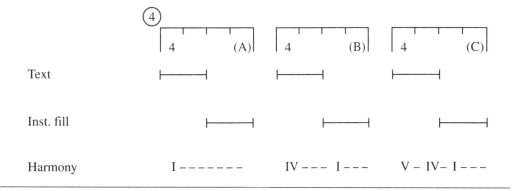

FIGURE 4.2 Opening lines of "Kind Hearted Woman Blues" text.

I got a kindhearted woman do anything in this world for me
I got a kindhearted woman do anything in this world for me
But these evil-hearted women man, they will not let me be

the text of phrases A and B. The first three phrases of "Kind Hearted Woman Blues" by Robert Johnson (Fig. 4.2), one of the major creators and performers of Delta Blues—an early precursor of rock and roll, is a good example.

The simple but effective harmonic changes which define the form serve to emphasize the message of the words. Phrase A uses only one chord. In Fig. 4.1 it is represented by the Roman numeral I [*the tonic chord*], and as in "Mary Had a Little Lamb," it is the home chord—a chord which creates no tension. While it can (and usually is) repeated several times within the phrase it never changes. Phrase B employs two chords. Its first two measures are harmonized by a chord represented by the Roman numeral IV [*the subdominant*], a chord which although not dissonant on its own, sounds a little "away from home" after hearing four measures of I. It serves to emphasize and perhaps give a slightly different flavor to the repeated text. The remaining two measures of phrase revert to I, the home harmony. Phrase C is the climax of the harmonic structure. Its text provides the answer to the statement of the first two phrases and is emphasized by the use of the chord represented by V [*the dominant*]. Again as with the IV chord, it is not dissonant and it does not create tension on its own. However when heard within the "home" created by the predominant harmony (the I chord), it creates considerable tension. The V chord is used in only the first measure of the phrase. Measure two returns to the IV chord (a little less tension) and the remaining two measures revert to the I chord. In other words, the blues form begins at home (phrase A), goes a short distance from home and returns (phrase B), travels farther away from home and, through somewhat of a winding road, finally returns home (phrase C). Fig. 4.3 is a "tension diagram" of the 12 bar blues form.

The first measure of phrase C, the climax of both the text and the harmonic tension, occurs at exactly the "right place." The symphonies of Mozart, the plays of Shakespeare, as well as well constructed "made for

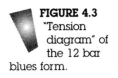
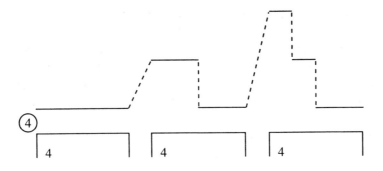

FIGURE 4.3 "Tension diagram" of the 12 bar blues form.

TV movies" inevitably feature climaxes which occur about 2/3rds of the way through the work.

In performance, the three phrases of the basic 12 bar blues form are usually repeated at least four times without pause. Different lines of text for each twelve measures allow the performer to reinforce his point or to develop the subject. The beauty of the form is in its simplicity. Accomplished blues creators and performers rarely remain slaves to the basic form. Robert Johnson's classic "Hell Hound on My Trail" stretches the four measure phrases to phrases of 5, 5-1/2, and 6 measures. These modifications are not only part of his individual style but are also used to emphasize certain words or groups of words.

As black musicians migrated to the urban centers of the north, their various styles of the blues continued to evolve. By as early as 1930, one of these styles, rhythm and blues (R&B) had become one of the predominant styles of black popular music. A minority music within the mainstream of white pop music, it was recorded by black owned record companies, broadcast by black owned radio stations, and danced to in black owned dance halls. To the vast majority of the white population it was completely unknown.

Because it was primarily dance music it had to be loud. It also had to be strictly structured—it's not easy to dance to music with phrases of 5-1/2 measures. Because it had to be audible in large venues, it was usually performed by bands of three or more. Although the resulting stability sacrificed some of the subtleties which could be produced by a single performer, R&B was no less unique. In fact, black musicians performed and created in all the forms and styles employed by white musicians. Opera singers, concert pianists, pop singers, and big bands all had their counterparts within the black community. However, R&B had no white counterpart. During the mid 1950s this void would be filled by rock and roll.

Rock and roll is (despite theories which name The Beatles, Elvis Presley, Alan Freed, and Jewish record producers and composers as its creators) Black R&B—especially black R&B as performed by white musicians. R&B was eventually discovered by white teens who were looking for an alternative to the pap which clogged the play lists of their parent's favorite radio stations. As thousands upon thousands of young people became attracted to their new "discovery," it became obvious to white musicians that there was money to be made from this black music. Consequently, the early 1950s witnessed the birth of the "covering" of R&B songs by white musicians. Covering, the re-recording of an existing record (sometimes with adjustments), was already widespread in the recording industry of the day. A recording of a hit song invariably spawned numerous covers. The real question was which white musicians would do the covering. The former members of the once dominant big bands were either working on Broadway, recording music for films, backing up canaries, or (in most cases) employed outside of the music business. Jazz musicians were working in a style which was far removed from R&B and were singlemindedly devoted to their art form. The musical style closest to R&B was performed by the members of another minority music—"hillbilly." Over a period of several hundred years, hillbilly musicians from the South and Southwest (decedents of early immigrants from the British Isles) had developed a large number of styles. Most were based on epic poetry—they told stories. Most were based on the song form known as strophic—lots of verses to the same music and refrains which remained unchanged throughout the song. By 1950 many hillbilly musicians had become proficient on the one instrument which seemed to be absent from much of R&B—the guitar. One style of hillbilly music, Western (or Texas) Swing exhibited the influence of both big band swing and R&B. Songs occasionally employed the 12 bar blues form and quadruple meters in which emphasis was placed on pulses two and four—the "backbeat." "Ida, Sweet as Apple Cider," recorded in 1936 by Milton Brown and his Brownies, featured electric steel guitar solos. Honky Tonk employed amplification for all instruments. This style was performed in honky tonks, large bars which featured a dance floor, mechanical bulls, and flying beer bottles. The band, usually placed behind a wall of chicken wire fencing, required amplification to be heard above the din. The shift from western swing or honky tonk to R&B was not only easy (a good hillbilly musician could "learn" a R&B song in an afternoon) but potentially lucrative.

While few can agree which R&B song was first covered by white musicians, Bill Haley's 1952 cover of "Rock the Joint" must have been one of the first. Formerly the Downhomers, Bill Haley and the four Aces of Western Swing (and by 1949) Bill Haley and the Saddleman, Haley changed styles in 1952 and became Bill Haley and His Comets. In 1954 he covered Jesse Stone's R&B classic "Shake, Rattle, and Roll" (Fig. 4.4). While covering the melodies and harmonies of most R&B songs was simple enough, the words were occasionally problematic. Part of the problem arose from the very nature of the style. R&B performers frequently changed the words from performance to performance. Words and entire verses were routinely adjusted to correspond to the nature of the audience or the mood of the performer. This inconsistency in the text and its frequent use of slang, sexual code words, and double entendre occasionally led to misunderstanding and even embarrassing results. R&B legend Joe Turner's 1954 recording of "Shake, Rattle and Roll" begins:

Haley's cover opens with:

> Get out in that kitchen and rattle those pots and pans
> Get out in that kitchen and rattle those pots and pans
> Well roll my breakfast 'cause I'm a hungry man

FIGURE 4.4 "Shake, Rattle and Roll" text.

> Get outta that bed, wash yo' face and hands
> Get outta that bed, wash yo' face and hands
> Well you get into that kitchen, make some noise with the pots and pans

Searching for Masterpieces From the 1950s **73**

While both versions paint the same scene (male dominance), Haley's adjustments to the grammar tend to take some of the bite out of the original. Turner's second verse goes a little farther.

> Well you wear low dresses, the sun comes shinin' through
> Well you wear low dresses, the sun comes shinin' through
> I can't believe my eyes all of this belongs to you

In it he evokes the open sexuality of a young lady positioned to revel womanly charms. Haley, or his recording company's sensors, felt the need to make adjustments in the corresponding text in his cover. The result,

> Wearin' those dresses your hair done up so right
> Wearin' those dresses your hair done up so right
> You look so warm but your heart is cold as ice

removes all of the steam of the original lines. Conversely, Turner's fifth verse,

> I'm like a one-eyed cat peepin' in a seafood store
> I'm like a one-eyed cat peepin' in a seafood store
> Well I can look at you tell you ain't no child no more

is filled with black slang and sexual innuendo. "One-eyed cat" and "seafood store" of course refer to male and female genitalia. Incomprehensible to Haley, he simply sings out the verse with no adjustments. Turner's seventh verse,

> I said, over the hill way down underneath
> I said, over the hill way down underneath
> You make me roll my eyes, Baby, make me grit my teeth

was simply avoided. Haley's cover of "Shake, Rattle and Roll," as well as many other white covers of R&B songs, is usually judged to be inferior to the original. Haley's version, despite the corruption of the original text and the impression he gives of working "too hard" at the creation of an attitude, does work. He re-creates the energy of the original. The musical abilities of the members of his band do seem to fit the style of the art form. Also striking is the double stop gliss which the guitar player plays on the first pulse of the song and repeats in selected places throughout the song. While this sounds impressive and technical, it is produced quite easily. The guitar player simply fingers the top two strings on the guitar (using two fingers or even one for both) and slides down the finger board. With additional help from the tenor saxophone and at a volume approaching distortion, the slide sounds continuous and somewhat menacing. Haley was quoted as saying, "We use country instruments, play R&B, and get *pop music*. As some have observed, it appeared that Haley didn't even know what he had created. The term "rock and roll" was not invented by Bill Haley or Alan Freed. The phrase was standard slang within the black community and referred to sexual activity. Certainly part of black culture as early as 1920, it first appeared in print in 1946 as part of a review of the song "Sugar Lump." The song was described as "Right, Rhythmic, Rock and Roll."

Elvis Presley's cover of Jerry Leiber and Mike Stoller's classic "Hound Dog" was even less successful than Haley's "Shake, Rattle and Roll." Of course, I mean successful in the musical sense, not the economic sense. Again, the words were problematic. The song, written for Willie Mae "Big Mama" Thornton, was a woman's lament regarding the wanderings of her man. The first verse with its dog itching to get outside (other women) and its reference to gratification at home and other sexual overtones sets the mood of the entire song. The song's last verse (with its sexual "weeps" and "moans") rounds out the lament.

Presley, whose manager and producers were desperately attempting to paint their young property as clean, pure, and honorable, made the required adjustments to the text. His cover steers clear of all mention of "weeps," "moans," "snoopin'," and "tail wagging." In fact, his version, which employs only adjusted versions of verses one and two—repeated in no meaningful order, excises the heart and thrust of the original. And while "Big Mama" stretched the 12 bar blues form—the third phrase of each verse actually consists of five measures (she had more to say); Presley's version is a slave to the textbook version of the form. The machine gun-like snare drum punctuation at the end of each phrase as well as the vocal harmonies which occur during both of the instrumental breaks become painfully predictable. Even fifty years later, there is still plenty of punch in "Big Mama's" recording. In an art form which emphasizes a certain authenticity and honesty in vocal quality (the same honesty required in the art form known as "rap") "Big Mama" set the standard. The fact that Presley's cover sold millions of copies while "Big Mamas" version remained in relative obscurity only serves to emphasize the importance of media exposure and the fact that the average thirteen-year-old did not care about the text. What teen even understood or cared about the meaning of another of Presley's million sellers—"Jail House Rock?" In fairness to Presley and many of the teen idols which would follow, it must be remembered that they were sailing in uncharted waters. No one knew exactly what a rock and roll star's career was supposed to look like. In addition, since rock and roll was, in the minds of many, a passing fad, most early rock and rollers assumed their early success would lead to careers in Hollywood.

Two Masterpieces

Despite the beauty of the Everly Brother's glow of sound, despite the power and colors of Little Richard's voice, and despite the attitude which Jerry Lee Lewis could bring to a performance or a recording, the vast majority of the R&B-based rock and roll which was created during the 1950s was simplistic, repetitive, and mildly offensive. I don't mean sexually offensive. I mean offensive in the sense that so much money and notoriety was made and derived from so little. Despite the pronouncements of socialists, the hype, and the best efforts of "The King," it is difficult to cite many musical masterpieces (masterpieces which can stand beside the best of the 1960s and later) which emanated from this first phase of rock and roll. There were two notable exceptions. Songwriters Chuck Berry and Buddy Holly each created at least one song which rose above the rest.

Chuck Berry, rock and roll's first important electric guitar virtuoso—and precursor of Jimi Hendrix, Jimmy Page, Jeff Beck, and so many more—was equally important as a song writer. Coming from the R&B tradition, Berry was able to manipulate its form and absorb new forms to create songs which went beyond the R&B norm and which went beyond the subject of male-female relationships. His "Roll Over Beethoven" (1956), a song in which Berry blasted snooty culture, employed the 12 bar blues form's phrase lengths and harmonic formula but featured constantly changing text—no automatic repetition of the words of phrase one in phrase two. "Sweetlittle Sixteen" (1958) was not R&B at all but the 16 measure phrase structure favored by hillbilly musicians. Berry's finest creation, and the closest we can get to a masterpiece from the 1950s is "Maybellene" (Fig. 4.5). Recorded in 1955, "Maybellene's" text and music create a world which is unmatched in the rock and roll music of the period.

Even a casual listen (or even a look) at "Maybellene's" text reveals a dichotomy. The refrain, which is always the same, seems to fit the text formula of the 12 bar blues form. The verses, which are all different, do not. In fact, the refrain is in the 12 bar blues form with its standard pattern of tension and release. The verses are static. That is, while they employ a lot of words, there is no harmonic change at all. Nor is there any change in melody. A case could be made for identifying these verses as rap—or at least a precursor of rap. Consequently, the verses are all tension and no release. Adding to this feeling is Berry's consistent use of a type of chord [*augmented*] which is neither major or minor—a chord which tends to create tension on its own. This dichotomy of intense tension and occasional release is amplified by the song's text and by Berry's vocal style. To emphasize the rural nature of the song's setting, he sings the refrains with a slight Creole accent. The verses are sung with a slightly different accent and with a more open vocal timbre. In addition (and further adding to the tension) the re-

Refrain

Maybellene, why can't 'cha be true?
Oh, Maybellene, why can't 'cha be true?
You done started back doin' the things you used to do.

Verse I

As I was motivatin' over the hill, I saw Maybellene in a coupe de ville
A Cadillac a-rollin' on the open road, nothing outrun my V-eight Ford
The Cadillac doin' 'bout ninety-five, we's bumper to bumper, rollin' side to side

(Refrain)

Verse II

The Cadillac pulled up to a hundred and four, the Ford got hot and wouldn't do no more
It then got cloudy and started to rain, I tooted my horn for a passin' lane
The rainwater blowin' all under my hood, I knew that was doin' my motor good

(Refrain—twice)

Verse III

The motor cooled down, the heat went down, and that's when I heard that highway sound
The Cadillac settin' like a ton of lead, a hundred and ten half a mile ahead
Cadillac look like it's settin' still, and I caught Maybellene at the top of the hill

Refrain

frains are in the present tense while the verses are set in the past tense. Berry employs even more subtle devices in the creation of tension. The words "road" and "Ford," which occur in line 5 are supposed to rhyme. They do not. His forced pronunciation of "Ford" to try to make it rhyme with "road" is not an error on his part. Berry, one of the best "rhymers" ever, is employing the literary devise known as assonance. In its most basic definition assonance simply means the rhyme "isn't quite right." Berry employs the device here, and in line 10 to pile on more tension.

Tension between the refrains and the verses is also revealed in the music and its effect on the text. Tempo is usually measured in "pulses per minute." That's what a metronome measures. Here, the tempo is extremely fast. The 48 pulses which make up the 12 bar blues form of the refrain move at over 250 pulses per minute. The tempo of the verses is the same. In way of comparison, Elvis' cover of "Hound Dog" moves at a tempo of about 190 pulses per minute. The breathless nature of the verses is enhanced by the fact that more words occur in each four-measure unit. The lines of the refrain vary from 8 to 11 syllables each. The lines of the verses contain as many as 24 syllables.

Throughout its history the automobile has been associated with sex. During the explosion of television as an advertising media sex was used to sell cars. As soon as the Baby Boomers were able to secure driver's licenses, cars became a symbol of escape, sexual freedom, and fun. While the subject of automobiles permeates the songs of the early 1960s it is surprisingly absent in the songs of the 1950s. The precise meaning of Berry's song is open to a number of interpretations, e.g. exactly what does happen when he catches Maybellene at the top of the hill? The "story" does not seem to have any conclusion. Does the use of a fade out, so common in music of the 1980s and 1990s but rare in the 1950s, indicate that the story continues somewhere beyond our ability to hear?

In "Maybellene" Berry sets up contradictions upon contradictions—contradictions which have been interpreted as white music vs. black music, sexual power vs. sexual jealousy, man vs. machine, and a host of others. In fact, Maybellene may not even be a woman at all. Maybellene may simply be a symbol for something elusive. In some ways that is Berry's final dichotomy.

The Crickets, formed by Buddy Holly in the mid 1950s, was rock and roll's first important band. Despite the fact that the band recorded only a small number of songs and despite the fact that Holly left the band in late 1958, its recordings were remarkable. They pointed the way to rock and roll's next level—a level achieved by The Beach Boys and The Beatles. The instrumentation of Holly's band, comprised of lead guitar, rhythm guitar (both electric), bass, and drums became the prototype of many bands of the future. Much has been made of Holly's vocal timbre or timbres. Early writers and critics reported that he was unable to control the sound and/or pitch of his voice. Others were convinced that he suffered from some sort of speech impediment. In fact, Holly was simply using his wide range of vocal timbres and inflections to enhance the meanings of his songs. The first important "studio band," Holly's songs were conceived with the recording studio in mind. Within the environment of the studio music can be created which contains subtleties of nuance and meaning—subtleties which cannot have their effect in live concerts which routinely include hundreds or thousands of screaming young people. "Peggy Sue" (1957)

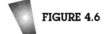
FIGURE 4.6

Verse 1

If you knew Peggy Sue, then you'd know why I feel blue
'Bout Peggy, My Peggy Sue
Oh well I love you gal, yes I love you Peggy Sue

Verse 2

Peggy Sue, Peggy Sue, Oh how my heart yearns for you
Oh-oh Peggy, my Peggy Sue
Oh well I love you gal, yes I love you Peggy Sue

Verse 3

Peggy Sue, Peggy Sue, pretty pretty pretty Peggy Sue
Oh-oh Peggy, my Peggy Sue
Oh well I need you gal and I need you Peggy Sue

Verse 4

I love you Peggy Sue with a love so rare and true
Oh Peggy, my Peggy Suh-uh-uh-uh-uh-uh-uh-uh-ue
Well I love you gal I want you Peggy Sue

Instrumental Break

Verse 5

Peggy Sue, Peggy Sue, pretty pretty pretty pretty Peggy Sue
Oh-oh Peggy my Peggy Sue
Oh well I love you gal yes I need you Peggy Sue

Verse 6

I love you Peggy Sue, with a love so rare and true
Oh-oh Peggy, my Peggy Suh-uh-uh-uh-uh-ue
Oh well I love you gal and I want you Peggy Sue
Oh well I love you gal and I want you Peggy Sue

(Fig. 4.6) is a perfect example of a song which was created in the studio—a song which was conceived of as a record. It was, as were most of the band's creations, a joint project. Holly, drummer Jerry Allison, and producer Norman Petty all contributed to the song's words, melodies, and harmonies.

The last lines of each verse are considered by some to be some sort of refrain. However, since they would not be the same length as the verses and since the words do change from verse to verse, they will be considered as part of the verses. On the surface the text and mood of "Peggy Sue" seems to resemble any number of the thousands of love songs which were created in the 1950s. However the deeper one looks, the stranger it becomes. Many love songs of the period concentrate on the physical attributes of the woman. There is none of this in "Peggy Sue." Instead, Holly concentrated on the feelings of the singer. Verse 1 seems to deal with the singer's feelings as expressed to someone else—perhaps a friend. In verse 2 Holly is now alone and expressing his feelings in terms he (and the average teen) is almost afraid to say. "My heart yearns" which sounds too adult is performed in Holly's famous "baby talk" style which amplifies the teen's fear of saying the words. In verse 3 Peggy Sue now seems to be present. The teen, unable to think straight in her real or imagined presence reverts to the repetition of "pretty, pretty, pretty," the only thing he can get out. Verse 4, the climactic verse of the first half of the song, presents the young lover at his most insecure. Filled with baby talk, high voice, and stuttering ("Suh-uh-uh-uh-uh-uh-uh-uh-ue") Holly uses the typical language of the teen magazines of the period ("With a love so rare and true"). After the instrumental break things are different. The repetitions of pretty in verse 5 seem to be more confident. The baby talk is absent and the stutter of verse 5 ("Suh-uh-uh") is now more soothing than nervous. And the last statement, lines 16 and 17 are in Holly's low voice—the only time he has used it in the song. These and additional factors seem to indicate that the song is not simply a love song but a song in which follows the maturation process. Holly exploits every element of music to this end.

For the most part the harmony of each verse uses alternating I and IV chords. I is home and IV creates little tension. Holly "saves" the V chord for a word which requires real tension. During the last line of each verse on the words "love" (or "need") and "Peggy Sue," Holly uses two different versions of the IV and V chords which both create considerable tension. Both chords [*IV7 and V7*] are not only dissonant in the "home" created by the I and IV chords but sound dissonant on their own. Both are used to emphasize important words. Each time the word "pretty" is repeated four times (lines 7 and 11), it is accompanied by an even more surprising chord. Although common in Western art music of the last 200 years, this harmony is extremely rare in rock and roll of the 1950s. It's relationship with the home harmony [*musicians identify it as a "third relationship"*] is not dissonant and the mood it creates within the home harmony is occasionally described as "feminine." Holly is using it as one additional way to look at Peggy Sue.

Within the course of the song the name Peggy occurs thirty times. Most of the time (twenty occurrences) the name coincides with the first two pulses of the measure—on the strong downbeat and the weaker second pulse (**PEG**-gy). This tends to make it sound direct, forward, and as some maintain—"masculine." Seven times it occurs not on the first pulse but spread over pulses three and four (Pe-eg-ey). This results in a less direct feel and is identified by some as "feminine." A third form occurs only three times. Here the first part of the name is actually sung just prior to the first pulse of the measure ('P '**HEG**-gy). This tends to place emphasis on the middle of the name and creates what is frequently referred to as Holly's "stutter."

Holly uses all of this in combination—the various vocal timbres and inflections, the wide array of chords and rhythms—to sing the name Peggy Sue in a wide variety of ways. What is striking is the fact that the "nervous" rhythm and vocal qualities generally occur during the first half of the song. After the instrumental break, Holly's rhythms and timbres (especially the low voice of lines 16 and 17) sound more direct, more confident, and more grown up. Adding to the effect is the fact that the music of the instrumental break includes many more examples of strong first pulses that occur in the first half of the song. It almost seems to function as some sort of outside agent for change—some force toward maturity. It is not too far a reach to see why a number of musicians view "Peggy Sue" as not just a simple love song but as a trip through the maturation process.

5 The Lean Years

Many students of the history of rock and roll maintain a relatively low opinion of the so-called "Teen Idol" (1959–1964) period. Others refer to this chapter in the history of the art form in terms of "the year the music died." Don J. Hibbard and Carol Kaleialih, in their book *The Roll of Rock*, refer to the period as the era of "pure puke." There is much truth to these opinions. The reasons for the death of the rock and roll of the 1950's seem obvious enough. Many of the major performing artists of the period left the business. Beside the tragic death of Buddy Holly, Elvis Presley was drafted into the armed services, Jerry Lee Lewis was hounded out of the business, Little Richard left voluntarily, and Chuck Berry was arrested for violations of the Mann Act. But there were other forces at work.

The major record labels, discovering that as much as 10% of record sales was going to rock and roll and hearing from their demographers that the population curve indicated that things would only get worse, attempted to crush the threat of rock and roll. This ploy taken by the major record labels and their proxies in the government and organized religion was not to be taken lightly. The September, 1958 issue of *The Instrumentalist*, a periodical which was read by virtually every member of the music education community, quoted Meredith Wilson, composer of such noted Broadway hits as *The Music Man*. He referred to rock and roll as "utter garbage" and a "creeping paralysis." He continued, "The people of this country do not have any conception of the evil being done by rock and roll; it is a plague as far-reaching as any plague we have ever had . . . My complaint is that it just isn't music. It's utter garbage and it should not be confused in any way with anything relating to music or verse." While there were isolated instances of "record burnings," this approach did not produce the desired results. Consequently, the major recording companies launched "Plan B." Simply reversing themselves they attempted to adapt their major recording stars to rock and roll—*Perry Como Rocks and Rolls!!!* In short, they attempted to join them. While this did not work any better than the first plan they, along the way, discovered that through mass hype via the new medium of television it was quite easy to control the teenage mind. They launched "Plan C." Through powerful images and trusted figures such as Dick Clark, they were able to "discover," develop, and sell new talent—talent they could control. While most of these "discoveries" had little or no musical ability or experience (Paul Anka was one notable exception), the constant exposure on pop radio and American Bandstand, and through the diversions created by the never ending sideshows usually referred to as "dance crazes," the sales of rock and roll were finally under their control.

While the vast majority of what was produced during the lean years was simply product, there is another way to look at this period—as a period of transition. There were, now that we have the benefit of hindsight, a number of developments which occurred during these five years which would have a direct impact on the developments of the rock and roll which occurred during the 1960's. Indeed, a number of the innovations which are frequently attributed to The Beatles and other "British Invasion" bands are already seen in a number of the songs produced in this era of pure puke.

This time period witnessed the final death of monaural recordings and their replacement by stereophonic recordings. In addition, there was a gradual switch from the 45 r.p.m. "doughnut" single to the 33-1/3 album. Phil Spector became the prototype of the "studio jock." Through his creative innovations in the use of overdubbing and a host of other recording techniques he paved the way for several generations of recording technicians.

This period also saw the founding and first flowering of Motown Records. While Motown was always more interested in sales volume and the bottom line, it did, nevertheless, record an amazing array of performing talent. Unfortunately, a successful recording usually meant additional clones. Even by 1964, and even though isolated masterpieces such as Marvin Gaye's recording of "I Heard it Through the Grapevine" were yet to come, Motown was exhibiting signs of stagnation.

On the other hand, there were signs of transition—signs of rock and roll's move to the next level. While the three young women who comprised the heart of the Shangri-Las were not accomplished singers (certainly no competition for the likes of Diana Ross or Gladys Knight), their product was nothing short of amazing. Two songs, "Remember (Walking in the Sand)" (Fig. 5.1) and "The Leader of the Pack" (Fig. 5.2) exhibited many of the stylistic features which would appear in the music of The Beach Boys and later, The Beatles. Dubbed by a number of critics "teen operas," they bristle with tempo and textural changes, unexpected harmonic changes, and additional features drawn from the world of "classical music." Both were written by professional song writer George "Shadow" Morton.

"Remember (Walking in the Sand)" begins with two "pick up" notes which both lead *down* to the first note of A. This two note leading down is a constant feature of this section of the song. It sets up a counterpoint to the vocal line which rises in every bar and tends to pull at the heartstrings even while the lyrics are talking about fond memories. D (only two bars) is a transition which leads to E. E is a complete change in tempo, texture

FIGURE 5.1 "Remember (Walking in the Sand)," George Morton, Structural chart.

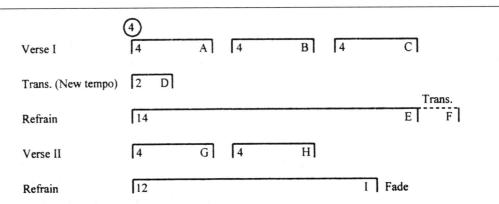

and mood. The tempo suddenly moves twice as fast. The instrumental accompaniment is stripped down to only bass, one voice and sea gulls! At least we assume that they're sea gulls (taped and dubbed in). Actually the function of the sea gull sound goes far beyond the mere suggestion of walking in the sand. Since the accompaniment is so bare, the forward motion they provide is essential to the movement of this section. Section E ends with one bar which acts as a transition back into the tempo and texture of the first part of the song. However the repeat of the first section is not complete and after eight bars (F and G), the song returns to the tempo and texture of the E section and fades.

"The Leader of the Pack" begins with a two-part introduction. Part one (A) seems to be in a slow four beats per measure. "Seems" because the instrumental accompaniment is limited to isolated chords that are not completely regular. Indeed, they are there to simply punctuate the single voice. This technique is borrowed from Italian opera. Yes, Italian opera! Italian opera of the 1600 and 1700's consisted of a series of songs (arias) which were interspersed among a series of musical sections called recitatives—literally recitations to music. Their function was to get a lot of words (the story) out in a short amount of time. The songs (arias) then comment upon these actions. In A, George Morton writes the equivalent of a short recitation. That is, in an efficient manner as possible, he sets out the subject of the entire song. The second half of the introduction (B and C) moves at a tempo which is about twice as fast and sets the speed for the rest of the song. The motorcycle sound at the end of C is, of course, to remind you that the song is about the leader of a motorcycle gang. However, it is also used as a structural feature throughout the song. It will appear again at the close of each major section.

Verse I is comprised of sections D, E, F, and G and is filled with details indicative of classical music. In the first lyrics (section D) the words "My parents are always putting him down" the answer in the backing vocals is "down, down, down." The melody is also literally down. That is, the answer is sung an octave lower than the statement. This technique is common in the world of classical music and is usually referred to as "text painting." The melody follows the sentiment of the words. When Bach wrote music to words like "and he ascended into heaven" the melody frequently went up. While it's one of those techniques that frequently goes unnoticed by the casual listener, once it is pointed out it is difficult to ig-

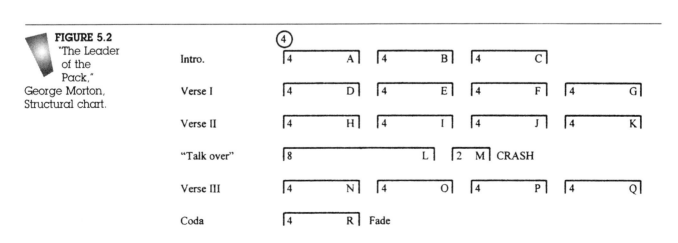

FIGURE 5.2 "The Leader of the Pack," George Morton, Structural chart.

nore. Of course, when the voice in section E says, "They say he came from the wrong side of town," the backing vocals do not repeat, "town, town, town" an octave lower. It would not make any sense. In fact, each of the opening statements in sections D–K is answered by a response using a different melody and/or texture. Section F and the corresponding section in verse II (section J) move to a completely different texture only to be "brought back to reality" in the last phrase of each verse. Section L is an eight-bar instrumental break which builds toward M—the CRASH. The crash is accomplished by an increase in volume and with the addition of some kind of pre-recorded sound of breaking glass. In addition, and probably unnoticed by the casual listener, the song moves up a whole step. Even if the listener is unacquainted with this technical element, he/she cannot help but be aware of a feeling of a "crash."

Great music? No. Sappy? Of course! Nevertheless, these and other "teen operas" which were written by George Morton for the Shangri-Las incorporated (for the first time) elements of music which would be used by The Beatles, The Jefferson Airplane, and many others as rock and roll began to move into its next phase of development.

The real rays of light which illuminated this period and pointed to a brighter future for rock and roll came from California. The Beach Boys was the first band in the history of rock and roll to develop. Their output would straddle the Lean Years and what would eventually be called "The Sixties." With the seeds for artistic rock and roll and its support by an active counterculture, e.g. baby boomers headed for college and isolated instances of transition in the music of The Shangri-Las and others what was needed was 1) some creative drive from outside of the music industry and 2) something to unify the "teen" population. The years which immediately followed this period witnessed both; the British Invasion and the war in Southeast Asia. Until then, the closest rock and roll came to its next phase occurred in the music of The Beach Boys. If Brian Wilson had been able to continue to develop as a composer, the world may have "not needed" The Beatles.

The music of The Beach Boys can be divided into two distinct "style periods." The first period, which runs from the formation of the band in 1962 to about halfway through 1965, is the style known to most listeners. It is the music which is most frequently played on "classic oldies" radio stations and the music which is associated with "surf music." Brian Wilson, the first complete musician to operate in the field of rock and roll, forged a sound which was unmistakable. His music featured continuous singing, relatively simple harmonies, and relatively simple instrumental backgrounds. The vocal texture came straight from male vocal groups such as The Lettermen. The instrumental style came straight from the garage band tradition with added influence from guitarist Duane Eddy. The lyrics were heavily influenced (with all open references to sex removed) by the songs of Chuck Berry. Brian Wilson, adding elements of his own, combined all of these influences and produced a series of songs which dealt with girls, cars, and surf. During the first style period the sun was always up and days were always carefree.

Something happened in mid 1965. Brian may have matured, he may have been influenced by the music of The Beatles, or he may have felt the first wave of the depression which would complicate future projects. Whatever the cause, the music he created began to evolve—to mature. Nowhere can this be seen more obviously than in his song "Wendy." Gone is the continuous singing and the simple forms. Gone is the optimism and carefree nature of the first style period. "Wendy" ushers in a new maturity in American rock and roll and a new style period for The Beach Boys. This new period will personify the music of The Beach Boys on the *Pet Sounds* album and in additional songs of 1966 and 1967.

"Wendy" (Fig. 5.3) begins with a most unusual introduction—an introduction not unlike that which is found in "The Leader of the Pack." What, on first hearing, sounds like isolated chords in the guitar and bass are in fact the downbeats of four measures of quadruple meter. The tempo is slower than the main body of the song. The fifth bar of what seems to be a phrase (A) is a little faster. Here, the drums here seem to push toward phrase B. The two measures of phrase B are now in the tempo of the rest of the song. Verse 1 is comprised of phrases C and D. Phrase C is straightforward—full vocal harmony and instruments in the background. Phrase D really divides into two units of four measures. In the first unit the texture changes. Now one voice stands out against the background vocal harmony. The remaining four measures of phrase D return to the texture of phrase C. On first hearing the second verse (phrases E and F) seem to do exactly the same thing. Vocally, until the very last measure, they are the same. However, the guitar adds an additional timbre by playing very short and dry chords on the downbeat of each measure. Until the very end phrase F repeats the music of phrase D. In contrast to the "high" ending of phrase D the last measure of phrase F leads "down" to the darker sound of the instrumental break. This darker sound is achieved by changing the mode from major to minor, limiting the short, dry chords of the guitar to the weaker second pulses of each measure, and giving the melody to the electric organ. By measure five of E the organ is playing the melody using two notes at a time [*in thirds*]. With very little imagination, it is easy to hear echoes of The Doors and their penchant for the minor mode, the use of the electric organ, and their fascination with "down subjects." Verse three is comprised of phrases H and I. Once again, while this verse may seem identical to verse one, there are differences in the details. The organ which was introduced in the instrumental break continues. Now it is in the background and limited to one note at a time. It adds an additional timbre to

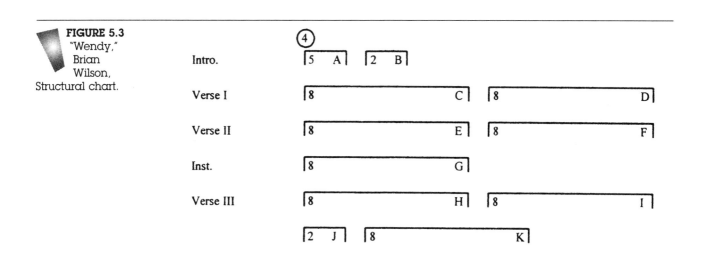

FIGURE 5.3 "Wendy," Brian Wilson, Structural chart.

the texture as well as lending additional "weight" to the thoughts. The chords in the guitar are now back on the downbeats but kept in the background. What happens at the end of phrase I is almost unheard of in early rock and roll. While verse 1 ends "high" and while the end of verse 2 leads "down," verse 3 ends in complete silence. Phrase J (only two measures long) is a repeat of the last two measures of the introduction (B). Phrase K is (with some surprising changes in the harmony provided by the guitar) like the first four measures of phrase C. These four measures are repeated three times in the form of a fade out.

"Wendy," and several other songs from this brief period of transition, e.g. "In My Room," begin to show Brian's interest in unusual timbres and textures. They also demonstrate his fascination with form—a fascination spawned by his ability to use the sophisticated devices of the recording and editing studios to overdub and to "cut and paste" from a number of "takes." As Brian continued to experiment with the new styles and concepts—styles and concepts which he would employ on subsequent recordings—he left many of the enthusiast fans of his early surfing days scratching their heads.

6 The Early Sixties

Part 1: Surf Beat

When the statement is made in so many rock documentaries, "As the fifties drew to a close, a series of events took place to *nearly* silence rock and roll forever," and is then followed by a discussion of Elvis in the army, Jerry Lee and his child bride, Little Richard and the church, and Buddy Holly and the plane crash—the *nearly* that is put in the sentence can only point in one direction . . . west. The American west coast, particularly southern California, was largely unaffected by the events at the close of the 1950s that shook up the rest of the country's music scene. The west coast had been brewing its own underground scene that plays a direct and utterly vital role in the direction of real, grassroots rock music.

In the late 1950s and early 1960s, while the radio stations around the country were filling the airwaves with over-produced, formulaic pop music by contrived rock-star idols, the collaboration and close friendship between Leo Fender and Dick Dale was about to introduce the next era of rock music. Not only did Dick Dale introduce the idea of a fast, hard-driving, heavy metal guitar sound in his introduction of surf rock to the world of music, but he was also the first musician to have the ability to play it loud—*very loud.*

Having Dick Dale, southern Californians were blissfully ignorant of the authentic rock void that the rest of the country endured until the British youths revived authentic blues in England and then in its home, America, in 1964 (with the exceptions of James Brown, what was happening at the Stax Records and Fame Recording Studio, and a few other bright stars of true rock grit that made high marks on the charts, i.e., *Louie Louie* in 1963). In fact, the very week before The Beatles claimed the number one spot on the Billboard Album Chart in February of 1964, the album they displaced for that spot was The Singing Nun. Not exactly hard driving rock and a perfect indicator of the direction the major labels preferred.

To southern Californians, however, who were packing 4,000 people per night for months in a row to see this "crazy maniac on guitar," this paradisiacal world of endless summer days of riding the surf and sun worshipping, and endless nights of dancing in beachside dance halls and around beach bonfires to a hard rock sound that was uniquely their own, was so far removed from the rest of America that they may as well have been on another planet.

Dick Dale and Leo Fender

The technological advancements that allow a guitarist to perform at a seriously high level of volume simply had yet to be worked out yet in the early 1960s. The whole concept of playing seriously loud was not really in the musicians' mindset, mostly because the best amplifiers of the day were low power amplifiers (5 to 20 watts) sold by Sears and Roebuck. The concept of loud, as in 100 watt or higher amplification, had still not been explored or exploited by rock and roll bands until Dick Dale met Leo Fender in the late 1950s. Together, they would help redefine every single bit of authentic rock music of the 1960s and beyond. Not only did Dale perform through the very first 100 watt amplifier in the late 1950s, he did so on a new breed of guitar, the solid body Fender Stratocaster, and in doing so, greatly helped to popularize the instrument.

Dick Dale (Richard Monsour) was born in Boston, Mass. on May 4, 1937, and moved with his parents to southern California in 1954. His father was Lebanese-born and introduced him to Middle Eastern modes and rhythms at a very young age. His parents fostered a musical environment as Dick was growing up, and he taught himself to play every instrument he could get his hands on. He never received formal training on any instrument, instead preferring to rely on his natural musical talent to guide his playing style on whatever instrument he picked up.

Today, Dale expresses tremendous pride in being able to make inborn talent alone work for him. Statements like "I don't know what I'm doing now, so why should I confuse myself?" and "I can't even play a scale! Who cares? But I can play every instrument there is and make a sound, and it comes from my soul." When told that if he played guitar the right way, he'd be the best guitarist on the planet, he replied, "Why fix it if it ain't broke?" These statements give an insightful view into the kind of grassroots musician that Dick Dale is.

Most impactful on the future surf guitar king was the drums and particularly the exotic, trance-like jungle drum playing of Gene Krupa. Dale still professes at every opportunity, "Gene Krupa was my first hero that I listened to on big band records, and he was why drums became my first instrument." When Dale switched to the guitar, he simply transferred everything he learned on the drums to guitar. In the same spirit as Bo Diddley, Dale plays the guitar as if he's playing the drums. Dick Dale's guitar style is, above all else, rhythmically driven. He keeps his frantically fast-tempoed songs rhythmically tight by employing a constant double-picking style he learned from his father's Middle Eastern influence, adding to that Middle Eastern melodic modes over frequently used minor keys (a darker quality than the standard major keys).

The most unusual aspect of Dick Dale's guitar playing, however, is that he played it upside down and backwards, meaning he turned a right handed guitar around to match his left-handedness, and left the strings the same, which placed the high strings near the top and the low strings near the bottom. Jimi Hendrix, a big fan of Dick Dale's music and frequent attendee at Dale concerts, not only played the instrument the same way, but would later get the same fluttering effects that Dale got through double picking by utilizing a heavy amount of trill. Dick Dale's combination of double picking with slow slides down the length of the guitar neck (glissando) gives his music a feeling of being under water, a natural effect reflecting Dale's own preoccupation with the ocean and surfing. Dale also owned lions and tigers, as well as just about any animal he could rescue from circuses and zoos, and you can hear the evening roars of his lions in the intros to many of his songs.

Dick Dale started out his stage career playing country hillbilly and western music in Boston. When Dick Dale's father noticed his strong innate talent, he moved the family to California, eventually starting the Del-Tone record label to release his son's records to the public. As Dale became more and more involved with the southern California surf and beach scene, he drifted away from rockabilly and started developing a style all his own . . . surf rock. In the late 1950s, Dick Dale and his father discovered an abandoned big band ballroom in Newport Beach called the Rendezvous Ballroom, capable of holding 4,000 people—an unheard of size for a rock audience at that time (even the big stars of the 1950s were still only playing for hundreds at a time). They went to the city's officials to get a permit to use it for live shows and were met with strong resistance against "the devil's music." The Dales were unrelenting and persuasive, and the city allowed the permits only if everyone who came wore a tie. Deal done, they bought boxes of cheap ties and handed them out to the barefooted, swim shorts clad surfers who showed up. Word spread fast and within weeks they went from a small handful of Dale's surfing friends to a packed house of 4,000 every night to see Dick Dale and the Del-Tones. Dick's father, seeing the potential, went around to other southern California towns to secure dancing permits for more shows. In a short amount of time, Dick Dale had all of southern California listening to his fast, maniacal, and completely original surf beat music.

In the age of fabricated teen pop idols, and overproduced "teen symphonies," Dick Dale and the Del-Tones were the vanguard of a new way of looking at grassroots, authentic rock music that has far-reaching impact right on up to today's heavy metal and hard rock styles. Some of the attendees at Dick Dale concerts included The Ventures, The Righteous Brothers (who, at that time, were performing some very authentic rock and roll themselves), Jan and Dean, some young lads who would become The Beach Boys, and one of Dale's biggest fans, Jimi Hendrix. Hendrix even dedicated the song *Third Stone from the Sun*, from his *Are You Experienced* album, to his hero after rumors had circulated that Dale was dying of cancer (he beat it) in 1966. Hendrix dubbed in the line, "You'll never hear surf music again" at a whisper, in tribute to the impact that Dale's music had on Hendrix's playing style. *Third Stone from the Sun* is also the only instrumental that Hendrix ever recorded in the studio. Considering how much of an impact Jimi Hendrix had on music, and still has, that's a pretty strong testimonial to the tremendous importance of Dick Dale and his surf rock guitar.

The large crowds Dale was playing before presented a problem in that their bodies were absorbing too much of the sound of the band (large crowds muffle a band's sound substantially). This is where the relationship between Dale and Leo Fender fully blossoms. Fender had given Dick Dale his first Stratocaster guitar and Fender amplifier. Dale kept blowing up the amplifiers trying to fill the big ballroom with sound. Fender kept giving him amps, and Dale would promptly blow them up by overdriving them. Finally Leo Fender went to see Dale perform at the Rendezvous and realized why he needed more volume when he saw the unprecedented number of people at the show. The result of the collaboration was the first high-power amplifier. Dick Dale still uses the amplifier that Fender built especially for him, a package containing two 15 inch JBL speakers powered by a 100 watt output transformer amplifier. Fender then marketed the amplifier as the Fender Showman Amp, which quickly became the dominant amplifier on the market, and in doing so, pushed rock and roll into the next era of loud, heavy metal rock.

Together, Dick Dale and Leo Fender changed the way rock music was played—fast, aggressive, and loud . . . VERY LOUD! (Dale still encourages his audience to wear earplugs while refusing to turn the volume down.) Fender and Dale also worked together to develop the first reverb unit. At first, Dale wanted it to create a warmer, rich full sound to his voice. Fender obliged with what became known as the Fender Tank Reverb, and it didn't take long for Dale to plug his guitar into it instead of the microphone.

Dick Dale had not only introduced a wholly new style of music based on Mid-East modes, performing styles, and rhythms combined with big band jazz drumming and rockabilly back beat, but he had pushed on the boundaries of possibilities with the first high-power amplification and a faster action, thinner necked, solid body guitar to carry rock and roll music into the age of hard rock. Today, Dick Dale sees himself as the "Johnny Appleseed" of grassroots, authentic and soulful rock music. As of this writing, he still maintains an aggressive touring schedule to bring the sounds of authentic rock music to all who will listen.

LET'S GO TRIPPIN'
MISERLOU
THE WEDGE
DICK DALE AND THE DEL-TONES

Dale is still performing his maniacal, energetic, and youthful brand of music decades after the artists, pop idols, and producers who dominated the music market of the early 1960s have been long forgotten except by historians and oldies radio stations. He's been around longer than the Rolling Stones and Bob Dylan, the only other nonstop rock acts from the 1960s that are still going strong. Dick Dale's music is as much alive today as it was in the 1960s, not only because people like Hendrix emulated him, but because he's actually still out there performing. He truly is the Johnny Appleseed of authentic rock music as he continues to inspire legions of guitarists through his live performances and relentless touring the world over.

The Ventures

Though there were many musicians who imitated the Dick Dale surf guitar style, and also many musicians who wanted to play grassroots rock as a backlash to the over-produced music of the hit parade, the most popularly successful of these groups was the Ventures. The Ventures were founded in 1960 in Seattle, Wash., also home of the Wailers, the Viceroys, and the Sonics. They hit it big rather quickly, releasing Top Ten hits *Walk—Don't Run* and *Perfidia* that same year. The Ventures cultivated a surf rock sound that was at once smooth and popularly accessible, while maintaining the authentic feel of surf beat in much of their music.

The Ventures were capable of playing both smooth and mellow surf beat, and twisted and disturbing sounds as well. *The Ventures In Space* album is loaded with some of the most hard-edged, demented instrumentals found anywhere in music (listen to *The Bat*), while their hit singles like *Walk—Don't Run* and *Perfidia* are some of the most accessible instrumentals in music and received some very heavy airplay nationwide. The Ventures had a similar element to them as Duane Eddy; their music was frequently so simple and direct sounding that it also helped to inspire teenagers nationwide to learn to play guitar.

The Ventures released over 50 albums in their career, never gaining a million seller, but every album sold over 100,000 copies, giving them a long and consistent stand as performers. Their style of accessible yet authentic sounding surf rock, while not as consistently hard-driving and gritty as Dick Dale, allowed them to pour any musical style into their surf cauldron. They took songs from such genres as blues, doo wop, R&B, hillbilly, science fiction movie themes, television themes, bosa novas, calypso, soul, and put their stamp on it. This ability to transform any song style into their own unique style allowed them unlimited material for all of those albums. The Ventures were also great explorers of musical elements, frequently employing minor tonality and other melodic modes, utilizing whatever studio tricks were available for atmospheric effect and framing it all in a sound that was uniquely the Ventures.

The Ventures enjoyed a very long, uninterrupted musical career, performing and touring from their inception in 1960 into the 1990s. Unlike Dick Dale, who did put vocals in some of his songs, the Ventures were a purely instrumental unit, which plays heavily into their high popularity in places like Japan and the Netherlands (where there is currently a surf beat revival in full bloom). Without words in their songs, there is no language barrier to prevent listeners from non-English speaking countries from relating to the music. It was pure music for music's sake, sacrificing vocals in exchange for the ability to create intense musical moods. Without vocals, the Ventures became rock and roll for the world.

 **Listen**

WALK–DON'T RUN
TELSTAR
THE BAT
WAR OF THE SATELLITES
THE VENTURES

Other Surf Beat Essential Listening:

MOMENT OF TRUTH
WIPE OUT
THE SURFARIS

LATINIA
THE SENTINALS

PIPELINE
CHANTAY'S

SURFIN' BIRD
THE TRASHMEN

Surf Beat Revival

Today, at the beginning of the 21st-century, the surf beat style of rock is enjoying a dramatic revival from musicians who are once again fed up with over-produced, fabricated pop idols and formulaic, cookie cutter "alternative rock" bands, which are neither alternative nor rock. Thanks to the efforts of people like Dick Dale, who feel a lifelong mission to dispense the sacrament of authentic grassroots rock music, new legions of converts are walking away from the turntables, the drum machines, the digital keyboards and effects processors, the loops and sampling machines, and re-embracing the authentic styles, techniques, and analog instruments and amplifiers used by the surf rockers of the 1960s.

Link Wray

At the same time that Dick Dale and Leo Fender were laying the groundwork for the hard rocking 1960s, there was one other guitarist working at the same time in a very different part of the country that would have a strong impact in his own way.

Though not a part of the west coast surf scene, Link Wray was a highly innovative guitarist who developed his own style of instrumental hard rock in the late 1950s that was also very influential to the rise of menacing hard, heavy, and loud rock music. A full-blood native American, Wray was born and raised in North Carolina, and relocated to the Washington, D.C. area with his brothers Vernon and Doug to form Link Wray and The Lazy Pine Ramblers in 1955. In 1958, with another brother, Ray Vernon, as producer, the now renamed The Ray-Men released the song *Rumble* on Cadence Records, and in doing so introduced the **power chord** to the world. A power chord is a hard, forceful, and full strumming of the guitar at high volumes. Other people had used the technique, but when *Rumble* climbed to number 16 on the national Billboard charts, the raw unrestrained nature of the style captured the imaginations of younger guitarists who would soon follow.

Rumble is a slow dirge instrumental that sounds like dark, menacing strip music. Archie Bleyer, who owned Cadence Records, gave the song its name because his daughter thought it sounded like the rumble scenes from *West Side Story*. The song became associated with big city street gangs simply due to its title, and (a song with no words) was actually banned from radio airplay in big city markets, including New York City, for that reason alone. *Rumble* has no real melodic line, except for a couple of turn around bridges back to the beginning of the song's form; instead, it relies completely on the rhythmic force of Link's power chords.

Other Link Wray songs from the same period, the late 1950s and early 1960s, reflect the same style, but at different tempos, peppered with uncomplicated searing, high-pitched guitar solos. The song, *Raw-Hide* (no relation to the television show theme), released in 1959 as an Epic Records single, uses the same power chord style in a fast, pounding, guitar driven rhythm and blues style instrumental. Link never really gained much fame after *Rumble* was released, but the damage had been done. Pete Townsend, guitarist of The Who (who still holds the Guinness world record as the loudest rock band ever), summed up the impact of Link Wray when he said, "If it hadn't been for Link Wray and *Rumble*, I would have never picked up the guitar."

Studio Production in the Early 1960s

By 1960, the hard edges and raw power of rock and roll had been eradicated by the major label music industry and were replaced by formulaic producers and songwriters, using interchangeable performers as recording artists. It may not have been hard-edged rock and roll, but it did open doors into production techniques and new technologies that would trickle down to the smaller independent studios and allow future rock musicians access to new recording abilities. When musicians go into a recording studio today, they take for granted the technology and recording techniques that surround them, though a line can be drawn from the high tech studios we use today right back to the music producers of the 1960s; and even more so, right back to Phil Spector.

Phil Spector and The Wall of Sound

Phil Spector had almost single-handedly reshaped the essence of the producer. No one, then or now, has ever shown the passion and drive of a self-made producer like Phil Spector. He was, simply put, the most unrelenting and daring producer of the time, a strategy that made him a millionaire by the age of twenty-one. When Phil Spector heard something in his head, he just did not stop until his vision was captured completely and clearly defined on tape.

Using the term "clearly defined" to describe what Spector did musically may seem a contradiction, as his approach to recording music was anything but. The whole essence of Spector's production style, known as the **Wall of Sound**, was to pack a lot of musicians, including not only standard rock and roll instruments, but also orchestral instruments like strings, brass, and timpani, into a relatively small studio. Then microphones were placed on all of the instruments. The mics for the violins would pick up not only the violins, but all other sound as well, a fraction of a second later. Likewise, the mics on the pianos (he used three of them at the same time) would pick up the pianos, and a fraction of a second later, the drums as well. When the musicians started playing, the sounds and rumbles of the other instruments would hit the ceiling and bounce into far away mics on the other side of the studio, again, a fraction of a second later.

Spector would also use **multitracking** (mixing together multiple recorded tracks) to fatten up the sound by essentially duplicating, even tripling, the already recorded tracks of the rhythm sections. When Spector came up with this idea of using large ensembles combined with large numbers of microphones displaced all over the studio, combined with multitrack mixing, the Wall of Sound was born, or as Spector himself put it, "That's the sound of gold."

Phil Spector reshaped the sound of pop music in America in the early 1960s, with his girl group phenomenon, Ronnie and The Ronettes' *Be My Baby*, and a fleet of other number one pop hits, including *Da Doo Ron Ron* by the Chrystals and *You've Lost That Loving Feeling* by the Righteous Brothers. The performers were largely interchangeable, as the driving popular force of any Spector-produced song was Spector's production, the Wall of Sound.

No other producer had ever captured the potential of authentic rock music and turned it into a popularly marketable product like Spector did, but in doing so, he also exposed the limits of his production style. Just how big of a sound can you create before it becomes too big? How many pianos, how many drum sets, how many orchestral instruments can be packed into a song before popular tastes shift away from them? Phil Spector's music was a vital exploration into the possibilities of the recording studio, but a shift back to authentic rock music performed by authentic, blues-based rock bands and individual musicians would dethrone the true king of pop music. After the British Invasion of 1964, Spector never regained the music industry authority and dominance he once claimed. The rules were being constantly rewritten, and the musical and cultural shifts of the later 1960s would usher in yet another new era in rock music.

Brian Wilson and The Beach Boys

Another of the extremely powerful forces in American music and production style in the early 1960s was Brian Wilson, founder and dominant figure for the Beach Boys. Taking their inspiration from the surf music scene of southern California, the Beach Boys popularized the ideals, youthfulness, and fantasy of surf culture to mainstream America. Up until the Beach Boys, kids in the rest of the country didn't really know about the surf culture lifestyle that was daily life for the southern California teenager, with the exception of the few authentic instrumental songs that gained national airplay. For the rest of America, authentic, instrumental surf rock didn't really *tell* them what was happening there. Though that music made complete sense to those who were a part of the culture, if you didn't live there, the instrumental surf beat was just another curious fad in rock music. But once the Beach Boys put the lifestyle into words and set those words in lush vocal harmonies on top of vaguely surfy music, America caught the "go west, young man" bug. Suddenly there were teenagers in the Midwest attempting to realize the surf cult fantasy.

Many would be so swayed as to make the move out west to be a part of it. This really isn't that surprising if you think about it, or if you're from the Midwest. The Midwest is cold a great amount of the year. There are no palm trees. There are no bikini clad girls or muscle boys. When the sun is shining in the Midwest, it's an event that makes the lead story on the nightly news. And probably most important in the eyes of Midwestern teenagers faced with the view of the southern California surf culture is that they would look around at their own lives, see their fathers sweating out a life in factories and other blue collar labor jobs, and see themselves in ten years if they didn't make some kind of change. Remember that this was a time when the idea of picking up completely and settling in a new land wasn't so foreign in our minds. A lot of midwestern teenagers were first or second generation Americans, meaning that their parents or grandparents were immigrants to America—people who had given up everything to start a new life in the New World.

Remember also that this was a time when people could still travel the country safely, quickly, and adventurously by simply sticking their thumbs out as they stood at the side of a highway (though a piece of cardboard with your destinations written boldly on it would get you a ride a lot faster). When the Beach Boys became popular nationally, California never looked so good in light of the options available to a kid trapped in small town, Midwestern America. If the people that run California had conspired to come up with ways to get Americans to move there, they couldn't have come up with a better promotional strategy than the Beach Boys.

The Beach Boys formed in 1961 in Hawthorne, Calif., a suburb of Los Angeles. As teens, they hung out at the beach concerts and ballrooms and absorbed the sounds, attitudes, and terminology of surf culture. They practiced and developed a vocal ensemble style based on 1950s vocal harmony groups like the Four Freshmen. Later, Brian Wilson would also list Phil Spector, and particularly the Ronettes' song, *Be My Baby* as prime inspiration for his arrangements and production style. Signed to Capitol Records, they released *Surfin' Safari* in 1962, which climbed into the Top Twenty, then *Surfin' U.S.A.* in early 1963, which put them in the Top Ten and catapulted southern California surf culture to the forefront of attention in the national music scene.

With vast popular support, Brian Wilson was able to guide the band into different musical directions by wrestling the job of producer away from a company-assigned studio producer. Now writing or co-writing the songs, performing them, and producing them as well, Brian Wilson had achieved an unprecedented position in rock and roll. Before this watershed in rock music, the popular music industry was set up so that there were always different people for each of those different roles. There are many cases of rock musicians who sang the songs they composed, like Little Richard, Chuck Berry, and so many others, but never did they produce them as well. Likewise, there were songwriters who produced their own songs when recorded by other musicians, like Lieber and Stoller. Wilson, however, had broken through a barrier that was built like a brick wall. Within a few years, when the psychedelic music scene stole the west coast spotlight, it was not at all uncommon for bands to produce or co-produce their own work in the studio.

The Beach Boys' popularity just kept getting higher and higher, until they finally claimed the number one album spot in the country in December of 1964, with *Beach Boys Concert*, but attitudes were changing fast in the music trends by then. In a sign of times and things to come, The Beatles had already beat them to that number one album spot by ten months. *Meet The Beatles!* not only claimed the number one album spot in February 1964, but *The Beatles' Second Album* (May 1964), *A Hard Day's Night* (July 1964), and *Something New* (October 1964) all charted for The Beatles into the Billboard Top Five Album Chart before *Beach Boys Concert* did. In 1966, in their struggle to maintain a strong presence on the charts, the Beach Boys released *Pet Sounds*. The album was a huge success critically and really showcased the talent of a studio producer Wilson had become. Though it did chart into the Top Ten, American tastes were headed in yet different directions; but not so overseas in England, where *Pet Sounds* earned The Beach Boys the title of best group of the year, beating out The Beatles on their home turf.

Eventually, they mostly gave up trying to keep up with the quickly changing music trends of the late 1960s and early 1970s and focused instead on polishing up their live show, getting top billing at the large festivals and stadium shows, but they did so playing the music that made them famous, which was sounding quite nostalgic by the mid-1970s. Exactly like his hero Phil Spector, Brian Wilson would also see his dominance in the American music scene dwindle in the face of the British Invasion, psychedelia, and hard rock. But whatever is said about Brian Wilson, don't forget to add the word "successful."

Part 2: Rebirth of the Blues

British Invasion

The British Invasion was really two distinctly separate musical events. One was The Beatles, a band, and their producer who was more like an accomplice, who would musically evolve so fast in such a short amount of time that there simply is no comparison anywhere in the history of American music. The other was everyone else. Out of the everyone else there were two camps as well: one, the authentic **blues revivalists** like the Rolling Stones and the Yardbirds (who would eventually spawn Led Zeppelin—one of the most blues dedicated hard rock bands of the 1970s) and the other, the more pop sounding and ever cute plethora of pop-idol Beatles imitator bands, like Herman's Hermits.

The question of how the British Invasion happened, and how a bunch of British youths were able to overtake and overwhelmingly dominate the

American rock music market is often hotly debated. The **Cultural Inferiority Theory**, one of the dominant theories in rock history circles, states that due to the growing sense of social upheaval, including the assassination of President John F. Kennedy in November 1963, and the brewing Civil Rights Movement, Americans had a "cultural inferiority complex" in the early 1960s, and that because of this inferiority complex, the American music market was ripe for the picking by foreign (but not too foreign) bands and performers. This theory certainly possesses some credibility. The assassination of JFK certainly did bring an adverse effect on all the people in the country. Even people who were six years old and in first grade at the time JFK was murdered remember it as the day all the grown-ups walked around crying. There is no doubt that in the 1960s America had never seemed so unsure of itself since the Depression and the American Civil War before that.

But, historically, when the chips are down, and a feeling of national pride and patriotism reawakens the people, it's a song that becomes the rally cry. For exactly the same reasons that would make a people ripe for lack of confidence and insecurity comes the rebellious spirit to rise above it all. Thus, the hard times and uncertainty would also make America ripe for a grassroots, favorite son or song to emerge, if there was one to emerge. Whenever and wherever in the world there has been a revolution in the last few centuries, there was always a song, songs, or a style of songwriting associated with the movement; a song that arises from the feeling of nowhere to go but up, as the downtrodden gather their strength and courage to act. *Yankee Doodle* during the American Revolution, *La Marsellaise* and *La Compatnole* during the French Revolution, *Battle Hymn of the Republic* for the North and *Dixie* for the South in the American Civil War, and the *Internationale* during the Russian Revolution are all prime examples of how a song can rally a people to action in the midst of an uncertain future.

The rally cries in America in the 1960s would soon come from so many musicians, but in the early 1960s, rock music wasn't yet associated with the Civil Rights Movement. It was not yet the true voice of the people, but instead, for the most part it was still just the voice of youthful ritual dance culture. It did help in bringing the races together in the 1950s, but it did so unconsciously. Soon though, in the latter part of the 1960s, songs would indeed bring the common people of America together. *We Shall Overcome*, *Feel Like I'm Fixing to Die Rag*, *Power to the People*, *Give Peace A Chance*, an even *Yellow Submarine* (three of those written by Brits), all became anthems sung en masse at protests against the Vietnam War and rallies for civil rights reform. How can a people who came predominantly from the lowest sectors of European society suffer a mass inferiority complex? Americans already knew they were the mongrel of the world and have always reserved a great sense of pride in that status. The grassroots people of America have always had a full understanding that they were the refuse and downtrodden of all the other countries of the world, and that together, all these different people were the ones who actually built and defended this country.

Antonin Dvorak even tried to tell American musicians to pay close attention to the grassroots music that was emerging here at the end of the 19th-century. Dvorak was a European composer who came to America in the 1890s to take a job in New York City as the Director of the National

Conservatory of Music in America, teaching university composition students the fine art of western music composition. In the three years he was in America, Dvorak spent the summer months traveling to and living with an immigrant Czech community in Iowa, teaching the young ones music. Remember, this is a time of horseback travel, so an adventurous trip from New York to Iowa would take weeks. Along his travels he absorbed gospel and Negro spirituals, blues, work songs, jazz, hillbilly, cowboy, and especially Native American music. He then would return to New York and teach his students that everything they needed to create a whole new music all their own was already here, as opposed to going off to Europe to study the classic masters. Dvorak then composed a symphony to fully illustrate the potential of what he heard in American music. His *Symphony from the New World*, composed in 1893, is heralded today as the model of that potential. Every single Hollywood western movie that ever came out pays tribute to that symphony and what it stands for. Simply listen to the *Symphony from the New World*, then listen to any western cowboy movie soundtrack, and the emulation is unmistakable.

However, the serious art music establishment of the collegiate system was not set up to send their students onto excursions into the backwoods, plains, and deserts of America, but to lock them up in the ivory towers of the east coast colleges or send them off to study the classic masters in Europe. Dvorak raised the ire of the establishment with his insightful view of the American landscape of possibility. He was promptly sent back home to Czechoslovakia (to be fair, he wanted to return home too) but, here again, the damage had been done.

Here was one of the world famous top name composers of the day telling Americans that their own raw and energetic grassroots music had extreme validity. If there is a long-standing national inferiority complex, it's not in the grassroots people, but in those guardians of the ivory towers who never left the big cities, or traveled the land to see what America was really about. When those who thoroughly embrace European culture are exposed to grassroots music, it is easy for them to look at a scruffy hillbilly playing a violin with a sawed down bridge, and playing the instrument tucked into his or her stomach, sawing away at breakneck tempos and not quite hitting the right pitches, as deprived of culture. From that vantage point it's easy to look down, an age old conflict and misunderstanding between classes. Ironically, it is a conflict that was exposed by Mozart and Beethoven, whom the ivory tower guardians hold up as idols.

There is another theory that we should consider in answering the question of how the British Invasion could happen. The **Theory of Contrivance** states that American youth had become overly accustomed to, or were simply tired of the lush, overproduced pop sounds, the contrived squeaky clean, respectable pop idols, and the soft-rock folk music that overtook authentic rock music in the early 1960s. There's certainly nothing wrong or bad about that music, it's just that the pendulum had swung back. That American youths were yearning for a little bit of authentic, hard-edged, and unrestrained grit and mud from the delta can be easily understood when compared against the bubblegum sounds coming out of the "ivory towers" of pop production of that era. Watch a movie of The Beatles performing in 1964 and compare that performance style against the Beach Boys at the same time period. The Beach Boys stand there quite politely, with nice clothes and properly trim hair, and deliver their music with that same polite and non-threatening style. The Beatles, on the other hand, had relatively long hair, played their instruments aggressively, and shook their heads all around while screaming into the microphones. When they took the stage, the energy and unrestrained performing became infectious to the audience. Even Brian Wilson said of The Beatles, "Suddenly we looked like golf caddies instead of rock stars." The Beatles simply performed with an energy and vitality that Americans hadn't seen for a few years.

The exact same argument can be used to explain the popularity of James Brown in the black community during the same period. When you saw Brown perform, you knew you were seeing something unrestrained and authentic. It was infectious, and it threw a glaring light on how much quaint, disposable consumer music there was out there, exposing the pop market hit parade for what it was, formulaic, contrived, and void of any real affinity to the common people. Once you heard James Brown, you would listen to what was being called soul music on the radio, and something just didn't jibe. And, worse yet for the major pop market, once you saw James perform, you certainly couldn't go back to viewing music, and even life, the way you used to. Performers like these show the rest of us what it's like to live on the edge, and what it means to do something full-throttle. How can these types of performers not steal the show?

Think of it this way. Who's going to have the biggest impact and get the most applause at the circus, the overly colorful and happy looking clown who juggles some balls and falls off his bicycle, or the shimmering, silver-clad trapeze artists who breathtakingly tempts fate, hovering alone in the spotlight high above the crowd's heads? The clowns may warm our hearts and make us laugh, because we can easily see a little bit of our own commonality and absurdity in them, but the lone trapeze artist takes our breath away, because in them we see the daring and certain intent that inspires individual dreams and action. We don't all become trapeze artists, but it's good to see that it's somewhere inside of us to be if we choose. Seeing that kind of intense, full-throttle performance can only inspire us as individuals. When these ideas are put to sleep, especially in the extroverted world of show business (let's face it, if you're an introverted music performer in any genre, you've picked the wrong career), as had been done in the early 1960s by the music industry in their mass marketing strategies, and are then reawakened, they awaken with vengeance and furor.

The Beatles, though not blues revivalists, and the Rolling Stones were just the vanguard of the invasion. Through the hole that they blew open in the American lines poured a revival of the blues and creative spirit that would shake the walls of rock music with the force of an earthquake, completely transforming, yet again, the musical landscape of rock and roll. From this point on, authentic blues music would regain its historical importance in the eyes of musicians and would become the dominant formal and interpretive factor in authentic hard rock music. That's a big way of saying that suddenly musicians wanted to understand and play with the intensity and soulfulness of the American blues man. It's not surprising that the musicians wanted to explore and expand on the blues, but that the American public wanted to hear it was a bit of a surprise for the industry and the musicians alike.

The blues revival movement explored the improvisational and formal possibilities within the framework of the blues, and there were literally hundreds of bands associated with it, but only a few stayed true to their blues quest, most opted for a shift into a more pop oriented sound and image. The great ones remained close to the blues. The Rolling Stones, Led Zeppelin, and Pink Floyd all evolved the language of rock music dramatically, pushing on the boundaries of what could be done, yet always maintaining a root essence of soulful blues and gospel in their music. They also were able to transform it into something new and fresh enough to make them all very successful, long after all the others had gone.

These sorts of bands didn't gain that kind of long lasting fame because of promotional strategies, though they were all certainly very good at self-promotion in their individual ways. There's something in their music, something that moves people emotionally. Without that music, no amount of promotional support can sustain the fan support that they enjoy. Long careers can, however, be sustained with enough corporate promotional support by having artists reinvent themselves to match the pop market trends as they age, but bands like the 'Stones, Led Zeppelin, and Pink Floyd built an intensely loyal fan base on their commitment to authentic, full-throttle performances and solid, creative, and imaginative songwriting and musicianship. They consequently did, and still do, have large corporate promotional support, but as the old saying goes, "It don't mean a thing if it ain't got that swing."

Once the blues revivalists reintroduced America to the blues, so many American musicians would follow their lead as well. Suddenly, being able to **jam** (improvising over a versatile formal structure) meant something. The British musician's term for jamming was **rave-up**, but it meant the same thing, which was basically that they would get a song started, then improvise and explore the ability of their instrument and talent over a repetitive rhythm section of just bass, rhythm guitar, and drums. After about twenty minutes, or sometimes much longer, of improvising and exploring, everyone clicks back into the song for an ending, all based on the blues. The people who danced to this music as well just wanted to, or needed to just dance all their frustrations out of their system. Suddenly, understanding where the mud of the Mississippi delta came from became important. Suddenly, the authentic voice of black America was again being embraced by young, white musicians and used as a stepping stone into new musical directions.

When the British Invasion happened, the bands swept to the top of the charts so fast, and displaced so many other American musicians, that there was a sense of shock among the Americans, like there had been some kind of catastrophic accident. It was obvious from the energy and excitement generated by the British bands that this wasn't just an overnight fad—that The Beatles represented something much larger. The Beatles had been called, "four Elvis Presleys" by the press, and maybe that says it all.

The British Invasion also motivated the American musicians out of complacency as they struggled to keep up with the changing trends. It also polarized the American music marketplace in a racial way. Black musicians were receiving heavy amounts of crossover airplay until then. Once the Brits came, there seemed to be a shift back to a sense of black music for black people and white music for white people. Not necessarily a bad shift, as, in the former system, a performer like James Brown was too raw for the major consumer market.

The invasion did displace many black performers who were recording highly produced songs written by hired songwriters, but it also allowed an authentic, hard-edged performer like James Brown to finally receive deserved attention because he was so far to the left of what the current hit parade's music was all about. Brown's music was so identifiably black that he was one of the only musicians untouched by the shift in focus. This was not the case for the black musicians recording music for the white marketplace, who saw almost every hit song drop off the charts. Once James Brown finally came into focus in the black community, he spilled over into the community of black and white musicians, and soon many would follow his lead into a wholly new style of music called funk. These periodic shifts and sense of competition, while they may or may not be good for individual artists, are vital to the life and vitality of rock music. If music starts getting too silly and contrived, there's always the threat that a new Elvis will come along and abruptly change the rules.

One more point about the British Invasion in general is something of food for thought. Think about the birth dates and geography of the musicians of the blues revival. So many of them had been born into the midst of the most brutal world war in human history. In their most formative years, Hitler was unrelenting in his attempt to bomb the life out of them. Then, after the war, as they were growing up, the hard life and industrial labor of rebuilding an utterly devastated country, both of its cities, and of its men lost to war, was the scenario that they emerged from. Maybe reflected in not only the shear loudness and raw edge to much of the music's feel, but certainly on much deeper levels as well, like the story portrayed of human nature and the darkness of insanity in Pink Floyd's, *The Wall*, with its intense imagery and analogy taken right from the World War II battlefront. *The Wall* was released in 1980. Pink Floyd formed in 1964. The story of *The Wall* took sixteen years to come out. It's worth listening to.

The Beatles

What can possibly be said about this band that hasn't already been said? The history of The Beatles has been so thoroughly documented in such extreme detail, told and retold so many times, that much of the extreme detailing hardly needs repeating here. But there are some very significant aspects of The Beatles, both culturally and musically as a group and as individuals, that warrant our attention.

When The Beatles rocketed to public attention in 1964, it seemed as if they had come out of nowhere, but by that time they had been performing together for seven long and hard fought years around England and Germany. Also, by the time they got to America, they had already developed their own musical style, but had done so over those seven years out of emulation of the early rock pioneers like Chuck Berry, Elvis Presley, and Little Richard. There were many bands like them, but through good management, and their relationship with their producer, George Martin, they had set themselves apart from the pack.

There were some early changes in personnel before The Beatles settled into their familiar fab four lineup. At the heart of the Liverpool band was the team of John Lennon (1941–1980) on guitar and Paul McCartney (b. 1942) on bass, who would soon become one of the most potent songwriting teams in music. Next in the lineup is guitarist George Harrison (b. 1943) who came into the band under the sceptical eye of Lennon, but soon would become one of the premier lead guitarists in rock music. Lastly is drummer Richard Starkey aka. Ringo Starr (b. 1940), whose steady rhythmic flow gave the band the solid and steady beat and backbeat they needed to step into the world of professional musicianship. There were a couple of other performers in the group before they settled into this line up. Stu Sutcliffe, a close friend of Lennon's, played guitar and bass, or at least posed with it as he couldn't really play, but looked good on stage. (He would die of a hemorrhage in 1962 due to a head injury sustained when The Beatles got beat up by some street punks in Germany.)

The Beatles, who had the earlier names of Johnny and the Hurricanes, the Nurk Twins, and eventually the Silver Beetles, settled on the misspelled Beatles by 1960. They frequently performed without any drummer at all, until Pete Best joined the group in 1960. Under Brian Epstein's management, The Beatles signed a one-year, four-album contract with EMI Records. Once Brian Epstein got them working with classically trained producer George Martin in the studio to create those recordings, Martin convinced them that Pete Best just didn't have the rock-steady beat needed for professional performances and studio work. Martin told Lennon and McCartney that they could use Pete on stage if they wanted to, but that he would bring in a different drummer for the recording sessions. That drummer, Ringo Starr, became their full-time drummer in 1962.

Their early days playing the clubs of Liverpool, England and Hamburg, Germany would toughen and season them as musicians and performers. They stayed in windowless back rooms, played for very little money. Any notion of superstardom was the farthest thing from their view of the future, as it was with all of the British Invasion bands. Success came at a high price, if at all, for these groups.

The Beatles' career can be viewed in four different periods. The **first period** was from their inception in 1960 until their first trip to America in February 1964. Here they learned to play rhythm and blues and rockabilly-based rock and roll music and developed as seasoned performers and musicians. It also includes the instillation of the songwriting team of Lennon/McCartney, and the unique appearance of a band that wrote their own songs. There was no leader of the pack in their imagery. A look at those early album covers shows the image of a real band in the truest sense; four equal members. This is also when George Martin was instrumental in getting them a recording contract.

The **second period**, the Beatlemania years that started with their arrival in America in 1964 until their last live public performance in August of 1966, was spent constantly touring and trying to survive Beatlemania. This is musically their "yeah, yeah, yeah" period, when their music was hard-driving, straight rock and roll, with nothing too thought provoking in the lyrics, with the exception of their first forays into iconoclasm with songs like *I'm a Loser*, and, of course the release of the album *Rubber Soul*, with its first strong indications that The Beatles were quickly evolving musically. With the release of *Rubber Soul*, it became apparent that they would not just keep playing the music that had made them famous. This was entirely unprecedented in the history of rock music.

Their **third period**, from the release of the *Revolver* album in 1966 until, and including the release of *Sgt. Pepper's Lonely Hearts Club Band*, the most critically acclaimed album of their career, was a time when they experimented heavily both with music and with life. Once they had stopped performing, a very wise move on their part, else Beatlemania would have literally torn them to shreds, they were able to focus on the abilities of the recording studio. Many people see this period as their most vital. With George Martin guiding the way, The Beatles incorporated into their music just about every instrument and every recording trick known to man. They used Bach trumpets, harpsichords, string quartets, sitars, and such studio effects as tape splicing and **backmasking**, the technique of playing prerecorded tape on the playback machine backwards.

The albums from this period are the high-water marks of what they were able to accomplish in the musical environment of experimentation that George Martin fostered. Of particular importance were the watershed events of the release of the song *Tomorrow Never Knows* on the *Revolver* album in 1966, and most importantly, the release in 1967 of the most impactful album of their career, *Sgt. Pepper's Lonely Hearts Club Band*. The other album from this period, *Magical Mystery Tour* in 1967 was a further perfecting of their explorations into studio production, and though it typically gets panned by historians and critics, some of the songs, like *I Am the Walrus*, *Strawberry Fields Forever*, and *Penny Lane* contain a richness of sound and seasoned quality that outshines *Sgt. Pepper* in many ways.

The **fourth period**, from 1968 until their official announcement of break-up in 1970, contains some of their best work as rock and roll musicians. This was also the period that gave indications that The Beatles might not be around as a band much longer. By the time they were recording material for *The Beatles* album, they were drifting far apart in individual visions of where they wanted to take their own personal lives. *The Beatles* double album (known popularly as the *White Album*) in 1968, was critically seen as disorganized and lacking any sense of direction, although it contains some of their hardest-hitting music and hardest-hitting lyrics to date.

This period also contains their largest selling single ever in *Hey Jude*, and the albums *Let It Be*, produced by Phil Spector and released as their last album in 1970 though it was recorded before their previous album release, and their true swansong album, and the last one they recorded together, *Abbey Road*. It does seem oddly fitting that the song *Let It Be* was released last, almost as a message to their millions of fans. They still worked with George Martin during this period, but gradually the direction of the music definitely heads straight back to their rock roots, this time funneled through their now extremely developed sense of musicianship and studio production. The penultimate song on their last recorded album, *The End*, segued (one song progressing nonstop into another) directly from the songs before it, *Golden Slumber* and *Carry That Weight*, is The Beatles at their purest, hardest-hitting rock and roll best, as if they wanted this to be how they would be remembered. In 1970, they called it quits and went out with as big a bang as when they came in.

The key to The Beatles' success was not just their music and performing talent, which was phenomenally large, but equally in their management by Brian Epstein, and the experimental production environment fostered by George Martin. Without George Martin, there would not have been the kind of musical growth that The Beatles had. The Beatles did have a natural magnetism toward experimenting with sound, but without Martin to help cultivate that attraction, they would not have had the availability of resources and depth of musical and technical knowledge to grow in that direction. With Martin as their overseer, they became like little kids playing in a candy store of sound. Eventually, as each of them drifted in different musical directions, John and Paul gradually stopped writing songs together, bringing in the other members of the band to record their individual compositions.

The Beatles' strongest qualities were their musical evolution and highly developed understanding of music, and their willingness to take chances with lyric content. Lennon's frequently iconoclastic and/or Salvador Dali-esque approach to lyric writing pushed hard on the boundaries of what could be written and still sell. The lyrics of Beatles' songs after the invasion years are full of word play and childlike playfulness in their imagery and metaphor use.

Lucy in the Sky with Diamonds, which will forever be associated with the acronym LSD whether Lennon intended it or not, is a prime example of how imagery could be set in rock music, and of how much The Beatles influenced other musicians to experiment with lyrics as well. This was definitely not *Teen Angel*, *Surfin Safari*, or even *I Want To Hold Your Hand*. The Beatles proved that it was OK to explore and experiment with the elements of lyric composition as well as those of musical composition, and proved it was OK to make people think.

The Beatles made their mark in music history by knowing that history and becoming familiar with the history of other music genres as well. Not only did they use orchestral instruments in creatively unique ways, they introduced westerners to many world instruments, music, and idealogy in their explorations in each.

After the death of manager Brian Epstein in August of 1967, The Beatles started their own record label, Apple Corp., Ltd., and announced that they would manage themselves. Though the company was not successful in the long run, it was an adventurous move for a group of young musicians to seize control of their own destiny in this way. This can only be expected from a band that in every step of the way rewrote the rules. When *Hey Jude* came out in 1967, radio was geared toward the three minute song format. It was unheard of to release a seven minute song, yet *Hey Jude* not only received heavy airplay, it was their biggest selling single ever.

In the end, The Beatles had paid a heavy price for all that unexpected vitality. Their timing was perfect for the era, but the era was fading. One by one, they all walked away from the band, only to be talked back into playing by Paul. When Paul no longer wanted to play that role, releasing his first solo album in 1970, The Beatles, the greatest and most influential pop rock band of all time was no more. In their parting shot, the band that had come so far to leave their mark on music and culture gave one final thought to their friends and fans—"let it be."

The Rolling Stones

The 1950s belonged to Elvis, the 1960s to The Beatles, and the 1970s to Led Zeppelin, but the whole rock and roll train belongs to the Rolling Stones. They are the survivors, the kings of the hill, and they did it embracing authentic blues every step of the way. The songwriting team (and friendship), of Mick Jagger and Keith Richards is the longest running in the history of rock music, and no band will ever have the kind of long lasting and far reaching impact on real rock music as the Rolling Stones.

The Rolling Stones were the spearhead of the blues revival, first in England, then in America. Their commitment to authentic delta and electric blues was actually typed up by cofounder Brian Jones in a Rolling Stones' mission statement early in their career. Even the name of the band was taken from the title of a Muddy Waters' song. They had built up a thriving blues scene in England, and when they came to America, the void that they left behind was quickly filled by others wanting to play the blues. Also when they came to America, their blues-based pop songs, and pop image would be transformed into what would again become the very essence of rock and roll; sex, outrageous rebellion, and full-throttle performing, after Mick Jagger first saw James Brown in concert. They would also make excursions to the Meccas of American blues and soul music, Chess Records in Chicago and Fame Recording Studio in Alabama.

The Rolling Stones and The Beatles were constantly compared to each other, with one main difference. The Rolling Stones portrayed an image of a bad-boy version of The Beatles. While The Beatles had cultivated a good guy image, and enacted damage control when they got bad press or a bad light was shed on the band, the Rolling Stones were busy staging outrageous publicity stunts to expand their naughty image. There's the famous airplane movie where the band members are carrying around a naked young lady; or the televisions thrown from hotel balcony windows; and the tour announcement press conference, where they told all the press to meet inside of a hotel in New York City.

Knowing that their fans would not be able to get into the press conference, they set up stage on a flat bed truck and pulled up in front of the hotel playing *Jumpin' Jack Flash* to the utter delight of their fans who were gathered outside and to the utter befuddlement of the press who were inside. They then drove around New York City performing for the people. There's also the attitude, completely irreverent and cute at the same time. Mick Jagger came across as a cute, lovable kid who needed a good spanking. Without the great music to back up their outrageous publicity stunts, no one would have cared. But they did have the music to back them up. Jagger and Richards, as a songwriting team, were able to develop a style that kept getting more popular with every album they put out. Regardless of how popular they became, they always maintained an edge and raw vitality to their music and irreverent performances that belies their immense songwriting talent and understanding of what it takes to write a hit song.

By far the most important aspect of the Rolling Stones is that they just keep going and going. They've been at it nearly 40 years, and they still show no signs of letting up. Though bassist Bill Wyman did recently retire before their Bridges To Babylon Tour of 1999, the rest of the band still performs with an energy and enthusiasm that many twenty-year old musicians would do well to study.

In fact, when the Stones were preparing for the Bridges to Babylon tour, all the press they were getting was making much fun of their age. Talk show hosts peppered their monologs with jokes about wheelchair access to the stage and tour sponsorship by Preparation H and Depends Diapers. The Stones certainly had the last laugh. At the beginning of the show, an overhead video was shown of the band members clad in black leather outlaw trenchcoats walking toward the audience. The dramatic stormy music swelled to a high volume, and out from the back of a very large stage ran a man at full speed clenching a guitar. At the middle of the stage he jumped into the air and slid the rest of the way on his knees to the very front edge of the stage, stopping just short of going too far, as he hit the introductory power chord of their first song of the night. That man was 55-year-old Keith Richards. For the next two and a half hours they performed nonstop, as if they were teenagers. The also 55-year-old Mick Jagger never stopped running around to every corner of the stage, its ramps and runways as he delighted the fans with one Rolling Stones hit after another.

The raw energy and irreverence is there more so today than ever in their careers. It even seems like the older they get, the more they enjoy snubbing their nose at conventional wisdom. The old adage about mellowing with age bears absolutely no impact on this band and even trembles under their shadows. Mick Jagger and Keith Richards are not going to get off the stage until they are carried off. And even when that happens, their status as the greatest pure rock band to ever take the stage is as solid as the earth itself.

The line up of the band has stayed pretty much consistent through their history, with a couple of exceptions. Original bassist Bill Wyman's (b. 1936) retirement is the most recent. Except for that, the position of rhythm guitarist went through a couple of changes in their early days, but the line up has been unchanged for almost 30 years. Mick Jagger (b. 1943) on vocals, Keith Richards (b. 1943) on lead guitar, and Charlie Watts (b. 1941) on drums have been there since the beginning as well. Cofounder of the band, Brian Jones dissolved into drug abuse and was booted out of the band in 1969. He died shortly thereafter of drug abuse, though it was officially listed as death by misadventure when he was found drowned in a swimming pool. In the period that Jones was in the band, the Stones released a catalog of hits that just wouldn't quit. Replacing Jones on guitar was Mick Taylor, catapulting the band into what many fans still think of as their most vital period, an amazing statement considering all of the hit songs they had under their belt up to that point. Taylor left the Stones in 1974 to pursue a solo career, a move that he still has a little trouble validating in press interviews. After Taylor left in 1974, Ron Wood, who was playing with Rod Stewart's Faces, became the third, and last, rhythm guitarist for the band.

One of the Rolling Stones' strongest impacts, besides convincing thousands of teenagers to start a band, was Jagger's iconoclastic lyric writing. Jagger has consistently taken shots at long-standing social mores, drastically distancing themselves and their fans from the previous generation. The song *Mother's Little Helper* in 1966 illustrates the schism between generations, with it's opening line of "What a drag it is getting old." From the very first line to the end, this song stabs ruthlessly at adult complacency and the tools used to achieve it.

MOTHER'S LITTLE HELPER
THE ROLLING STONES

Ouch! But Jagger didn't stop there. After they had solidified their status in rock music with such tremendously popular hits as *I Can't Get No Satisfaction* and *Get Off Of My Cloud* in 1965, *Let's Spend the Night Together* in 1967, and the immortal *Jumpin' Jack Flash* in 1968, they released the *Beggars Banquet* album in 1968. Most of the songs on *Beggars Banquet* are pure delta blues, electric blues, or country influenced songs

The Early Sixties **105**

with little deviation from their authentic intent, with the exceptions of the rocking *Street Fighting Man*, *Factory Girl*, and their ultimate iconoclastic work, *Sympathy for the Devil*.

In *Sympathy for the Devil*, Jagger takes on the acting role of portraying human evil, sometimes called the devil, or Satan. He even took flack from people who couldn't see the obvious metaphor at work, claiming that Jagger thought that he himself was the devil. The song lyrics detail some of the darkest moments in human history, using first person association. Jagger, portraying the devil, or evil, is saying in essence, I was there when this bad thing happened, and that was me when that bad thing happened. His point is obvious, that evil comes from the hearts and minds of men and women, not gods or demons, and that it happens because we allow it to happen by not standing up against it. "I shouted out, who killed the Kennedys, when after all it was you and me." Interestingly, after the disastrous events that took place at the Rolling Stones' Altamont concert at the end of 1969, where four people lost their lives and band members from Jefferson Airplane were beat up at the hands of Hell's Angels, the Rolling Stones refused to perform *Sympathy for the Devil* for six years.

Controversy aside, there is no diminishing the Rolling Stones' influence on rock music. Mick Jagger was the first real punk. In the early 1970s, as future punk rock musicians were learning how to play hard, no frills rock, they did so by playing covers of Rolling Stones' songs. Their songs were musically simple, but had such strong hooks built into them, and a properly irreverent attitude that they made perfect learning tools for young rock musicians. Unlike The Beatles, who developed such complex production qualities that their music seemed untouchable, the Rolling Stones music was completely accessible to young musicians. All you had to do was learn the I-IV-V progression in a handful of keys and you were well on your way to learning their songs. Plus it was almost all guitar, bass, drums, and vocals, with a few seemingly misguided treks elsewhere, unlike The Beatles who evolved to such a point that they couldn't even perform their own material live if they wanted to.

Sure they influenced countless future musicians, and sure they struck at hard-hitting social commentary in their lyrics, but when all is said and done, the reason for their immense fame still comes down to the fact that the ever youthful Rolling Stones don't get older, they just get better, and they do it by maintaining a close relationship with authentic American blues. Peel away the layers of finely honed rock writing style, and there you'll find the blues. Maintaining a direct link to the roots of rock music has served them well, and secured a very high place for them in the history of this music. When all the others have disappeared or faded into solo careers of constant reinvention to keep up with trends, the Rolling Stones just keep rolling their stone. How long can they go? This author is willing to bet there's still at least one more tour in the new millennium. If Mick Jagger and Keith Richards still breathe, there's always one more tour.

Other Significant Voices of the Invasion

Them

Led by George Ivan "Van" Morrison, Them formed in Belfast, Ireland. Born into a family of blues-playing parents, and a life in industrial post-war Ireland, Morrison could relate to the plight of the American blues man, thus the music made a perfect match to express himself. Van Morrison was one of the most vocally intense and raw singers to come out of the blues revival.

The first release for Them, *The Angry Young Them*, in 1965, contains some of the most powerful music of the era. On songs from that album, like *Mystic Eyes* and *Baby, Please Don't Go*, Morrison's voice communicates an urgent sense of anger and intensity that is a direct relative of the music of bluesmen like Son House. Yet on his sultry versions of Screamin' Jay Hawkins' *I Put a Spell on You*, and T-Bone Walker's *Stormy Monday Blues*, Morrison croons, moans, and scats like a seasoned, if gruff sounding, jazz singer. But for full-throttle, pure power, anger, and raw intent, listen to *Gloria*. The pulsing repetitive three chord progression is a perfect example of a good rave up form. It's laid back when it needs to be to make way for the vocals, then builds to a frantic rhythmic frenzy.

The Animals

Led by Eric Burdon, the Animals added more anger and attitude to what was coming out of the blues revival. Burdon's voice on the Animals' recordings harkens back to the early American blues men, with a proper edge and raw power dictated by the style, while also having the ability to lay back and croon a bit in the softer sections, just to explode again when a song builds to a fever crescendo. The Animals knew how to write a hook into a song, unlike many of the revivalists that are now forgotten in time. They weren't around very long as a band, but the impact of a few songs will carry their name into the history books.

The Animals were also adept at iconoclastic lyric content in songs that made it into the charts. The important thing about that ability is that, it's one thing to write a song about some social absurdity or injustice (Frank Zappa made a whole career out of it), but quite another to frame it musically so that it garners heavy airplay and is heard by the masses. The British Invasion bands not only did this, but were the first to do it. Nobody in American music was taking shots at the industrial military complex, or really, at any of the social ills of the world until the British bands came over. Then everything exploded. Suddenly everyone in music was a social commentator. The west coast groups associated with psychedelia and the civil rights and anti-war movements would take much credit for opening people's eyes, but it was actually a scruffy bunch of British bohemian street urchins left over from the remnants of Hitler's attempted annihilation of England that introduces the idea of serious social commentary in popular music.

The Animals' song, *Sky Pilot*, is a seven-and-a-half-minute long stab at not just the futility of war, but also the absurdity of the idea of divine providence in war, searing not only in its words, but even more so in the musical setting. Burdon delivers the first verses in a normal musical setting like any song. This is followed by a full two minutes of collaging the music into the sounds of a battle, complete with bomb explosions and dive-bombing planes, and ending with a pan out of the war scene as the sounds of bagpipes pan in. The battle is over, and now the calming music of a string quartet over the original beat portrays a sense of the calmness and sadness of post-battle shock. Throughout this part of the song, a battle is fought, ends, and the quiet remnants of war lay before you. The last verses are sung over this setting, and the song gradually builds to its

Listen

SKY PILOT
THE ANIMALS

original fever rock pitch as the chorus is sung over and over, gradually fading away to nothing on the repeated last line, "never reach the sky."

This kind of in-your-face commentary was simply not popular when it came out in 1968. Though the song has a very catchy hook to its melodic line, which would get it airplay, when you got around to listen to the words beyond the "sky pilot" chorus, there was a hard-hitting message directed at the establishment. This song, and a few others like *For What It's Worth* by Buffalo Springfield, were direct shots across the bow of the industrial military complex. Many would follow this lead as the war in Vietnam, and opposition to it escalated throughout the 1960s.

The Animals also utilized a unique strategy to gain a foothold in the marketplace, and a place in the hearts of every garage band. Their cover version of *House of the Rising Sun* is a slow, haunting tribute to the roots of the music. It came about when the Animals were booked onto a Chuck Berry tour. Knowing that all the other bands on the bill would try to out-rock Chuck Berry (a futile effort if there ever was one), the Animals decided to perform a song that would be unique in the show, or as Burdon put it, "The audience would remember the one song that was different." Their version of *House of the Rising Sun* is certainly that. The organ and guitar slowly arpeggiates up and down in the dark D minor key, and Burdon's haunting vocals portray a sense of distance as he sings about "the ruin of many a men" at a place in New Orleans called the "House of the Rising Sun." The Animals also did a version of Screamin' Jay Hawkin's *I Put a Spell on You*, helping to place it in the standard repertoire of blues revivalists.

Yardbirds

The graduate school of rock guitar, the Yardbirds emerged in England from the vacuum created by the Rolling Stones' success and subsequent departure to bigger markets. In live performances, they would play extended rave ups in classic blues songs, improvising for hours on hypnotic electric blues rhythms. In the studio, however, the band tried for pop market success in songs like *For Your Love*. The pop side of the Yardbirds would chase away their innovative first guitarist, Eric Clapton, in 1965, into other more purely blues based projects like John Mayall's Bluesbreakers and Cream.

Their next lead guitarist, Jeff Beck, was building up his own reputation as a blues guitarist with the Tridents when he was asked to audition for the Yardbirds. He came into the audition, where there were a roomful of guitarists hoping for their chance for fame, played a few authentic blues riffs, and the rest of the guitarists were sent home. Beck pushed the group into a period of innovation and success with his experimental approach and heavy use of special effects like feedback, reverb, and distorted fuzz tones to his guitar playing.

But soon another guitarist would join the Yardbirds that would lead them in yet newer directions. When Jimmy Page joined the band, first as a bassist, then as a second guitarist, his extreme talent gave even Jeff Beck an inferiority complex that wouldn't quit. Beck had a nervous breakdown on stage during their first tour with Page in the lineup, smashed his guitar and walked out of the group. The Yardbirds continued on with Jimmy Page as their lead guitarist. Page had already been using his patented violin bow on the guitar technique, most associated with his work in Led Zeppelin, to go along with his virtuosic fingerboard talent and plethora of special effects.

In 1968, Page formed a new band after the Yardbirds split up, first calling it the New Yardbirds. Legend has it that Who drummer Keith Moon had seen one of their first performances and commented to the band members, "That's going to go over like a lead zeppelin." Now they had a name that fit their slow, plodding distorted and soulful blues sound. Though the term was first associated with Jimi Hendrix, Led Zeppelin would soon become the very embodiment of heavy metal music. They would dominate the authentic rock music scene in the 1970s like The Beatles dominated the 1960s, and Elvis Presley in the 1950s, and inspire yet more legions of musicians and bands to follow.

The Yardbirds had delivered to the world three of the premier, hardest playing and highly talented guitarists in rock music of the 1970s. The Yardbirds were the classroom where Clapton, Beck, and Page learned and developed their craft of blues-based electric guitar, their sense of direction for their own individual careers, and their stage presence. The Yardbirds weren't around very long, but their influence with Clapton, Beck, and especially Page on guitar echoed strongly into the 1970s as each formed their own projects and solo work.

 **Listen**

GLORIA
MYSTIC EYES
I PUT A SPELL ON YOU
THEM

HOUSE OF THE RISING SUN
SKY PILOT
I PUT A SPELL ON YOU
THE ANIMALS

TRAIN KEPT A-ROLLIN'
FOR YOUR LOVE
I'M A MAN
THE YARDBIRDS

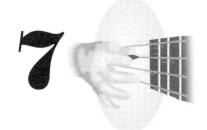

The Beatles and The Stones

Seen from afar and through a haze, The Beatles and The Rolling Stones seem to be quite similar. After all, both were British rock and roll bands, both created the vast majority of the music which they performed and recorded, both were wildly popular, and both came to America as part of what is commonly referred to as "The British Invasion." However, as the haze clears the difference between the two becomes quite obvious. While The Beatles created a body of work which has yet to be surpassed they had remarkably little influence on future rock and roll musicians. (You don't just run up stairs and write a tune in the style of The Beatles.) The music of The Beatles is self contained—that is, their songs' melodies, harmonies, and other elements of music transcend the performance. The "guts" of *Yesterday*, *She Said, She Said*, or *Here Comes The Sun* are not lost when they are performed on the piano or by an orchestra or a marching band. The very nature of each song is in the music—not in the performance. It is no coincidence that after 1966 The Beatles retreated into the recording studio and avoided live performances.

The songs created by The Rolling Stones are fundamentally different. They are vehicles for live performance—performance by The Rolling Stones. Without the performance and the attitude and atmosphere which it creates, their music pales next to the music of The Beatles. But, when all is said and done, their influence on the future of rock and roll—how it would look, how it would sound, and what sort of attitude it would present—far surpassed that of The Beatles.

The Beatles

The musical career of The Beatles falls into five distinctive style periods.

I.	1958–1961	Imitative
II.	1962–1964	Beatlemania
III.	1965–1967	Maturity
IV.	1968–1970	Decay
V.	1970–Present	Apart

During the imitative period the band's personnel stabilized, they performed covers of American R&B and several British pop styles, and (through an endless succession of "gigs") learned their trade. While the period usually referred to as "Beatlemania" was characterized by the hysterical audiences, the number one records, and the appearances on Ed Sullivan's *Toast of the Town*, the important musical development was reflected in the growing songwriting skills of Lennon and McCartney. It was their songs which "ruled the charts"—not their covers. The third period is dominated by their retreat into the recording studio, their association with musician and producer George Martin, and the production of three of the most important albums in the history of rock and roll: *Rubber Soul, Revolver,* and *Sgt. Pepper's Lonely Hearts Club Band.*

Period IV is characterized by infighting, wandering interests, and, with the exception of the *Abbey Road* album, music of uneven quality. After 1970, despite numerous rumors of a reunion, each went his own way. While each produced a wide variety of musical and non-musical projects, the magic and the unity of their music of the mid 1960s was never recaptured.

Lennon and McCartney were not a songwriting team in the tradition of Rodgers and Hammerstein or Lerner and Lowe. That is, one was not the lyricist and the other the musician. While most songwriting teams do, in fact, divide the labor, Lennon and McCartney helped each other with both aspects of songwriting. Most Lennon/McCartney songs were primarily the work of one with the encouragement and/or contribution of the other. Most are identified as either "John's song" or "Paul's song."

During the early 1960s Lennon and McCartney abandoned their covers of R&B and began to record songs of their own. *Please Please Me* (1962) (Fig. 7.1) is a good example of their early work. It also foreshadows their future creations.

The four-measure introduction (A) presents a simple descending melody in the lead guitar (Harrison) and harmonica (Lennon). Verse one is in two contrasting halves. In phrase B Lennon sings the melody heard in the introduction. Its words start on the weaker second pulse of the measure and fill only three measures. Measure four of B is an amazing miniature instrumental break which sounds suspiciously reminiscent of harmonies used by The Everly Brothers. Measures five through eight are a repeat of measures one through four. In phrase C (the second half of the verse) things change. Now the melody goes up and as Lennon sings, "Come on, come on, come on," the harmony becomes more and more complex. Without diving into the intimate complexities of the song's harmony it is obvious that Lennon has moved beyond the I/IV/V harmonies of R&B based rock and roll. During the brief instrumental break (measure four of B) he uses the harmonies III/IV/V (all in the same measure) before returning home to I. The III chord, very rare in rock and roll of the period, is used

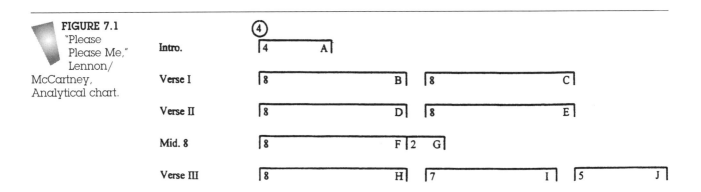

FIGURE 7.1 "Please Please Me," Lennon/McCartney, Analytical chart.

as a "color" and is, in fact, the same chord used by The Everly Brothers in their song *Bird Dog*. The harmony in C is even more dramatic. As Lennon's pleading melody ascends it is harmonized in the accompanying voices and instruments as follows: IV/ii/vi/IV before returning home to I. Lower case Roman numerals refer to chords of the minor mode.

Verse two (phrase D and E) consists of different words set to the same music. Phrase F (frequently referred to as "the middle eight") presents a contrasting melody. G is two measures which are "borrowed" from the song's introduction. Verse three (phrases H and I) is, with the addition of harmonizing vocal lines (McCartney and Harrison), the same as verses one and two. J is an extension of phrase I. In its closing three measures, under the word, "You" the harmony again uses some of the exotic chords heard earlier. In the tradition of American R&B, the song comes to a distinct end—no fade out.

When the music of The Beatles first became known in America, many said there was "something different about," "something fresh about it." The real difference could not be accurately identified or agreed upon—but there was something different. Now, after years of listening to and examining their music, "the difference" becomes quite obvious. It was not the hair, or even the Liverpuldlian accents—it was how they used the basic elements of music. Even in "Please Please Me," one can observe the sophistication in the use of harmony as it supports the meaning of the words, the shaping of melodies within the overall form of the song, and Lennon and McCartney's fascination with word play—*Please Please Me*.

The Beatles brought something else which made them sound different and fresh. Throughout the 1950s and during the lean years, the texture produced by pop music groups fit into two distinct styles. Performers such as Little Richard, Chuck Berry, and Elvis Presley were solo singers backed up by a band. While their arrangements occasionally employed vocal backgrounds, the unique timbres of their voices were always of primary importance. Their fans had to be able to recognize the distinctive sounds of their voices. Conversely, vocal groups strived for a homogeneous (blended) sound. The members of groups as widely separated in musical style as The Kingston Trio (folk), The Ronettes (do-wop), and The Beach Boys sacrificed the individual colors of their own voices to the blend of the group.

The vocal texture and timbre of the Beatles did not fit either model. While Lennon, McCartney, and Harrison all sang within the same vocal range, the timbres produced by their voices were remarkably diverse. Instead of attempting any form of blend, they played off these differences. The determination of "who sang what" was generally determined by "who wrote what." *A Hard Day's Night* (1964) (Fig. 7.2) is an excellent example of this "new" texture and timbre.

The first two phrases of Verse I (phrases A and B) are sung by Lennon. Phrase C adds McCartney. Although they are singing in close harmony [*chromatic thirds*] their voices do not blend in the manner of other vocal groups, e.g. The Everly Brothers. Their two distinct vocal qualities mix to form a new timbre. The middle eight was written by McCartney and, consequently, it is sung by him—a third vocal timbre. Within *A Hard Day's Night*, one hears three distinct vocal timbres; 1) Lennon solo, 2) Lennon and McCartney together, and 3) McCartney solo. Because each individual timbre is associated with one and only one structural unit, the timbres themselves become important structural components.

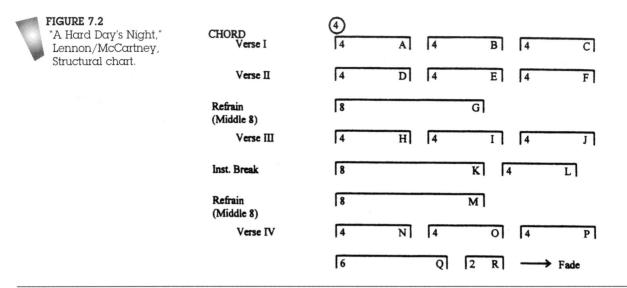

FIGURE 7.2
"A Hard Day's Night," Lennon/McCartney, Structural chart.

A Hard Day's Night opens with a most unusual "introduction." Both guitars and the bass slam into a single shocking chord. Unlike anything in pop, this chord [*stacked fourths and fifths*] is an "attention getter"—perhaps the slamming of a door upon returning from a hard day's night. The melodic line of Verse I is a classic example of text painting. While the melody of the first two measures of phrase A is static—all sung on the same note, Lennon moves up [*a minor third*] in the third measure on the word "working." The note he sings and the chord which accompanies it [*flat-III*] are far removed from the home tonality of the song. He does the same thing in measure three of phrase B—on the word "sleeping." In both cases the tension created corresponds to and emphasizes the key words, "working" and "sleeping." Phrase C, the poetic center of the verse pulls out all the stops. Here, the first two measures (now sung by Lennon and McCartney) of the melody climb higher and higher and move in quicker notes—notes of shorter duration. Aided by the familiar harmonic progression IV/V, the tension becomes almost unbearable until it is released in the last two measures of C. Here the melody comes down, McCartney's voice leaves the mix, and the harmony returns to I (home.) Except for new text verse II is the same as verse I.

McCartney's middle eight switches to the minor mode for four measures before returning to major for the remaining four measures. The last bar of G does not return home harmonically. Instead McCartney leaves the listener "hanging" on a tension filled chord [*V 7*]. Of course this makes the return to home at the beginning of verse III all the more satisfying.

The song ends with what musicians call a "coda." Coda means tail in Italian. It refers to a brief musical extension at the end of a piece. Here it lasts for six measures (Q) and is extended into a brief fade (R). As with so many of The Beatles songs, even what seems insignificant is usually remarkable. In *A Hard Day's Night* the coda contains music (repeated figures in the lead guitar) which appears nowhere else in the song. While similar in harmony to the shocking harmony of the introductory chord, the notes are now played one at a time and the harmony, while never quite reaching home (I), contains less tension. While *A Hard Day's Night* is a product of the Beatlemania period it nevertheless exhibits structural, melodic, and harmonic details which will come full turn within the next year and a half.

In many ways *Rubber Soul* (1965) was rock and roll's breakthrough album. In one quick gesture it turned away from rock and roll's R&B heritage. It also moved away from rock and roll's traditional focus—male/female relationships. In addition, it ushered in a new raison d'être for the album format and it severed its traditional relationship with dance. To the dismay and even shock of Beatlemanias, The Beatles had changed. With *Rubber Soul* the Beatles entered a new world of sound, style, subject matter, and purpose.

Throughout this transformation, the assistance received from George Martin (musician and producer) cannot be overstated. As a classically trained musician he could translate Lennon and McCartney's ideas into musical notation, make suggestions regarding the use of instruments, and act as a liaison between The Beatles and the guest performers which would appear on the next several albums. As a producer, he was able to produce finished products which were remarkably well mastered—much "cleaner" and more professional than even Brian Wilson's best efforts.

Rubber Soul opens with *I've Just Seen A Face*. From the outset, this does not sound like Beatlemania Beatles. Gone is the domination of the electric guitars and electric bass. Percussion is limited to a minor supporting role and McCartney does not even take the bass out of its case. That is not all. The song opens with two descending notes from the acoustic guitar which lead into a ten measure introduction (acoustic and electric guitars) which does not start in the home harmony—or even in the primary mode of the song—major. After ten winding measures it finally makes its way to the home harmony and the beginning of verse I. The fact that the introduction is in a slightly slower tempo than the rest of the song only serves to maintain the tension (Fig. 7.3).

Verse I consists of phrases B and C. Each is twelve measures of quick duple meter. McCartney's solo voice is accompanied by acoustic guitars and restrained drums. The drums are hit with brushes—a type of drumstick which actually looks like a brush. During the refrain, McCartney is

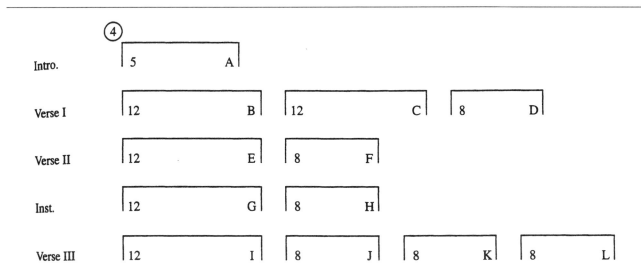

FIGURE 7.3. "I've Just Seen A Face," Lennon/McCartney, Structural chart.

joined by Lennon in close harmony while the instruments remain the same. During the third return of the refrain McCartney even performs a few "cowboy yells"—just in case you don't recognize the "country" style. G is an instrumental break which leads to another rendition of the refrain. J, K, and L are additional repetitions of the refrain. The seemingly simplistic and rustic nature of the music is countered with the sophisticated harmony and, above all, the text (Fig. 7.4).

FIGURE 7.4 "I've Just Seen A Face," Lennon/McCartney.

Verse I
I've just seen a face
I can't forget the time or place where we just met
She's just the girl for me
And I want all the world to see we've met
Mn mm mm mm

(Refrain)

Falling
Yes I am falling
And she keeps calling me back again

Verse II
Had it been another day
I might have looked another way
And I'd have never been aware
But as it is I'll dream of her tonight
La la la la

(Refrain)

Verse III
I have never known the like of this
I've been alone and I have missed things and kept out of sight
For other girls were never quite like this
Da da da da

(Refrain)

Strange. Could this possibly be a love song? As subsequent songs will clearly demonstrate, *I've Just Seen A Face* is anything but a traditional love song.

With *Norwegian Wood*, (Fig. 7.5) the album's second song, the listener is ushered into a completely different world of timbre, tempo and rhythm. The meter employs twelve pulses per measure. Not unlike the meter used in The Shangi-Las *Walking in the Sand*, the pulses come quickly enough to be heard as four principal beats with subdivisions—**1** 2 3/**4** 5 6/**7** 8 9/**10** 11 12. This is referred to as compound meter [*in this case 12/8*]. While the four strong beats are of primary importance, the "accompanying" subdivisions are crucial to the song's feel and mood. A quick glance at *Norwegian Wood's* structural chart reveals that the song is composed of relatively few measures. However, since the tempo is quite slow, its duration is actually longer than that of *I've Just Seen A Face*.

The introduction is comprised of two phrases—A and B. Phrase A is for acoustic guitar only. The entrance of the sitar in phrase B shocks the listener into a different world. An instrument of Indian origin, the sitar looks, from a distance, like a guitar. However, a closer examination reveals

FIGURE 7.5
"Norwegian Wood," Lennon/McCartney, Structural chart.

			⑫		
Intro.	2	A	2	B	
Verse I	2	C	2	D	
Refrain	2	E	2	F	
Verse II	2	G	2	H	
Inst.	2	I	2	J	
Refrain	2	K	2	L	
Verse III	2	N	2	N	
	2	O	FADE		

that its frets (the little bumps on the finger board) are moveable. In addition its four to seven strings are strung more loosely than the modern guitar, tuned to different notes, and are usually complemented with extra strings for sympathetic vibrations. It is plucked with a pick and the melody is played on one string at a time while the others serve as a drone. Although Harrison's performance is anything but authentic (he retuned the strings to conform to the tuning of the modern guitar), the unique timbre of the sitar, as heard here and on subsequent recordings by The Beatles, quickly made it the trademark sound of the 60s counterculture and it quickly became associated with all things psychedelic.

Verse I (sung by Lennon) is an excellent example of the innate contradictions which will become one of the principal features of songs of the third style period. Again and again Lennon and McCartney will compose texts which feature a statement which is immediately contradicted. "I once had a girl/Or should I say she once had me" and from the refrain (phrases E and F), "She asked me to stay, and she told me to sit anywhere—So I looked around, and I noticed there wasn't a chair."

The rhythm of the refrain is no less innovative. In the first measure of C, Lennon and McCartney sing in open harmony—that is, the two voices are relatively far apart [6ths and 5ths]—while the guitars, bass, and drums accentuate the principal beats and their subdivisions. They firmly establish the twelve beats per measure. In the second measure of C, in what appears to be a response to the contradictory nature of the text, the bass drum suddenly switches to eight pulses. Longer in duration that the "twelve" of the other instruments and spread out evenly within the measure, the result gives the impression of total confusion. In fact, the combined rhythm creates what musicians refer to as a polyrhythm [*in this case*

3 against 2]. Because of the difficulty in performing them accurately, many rock and roll bands of the 1970s and beyond will employ the technique for no particular reason—except to show off. Here, the use of the polyrhythm in conjunction with the "confused" words makes perfect sense.

The text is at least as elusive as that of the previous song. What exactly is Norwegian Wood? What exactly was set on fire? Interpretations have ranged from unrequited love to arson. Adding to the confusion is the fact that the last line of text, "Isn't it good Norwegian Wood?" is punctuated with a question mark. It is a question—not a statement.

Buried on the second side of the album is the song *Girl*, (Fig. 7.6). In several ways, it is the key which unlocks the meanings of a number of the album's songs.

Here, the function of the verses and the refrain is deeper than simply presenting a story and punctuating it with a repeated text. The texts of all three verses (and the middle eight) tell a similar story and relate a similar mood. Lennon's "girl" is troublesome. She's difficult to leave. All this angst is reflected in the music. The somewhat jagged melody is in the minor mode and is sparsely accompanied. In complete contrast, the refrain (phrase B) switches to major [*c minor to E-flat Major*] and smoothes out the melody. In addition, Lennon is joined by McCartney and Harrison in harmony. In measures two and four of the refrain all singing stops and is

FIGURE 7.6
"Girl,"
Lennon/
McCartney.

Verse I
Is there anybody going to listen to my story
All about the girl who came to stay?
She's the kind of girl you want so much it makes you sorry
Still you don't regret a single day

(Refrain)

Ah, girl
Girl, girl

Verse II
When I think of all the times I tried so hard to leave her
She will turn to me and start to cry
And she promises the earth to me and I believe her
After all this time I don't know why

(Refrain)

Middle Eight

She's the kind of girl who puts you down when friends are there
You feel a fool
When you say she's looking good
She acts as if it's understood
She's cool, ooh, ooo, ooo, ooo

(Refrain)

Verse III

Was she told when she was young that pain would lead to pleasure?
Did she understand it when they said?
That a man must break his back to earn his day of leisure?
Will she still believe it when he's dead?

(Refrain)

FIGURE 7.7
"Girl," Lennon/McCartney, Structural chart.

replaced by a heavy inhaling sound. In each repetition of the refrain (D, H, and J) the breathing becomes increasingly obvious.

In *Twilight Of The Gods*, British musicologist Wilfred Meller's landmark study of the music of The Beatles, the author addresses these breathing sounds; "The melismata [the melody of the refrain] are 'cool,' the sighs verge on the ludicrous; yet this paradoxically intensifies the loving pathos of the lyrical tune . . . since life is a tangled mesh of hopes and disappointments."

Really? Clues to the song's actual meaning abound on the album's jacket. From the psychedelic balloon lettering of the title and the somewhat foreshortened photograph of The Beatles (the name of the band does not appear on the front of the jacket) against a background of greenery to the collection of individual black and white photographs on the back the message is screamed loudly and clearly. Why are the plants "growing" out of Lennon's head? Why does the cigarette which McCartney is smoking look home-rolled? The heavy breathing of the refrains are, in fact, the inhalation of marijuana. Replace the word "girl" with the word "pot" and the song makes much more sense. It is not difficult to imagine Ringo saying to John something like, "Do you think we'll really get away with it?"

With *Girl* The Beatles produced their first "drug song." But it is much more than that. Here, in musical terms, they examine pot's pros and cons. Despite the fact that "girl" was a popular street name for pot, the symbolism and double meanings should not be overlooked. By comparing the innate nature of girls (yes, not exactly PC) to the innate nature of marijuana, Lennon creates a universal symbol. One hundred years from now (when who knows what sort of drugs may be in popular use) marijuana may be known only to historians. On the other hand, the concept of girl ("She's the kind of girl who puts you down when friends are there") will likely remain unchanged. It will probably also apply to whatever drugs the future holds. With the alternation of minor and major modes and the alternation of "negative" and "positive" words, Lennon delineates his thoughts about and his relationships with marijuana. The accompanying voices of the middle eight ("Tit, tit, tit, tit . . .) only serve to reinforce the symbolism and add a measure of satirical punch.

Girl also serves up clues as to the meaning of a number of the album's songs, e.g. *The Word*, *I'm Looking Through You*, and perhaps even *Norwegian Wood*. Replace *I've Just Seen A Face*'s vague references to the meeting of a new girl with the concept of meeting a new experience—pot. Suddenly the song's meaning becomes clear and straightforward. With *Rubber Soul* The Beatles became not only one of the symbols of the 1960s counterculture but also one if its principal prophets.

NOTE: The contents of the English version and the American version of *Rubber Soul* differ slightly. The British version does not include the song *I've Just Seen A Face*.

The following are classical composers from the past: Antonio Salieri (1750–1825), Giacomo Meyerbeer (1791–1864), Johann Hummel (1778–1837). They all share one thing in common. While they were widely admired and performed in their day, their music is pretty much ignored today. It is never played by major orchestras and the details of their careers are known only by music historians. This is not because listeners are fickle. It is because it takes time to make real value judgments. Judgments made at the time of a musician's popularity are frequently colored by sales, publicity, and national bias. It takes the distance of time to get by all this baggage. The same his been true throughout the history of rock and roll. Nowhere is this more obvious than history's judgments of the album *Revolver*. In its August issue of 1987 *Rolling Stone* magazine presented its *100 Best Albums Of The Last Twenty Years*. Topping the list, and coming as a surprise to very few, was The Beatles album *Sgt. Pepper's Lonely Hearts Club Band*. Given the hype created around the album's release (1967) and its subsequent elevation to the status of Godhood, few critics would dare to vote for anything else—walls would bleed. Even ten years later, as *Rolling Stone* presented its top 200 (*The Definitive Library of the Best Albums Ever Made*), the Beatles were represented by: *The Beatles/1962–1966* (a compilation set), *Rubber Soul, Sgt. Pepper's Lonely Hearts Club Band, The Beatles* (the so-called White Album), and *Abbey Road*. Even as musicians and music historians began to discover and espouse the musical superiority of the *Revolver* album, critics and reviewers could not get past the baggage of their earlier pronouncements.

The crowning achievement of The Beatles' third style period was the album *Revolver*. Released in 1966, it is a testament to The Beatles' maturity as songwriters, the depth of their studio creativity, their collaboration with George Martin, and their position as leaders among the 1960s counterculture. The album's packaging which is nothing short of amazing quickly became the standard against which all future album covers would be judged. Designed by graphic artist musician Klaus Voormann, the *Revolver* cover features a combination of line drawings and black and white photographs. The line drawing faces of The Beatles are monumental, all knowing, and serene. Resembling the faces carved into Mount Rushmore, they are masters of all they purvey. Within, and "growing" out of their hair, are line drawings of the faces of The Rolling Stones. They are much less imposing and considerably less serene. They are surrounded by a montage of individual photographs of The Beatles—many of which appeared on previous albums. Once again the name of the band does not appear on the front of the jacket. The reverse side presents a single (again black and white) photograph of the four Beatles grouped around an open grand piano—the kind of classical musical instruments. Gone is the clowning of earlier cover photographs. Here, The Beatles are presented as mature musicians who are confident in their craft.

For once, the packaging was indicative of the contents. While a number of the songs which appeared on the *Rubber Sole* album reflected the influence of Dylan, *Revolver*'s songs go a step further. While absorbing Dylan's thoughts, his use of symbolism, and his passion for painting pictures with words, the resultant product (what "comes out" on the other side) is strictly Beatles. The same process drives the music. That is, the musical influences upon the *Revolver* songs (classical music, folk music, jazz, commercial music, non-Western influences) all pass through a sort of Beatles filter and emerge as something entirely new—Beatle Music.

Taxman, the album's opening song, serves notice to the fact that The Beatles will be addressing subjects which go far beyond the scope of the R&B tradition and even far beyond the scope of their own *Rubber Soul* album. Gone are the male/female relationships of *I Want To Hold Your Hand* and *If I Fell In Love With You*. Here are social commentary, cosmic realities, and the spaces between people.

Taxman opens with what sounds like a "count off"—a verbal indication of the tempo and mood, à la The Beatles recording of *I Saw Her Standing There*. But it is all wrong. The tempo is considerably slower than the song. In addition, the voice (Harrison) seems to be non-committal and is hardly in the style of the song. It is, in fact, not a count off at all. Harrison is imitating a bored, probably underpaid, and somewhat resentful company paymaster as he doles out the weekly wages to his company's employees. Accompanied by a dense hodgepodge of musical and non-musical sounds, it is a perfect introduction to Harrison's song about the crushing nature of Britain's tax system.

Harrison's depression is reflected in the music. A quick glance at the song's structural chart (Fig. 7.8) reveals the constant use of asymmetrical phrases—anything but relaxing. Throughout the song, both the bass and the guitar parts feature a rhythmic melody (riff) of only six notes. It is repeated, and repeated, and repeated over and over again. Classical composers refer to this compositional technique as ostinato. It means the same thing over and over. The term is derived from the root word from which we glean the word obstinate. Here, it is just that. By hammering the same musical figure (when the harmony changes the ostinato is simply adjusted to fit the new chord), Harrison hammers away at the tax system. While phrase E is a perfect foil for the intensity of the verses and refrains,

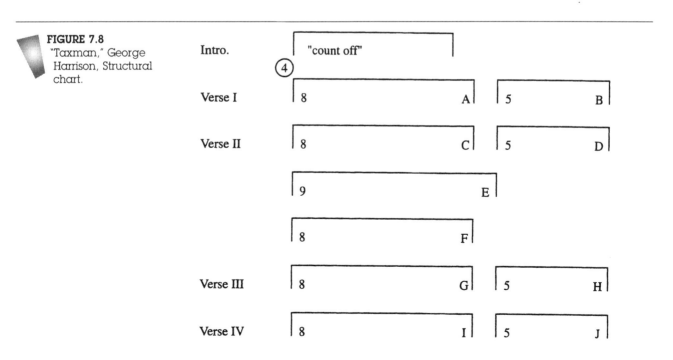

FIGURE 7.8
"Taxman," George Harrison, Structural chart.

there is no let up in Harrison's diatribe. Lennon and McCartney (singing in a very seductive harmony) set up Harrison's ironical responses.

There is more than just "ostinato" tension in the verses. Never, **never**, throughout the entire duration of the song is there any feeling of harmonic relaxation. Never does the harmony come to a rest at "home." Even in the quasi refrains (phrases B, D, and H) the harmony is nervous and edgy [*seventh and ninth chords*]. Throughout (especially in the instrumental break (F) and the coda (J)) is Harrison's incessant psychedelic guitar.

Rarely in the history of recorded popular music has there been a larger contrast than between *Taxman* and the album's second song—*Eleanor Rigby*.

FIGURE 7.9 "Eleanor Rigby," Lennon/McCartney.

Ah! Look at all the lovely people
Ah! Look at all the lovely people

Verse I
Eleanor Rigby picks up the rice in a church where a wedding has been, lives in a dream
Waits at the window wearing a face that she keeps in a jar by the door, who is it for

(Refrain)

All the lonely people
Where do they all come from
All the lonely people
Where do they all belong

Verse II
Father Mackenzie writing the words of a sermon that no one will hear, no one comes near
Look at his working darning his socks in the night when there's nobody there, what does he care

(Refrain)

Verse III
Eleanor Rigby died in the church and was buried along with her name, nobody came
Father Mackenzie wiping the dirt from his hands as he walks from the grave, no one was saved

Ah! Look at all the lovely people   All the lonely people, Where do they all come from
Ah! Look at all the lovely people   All the lonely people, Where do they all belong

---

McCartney's song, *Eleanor Rigby*, is about the space between people. It's about the unwritten social dictates which, within a class conscious society, regulate the relationships between those of differing socio-economic backgrounds, different ethnic backgrounds, and different races. To reinforce the pathos of the song, McCartney makes it personal. Eleanor Rigby (verse I) works at the church—she is a cleaning lady. The verse could have begun, "Little old lady picks up the rice . . ." By attaching a name to the lady McCartney makes her a real person. Most people know at least one *Eleanor Rigby*.

While Father Mackenzie's (verse II) position and/or denomination is never specified, it hardly matters. He is clearly of a higher social class than Eleanor Rigby. While they have apparently "worked together" for a considerable period of time they can never really be together. Even though she would kill to darn his socks such a thing could never happen.

The song virtually boils over with the contradictions and ironies so loved by The Beatles. Each line of each verse makes a statement which is

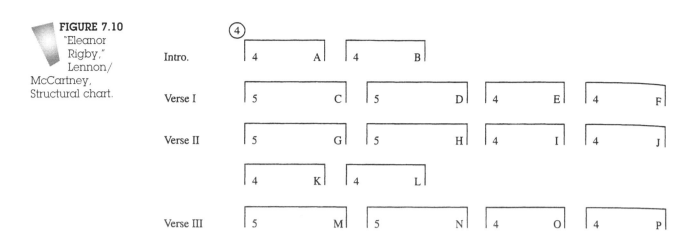

FIGURE 7.10 "Eleanor Rigby," Lennon/McCartney, Structural chart.

immediately contradicted or challenged. Perhaps most striking is verse I. Eleanor Rigby cleans up after a wedding—not her wedding—but lives in a dream world. While the listener is not really sure of the nature of the dream, it is certainly something beyond the life of a janitor. Verse I's second line is pure Dylan. Who indeed is the face for—the face which she keeps available should the situation arise? It is, of course, for Father Mackenzie.

Meanwhile, through more of McCartney's contradictions, verse II paints an inside look at one of social standing. Beneath the veneer of the church, his robes, and his rank, Father Mackenzie is a lonely man. No one really listens to his sermons and no one will administer to his most mundane needs. Of course, Eleanor Rigby and Father Mackenzie do have a rendezvous with destiny. Her death, which no one mourns, required his professional attention. Even so, he symbolically "Wipes up the dirt from his hands as he walks from the grave." If it was not part of his job he would not have been there either. Such is the nature of a class conscious society.

Each phrase of each verse is five measures in length. The "extra" measure is for the contradiction. Even if the listener is not counting pulses or measures, it is obvious that there is something extra in each line. Interspersed among the five measure phrases of the verses are the four measure phrases of the introduction (A and B), the refrain (E and F, and I and J), and the middle eight (K and L). Permeating all is the contrast between "lovely people" and "lonely people." The coda, by combining the two, confers the primary message of the song. As the lines, "All the lonely people/ Where do they all come from," and, "Ah! Look at all the lovely people," are finally brought together (and performed in counterpoint) it becomes obvious that the difference between the two—between social classes—is not so obvious after all. The spaces between people are not only harmful but self inflicted.

McCartney's music is equally full of contradiction and irony. The song's instrumental accompaniment is played by eight string instruments—no "rock and roll" instruments and nothing played by a Beatle. McCartney's melodies and ideas were sung and played (piano) for George Martin who, in turn, notated the parts in standard musical notation for eight professional (classical) string players. While theories abound as to the rationale behind McCartney's choice of string instruments—to make it sound "churchy," to make it sound old—it hardly seems to matter. The very nature of the music's structure and pathos seem to fit the color of the string instruments. Again the contradictions within the details of the music are startling. The texture of the string accompaniment changes with each verse. At one moment a single instrument stands out as a solo voice and, at another, all instruments hammer away at the same time, and, as in verse III, several melodies occur simultaneously. While the texture of the "string bath" is constantly changing, the harmony is amazingly static. One chord dominates the entire song. Imagine, Chuck Berry was belittled for using only three different chords in each song. Here, one chord [*e minor*] harmonizes the entire song. The only reprise is a *very* brief change to major on the words, "Ah! Look at all the lovely people."

While the harmony (at least on paper) appears to be boring, the melody is incredibly expressive. In measure one of each verse the name "Eleanor" or "Father" always coincides with the measure's strong downbeat. Conversely, the second names (Rigby and Mackenzie) occur on the syncopated second half of the weaker second pulse. In the following portion of each line, the "important" words do not fall on the strong pulses, e.g. "Picks up the **RICE** in the **CHURCH** where a **WEDDING** had been." The addition of instrumental accents to these syncopations (especially in verse III) only add to the anguish. McCartney adds one additional contradiction in the song's first line. Listen to the assonance as he "rhymes" the word "been" (pronounced "bean") with the word "dream."

According to Lennon, *She Said She Said* (Fig. 7.10) was written after and inspired by an acid (LSD) trip. True or not, it hardly matters. *She Said She Said* explores yet another world of timbres and rhythms. Both heighten the psychedelic nature of the words. Following the opening songs on the album, the listener is immediately struck by the active nature of the drumming and the extensive use of the cymbals. While Ringo is occasionally referred to as the weak member of the band and is held in rather low regard as drummer, a closer examination of his recorded performances tells another story. Instead of "ruling" with power and speed, his contributions are far more subtle. The remarkable nature of his drumming is frequently the result of what he leaves out as opposed to what he adds. Throughout the *Rubber Soul* album the drums are noticeably quiet. *Revolver* continues in the same fashion. Even in Harrison's driving *Taxman*, the drums are relatively subdued. The cymbals are used for color only. In *She Said She Said* they explode—not in volume—but in importance. While they color the verses they also punctuate important aspects of the rhythm.

The first eight measures of verse I (quadruple meter) feature Lennon and McCartney singing a stepwise melody. It is accompanied by active guitars and very active drums—including a long cymbal crash on the downbeat of every other measure. In measure 7 (phrase I) Lennon and McCartney sing exactly the same melody—no harmony. Here, the words are sung to a syncopated rhythm which is emphasized by cymbals on the words, "feel," "never," and "born." This rhythm is repeated (without words) in the last two measures of verse I. While they may sound like "extra measures" their function is to further establish the syncopation and make the rhythm feel a little "unglued." The effect is heightened by the timbre of the cymbals—a timbre which rings and which seems to have little "center"—

little to "hang on to." This uneasy rhythm also prepares the listener for the meter shift which occurs later. Verse II is the same music with new words. Although phrase D is eleven measures in length, it functions as a middle eight. Its first two measures continue the quadruple meter of the verses. However, by measure three the meter has switched to triple. Verse III, the same music as the two previous verses, reverts to quadruple meter. It is followed by a repetition (with meter change) of the "middle eight." The text of the coda (H) reiterates the lines, "I know what it is to be dead," with Lennon and McCartney answering back and forth. The syncopation, the changes of meter, and the active cymbals are openly psychedelic and are effective in recreating the LSD experience. However, there are additional subtle (and technical) devices at work which also heighten the experience. First appearing in verse II (and way in the background) is a single held note played on a small electric organ. This sustained note is high [*B-flat above the treble staff*] above all of the other instruments and voices. It stays constant as other notes change. Identified by classical musicians as an inverted pedal, its "job" is to create a different degree of tension between the notes it "sounds against." In the "middle eight" (D) it changes function. For four measures it plays its own melody and then (measure five) joins the guitar. While your ear has to listen closely to hear it, your mind knows that it is there.

The nature of the harmony also enhances the psychedelic atmosphere. While the song is harmonized with the familiar I/IV/V chords (the same chords used by Chuck Berry) they are not in their pure form. That is, each one has an additional note which causes each chord to sound mildly dissonant. Consequentially, each one of these chords [*I7/IV7/V7*] contains its own tension. There is no real release anywhere. Even the coda (harmonized with the I chord plus an added note) never sounds at rest—never really goes "home."

The remaining songs of *Revolver*—many of which are masterpieces in their own right—drive home the following two points. 1) There is no such

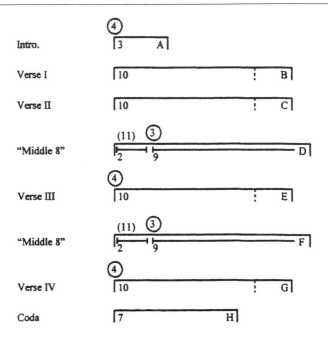

FIGURE 7.11
"She Said She Said,"
Lennon/McCartney,
Structural chart.

thing as a typical "Beatles song" and 2) Any attempt to identify individual stylistic tendencies between Lennon and McCartney is fraught with myriad exceptions. That is, pronouncements such as, "Lennon's songs speak to the head while McCartney's songs speak to the heart" are so fraught with instances which demonstrate the opposite that they are pointless. The two points which are obvious and which do impact upon the contents of *Revolver* are style and diversity. Much to the horror of Beatlemania fans, The Beatles moved away from what most would identify as mainstream rock and roll. By late 1966, The Beatles are actually appealing to two entirely different generations. While the teens of the early 1960s had moved on to college and on to a more sophisticated appreciation of pop music, a new crop of teens replaced them. While the new generation reveled in their heroes (Motown, The Bee Gees, The Box Tops, etc.) they also treasured The Beatles of the Beatlemania period. The diversity of material on the *Revolver* album is staggering. While this diversity is obvious in the terms of content and style, e.g. *Taxman* (a rare Beatles political statement), *Eleanor Rigby* (string accompaniment), *Love To You* (Indian influences and Harrison's emergence as a skilled songwriter), it is equally dramatic in the technical details of the album's songs.

As with so much of the music by The Beatles, the details are filled with contradictions. *Tomorrow Never Knows*, Lennon's deceptively complex song is, once the listener gets past the veneer of sound, really quite simple. It is comprised of seven verses (all eight measures in length) which are all harmonized by the same single chord. For once the harmony is almost "too simple." The single chord employed is the I chord—"home." The melody is composed of (with one exception) only the notes which are within the "home" chord [*diatonic*]. The one note which is alien to the chord [*the B-flat in measures five and seven*] is still harmonized with the I chord and creates only a minor amount of tension. In addition, the repeated bass line and drum figures remain unchanged throughout the song and the timbre of the sitar colors the entire background. The only variants are a single sustained chord in the organ during the second half of each verse and a brief appearance of the piano in the coda. Of course, this is all simply a foundation for Lennon's words and for the sea of other "outside" sounds. Lennon's text, sung through a rotating loudspeaker, is derived from *The Psychedelic Experience*—Timothy Leary and Richard Alpert's interpretation of the Tibetan Book of the Dead. It is the first song by The Beatles in which there is no attempt to forge the words into some sort of rhyme scheme. The other sounds, tape loops of noise, other Beatle's songs, musical excerpts and extraneous sounds (all dubbed in at different speeds and, in several instances, backwards) complete Lennon's music landscape.

On the other hand, McCartney's *For No One*, is deceptively simple. While, on the surface, an uncomplicated song about lost love, it is, in its details, far more complex than *Tomorrow Never Knows*. The song's opening employs three devices which are designed to tug at the heartstrings. McCartney's melody, structured so that the downbeat pulses are never stressed in the voice and so that "important" words never correspond to the strong pulses, create a disparate—even weeping—persona. While the melody line ascends through most of the verse the bass descends in a stepwise manner. That is, the two elements (voice and bass) move in opposing directions. Surrounding the two lines is a harmony which is full of frequent and (although pleasing) unusual chord changes. I goes to III to vi and so on—harmonies well outside the world of R&B based rock and roll. A short solo by the French horn (performed by professional hornist Alan Civil) leads to a contrasting section which is an entirely new tonality [*B-flat Major to c-sharp minor*]. While the song eventually returns to its "home" key, it ends in the V chord—it never returns home and never releases its pent up tension. With all its innate complexities, *For No One* is performed by only three people. Alan Civil's contribution is limited to two brief excerpts. Everything else is performed by McCartney, bass, piano, and voice and Starr, drums and tambourine—just two Beatles! This tendency toward total "control" of their own material would become one of the wedges which would eventually split The Beatles apart.

If ever a rock and roll album was greater than the sum of its parts it was the third album of The Beatle's *Maturity* style period—*Sgt. Pepper's Lonely Hearts Club Band.* Eagerly awaited, performed world-wide (and almost non-stop) during the 1967 *Summer of Love*, hailed as the first concept album (few remembered *Pet Sounds)*, and eventually anointed as the greatest rock and roll album of all time, it is an album who's luster has only recently begun to fade—at least a little.

While *Sgt. Pepper's* concept seems straightforward enough its messages prove to function on several levels—a number of which are quite elusive. In fact, there is more unity in the packaging than in the contents. Much (perhaps too much) has been made of the jacket's water pipe, plants, personalities, art work, "inside" photograph of The Beatles in their psychedelic Edwardian band uniforms, and enclosed Sgt. Pepper "cutouts." More important to the collective concepts is the format of the concert within a concert. In the guise of rock and roll The Beatles assume the persona and certain aspects of the style of an Edwardian (reign of King Edward VII—1901–1910) band. Key to this aspect of the concept is the "concert program"—the order in which the songs appear on the album.

Side One

Sgt. Pepper's Lonely Hearts Club Band
A Little Help From My Friends
Lucy In The Sky With Diamonds
Getting Better
Fixing A Hole
She's Leaving Home
Being For The Benefit Of Mr. Kite!

Side Two

Within You Without You
When I'm Sixty-Four
Lovely Rita
Good Morning, Good Morning
Sgt. Pepper's Lonely Hearts Club Band (Reprise)
A Day In The Life

The band's "theme song," *Sgt. Pepper's Lonely Hearts Club Band*, opens and closes the show. Lucy of *Lucy In The Sky With Diamonds* and Rita of *Lovely Rita* are the only two women mentioned on the album. Each is placed in the same position on their respective sides of the album. *Being For The Benefit Of Mr. Kite!*, which rounds out the band's first "set," is quite similar in flavor and texture to the carnival atmosphere, the crowd noises, and the master of ceremonies of "Sgt. Pepper." *With A Little Help From My Friends*, *Getting Better*, and *Fixing A Hole* all feature the same rhythm and all have similar melodies. *She's Leaving Home* and *When I'm Sixty-Four* deal with different sides of the same issue and both are dominated by the timbres of non-rock and roll instruments. While the words to both "Mr. Kite" and *A Day In The Life* are drawn from media sources, their function within the cycle is quite different. *A Day In The Life* is, in fact, an encore.

Adding to the album's unity is the fact that many of the songs "bleed" *[segue]* into each other. In some cases, e.g. *Sgt. Pepper's Lonely Hearts Club Band* into *A Little Help From My Friends* the music never really stops—it sounds like the second part of the same song. In other cases, e.g. *A Little Help From My Friends* into *Lucy In The Sky With Diamonds*, the transfer is more subtle. Here the sound of the acoustic piano is altered electronically. After a moment of silence the same note is picked up in the electric organ. Others are even more creative. Listen to the way the sound of the rooster at the close of *Good Morning, Good Morning* is picked up by the electric guitar at the beginning of *Sgt. Pepper (Reprise)*.

Although there has been much (perhaps too much) written regarding the order of the songs within the "show," e.g. *Strawberry Fields Forever* was originally intended to open side two and the order on side one was to be different than the published version, the debate is really pointless. As with the classical masters, the first published version of a work is usually the most trustworthy. While there is always the possibility of minor typos, the composer was afforded the opportunity to "read a proof."

After establishing a "concert" setting complete with crowd noises and orchestral warm ups and tuning, *Sgt. Pepper's Lonely Hearts Club Band* (Fig. 7.12) begins with a four measure introduction which is all electric, on the verge of feedback, and sufficiently psychedelic. In verse I (B) the solo voice (McCartney) is accompanied very sparsely by guitars, bass, and drums.

C is an interlude played by a brass band—Sgt. Pepper's Band? Actually the brass band consists of four French horns. The horn interlude is followed by, what on first hearing, seems to be a refrain. The eight measures of D are divided in two. The first three measures are punctuated in measure four by static strumming in the guitars and bass. The last three are rounded out (measure eight) by the horns. Here, (D), The Beatles are singing in three voice harmony as opposed to the solo voice of the opening verse. In the first verse the solo voice assumes the role of a carnival barker or emcee. The rhythm follows the natural speech patterns and inflections of the English language. The tri-part harmony of the "refrain" is more calculated. By the clever use of syncopation the word "sergeant" lines up with the downbeat (first measure of D) but the words "heart's," "club," and "band" do not. The opening text of phrase E begins to reveal the

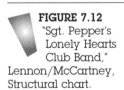

FIGURE 7.12
"Sgt. Pepper's Lonely Hearts Club Band," Lennon/McCartney, Structural chart.

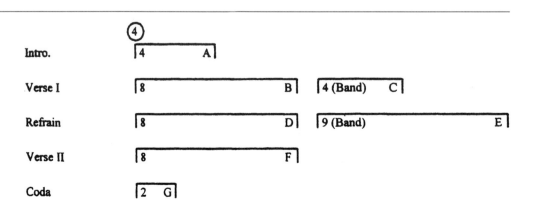

themes within the album's principle concept. "Sgt. Pepper's Lonely, Sgt. Pepper's Lonely, Sgt. Pepper's Hearts Club Band," hints to the fact that, indeed, even Sgt. Pepper is lonely. This word play will become even more obvious in the song's reprise at the close of the "concert." Measure five of E brings back the band (horns) but now in a supporting role as the standard gab from the emcee continues. Verse II (F) returns to the music of B. Here the solo voice begins the incredible build up which will introduce the band's singer—Billy Shears and the beginning of the "concert." Any effort to delineate *Sgt. Pepper's Lonely Hearts Club Band* in terms of averse and refrain format is pointless. The length and functions of its various phrases are determined more by the number of words needed than by any pre-set form.

The enormous build up (volume, texture, and harmonic tension) leads into the concert's first offering and sets the stage for at least one of the album's sub-concepts. The build up leads directly into *With A Little Help From My Friends*. Sung by Starr (the non-singer of the band), it is simple and in many ways quite poignant. Here, Starr, with an accompaniment of piano, guitar, bass, and drums (and with a voice which seems uncomfortable) faces the world with only one question—the question of a child. Will you still like me if I screw up? He will, of course, get by with a little help from his friends—even get high with a little help from his "friends." It is almost impossible to overlook the drug influence.

Throughout the concert there is surprisingly little rock and roll. Only the refrain of *Lucy In The Sky With Diamonds* and certain aspects of *Good Morning, Good Morning* reflect the fact that The Beatles are a rock and roll band. *Getting Better*, *Fixing a Hole*, and *For The Benefit Of Mr. Kite!* all feature a rhythmic pattern which is far more at home in the British music halls of the Edwardian period. *She's Leaving Home* is accompanied by harp and strings while *When I'm Sixty-Four* is bathed in the sound of clarinets and bass clarinet. The only two timbrel unifiers (and even here the unification is not complete) are the bass and drums. The bass (electric bass—McCartney) is the foundation for every song except *She's Leaving Home* and *Within You, Without You*. Great care has been taken with the bass's timbre. Through the judicious use of filters and other studio trickery, the instrument's timbre changes from song to song. In fact, a great deal of the variety in timbre which pervades the album is the result of studio adjustments as opposed to performance adjustments or changes in texture. The same is true for the voices. Compare the timbres of Lennon's voice in "Lucy" and *For The Benefit Of Mr. Kite!*

A great deal of attention to timbre was taken with the album's second unifying factor—the drums. They were taken apart, stuffed with rags, covered with blankets, and more in an effort to achieve a thudding (hollow) sound which had a strong impact. This sound is most obvious in the short (one measure) "drum breaks" which occur in *With A Little Help From My Friends*, *Lovely Rita*, and *A Day In the Life*. Far removed from the monster breaks of Led Zeppelin, etc. they are the ultimate in style and taste. The only exception is in *Good Morning, Good Morning*. Here the drumming (heavy on the snare drum) fits the style of the quasi-blues band which accompanies the song and which takes the listener "out of the concert."

Much has been made of the *Lucy In The Sky With Diamonds*' LSD acronym. While the drug reference and psychedelic nature of the music and text seems obvious enough, Lennon insisted that it was simply a coinci-

FIGURE 7.13
"Lucy In The Sky With Diamonds," Lennon/McCartney, Structural chart.

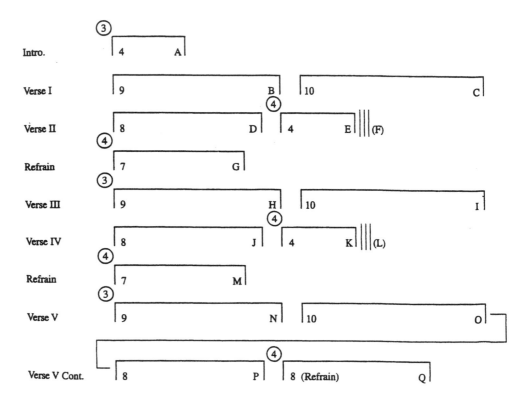

dence. Whether inspired by his son's drawing of a flying Lucy surrounded by diamonds, or LSD, or a combination of the two, it hardly matters. The song's text and dreamlike atmosphere can be interpreted as the inside of an LSD trip or it can be seen as the observations of the uncluttered mind of a child. It works both ways.

The song is introduced by a four-measure introduction. While the atmosphere created by the organ timbre (distorted almost beyond recognition) persists throughout all the verses, the organ melody itself is an important structural element. The meter is triple and while there are subtle differences in the harmony used in each measure the "home" chord (I) is firmly established. While the phrases are clearly delineated the verse structure is not so clear. The two phrases which constitute verse I are not the same length. Verse I begins with solo voice (Lennon) accompanied by bass (one note per measure) and the four-measure organ melody from the introduction. In fact, the organ melody now becomes a countermelody. Although phrase one of Verse I is nine measures long, only eight are devoted to text. The "extra measure" corresponds to a pause in the text (a time for reflection?). It is filled with brief flashes of color from the cymbals and tamboura—a lute-like instrument from India which produces drones. With phrase two (C) the melody and its countermelody begin anew. While the first eight measures are the same as B, C adds two "extra measures." Here the bass becomes more active—three notes per measure. During the extra measures the song actually changes tonality. It moves up a half step [A to B-flat] and leads into the second verse (D). Now the bass remains active but the countermelody in the organ is gone. A new timbre is provided by the slide guitar playing exactly the same notes as the vocal

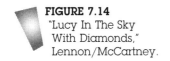

FIGURE 7.14
"Lucy In The Sky With Diamonds," Lennon/McCartney.

Picture yourself in a boat on a river,
With tangerine trees and marmalade skies
Somebody calls you, you answer quite slowly,
A girl with kaleidoscope eyes.
Cellophane flowers of yellow and green,
Towering over your head.
Look for the girl with the sun in her eyes.
And she's gone.

Refrain

Lucy in the sky with diamonds

Follow her down to a bridge by a fountain
Where rocking horse people eat marshmallow pies,
Everyone smiles as you drift past the flowers,
That grow so incredibly high.
Newspaper taxies appear on the shore,
Waiting to take you away.
Climb in the back with your head in the clouds,
And you're gone.

Refrain

Picture yourself on a train in a station,
With Plasticine porters with looking glass ties,
Suddenly someone is there at the turnstile,
The girl with kaleidoscope eyes.

melody. Although D is eight measures in length the text occupies only seven. While the next phrase (E) begins exactly the same way and gives every indication that it will be a duplicate of D, it is interrupted by three heavy drum beats (F) which push into the refrain. The details of the refrain are almost the exact opposite of the details of the verses. The meter is now quadruple, the melody, "Lucy in the sky with diamonds," is sung in two-part harmony, and the drums explode into a stereotypical rock and roll drum pattern. In addition, the harmony, which has previously avoided any references to rock and roll, now falls into one of its standard formats—I/IV/V/I. The musical jolt which occurs in the refrain has been interpreted in a number of ways, e.g. Lucy being brought down to earth, or the visions of a child facing the real world. Again, it hardly matters—the text "works" on multiple levels. Verse III (H) returns to the triple meter and the timbre of B. The return of the refrain presents the same jolt as before. Verse V is, once again, similar to verse I. In Q, the refrain functions as a coda. It is repeated (with minor variations) and faded.

Trivia

During the summer of 1974 a team of paleontologists working in Hadar (Africa) excavated the first fossils of a species which would become known as Australopithecus afarensis. Standing three and a half feet high and dated at 3.5 million B.C., it was assumed to be the, or one of, the "missing links." While fossils have long scientific names and are, upon discovery, assigned acquisition numbers, many are also given nicknames. Because the crew played "Lucy In The Sky With Diamonds" almost nonstop during the dig the Hadar Australopithecus (AL 288-1) was quickly nicknamed "Lucy." As the expedition's leader Donald C. Johanson explained in his book *Lucy: The Beginning of Humankind*, "We were sky-high from finding her."

The reprise of *Sgt. Pepper's Lonely Hearts Club Band* is a brief concert closer. The timbre and the style are pure rock and roll—no French horns or music hall styles. However, the harmonic language and the truncated nature of the form are not. There is no verse and refrain structure. While the texture (electric instruments and three-part vocal melody remains unchanged throughout, the harmony takes the most amazing twists and turns. The song's opening text, "We're Sgt. Pepper's Lonely Hearts Club Band," is first harmonized with I/flat—III/IV/V—except for the second chord, not too strange. On the repeat of the text the harmony changes to I/flat—III/IV/I/II/V 7. Don't be intimidated by all the chord symbols. All they really indicate is the fact that the harmony is a little unusual—at least for rock and roll. What happens next is a most interesting and unexpected harmonic "trip" on the repeated words, "Sgt. Pepper's Lonely." The downbeat of each measure (on the word "Sergeant") changes harmony—IV/I/II/VI. Each harmonic twist drives home the point that Sgt. Pepper is, in fact, lonely. By the fifth "Sergeant" the song has changed tonality [F to G] and returned to the original tonality of the show's opener. Now, with the crowd noises and a return to the original tonality, the cycle is complete. Although the album could have easily ended right here, The Beatles have more to say. It is said in the encore, *A Day In The Life*.

At first thought to be two incomplete songs (one by Lennon and one by McCartney) fused together as one, analysis reveals it to be a complete song by Lennon with an incursion—a fragment of a song by McCartney.

The crowd noises and psychedelic finish of *Sgt. Pepper's Lonely Hearts Club Band (reprise)* gives way to the four-measure introduction (A) of *A Day In The Life*. After two measures the acoustic guitar is joined by electric bass and piano (no drums). Verse I introduces Lennon's solo voice. The vocal timbre is breathy, far away, and somewhat sarcastic. In words, taken from actual newspaper articles, are delivered in rhythmic patterns which imitate natural speech patterns. In verse II, nine measures in length (here

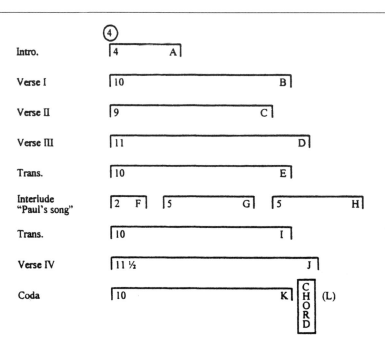

FIGURE 7.15 "A Day In The Life," Lennon/McCartney, Structural chart.

and throughout the song the number of words in the text determines the length of the phrases), the piano becomes more active and the pauses between groups of words are filled with drum breaks. These breaks, more color than rhythm, are all different and do not emphasize the pulses. In verse III (D) the nature of the piano accompaniment changes once again and the drums (now playing every measure) take a more active role in the declination of the rhythm. What follows (with the words, "I'd love to turn you on. . ."—usually interpreted as some sort of drug reference) is unique in the world of rock and roll. In this ten-measure transition (E) McCartney instructed an assembled orchestra of classical musicians to gradually ascend from the lowest note on their instruments to the highest. The resultant "sound" is over dubbed several times and creates what classical composers of the Twentieth Century e.g., Krzysztof Penderecki, Karlheinz Stockhausen refer to as a "transient sound wall." In fact, this compositional technique known as sound mass composition was not invented by McCartney or even George Martin. However, its incorporation into the structure of the album's final song is both amazing and effective. Its final "destination" is the brief song fragment by McCartney (F–H). Here, in three brief and asymmetrical phrases, McCartney's words move away from Lennon's ethereal ruminations about a day in the life of the world and focus on the mundane. I can be described as a transition back to Lennon's world—perhaps a dream sequence. His last verse (J) rounds out the album's concepts with one final thought.

FIGURE 7.16
From: "A Day In The Life," Lennon/McCartney.

I read the news today oh boy
Four thousand holes in Blackburn, Lancashire
And though the holes were rather small
They had to count them all
Now than know how many holes it takes to fill the Albert Hall
I'd love to turn you on

The verse relates the details of a newspaper article about pot holes. Someone actually counted (or estimated) the number of pot holes in Blackburn, Lancashire (Blackburn, in Lancashire County, is located about 30 miles north east of Liverpool). Then multiplying them by their average volume, calculated that they would equal the interior volume of the Royal Albert Hall—one of the largest indoor theaters in the world. Of course, Lennon's message is quite poignant—"This is the sort of thing which received press coverage?" The last verse is followed by a second transient sound wall. Upon reaching its "top," it gives way to a huge I chord played by several pianos. The volume control in the recording equipment is adjusted to lengthen the natural decay of the piano sound.

With *Revolver* and *Sgt. Pepper's Lonely Hearts Club Band* The Beatles reached the zenith of their creative powers and their ability to function as an ensemble. While the music created between the end of 1967 and 1969 is dizzying in its variety, the quality is uneven. In addition, a number of "solo" projects, e.g. Lennon and Yoko Ono's concept art album, *Two Virgins*, border on the embarrassing. Despite *Abby Road's* elegant *Come Together* and the ensemble of interrelated songs which comprise the album's second side, the magic which was created in 1965–1967 was never recaptured.

The Rolling Stones

The differences between the bodies of work and the careers of The Beatles and The Rolling Stones can be attributed to two separate and distinctive factors: the strengths and weaknesses of each band and the attitude toward music as proffered by each band. The songwriting abilities of The Beatles drove them into the recording studio. The fact that the studio became their performance vehicle influenced the nature of their creations. Their songs were created to be of finite length. That is, each song had a beginning, a middle, and an end—pattern of tension and release which caused climaxes to occur in predictable locations. Also, they had to fit on a given amount of vinyl. The chosen venue of The Rolling Stones was not the recording studio—it was live performance. One of the reasons for this dichotomy was improvisation—The Beatles could not do it and The Rolling Stones could.

Improvisation, simply put, is the art of creating something new within the context of something old. Since the Renaissance (and probably before), improvisation has been a factor in Western Music. Composers of Bach's day (1685–1700) frequently "wrote" compositions which were little more than sketches—blueprints if you will. It was assumed that the performer would add additional notes based on the given foundation. It saved ink, saved time, and offered the performer a degree of creativity. In many cases the performer was the composer. Of course, when these compositions are performed today, even experts cannot agree on the nature of the filled in (improvised) material. Perhaps Western Music's most obvious use of improvisation occurs in the world of jazz. Here performers create new melodies, new rhythms, and new moods based on a set of given chord progressions—usually the chord progressions of a well known song. The real art of jazz is the creation of something new (based on the skill and attitude of the performer) out of something old. Improvisation is the act of creating music spontaneously. Consequently, no two improvisations are, or should be, the same. You frequently hear jazz musicians say something like, "Man! Listen to what he does with it!" On the simplest level, jazz musicians anticipate the chords they will hear and make sure that the notes "fit" the notes of the chords. Music (especially jazz) is slippery stuff. There are few absolute "rights and wrongs." Deciding what fits and what does not fit is a matter of taste, knowledge, and sophistication. Frankly, that is one of the things which makes jazz so attractive to creative musicians.

Rock and roll and jazz evolved from the same general sources, e.g. the blues. Rock and roll of the 1950s was, in terms of harmonic language and rhythmic complexities, relatively simple. The performers of the 1950s were, with the exception of Chuck Berry, not skilled enough or creative enough to participate in any form of improvisation. Even Chuck Berry's improvisations were brief, followed simple patterns, and were not central to the song or the performance. The Beatles, who while influenced by R&B, quickly incorporated additional outside influences, created songs who's words were on an equal footing with the music, and strived for subtle effects, successfully avoided improvisation. Even during the live performances of Beatlemania, instrumental breaks were limited to eight measures (eight planned out measures)—no improvisation.

Improvisation quickly became one of the cornerstones of the music of the Rolling Stones. It was also an important ingredient of their on stage attitude. It also accounted for the difference between the careers of the two bands. Songs which, "on paper," looked to be the same length as those of The Beatles were regularly extended through improvisation. Songs with recording times of less than three minutes were, in live performance, frequently extended to twenty minutes or more. The improvisations of Richards and Jones over known chord progressions gave plenty of time for Jagger's gyrations, ad-lib vocal comments, and attitude.

While the set up of The Beatles and The Rolling Stones looked the same "on paper"; lead guitar, rhythm guitar, bass, and drums, the reality was quite different. The Beatles consisted of three "singers"—each with his own distinctive vocal timbre; Jagger dominated the vocal sound of The Rolling Stones. While Harrison was The Beatles only strong guitar player (and his improvisational skills were somewhat limited), The Rolling Stones had two. Both Richards and Jones were skilled at improvisation. With Jagger "free" from any but the most elementary participation (e.g., occasional tambourine), he was free to create a stage persona which went far beyond the outlaw attitudes of Presley, Little Richard, and even Jerry Lee Lewis.

While The Rolling Stones use of the elements of music grew out of their interest in American R&B, it was also heavily influenced by American Blues. The band limited itself to one vocal timbre—Jagger. Although he is able to produce a variety of sounds, his voice is immediately recognizable. The drums, tuned loosely and emphasizing the lower part of the set (bass drum and tom toms), create a dark and thick sound. In addition, the guitars tend to concentrate on the lower strings. This thick, high density sound (offset by Jagger's medium high voice) is unlike anything encountered in 1950s rock and roll.

While The Beatles experimented and incorporated rhythmic complexities, harmonic complexities, and subject matter which went far beyond early rock and roll, The Rolling Stones (with a few notable exceptions) maintained the formula which they developed during the mid 1960s. The Rolling Stones is a perfect example of a band which lasted too long. The world of classical music is filled with examples of composers and performing musicians who died too soon—musicians who died at the height of their creative and performing powers, e.g. Mozart, Schubert. It is also replete with musicians who died at just the "right time." Felix Mendelssohn who, after the masterpieces of his youth, began to compose mundane and uninspired music. Then he died—just in time. Unfortunately, there are numerous examples of composers who lived "too long." Gioacchino Rossini, who after a career of operatic triumphs, e.g. *William Tell, Barber of Seville,* grew stale. However, instead of dying at the "right time," he continued to compose unremarkable music for another twenty years.

As with The Beatles, the career of The Rolling Stones can also be divided into several style periods. During the early 1960s the band covered American R&B. By 1964, with the albums *12 X 5* and *Out Of Our Heads,* they emerged as songwriters. 1966–1969 is usually identified as The Rolling Stones "classic phase"—the albums *Aftermath, Between The Buttons, Their Satanic Majesties Request, Beggars Banquet,* and *Let It Bleed.* Here, The Rolling Stones combined electric performances with creative songwriting and creative packaging. They also brought the "bad boy" image (with hints of Satanism) to full flower. Instead of following the example of The Beatles—breaking up in 1970—they simply took a brief hiatus.

1971 produced an additional style period—one which The Beatles never experienced—a "jazz" period which included the albums *Sticky Fingers* and *Exile On Main Street.* 1972 marks the beginning of their decay. Again, instead of breaking up, they continued for another thirty years. The albums produced throughout this period were lackluster and often embarrassing but did not impact on the popularity of the band. While concerts frequently resembled impersonations—impersonations of their 1960's persona—it hardly mattered. In the end, The Rolling Stones were (and are) much more about attitude and performance than substance.

While The Rolling Stones was a performance oriented band, the marketplace demanded recordings. Between 1964 and 1991 they produced at least 28 original albums. In addition, their producers flooded the market with a number of "Best Of" and "Greatest Hits" albums. Even the best *Aftermath, Between The Buttons, Beggars Banquet,* and *Sticky Fingers* do not show The Rolling Stones at their best as entertainers. However, because of the time constraints of the recording process, these albums show them at their musical best. While few would argue the value of musical performance, the legacy and the body of work which is left behind is based upon recordings.

A "riff" (or "hook") is a melodic fragment. It is usually brief (no more than two measures) and simple—easy to remember. Short groups of notes (usually referred to as motifs) have been a part of Western Music for centuries. Perhaps the most famous is the opening motif from the Symphony No. 5 of Beethoven. It lasts only two measures and uses only four notes. Nevertheless, once you have heard it you never forget it. However, motifs as used by Beethoven, went through many changes throughout the duration of the piece. They were, as musicians say, developed—played by different instruments, played in different tonalities, even played backwards. Riffs in rock and roll are not expanded upon—they do not develop. Their function is to make sure the listener remembers the song. The two-measure riff which is the foundation of the introduction of The Beatle's *Please Please Me* is not particularly memorable. What gives it its distinction is the timbre produced by the harmonica. Far more memorable is the recurring riff in *I Heard It Through The Grapevine.* Because it is melodically simple yet harmonically interesting it has a way of remaining in the brain. It is such a part of rock and roll history that simply hearing its two measures recalls the entire song—melody, words, and mood.

The two-measure riff which begins, ends, and permeates the entire body of *(I Can't Get No) Satisfaction* is of equal power—perhaps the most memorable in all of rock and roll. As such, it deserves detailed examination. Virtually every element of music contributed to its power. During the first measure (quadruple meter) the melody gradually moves up two steps [*B to D*]. The rhythm is designed so the highest note does not correspond to one of the measure's pulses. It occurs right after pulse number four creating a syncopation. After reaching the high note it (in the second measure) works its way back down to the original note. Measure one goes up—measure two goes down. But the rhythm is not the same in each measure. On repeated hearings it becomes obvious that the first measure of the riff is the most important—the "thrust up." The harmony adds to the tension. While the first measure begins with the I chord ("home"), it quickly moves to the flat—VII—lots of tension. Additional tension is created as each of the notes in the second measure grinds away at the flat—VII chord on the way back to I—home. That's not all. The timbre created by the electric guitar in the low range and played with fuzz tone (an electronic device placed on the floor and activated with a foot pedal) engraves itself on the memory. *[The fuzz tone device changes the sine wave to a square wave enhancing the overtones of the guitar timbre].* This timbre combined with the syncopation of the rhythm, the asymmetrical design of the melody, and the tension created by the harmony creates a riff which is not only memorable but (as it crawls under your skin) sets the mood of the body of the song. It is a perfect counterpart of Jagger's vocal quality and words.

The overall simplicity of "Satisfaction" is remarkable—and is an integral part of its success. The drums play only the most basic rhythmic patterns. In fact, for most of the vast majority of the song, they simply bang away at the basic pulse. Even the "drum breaks," serve to do little more than emphasize the pulse. The bass is active but in the background. When not playing the riff, the electric guitar turns off the fizz tone and slips into the background. The rhythm guitar (acoustic) is heard as little more than color. The song is dominated by the riff, Jagger's voice, and the pounding drums.

The introduction (A and B) (Fig. 7.17) consists of two phrases of four measures each. Phrase A gives just a hint of what will eventually become extremely common in "Stones" introductions. The guitar riff begins at the outset. It is followed one measure later by the bass. The drums begin in measure three. While at live concerts this introduction will occasionally be expanded to as much as five minutes, the order of the "entrance" of the instruments will remain unchanged. Listen to the recorded version of *Gimmie Shelter* (the *Let It Bleed* album). It is a natural expansion of the "Satisfaction" introduction. Over the space of X measures (instead of "Satisfaction's" two measures) each instrument is introduced.

FIGURE 7.17 "Satisfaction," Jagger/Richards, Structural chart.

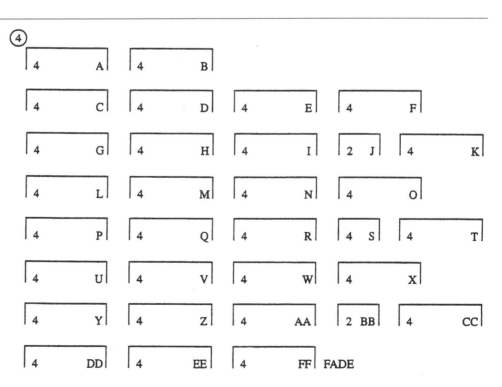

The introduction is not followed by Verse I but by the refrain. While the songs created by The Rolling Stones are frequently simple and repetitive, they are constructed in a wide variety of forms. As with Dylan's songs, the refrain can be a separate entity, it can be so short that it sounds as though it is part of the verse, it can dominate the song, and it may not exist at all. The four Rolling Stones songs examined in this chapter exhibit several of the above.

"Satisfaction" emphasizes the refrain. In addition, it is the text of the refrain which hammers home the lack of satisfaction. That said—there is plenty of repetition. Phrases C and D feature the low voice answered by the low guitar. In phrase E the voices (perhaps Jagger over dubbed but more likely Jagger and Jones) climb to the highest note in the vocal line—the first note of phrase F. While this climb on the words, "Cause I try and I try and I try and I try," may seem reminiscent of the same kind of climb found in The Beatles *Please Please Me* ("Come on, come on, come on, come on"), the harmony is fundamentally different. In the Stones' climb the harmony is relatively simple—I/V/I/IV. The Beatles' climb is harmonized with a more complicated and sophisticated progression of chords—IV/ii/vi/IV/I—a good example of the musical difference between the two bands. The high point of the Stones' climb (phrase F) is emphasized by the return of the riff. The riff dominates the music of Verse I as Jagger spells out his lack of satisfaction. J, a two-measure drum break, serves to separate the verses last line of text from its first six. The remainder of the song (except for changes in the text) consists of three more repetitions of the music of the refrain and verse. The fade at the end is simply four (or more) repetitions of the last phrase of verse III.

While the form is somewhat predictable, there are interesting details within. During the refrain, the beginning of the text never corresponds with the downbeats. The important words, "I" and "Satisfaction" always "land" on the weaker second pulse. Even rhythmically, Jagger can't get no satisfaction. The song's satisfaction (or lack thereof) has been interpreted as masturbation, sexual gratification, lack of respect, lack of self esteem, and a host of other "lacks of." In the final analysis, it is the power of the refrain which dominates the song—not the words. The listener can apply whichever interpretation hits closest to home.

While *Paint It Black* (*Aftermath*, 1966) is just as simple and repetitious as "Satisfaction," a detailed analysis of the song reveals the vast degree of difference between the two. While timbre is crucial to the effect created by *Paint It Black*, it is not dominated (as was "Satisfaction") by one color. Compared to "Satisfaction," it is, in fact, a "color showpiece." The sitar, played by Jones, is retuned to "guitar tuning" and attacked like a guitar. There is no pretense of authentic Indian performance. It is introduced immediately—phrase A (Fig. 7.18).

A, which does not really establish a steady pulse, ends with a short hold—a chance to let the sound of the sitar sink in. The second half of the introduction (B) introduces the basic pulse (quadruple meter) and the minor mode. Verse I consists of four phrases of four measures each. The first two (C and D) remain in the minor mode and feature Jagger's voice in the low range and somewhat subdued. In phrases E and F the mode changes to major and Jagger's voice explodes into the high range. While it may be tempting to assign E and F the role of a refrain they really do not function as such. The text of E and F and that of their counterparts

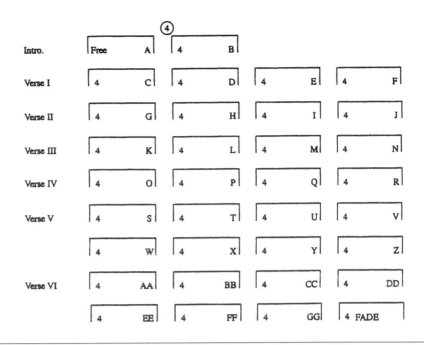

FIGURE 7.18 "Paint It Black," Jagger/Richards, Structural chart.

in verses II–V not only change with the verse but do not seem to comment directly upon the words of their respective verses. The "refrain" is felt in sound and mood only.

Verses II and III are (with the exception of the changing words) musical copies of verse I. The color action begins with verse IV. Here the sitar and a selection of rattles (some played by Jagger) color O and P. In verse V, the subdued voice of C and D is replaced with "full voice." In verse VI words are replaced by humming. The central focus on the voice (and text) is replaced with a "showcase" of color. In phrase W the bass changes from single notes to slides. Given a certain amount of imagination you can almost "feel" your stomach growl. Phrase X introduced the rhythm (in the drums) of the Spanish dance known as the Bolero. It adds intensity and, in the spirit of this dance, seems to move the song ahead. In phrase Y the Bolero rhythm is picked up by the guitar and in phrase Z the sitar explodes into a non-rhythmic splash of color.

Verse VI is a repetition of the music in verses I–III. This is a good place to incorporate your own fade out by simply turning down the volume control to nothing. This way the coherence of the words and the bite of their meaning remains "tight." The text of verse VI is not formally set. It is, in fact, a series of ad libs. In concert, the extension of this phrase as well as the introduction and the fade frequently expanded the overall duration of the song to well over ten minutes. Even in the recorded version (2 minutes and 33 seconds) the ending fade lasts too long. It robs the song of the punch of its words. But at a Stones' *concert* who is thinking about that?

The two major albums of 1967 saw The Rolling Stones move ever closer to The Beatles. *Between The Buttons* incorporated the use of extra musicians—classical musicians. A number of the songs included exotic percussion, harpsichord—*Yesterday's Papers*, and orchestral instruments. Additional "Beatleisms" included asymmetrical phrase structures and more exotic harmonic progressions. With the release of *Sgt. Pepper's Lonely*

Hearts Club Band, The Rolling Stones, feeling the challenge to keep up with The Beatles, released their own concept album. While panned by most critics, *Their Satanic Majesties Request,* the album's concept was actually more well defined than that of *Sgt. Pepper.* Packaged in an album cover which featured a primitive hologram, a maze which went nowhere, and a collection of images as wide ranging as the Mount Palamar Telescope and Leonardo da Vinci's portrait of Ginevra de' Benci, *Their Satanic Majesties Request* was about travel: travel from place to place, from time to time, and from state of mind to state of mind. In addition, its songs were arranged in a format far more rigorous that those of *Sgt. Pepper.* Each was matched to its counterpart on the opposite side of the LP. A huge collection of orchestral instruments provided a wide variety of timbres and served as a background and provided album unity. Despite sloppy editing and the overuse of certain instruments, e.g. various types of shakers and maracas, the album was successful in capturing a sense of mystery and timelessness. But it was not The Rolling Stones. It was not what they did best. With *Beggers Banquet* (1968) they turned their backs on high art (and trying to follow the lead of The Beatles) and created their best album from The Stones "Classic" period.

The album's opening song, *Sympathy For The Devil,* set the tone for the entire album and, with its satanic references, set the tone for The Rolling Stones' stage performances. *Sympathy For The Devil* and a number of the album's other offerings, deal with puzzles—life's puzzles. The text, exhibiting the influence of Dylan, falls into three major sections. Verse I is concerned with the introduction of the Devil—although the listener is not yet supposed to make the identification. To emphasize his eternal nature he evokes the torment of Jesus. A longer middle section, verses II and III detail (in chronological order) his satanic activities—World War I, World War II, and political assignations. The final is, as with so many Dylan songs, the crown of the song. Life is a puzzle—cops are criminals and sinners are saints. Each verse is punctuated by what turns out to be a refrain. Okay—all right—it's not Dylan. However, the music which surrounds the text brings the meaning home and creates an atmosphere unlike anything else in rock and roll.

The rhythmic pattern which permeates the entire song is that of the Latin dance known as the Samba. While the tempo of the basic pulse (quadruple meter) is not particularly fast, each pulse is subdivided into several additional pulses. Musicians call this detailed subdivision. To the average listener the rhythm sounds busy and thick—and it is. Each pulse is accompanied by additional percussion sounds.

The long introduction (even longer in live concerts) is designed to introduce instruments one at a time (e.g. maracas enter in measure four), and to allow for ad lib sounds and words from various members of the band.

Verse I (Fig. 7.19) features solo voice (Jagger), a host of percussion instruments, piano, and bass. The harmony is heard in the piano. All four phrases of verse I (B, C, D, and E) are set to the same harmonic progression—I/flat III/IV/I. While the second chord is somewhat unusual, it is not dissonant and it creates little tension. The "extra measure" in E is a simple instrumental extension which helps to set off the refrain (F and G). The refrain's harmony (V/I) is noticeably different from that of the verses and places increased emphasis on its words. Verse II is a repeat of the

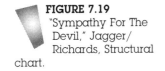

FIGURE 7.19 "Sympathy For The Devil," Jagger/Richards, Structural chart.

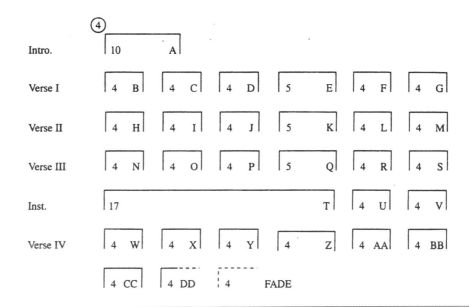

music of verse I. Verse III introduces two additional voices singing, "Ooh, ooh" in harmony and in the background. They continue through the rest of the song—even throughout the instrumental break (I). CC is phrase one of the verse repeated many, many times and is accompanied by additional vocal ad libs. Once again, a quick turn down of the volume control to produce an early fade out enhances the song and tightens the message of the text.

After the debacle at the Altamont Music Festival, the death of Brian Jones, and a brief hiatus from the recording studio, The Rolling Stones re-entered the world of recorded rock and roll with *Sticky Fingers* (1971). Here the satanic image is dropped, improvisation plays a more important role, and the drug references and the anti-woman statements are more open and more virulent. At its best—*Brown Sugar* (an expose of the slave trade) and *Sway*—the music of *Sticky Fingers* is a powerful blend of R&B and jazz. At its worst—*Moonlight Mile* (with its sophomoric string arrangements) it is disappointing.

The album's best offering, *Sister Morphine*, is, in a number of notable ways, ahead of its time. A number of aspects of its form and its mood will be incorporated into the musical language of a number of important bands of the mid-1970s, e.g. Pink Floyd and Led Zeppelin. *Sister Morphine* is unlike previous successful "drug songs." In *Girl*, The Beatles waiver between trusting and mistrusting marijuana. In the next chapter The Jefferson Airplane *(White Rabbit)* will sound an open endorsement for marijuana while The Velvet Underground *(Heroin)* will graphically depict the heroin experience. In *Sister Morphine*, The Rolling Stones simply explore reality.

The tempo is slow—what the 1970s will refer to as "slow rock"—a tempo which will permeate the music of Pink Floyd. While the mood of the text "winds down" and moves ever closer to the acceptance of inevitable death, the music does just the opposite. In fact, the structural chart of *Sister Morphine* (Fig. 7.20) is amazingly similar to that of Led Zeppelin's *Stairway To Heaven*.

The song's four-measure introduction is for acoustic guitar alone. In verse I the acoustic guitar is joined by the electric guitar. F is a short break

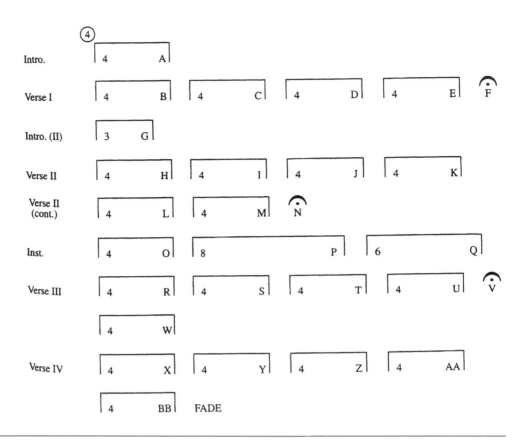

FIGURE 7.20 "Sister Morphine," Jagger/Richards, Structural chart.

of dead silence. G acts as a second introduction. The bass does not enter until phrase three (J) of verse II. P is an instrumental break featuring a collection of "electronic" sounds created by enhancing the sounds of scraped guitar and bass strings. Finally, *finally* (over halfway through the song), the drums enter. But what an entrance—they literally explode. Exactly the same type of drum entry occurs in *Stairway To Heaven*.

In the last verse—as the words are dying away—the music takes over. Once again the fade out (even on the recorded version) is much too long. Again it tends to distract from the punch of the text. Another "manual fade" will enhance the effect of the song. *Sister Morphine* is an example of The Rolling Stones at their musical best. Its feel for color, its sense of musical pacing, and its use of silence is not only extraordinary but, quite ahead of its time. Many aspects of the rock and roll of the 1970s and 1980s owe a great deal to the music of *Sister Morphine*. While likely coincidental, the first line of verse III, will appear virtually unchanged in Pink Floyd's *Sheep*. (*Animals*, 1977)

8 Folk and Related Styles

Introduction

By strict definition, folk music is the music of the people. It is handed down from one generation to the next usually by aural tradition. It is a regional music and expresses the beliefs and feelings of a particular group. The music is generally simple. It is most often a vocal music, so the lyrics are generally more important than the music. Structures tend to be strophic, several verses sung to the same melody. Folk music in its pure form (i.e., non-commercial) appeals to a small audience. "Whenever folk music takes on popular dimensions, that is, commercial value, it is usually because the particular themes being expressed have meaning for the society at that time."[1]

There are several styles of rock that derived from folk in the 1960s and 1970s. This chapter deals with the styles closely associated with folk, namely folk rock, country rock, and Southern rock.

Folk

The folk music style that was popular in the early 1960s was modeled after the Appalachian folk-ballad style, an Anglo-Scottish-Irish song type that developed in the south. The instrumentation typically consists of acoustic string instruments almost exclusively: guitars, banjo, mandolin, string bass that accompany one or more vocalists. Early 1960s folk music is quite different from 1950s rock 'n' roll styles:

- Voices generally had good vocal control.
- Lyrics were pronounced clearly and usually carried a message: peace, racial equality, and love.
- Music to listen to and to think about rather than music to dance to and party with.
- Harmony is simple but generally avoids the 12-bar blues progression and the doo wop progression of rock 'n' roll
- Rhythm is kept deep in the background. The rhythm is supplied by the strummed instruments.
- There is no strong backbeat as in rock 'n' roll, the downbeat is usually emphasized, and there is very little use of syncopation.
- Folk musicians used acoustic instruments exclusively; no electric guitars or basses. They may include smaller percussion instruments such as tambourines or bongos.

- In the studio folk groups went for the true, honest sound of the studio rather than elaborate productions and recording techniques such as double-tracking, overdubbing, echo and reverb effects, etc.
- Folk music in general appealed to college age people and older (roughly 18 to 24 year olds). Folk music, on the other hand, was more easily available on LP albums, which were affordable to the 18–24 year old age group.

The folk music of the 1950s and 1960s was performed either by solo singers accompanying themselves on acoustic guitars or by groups who harmonized a lead vocalist and accompanied themselves on acoustic instruments. Many of the groups, such as the Kingston Trio, were formed on college campuses, often starting as amateur groups to perform at fraternity/sorority houses or other school functions. They gradually became involved as professional recording artists as record labels vied with each other for the newest trend. Many of the solo artists, such as Joan Baez or Phil Ochs, also began their careers on college campuses, often in coffee houses that catered to college-age clientele and, more than the groups, were seriously concerned with social and political topics. Their music was based on the folk music of the 1940s, particularly the songs by one of the principal folk singers from the 1930s until his death in 1967, Woody Guthrie.

Woody Guthrie (1912–1967)

Woodrow Wilson "Woody" Guthrie, from Oklahoma, was a traveling songster, riding the rails (hopping freight trains) to get around. He wrote songs about his personal experiences in the Great Depression, during the Dust Bowl days, and World War II and his experiences with labor unions. He also published his autobiography, *Bound for Glory*, in 1943. With Pete Seeger (b. 1919), Guthrie formed the Almanac Singers in 1940. This group toured the U.S., often giving free performances at union meetings and at strike demonstrations.

Guthrie was an outspoken political and social critic. He wrote several articles for the Communist party *Daily Worker and People's World*. He published over a thousand songs and recorded many albums in his nasally Oklahoma voice. Other stylistic traits of Guthrie include:

- Self-accompanying acoustic guitar, strummed and finger picked.
- Frequent irregular measures.
- Some use of yodeling technique.
- Generally clear pronunciation of words.

Many of Guthrie's songs are well-known as examples of the American folk style, including *Pretty Boy Floyd*, *This Train Is Bound for Glory*, *Roll On, Columbia*, *Grand Coulee Dam*, and *The Sinking of the Reuben James*. Perhaps his most well-known song is *This Land Is Your Land*. It is interesting that today *This Land Is Your Land* is almost accepted as a national anthem, with school children still learning to sing the song in elementary music classes; Guthrie's original message for the song was to the average citizens, warning them to beware of government and big business taking over all the land that is America and leaving nothing for the citizenry. The harmony of the song is a simple pattern using only tonic, subdominant, and dominant chords.

Listening Timeline 8-1

THIS LAND IS YOUR LAND (1940)
WOODY GUTHRIE
from *This Land Is Your Land: The Asch Recordings Vol. 1*
Strophic song form
Original progression in E-flat
Smithsonian Folkways
SF CD 40100, 1997
2:16

Time	Section	Notes
0:00	Introduction	Solo acoustic guitar using a finger picking pattern with many hammer-ons.
0:06	Chorus ("This land is your land . . .")	Solo voice.
0:27	Verse 1 ("As I went walking . . .")	
0:45	Guitar instrumental fill	
0:54	Verse 2 ("I roamed and rambled . . .")	
1:15	Verse 3 ("When the sun comes shining . . .")	
1:36	Chorus	
1:55	Verse 3 repeated	
2:13	Begin fade out	

By 1948, Guthrie was dying of Huntington's chorea, a degenerative disease. He was bedridden for most of the last two decades of his life. His lyrics and his sociopolitical views inspired many folk musicians of the 1960s, most notably Bob Dylan who sang Guthrie's songs and copied Guthrie's singing style.

After Guthrie left the Almanac Singers, they regrouped under Seeger and called themselves the Weavers. They were associated with left-wing political causes and organizations and were blacklisted as subversives during the McCarthy era. The group disbanded in 1963 and Seeger went on as a solo performer. He wrote several songs that became important representatives of the 1960s folk music style including *If I Had A Hammer, Where Have All The Flowers Gone*, and *Turn Turn Turn*.

In the late 1950s and early 1960s, there were several folk groups that were recording and playing at colleges and coffee houses. Some of the more important of these include the Kingston Trio, the Brothers Four, the Highwaymen, the New Christy Minstrels, and others. These were not rural folks but were instead urban, college-educated groups. Yet they provide a chronological link between the folk music of the 1940s and the folk music of the 1960s.

Peter, Paul, and Mary

The next development in folk music was the political protest movement. The performers of the movement did not have the same "Ivy League" college look of their predecessors; they looked like they were more from the beat generation of the 1950s. Their music was geared toward the older college-age students and young adults and recordings set the tone for the folk protest movement in proclaiming that their music was authentic, sincere, and honest.

They represented the new youthful attitude toward politics that began with the election of Kennedy, the idea that politics were not just for the "graybeards." It was a new socio-politically conscious movement that wanted music with a message. They acted on the messages of the music through social protest. Some of the important figures in the protest movement were Joan Baez, Phil Ochs, and Buffy Sainte Marie. The most commercially successful of the early protesters, thereby bringing the music and socio-political concerns to a wider audience, was the trio Peter (Yarrow), Paul (Stookey), and Mary (Travers).

The music of Peter, Paul, and Mary spoke to the ideas of social protest, against war (*Where Have All The Flowers Gone?*) and against injustice (*If I Had A Hammer*), both from their first album (1962) and written by Pete Seeger.

Peter, Paul, and Mary's style consists of very simple vocal harmonies; sometimes they sing in unison/octaves. They are accompanied by two acoustic guitars played by Peter and Paul, strumming simple chord structures that are developed from the melodies; there is no back-up band in the early albums, keeping true to the "honest sound" that the folk movement was after. The songs are strophic, new words sung to the same music. A good example of the sound of Peter, Paul and Mary is the Pete Seeger-composed song *Where Have All the Flowers Gone?* which was released on their first album *Peter, Paul, and Mary* (1962). The harmonic progression, although following the pattern of the doo wop progression (I-vi-IV-V), was written to emphasize the sadness of the lyrics (the minor chord) rather than as a commercial use of the doo wop progression. The lyrics form a cyclic pattern with the answer to each verse's question leading on to the next verse's question until we have come full circle to "where have all the flowers gone" once again.

Listening Timeline 8-2

WHERE HAVE ALL THE FLOWERS GONE?
(1962)
from *Peter, Paul, and Mary*
Strophic song form
Modified doo wop progression in B-flat
Warner Brothers 1449
3:50

0:00	Introduction	Acoustic guitars strum syncopated pattern, alternate B-flat and G minor (I and vi).
0:09	Verse 1 ("Where have all the flowers gone . . .")	Sung in unison and octave; Mary answers the question as a solo line.
0:42	Verse 2 ("Where have all the young girls gone . . .")	Alternate solo (Mary) call with harmonized response.
1:22	Verse 3 ("Where have all the husbands gone . . .")	Sung unison/octave; gradually louder in volume. Solo (Mary) answers question.
1:58	Verse 4 ("where have all the soldiers gone . . .")	Voices in three-part harmony; volume is much louder, angry; Solo male voice answers question.
2:31	Verse 5 ("Where have all the graveyards gone . . .")	Solo Mary elides with harmonized ending of preceding verse, response is harmonized and more emotional and louder; the men sing harmonized "ahs" to Mary's solo melody; the answer is in three-part harmony.
3:08	Verse 6 ("Where have all the flowers gone . . .")	Voices once again in unison and octave; volume level is very subdued, quiet. Ends with strummed rhythm.

In 1963 they began recording the songs of Bob Dylan, notably *Blowin' In The Wind* and *Don't Think Twice, It's Alright*. They had a more polished style than Dylan had at that time and in general were probably more acceptable than Dylan was. Other notable hits by Peter, Paul, and Mary include *Puff The Magic Dragon* (1963) and *Leaving on a Jet Plane* (1969), their only number one hit. They disbanded shortly after the release of *Jet Plane*, but have since reunited for anniversary type concerts.

Bob Dylan (b. 1941)

Bob Dylan was born Robert Zimmerman in Duluth, Minnesota and grew up in Hibbing, Minnesota. As a teenager, Dylan was captivated by the new sounds of rock 'n' roll and according to friends and relatives was constantly trying to put together a rock 'n' roll combo. He taught himself to play guitar and piano while in high school. During his high school years his biggest influence was Buddy Holly, though he was also familiar with the music of Jerry Lee Lewis and Elvis Presley.

After graduating high school, Dylan attended the University of Minnesota for a short time but dropped out in 1960. It was at this time that he began to listen more to folk and country blues recordings, switching his allegiance from rock 'n' roll to folk. He learned the music of Woody Guthrie, whom he greatly admired, and immersed himself in Guthrie's autobiography, *Bound for Glory*. He decided to reinvent himself for the folk scene and began calling himself Bob Dylan. Contrary to popular belief, the origin in his pseudonym was not from Welsh poet Dylan Thomas, but rather a combination of Bob's admiration for television character Matt Dillon (from the television program *Gunsmoke*) and a Hibbing pioneer family named Dillion.[2] In admiration for Guthrie, Dylan invented a fictional past for himself as a runaway with an Okie background and began telling people that he had spent a lot of time "hoboing" or hopping freight trains as Guthrie had done.

In December 1960 Dylan moved to New York City in order to be close to Guthrie, who was by then in the hospital with Huntington's disease. He became acquainted with the folk music circuit in New York, hanging out at coffee houses and clubs singing and playing where he could and getting to know the people (particularly the club owners) of the folk scene. He naturally absorbed a good deal of folk music influence there and met several folk singers with whom he could sing and play. He was hired to play harmonica on a couple of songs for a friend named Carolyn Hester; her self-titled album was released by Columbia Records, which put Dylan in contact with Columbia's Artist and Repertoire agent John Hammond.[3] Hammond hired Dylan to play background harmonica on the title cut of Calypso singer Harry Belafonte's *Midnight Special* album in 1961; Hammond quickly signed Dylan to a recording contract with Columbia.

Under Hammond's guidance, Dylan recorded his first album, the self-titled *Bob Dylan* (1962) consisting of just Dylan, his guitar, and his harmonica. The songs on this first album were mostly covers of favorite folk songs such as *House of the Risin' Sun* and *See That My Grave Is Kept Clean*, but in Dylan's distinctive vocal style. This album also included two examples of Dylan's original material: *Talkin' New York* and *Song To Woody*, an homage to his hero Woody Guthrie. Although Dylan was hailed in folk circles as the new artist to reckon with, the first album sold a miserable 5000 copies in its first year.

The song *Talkin' New York* is an excellent introduction to the songs of Bob Dylan. The song is written in the story-song style popular with folk singers, a style which is said to have originated with blues singers/songsters such as Leadbelly. The song is performed in a kind of speechlike delivery, not really sung, unlike clear vocal style of other folk singers and, as with most folk songs, it is a strophic form with several verses sung to the same music. The song also demonstrates Dylan's great wit and his talent for working with words; a very sarcastic sense of humor rises in the final lines of several verses.

Listening Timeline 8-3

TALKIN' NEW YORK (1962)
BOB DYLAN
from *Bob Dylan*
Strophic song form
Simple I, IV, V progression in G
Columbia CK 08579, 1962
3:15

Time	Section	Notes
0:00	Introduction	Guitar and harmonica
0:11	Verse 1 ("Ramblin' out of the wild west . . .")	Note the "hayseed" wonder at the marvels of New York City's subways and skyscrapers ("ups and downs").
0:25	Instrumental fill	
0:33	Verse 2 ("Winter time in New York town . . .")	Note Dylan's sarcasm concerning the weather and the *New York Time's* weather report.
0:52	Instrumental fill	
0:59	Verse 3 ("I swing on to my old guitar . . .")	His sarcasm is directed at the New York folk scene.
1:12	Instrumental fill	
1:22	Verse 4 ("I walked down there and ended up . . .")	Continues his sarcastic commentary on the New York folk scene.
1:37	Instrumental fill	
1:48	Verse 5 ("Well I got a harmonica job . . .")	Referring to his first recording gig; the man who liked his playing ($1 a day's worth) is John Hammond.
2:02	Instrumental fill	
2:11	Verse 6 ("After weeks and weeks of hanging around . . .")	
2:21	Verse 7 ("A very great man once said . . .")	Reference to Woody Guthrie; the line "some people rob you with a fountain pen" is from Guthrie's *Pretty Boy Floyd*.
2:41	Instrumental fill	
2:48	Verse 8 ("So one morning when the sun was warm . . .")	Return to sarcastic observations. Our hero wanders back west, from New York City to East Orange, New Jersey.
3:06	Coda: Instrumental fill with fade	

Dylan's next album, *The Freewheelin' Bob Dylan* (1963), contained almost completely original material and definitely caused the folk music community to sit up and take notice of him. Dylan saw that folk music was beginning to lean toward civil rights and anti-war and many of the songs on this album reflect this attitude. The album includes *Blowin' in the Wind*, which was a number two hit for Peter, Paul and Mary, *Masters of War*, which is one of Dylan's most bitter anti-war songs, and *Don't Think Twice, It's Alright*, an example of a bitter/sarcastic Dylan love song. *Masters of War* is the song which supposedly catapulted Dylan into the forefront of the anti-war movement. The song exhibits a lot of rage towards both those who make weapons and those who order others to use them.

Listening Chart 6

MASTERS OF WAR (1963)
BOB DYLAN
from *The Freewheelin' Bob Dylan*, Columbia CK 8786, 1963.
Bob Dylan, vocal, guitar, and harmonica.

Sound:	Acoustic guitar, capoed at the third fret to accommodate D minor-shaped chords in the proper key. Single male voice, high tenor range, with a nasal tone quality.
Form:	Strophic song form consisting of eight verses with a brief, two-measure introduction and a coda.
Harmony:	An F minor chord is played throughout with hammer-ons and pull-offs on the treble strings; the bass strings emphasize the tonic (F) and the flat seventh (E-flat) of the key. The subtonic chord (E-flat) is used at the ending phrase of each verse.
Rhythm:	Strummed in a fast triple meter, between 160 and 168 beats per minute. The strummed rhythm becomes hypnotic, reinforced by the surface-level syncopations of the pull-offs and hammer-ons, and by the alternating bass strings. The fast tempo does not allow for much beat subdivision, but that which is there is even.
Melody:	A narrow, almost static, melodic range. Each verse starts in the lower range and gradually builds to a higher range by the end of the third line; the voice then descends to the starting range by the end of the last line in each verse.
Text:	One of Dylan's angriest and most frustrated songs directed at those in business who supply weaponry for wholesale slaughter, but are safe in the background when the fighting starts. The rage of the lyrics has been described as cathartic, "a way of getting temporary relief from the heavy feeling of impotence that affects many who cannot understand a civilization which juggles its own means for oblivion and calls that performance an act towards peace."[4] The mode of the song is one to another—Dylan to the "Masters of War"—and takes place in the present.

By the time he released his next album, *The Times They Are A-Changin'* (in February 1964), Dylan was established as a major figure in the folk movement. This album included original songs against war *(Only a Pawn in Their Game)* and racial prejudice *(The Lonesome Death of Hattie Carroll)*; the title cut seemed to warn the establishment that a new wave of youths were becoming a force to be reckoned with, and they (the establishment) had best adapt or be washed out.

This album was followed by *Another Side of Bob Dylan* (August 1964). The songs on this album have been described as Dylan's first step toward rock, with the lyrics more self-oriented, emphasizing personal rather than political sentiments, as in the song *My Back Pages*. In this strophic song, Dylan seems to question his earlier self-assuredness, his youthful cocky attitudes. But his lyrics are becoming more and more poetic with each successive album release.

Listening Timeline 8-4

MY BACK PAGES (1964)
BOB DYLAN
from *Another Side of Bob Dylan*
Strophic song form
Original progression in E-flat
Columbia CK 8993, 1964
4:20

0:00	Introduction	Solo guitar sets the tempo, meter, and key.
0:05	Verse 1 ("Crimson flames tied through my ears . . .")	
0:48	Verse 2 ("Half-racked prejudice leaped forth . . .")	
1:31	Verse 3 ("Girls faces form the forward path . . .")	
2:14	Verse 4 ("A self-ordained professor's tongue . . .")	
2:56	Verse 5 ("In a soldier's stance I aimed my hand . . .")	
3:37	Verse 6 ("Yes my guard stood hard when abstract threats . . .")	

Another Side of Bob Dylan was mildly surprising to Dylan's established protest audience. His next album, *Bringing It All Back Home* (March 1965), was even more shocking. The problem here wasn't that the lyrics were more personal than political; the problem was the music itself. To the hardcore folk music adherents, Dylan had sold them out, becoming more commercial. He used drum sets and electric guitars on this album and the style was suspiciously rock-like. At the 1965 Newport Folk Festival, Dylan horrified the folk purists by stepping onstage with an electric guitar. One of the songs on *Bringing It All Back Home* is the incredibly witty *Subterranean Homesick Blues*.

Dylan's next album, *Highway 61 Revisited* (August 1965), featured Dylan's first truly successful song *Like A Rolling Stone*, which reached number two on the charts. Besides being Dylan's first major hit, the six-minute song broke the standard radio station/45 single norms of two-and-a-half minute songs.

Never one to let his critics deter him or make him change his style, Dylan's next album, *Blonde on Blonde* (1966), contained one of his biggest hits, *Rainy Day Women #12 & 35*. This song opens up the double album (the first rock double album), and notes that people will criticize no matter what one does. It has been said that the songs on the album in general are characterized by lyrics that are intense poetic interpretations of drugs, dreams, and nightmares.

The recording of *Blonde on Blonde* took place in Nashville and included some of the foremost session musicians from Nashville, including pianist "Pig" Robbins, guitarist Charlie McCoy, and bassist Joe South. This was Dylan's first recording venture in Nashville and it will set the pace for his late 60s albums, *John Wesley Harding* and *Nashville Skyline*. The recording session for *Rainy Day Women #12 & 35* is described as a party going full force.[5]

Listening Chart 7

RAINY DAY WOMEN #12 & 35 (1966)
BOB DYLAN
from *Blonde on Blonde*, Columbia CGK 841.

Bob Dylan, vocal, harmonica, acoustic guitar; J. Robbie Robertson, electric guitar; Wayne Moss, guitar; Jerry Kennedy, guitar; Al Kooper, tambourine; Joe South, bass; Hargus "Pig" Robbins, piano; Kenney Buttrey, drums; Charlie McCoy, trumpet; Wayne Butler, trombone; All, assorted whoops and hollers and laughter.

Sound: A general party atmosphere; a nasally tenor-range vocal accompanied by an amateur sounding band: snare drum is muffled, the horns are played slightly out of tune. Lots of laughter and background comments from the band.

Form: A strophic song form consisting of five verses and an instrumental introduction (the intro is fourteen measures long). There are instrumental passages (like the introduction) between verses 3 and 4 and between verses 4 and 5. A brief

	coda based on the introduction is played after the fifth verse with a fadeout beginning on the fifth measure.
Harmony:	12-bar blues progression in F.
Rhythm:	In 6/8 time, with no strong backbeat; a march-like bounced feel is felt with a stronger emphasis on beats 1 and 3. The tempo is between 96 and 100 beats per minute. The surface rhythms of the melody are mostly even subdivisions of the beat.
Melody:	Very narrow range, almost static. Noticeable laughing in the lead vocal in several verses. Great and extensive use of blue notes in the melody line.
Text:	Essentially, Dylan is railing back at his critics: you can't please everyone all of the time, so what's the use of trying to do so? Just be yourself and do what you do best. Dylan is using the term "stoned" on different levels: the critics "stone you" in the Biblical sense (i.e., throw rocks at you literally), and of course the party atmosphere of the song in which everyone sounds stoned. The mode is one to the world and in the present tense.

In the summer of 1966, Dylan was involved in a motorcycle accident and he disappeared from the music scene to recuperate from a broken neck. All the while, rumors of death and drug addiction abounded. While recovering, Dylan recorded *The Basement Tapes* with the Band, although this was not officially released until 1975.

Dylan released the album *John Wesley Harding* in early 1968. This album was recorded in Nashville and used Nashville session musicians Charlie McCoy (bass) and Kenney Buttrey (drums), also with steel guitarist Pete Drake on two cuts. From this album came the song *All Along the Watchtower*, which was later covered by Jimi Hendrix.

Dylan's last album of the 1960s was *Nashville Skyline* (1969). This album was also recorded in Nashville and included Charlie Daniels (fiddle) and David Grissman (mandolin) as backup musicians, and also included a duet with Johnny Cash on the remake of *Girl from the North Country*. The album was more in a country vein than in a folk or folk-rock style and it yielded one of Dylan's biggest hits, *Lay Lady Lay*.

In the 1970s, Dylan returned to the more rock-influenced folk style he had reached in 1966 with *Blonde on Blonde*. His music remained in pretty much the same vein throughout the 1970s: rock-influenced folk style with uncommonly good, insightful lyrics for the most part. The biggest change in Dylan's style came in 1979 with his conversion to Christianity and the release of the gospel-inspired *Slow Train Coming*. An interesting cut from *Slow Train Coming* is the opener, *Gotta Serve Somebody*, which combines the message lyrics of folk music, the instrumentation and pronounced backbeat of rock, and the emotion and performance style (call and response) of gospel music. The harmony is a 16-bar blues with a verse (8 measures on the tonic) and a refrain (two measures each subdominant and tonic, one measure each dominant, subdominant, and two more tonic).

0:00	Introduction	Electric piano, bass, and drums.
0:11	Verse 1 ("You may be an ambassador . . .")	Adds lead vocal and guitar.

Listening Timeline 8-5

GOTTA SERVE SOMEBODY (1979)
BOB DYLAN
from *Slow Train Coming*
Strophic song form
16-bar blues in A minor
Columbia CK 36120, 1979
5:14

0:31	Refrain ("Well you gotta serve somebody . . .")	Guitar fills more prominent.
0:51	Verse 2 ("You might be a rock 'n' roll addict . . .")	Piano and organ become more active.
1:12	Refrain	Add women's chorus, call and response.
1:32	Verse 3 ("You might be a state trooper . . .")	
1:52	Refrain	Increase in volume and excitement.
2:13	Verse 4 ("You may be a construction worker . . .")	Guitar more active.
2:33	Refrain	Organ more prominent.
2:53	Verse 5 ("You might be a preacher . . .")	Softer volume with crescendo going into refrain.
3:13	Refrain	
3:33	Verse 6 ("Might like to wear cotton . . .")	Rhythm becomes more insistent.
3:53	Refrain	
4:14	Verse 7 ("You may call me Terry . . .")	
4:34	Refrain	Backup vocals more pronounced.
4:54	Coda	Women's chorus and instrumental riff on electric piano, bass, and drums with organ fills; fade.

Dylan is one of the most important musicians in rock music, with his songs covered by many groups and individuals including the Byrds, the Turtles, Peter, Paul, and Mary, Johnny Cash, Jimi Hendrix, and Joan Baez. As a lyricist, he is a definite influence on The Beatles, especially on Lennon, and he is an influence on The Rolling Stones as well. He is certainly the most eloquent of the folk musicians of the 1960s. Still creating and releasing new material, such as *Time Out of Mind* (1997), and still touring, Dylan's influence is certainly one of the most far-reaching in rock music.

Folk-Rock

Introduction

Folk-rock is a wide category of music that began in the mid-1960s and is a vague, generalized style of rock music. It is a blending of the message-laden, or profound, story-telling lyrics and tuneful melodies of folk music with the electrification, ostinato bass, and hard-driving backbeat of rock music. Purists on both sides were put off by the fusion of the two: the folkies by the commercialism and the rockers by the social messages.

There is a wide range of artists and personal styles in folk-rock. Some of the performers who fit in this style include the Byrds; Buffalo Springfield; the Mamas and the Papas; the Lovin' Spoonful; Crosby, Stills, and Nash (and Young); Simon and Garfunkel; Donovan; and the Turtles. Some sources also include Sonny and Cher, Barry McGuire, and the Grass Roots. So a very wide variety of musicians are represented in this category.

It is difficult to say who or which group originated the folk-rock style. Most authorities consider the first folk-rock song to be the Byrds' recording of Dylan's *Mr. Tambourine Man*, which was released in March 1965. It entered the charts in early June 1965 and hit number 1 later that month; it is the first folk-rock song to reach number one. Dylan's 4th album, *Bringing It All Back Home*, was also released in March of 1965; Dylan used electric instruments on most of the songs on the album including *Subterranean Homesick Blues*, and *Subterranean Homesick Blues* hit the charts in May 1965 although it only went to number 39, barely breaking into the top forty. And besides, Dylan wrote *Mr. Tambourine Man*. In fact, Dylan wrote most of the songs that were covered by the folk rock groups: *My Back Pages*, recorded by the Byrds, *It Ain't Me, Babe*, recorded by the Turtles, *All I Really Want To Do*, recorded by Sonny and Cher, and so on. Both Dylan and the Byrds can be considered pioneers of the style.

The Byrds

Roger McGuinn (lead guitar, vocal), David Crosby (rhythm guitar, vocal), Gene Clark (vocal), Chris Hillman (bass), and Mike Clarke (drums); group formed 1964. Considered by some to be comparable to the Beatles and Dylan, the Byrds never amounted to their full potential primarily because of constant fighting within the band and the subsequent personnel changes that resulted from this.

Their first album, *Mr. Tambourine Man* (1965), contained four songs by Dylan (including the title cut), some original material by Gene Clark, and other songs (including a rock version of *Oh Susanna*). Their second album, *Turn Turn Turn* (1965), also contained a similar mixture of Dylan covers and original music. The title cut was a song by folk singer Pete Seeger, who adapted the lyrics from the Book of Ecclesiastes, from the Bible; *Turn Turn Turn* hit number 1 on the charts in December 1965.

The early folk-rock sound of the Byrds is exemplified by their recording of *Mr. Tambourine Man*. Note 12-string guitar sound from McGuinn. For this version, the group recorded only the second verse and the chorus from Dylan's original song.

Listening Timeline 8-6

MR. TAMBOURINE MAN (1965)
THE BYRDS
from *Greatest Hits*
Strophic song form
Original progression in D
Columbia CK 9516, 1967
2:17

0:00	Introduction	Solo 12-string guitar for two measures, bass and tambourine come in next two measures; drum kick into chorus.
0:09	Chorus ("Hey Mr. Tambourine Man . . .")	Harmonized vocals, add drums and rhythm guitar.
0:42	Verse ("Take me for a trip . . .")	Solo lead vocal, enhanced by echo.
1:31	Chorus	
2:01	Coda	Solo 12-string guitar for two measures, add bass and fade.

Later recordings by the Byrds further illustrate the combination of rock and folk, including *Eight Miles High* from the album *Fifth Dimension* (1966). This song suffered from radio bans because it was thought that the lyrics were drug-oriented. *Eight Miles High* has a definite "other-worldly" sound caused by electronic sound manipulation—e.g., lots of reverberation helps create a dream-like atmosphere for the song, a characteristic of the psychedelic sound of rock groups from San Francisco around the same time.

The Fifth Dimension album was followed by the albums *The Notorious Byrd Brothers* (1968) and *Sweetheart of the Rodeo* (1968), both of which are distinctly country flavored and form the foundation of the 1970s country rock style, influencing such groups as the Eagles (at least up to their *Hotel California* album) and Poco (see below).

Beginning in 1966, the group underwent several personnel changes: Gene Clark left the group (March 1966); questions of leadership lead to the firing of David Crosby (October 1967); Crosby was replaced by Clark, who quit again three weeks later; Mike Clarke quit shortly after Gene Clark quit the second time; McGuinn and Hillman recruited Kevin Kelley (drums) and Gram Parsons (vocal, guitar) (early 1968); Hillman left after dispute with McGuinn (late 1968); McGuinn assumed full control of the group until the group disbanded in 1970. Recent reports indicate that Crosby and Hillman are trying to reform the original group, but have yet to convince McGuinn to join them again.

The Byrds was an important group both in regard to their sound and in the songs they developed and in the personnel the group cultivated: some of the groups in the 1970s that included ex-Byrds are Crosby, Stills, and Nash (and Young), Manassas, Souther-Hillman-Furay, the Flying Burrito Brothers, and Firefall.

The Buffalo Springfield

Neil Young (guitar, vocal), Stephen Stills (guitar, vocal), Richie Furay (guitar, vocal), Dewey Martin (drums, vocal), and Bruce Palmer (bass); group formed 1966. This group was in the same folk-rock/country-rock mold as the Byrds. Again, due to internal struggles, the group was very short-lived. Like the Byrds, Buffalo Springfield also went through many personnel changes, including replacement of Palmer with Jim Messina. Buffalo Springfield is more important for the groups that its members later spawned: Crosby, Stills, and Nash (and Young), Poco (Furay and Messina, with future Eagle Randy Meisner), and Loggins and Messina.

Neil Young wrote several good songs that the group recorded, including *Mr. Soul, On the Way Home,* and *Expecting To Fly.* But the group is probably best remembered for their top ten hit from their first album, *For What It's Worth*, written by Stills and which reached number 7 on the charts. The overall sound of the song is an example of the harder edged sound of the Springfield; especially interesting is Young's meandering guitar solo, which sounds somewhat influenced by the then-current rock interest in Indian music.

Listening Timeline 8-7

FOR WHAT IT'S WORTH (1967)
THE BUFFALO SPRINGFIELD
from *Retrospective*
Strophic song form
Original progression in E
Atco 38-105-2, 1969
2:35

0:00	Introduction	Guitar plays ringing harmonics of E (12th fret) and B (5th fret) accompanied by bass and drums; acoustic guitar enters measure three.

0:10	Verse 1 ("There's something happening here . . .")	Solo vocal (Stills) over accompaniment.
0:21	Chorus ("Think it's time we stop . . .")	Harmonized vocals, a bit louder volume.
0:36	Interlude	Instrumental, like introduction.
0:44	Verse 2 ("There's battle lines being drawn . . .")	Solo vocal with harmonized vocal on last phrase ("from behind").
1:03	Chorus	Harmonized vocal; add electric guitar obligatto (Young).
1:10	Interlude	Features electric guitar playing modal melody, with reverb.
1:18	Verse 3 ("What a field day for the heat . . .")	Solo lead vocal with harmonized "oohs"; electric guitar drops out.
1:37	Chorus	Harmonized vocals; electric guitar returns.
1:43	Interlude	Modal melody in electric guitar; note long bent notes.
1:52	Verse 4 ("Paranoia strikes deep . . .")	Harmonized lead vocal; electric guitar continues countermelody; hand claps at the end of every sung phrase.
2:11	Chorus/Coda	Harmonized vocal, sung four times with fade, guitar continues in forefront, then fades also.

Crosby, Stills, Nash, and Young

Considered one of the first "super groups" because it consisted of exceptionally talented composer/performers who were involved in earlier major groups; Nash started out as a vocalist and guitarist with the British group the Hollies, Crosby was from the Byrds, and Stills and Young were in Buffalo Springfield.

This group began as a trio (without Young), and they released their first album (self-titled) in 1969; this contained the songs *Marrakesh Express* and *Suite: Judy Blue Eyes*, the latter song for Steve Stills' then love-interest Judy Collins. The album is characterized by tight vocal harmonies, especially between Crosby and Nash. They soon recruited Stills' ex-Springfield partner Neil Young, whose guitar playing added a bit more edge to the overall sound and whose songwriting abilities provided some excellent repertoire.

With this line-up (and bassist Greg Reeves and drummer Dallas Taylor), they recorded their best album *Déjà vu* (1970). This album contains some great material by Crosby *(Almost Cut My Hair)*, Nash *(Teach Your Children)*, Young *(Helpless, Country Girl)*, and Joni Mitchell *(Woodstock)*. The song that best shows the folk and rock roots of C, S, N, and Y is the Steve Stills opener *Carry On*. The song is in E-flat, but the guitar is capoed at the first fret, and the lowest string is dropped to D, in order to use the chord forms of D and D minor.

Listening Timeline 8-8

CARRY ON (1970)
CROSBY, STILLS, NASH, AND YOUNG
from *Déjà vu*
Two-part strophic form
Original progression in E-flat mixolydian (part 1) and E-flat dorian (part 2)
Atlantic 82649-2, 1970
4:23

0:00	Introduction to part 1	Acoustic guitars.
0:14	Verse 1 ("One morning I woke up . . .")	Harmonized vocals with solo voice (Stills) singing last phrase of each line; bass added.
0:38	Interlude	Add electric guitar fills.
0:45	Verse 2 ("The sky is clearing")	Electric guitar continues countermelody.
1:09	Interlude	Add conga drums.
1:16	Verse 3 ("The fortunes of fables . . .")	
1:40	Interlude extended	Double in length of previous interludes.
1:54	Transition ("Carry on . . .")	Four-part harmony, sung a cappella.
2:11	Introduction to part 2	Organ, congas, bass, drums; electric guitar added measure nine.
2:43	Verse 1 ("Where are you going now my love . . .")	Harmonized vocals.
3:12	Interlude	Electric guitar uses wah-wah pedal.
3:28	Verse 2 ("Girl when I was on my own . . .")	Second electric guitar plays counter to first electric guitar and organ.
3:56	Coda	Based on interlude, featuring guitar with wah-wah, gradually fades out.

The group disbanded shortly after the release of *Déjà vu*, but managed to release two more albums: the greatest hits package *So Far* (1974) and the live double album *Four-Way Street* (1971). *Four-Way Street* is very much like the title implies: four very talented individuals going their own way, which is why the group did not work very well. The various members went on to various solo and collaborative projects, Crosby and Nash released a couple of albums and Stills and Young got together as the Stills-Young Band and released *Long May You Run* (1976). Crosby, Stills, and Nash got back together a few of times over the years to release albums and tour to promote these albums. In 1999 they reunited once more to record the album *Looking Forward*.

The Band

The Band is another very talented folk rock group to arise in the 1960s. Originally organized as The Hawks, the group supported 1950/1960 rock 'n' roll singer Ronnie Hawkins. The group was formed by Arkansas native Levon Helm (drums, vocals) and Canadians Jaime Robbie Robertson (guitar, vocals), Garth Hudson (keyboards, vocals), Rick Danko (bass, vocals), and Richard Manuel (keyboards). In the mid-1960s, the group (now calling themselves Levon and the Hawks, having left Hawkins) were introduced to Bob Dylan. They were hired by Dylan in the summer of 1965 to tour with him as his first official electric band. At the end of 1965, Helm retired momentarily from playing.

In the meantime, the remaining members continued working and composing, completely changing their sound to a more electrified funk folk hybrid. Dylan used Robertson's guitar talents on his 1966 album *Blonde on Blonde* (see Listening Chart 7, *Rainy Day Women Nos. 12 & 35* above). After Dylan's motorcycle accident in 1966, he moved to Woodstock in upstate New York to recuperate. In 1967, the four remaining members of the Band (as they were now calling themselves) re-recruited Helm to come back and play and sing with them as they too moved up to Woodstock to be with Dylan. Living communally in a large, pink house (which they called Big Pink), Dylan and the Band began writing and recording a huge number of songs (this is the source of Dylan's *Basement Tapes*, for the longest time one of the most well-known bootleg recordings in rock music, ultimately released as an official album in 1975 by Columbia Records).

While Dylan composed a number of songs for his own releases in subsequent years, the Band were also writing prolifically. The results were songs that were released on the albums *Music from Big Pink* (1968) and *The Band* (1969). Both albums consisting of a number of good songs (*Up on Cripple Creek*, *The Night They Drove Old Dixie Down*, and *Tears of Rage* for example), an interesting example is Robertson's *The Weight*, which he said was inspired by the surreal film style of Spanish film maker Luis Bunuel.[6]

Listening Timeline 8-9

THE WEIGHT (1968)
THE BAND
from *Music from Big Pink*
Strophic form
Simple I–IV progression in A
Capitol 72435-25390-2-4, 2000
4:33

0:00	Introduction	Solo acoustic guitar (Robertson), joined by drums, bass, and piano.
0:10	Verse 1	Solo voice (Helm) with the band.
0:37	Chorus	3-part harmonized vocals (Helm, Danko, and Manuel); piano becomes more prominent.
1:00	Verse 2	Return to solo voice.
1:26	Chorus	As before.
1:49	Verse 3	Solo voice/band
2:16	Chorus	As before.
2:38	Verse 4	Solo voice switches to Danko
3:05	Chorus	As above, except the descending interlude at the end (from the introduction) is played twice.
3:35	Verse 5	Two voices (Helm and Manuel) in harmony.
4:01	Chorus	Continues two-part vocal harmony.
4:24	Coda	Instrumental repeat of the descending interlude from the introduction.

The Band remained active for the rest of the 1960s and the first half of the 1970s, recording and touring by themselves as well as with Dylan. In 1976, they decided to call it quits and at Thanksgiving of that year, they held a retirement concert featuring themselves and a variety of friends, including Dylan, Ringo Starr, Ronnie Hawkins, Eric Clapton, Joni Mitchell, Muddy Waters, and others. The performance was filmed by Martin Scorsese and released as *The Last Waltz*. The members of the Band went their separate ways, Robertson and Helm both trying their hands at acting as well as maintaining musical careers. Richard Manuel committed suicide in 1986, and Rick Danko passed away in 2000.

Folk and Related Styles

Simon and Garfunkel

The folk rock duo Paul Simon and Art Garfunkel first teamed up in 1957 under the name Tom and Jerry. As Tom and Jerry, they modeled themselves after The Everly Brothers, singing two-part harmonized rock 'n' roll, however, they were not very successful. They later teamed up again in 1964, this time using their real names and singing traditional folk songs, covers of Bob Dylan folk songs, and original songs by Simon.

They released their first album, *Wednesday Morning 3 A.M.*, as a folk duet in 1965. Besides a few covers of folk songs, this album contained mostly original material written by Simon, including the first version of what became their first hit single, *The Sounds of Silence*. This album did not sell well, prompting Simon to go to England to try to get his career rolling. In the meantime, Columbia Records producer Tom Wilson, who had been instrumental in electrifying Bob Dylan on record and who was inspired by the new rise of folk rock in America, decided to remix the single *The Sounds of Silence* with electric bass, electric guitars, and drums. This new version was released as a single and on an album of the same name; the single hit the number one spot on the *Billboard* pop music chart January 1, 1966 where it remained for two weeks.

Listening Timeline 8-10

THE SOUNDS OF SILENCE (1966)
SIMON AND GARFUNKEL
from *Sounds of Silence*
Strophic song form
Original modal progression in G-flat/E-flat minor
Columbia CK 9269, 1966
3:03

0:00	Introduction	Solo acoustic guitar picks one measure, overdubbed electric guitar added second measure.
0:04	Verse 1 ("Hello darkness my old friend . . .")	Harmonized vocals.
0:37	Verse 2 ("In restless dreams I walked alone . . .")	Add drums, bass.
1:12	Verse 3 ("And in the naked light I saw . . .")	Volume a bit louder.
1:47	Verse 4 ("Fools said I you do not know . . .")	Second electric guitar adds countermelody, very softly.
2:21	Verse 5 ("And the people bowed and prayed . . .")	Loudest volume; gradual decrescendo in volume and ritardando in tempo;
2:52		Sustained note on "sounds" then
2:55		Slower tempo resumes on "of silence" as guitars pick tonic chord slowly, ritardando in tempo to final strummed chord.

Simon and Garfunkel became greatly popular during the folk rock boom of the mid-1960s. Their next album, *Parsley, Sage, Rosemary, and Thyme* (1966) contained the top twenty hits *Homeward Bound* and *Scarborough Fair*. Their next release was *Bookends* at the end of 1966 which contained the number one single *Mrs. Robinson* from the film *The Graduate*. These albums established Simon's reputation as a literate, poetic, and aggressive lyricist. Simon's lyrics are powerful, filled with introspection and irony, and are very well-suited for the smooth harmonic blend of their voices.

The duo's last album was *Bridge Over Troubled Water*, released in 1970. This album shows a great deal of thought in the lyrics, particularly in the title cut which reached the number one spot on the pop chart. The album also contained the top twenty singles *El Condor Pasa*, *Cecilia*, and *The Boxer*.

Despite their chart success, Simon and Garfunkel felt constrained by the image they projected and they split in 1970. They maintained a good working relationship and friendship, coming together every so often to help each other on recording projects and concerts, reuniting in 1981 for a well-received concert in Central Park. In the meantime, Garfunkel had a brief solo recording career and tried his hand at acting while Simon continued recording his songs in a successful solo career.

Country Rock

Country rock is a style that developed largely in southern California in the late 1960s and early 1970s, based primarily in the studios of Los Angeles. It is distinctly different from the Memphis country rock style of the 1950s: Memphis country rock, as a 1950s rock 'n' roll style, was created from a mixture of country and western with rhythm and blues, that is, two distinct musical genres. Southern California country rock combines elements of rock, which is already a combination of two or more 1950s rock 'n' roll styles, with country and western. In essence, country rock of the 1970s is a rock style that turns to country techniques and lyrics for inspiration. The most notable characteristics of country rock are:

- Incorporation of the basic country string band with the electric band of rock.
- Prominent use of country-style pedal steel guitar.
- The bass often plays two-beat bass lines, though they may be decorated with runs and bounced notes.
- Twangy lead guitar sound.
- Nasally vocals with southern or country accents.
- Close vocal harmonies.
- Stiff country rhythms.
- Steady, evenly subdivided beats.
- Lyrics are very much like country lyrics—a "love gone bad" type of song, perhaps accompanied by crying in one's beer.

The Byrds

The principal founders of the southern California country rock style was the Byrds; the release of their psychedelic-oriented album *Fifth Dimension* (1966) was followed by the albums *The Notorious Byrd Brothers* (1968) and *Sweetheart of the Rodeo* (1968), both of which are distinctly country flavored. By 1968, after the departure of David Crosby, Gene Clarke, and Mike Clark, McGuinn and Hillman recruited Kevin Kelly (drums) and Gram Parsons (vocal, guitar) to join the band. A classic example of the Byrds' country rock style is Gram Parsons' *You're Still on My Mind*, from *Sweetheart of the Rodeo*.

Listening Timeline 8-11

YOU'RE STILL ON MY MIND (1968)
THE BYRDS
from *Sweetheart of the Rodeo*
Strophic song form
Simple I, IV, V progression in A
Columbia CK 65150, 1968
2:22

0:00	Introduction	Starts with steel guitar, add drum, bass, and rhythm guitar.
0:09	Verse 1 ("The jukebox is playing . . .")	Solo vocal (Parsons), piano playing country honky tonk style with lots of rolls, trills, etc. In second half of verse, steel guitar returns with fills. Hook line of song (title) is harmonized by McGuinn.
0:40	Instrumental fill	Honky tonk piano for first half, steel guitar for second half.
0:54	Verse 2 ("The people are dancing . . .")	
1:24	Instrumental fill	
1:39	Verse 3 ("Alone and forsaken . . .")	
2:09	Coda	Extension of song by repetition of harmonized hook.

The troubles of the Byrds continued to grow in the late 60s. After a dispute with McGuinn, Chris Hillman left in late 1968. McGuinn assumed full control of the band until the group formally disbanded in 1970; McGuinn carried on for some time as a solo act.

The Flying Burrito Brothers

After the dissolution of the Byrds, the various members went on to form new bands. Parsons and Hillman (who switched to guitar) teamed with steel guitarist Pete Kleinow and bassist Chris Etheridge to form The Flying Burrito Brothers in 1968; in 1969 ex-Byrd drummer Mike Clarke also joined the group. The Flying Burrito Brothers recorded two albums under the leadership of Parsons before he left the band for a solo career; a third album with Parsons' work, *Sleepless Nights*, was released after Parsons' death. Included on this album was Parsons' *Close Up the Honky Tonks*.

Listening Timeline 8-12

CLOSE UP THE HONKY TONKS (1976)
THE FLYING BURRITO BROTHERS
from *The Best of the Flying Burrito Brothers*
Strophic song form
Simple I, IV, V progression in A
A&M CD 5216, 1988
2:15

0:00	Introduction	Begins with solo steel guitar pickup to the downbeat; bass, playing an active walking line, enters on the downbeat.
0:08	Verse 1 ("She's in some honky tonk tonight . . .")	Solo vocal (Parsons) enhanced with echo; steel guitar plays fills.
0:31	Chorus ("So close up the honky tonks . . .")	Harmonized vocals (add Hillman).
0:55	Solo steel guitar	Kleinow.
1:06	Solo electric guitar	Parsons, country finger-picking style.
1:18	Verse 2 ("I wish I had the power . . .")	
1:41	Chorus	
2:05	Coda	Repeats final line (hook) of chorus.

Like the Byrds, however, the Burritos never seemed to reach their full potential because of the constant personnel changes. After the release of their first album, *The Gilded Palace of Sin* (1969), Etheridge left to return to studio sessions, Hillman returned to the bass, and the group was joined by multi-instrumentalist Bernie Leadon. Parsons left after the release of their second album, *Burrito Deluxe* (1970), to pursue a solo career; as a soloist, Parsons released the albums *G.P.* (1972) and *Grievous Angel* (1973). While rehearsing in September 1973, Parsons died. Other members of the Burrito Brothers left to pursue their own careers: Leadon formed the Eagles, Kleinow went back to studio sessions, Clarke retired to Hawaii, and Hillman joined various bands including Manassas (with Stephen Stills) and the Souther-Hillman-Furay Band with songwriter J.D. Souther and Richie Furay (ex-Buffalo Springfield).

Creedence Clearwater Revival

Formed in 1965 in El Cerrito near San Francisco Bay by the Fogarty brothers John and Tom, the group was originally named the Golliwogs, supposedly in an attempt to cash in on the British Beat boom. John played lead guitar and sang the lead vocals, Tom was the rhythm guitarist. They were joined by friends Doug Clifford (drums) and Stu Cook (bass). After signing with Fantasy Records, the group began to develop their own sound which is a mixture of rhythm & blues and cajun music. In 1967 they persuaded their record label to let them change their name to Creedence Clearwater Revival. Their new sound and their look coincided with the up and coming psychedelic movement then happening in San Francisco.

CCR scored their first big hits with covers of two old rock 'n' roll classics: Dale Hawkins' *Susie Q.* and Screamin' Jay Hawkins' *I Put a Spell on You*, both released in 1968 on their debut self-titled album. Subsequent albums, produced, arranged, and primarily written by John Fogarty, further developed CCR's so-called "swamp rock" sound: *Bayou Country* and *Green River* (both released in 1969) each contained some of their classic songs including *Bad Moon Rising, Lodi, Green River, Born on the Bayou*, and especially *Proud Mary. Bad Moon Rising* is a clear example of the band's hybrid cajun/R & B roots and demonstrates their California-based country rock sound.

Listening Timeline 8-13

BAD MOON RISING (1969)
CREEDENCE CLEARWATER REVIVAL
from *Chronicle*
Strophic song form
Simple I, IV, V progression in D
Fantasy FCD-CCR2-2, 1991
2:16

0:00	Introduction	Solo electric guitar (J. Fogarty) joined by drums and bass to set the harmony and the tempo.
0:06	Verse 1	Solo male vocal (J. Fogarty) accompanied by band.
0:27	Chorus	
0:38	Verse 2	2nd guitar added with fingerpicked fills.
1:10	Solo	Lead guitar (J. Fogarty) using double stops plays half of the verse progression and the chorus progression. The guitar has a twangy Rockabilly kind of sound, with stiff rhythms and country-style finger picking in the 2nd guitar.

1:31	Verse 3	
1:52	Chorus	
2:03	Coda: repeat of chorus with final cadence.	

Creedence remained a fairly popular group in the early 1970s with albums like *Willy and the Poorboys* and *Cosmo's Factory*. After citing personal problems with the group, Tom Fogarty left to pursue his own career, forming the group the Blue Ridge Rangers. He died of complications from tuberculosis in 1990. CCR continued on for some time as a trio, finally disbanding in 1973 after releasing a live album from their European tour. John Fogarty has continued playing and recording, releasing the critically acclaimed album *Centerfield* in 1985.

The Eagles

The most commercially successful of the southern California country rock bands was the Eagles, formed in 1971 by Bernie Leadon (guitar, banjo, vocals), Glenn Frey (guitar, vocals), Don Henley (drums, vocals), and Randy Meisner (bass, vocals). Leadon had recently left The Flying Burrito Brothers and had teamed with Meisner (recently with Poco), Henley, and Frey playing backup for Linda Ronstadt on her album *Linda Ronstadt* (1972). The Eagles' first two albums, *The Eagles* (1972) and *Desperado* (1973), were received favorably by fans and critics as the successors of the country rock style. They added second lead guitarist Don Felder for their third album, *On the Border* (1974); the opening cut, *Already Gone* by Frey, demonstrates the country rock sound of the Eagles.

Listening Timeline 8-14

ALREADY GONE (1974)
THE EAGLES
from *On the Border*
Strophic song form
Simple I, V, IV progression in G
Asylum 7E-1004-2, 1974
4:13

0:00	Introduction	Solo lead guitar one (Felder) plays pickup measure, joined by drums, bass, and rhythm guitar playing stop time chords on downbeats; lead guitar two (Frey) enters measure 5 playing country-like riff counter to guitar one.
0:16	Verse 1 ("Well I heard some people talking . . .")	Solo lead vocal (Frey) band is soft, lead guitars drop to a rock 'n' roll rhythm accompaniment; note syncopated drum fills and bass runs between sung lines; bass plays decorated two-beat bass line; lead guitar one returns at end of last line to lead into chorus.
0:42	Chorus ("Well I'm already gone . . .")	Sung in three-part harmony; accompaniment from introduction with two lead guitars returns; bass line more active outlining chords.
1:08	Verse 2 ("The letter that you wrote me . . .")	Return to solo voice; lead guitar one more prominent; harmony vocal joins for last half of verse.
1:35	Chorus	Bass more animated.

2:01	Solo	Lead guitar one begins, answered by lead guitar two; solo continues featuring dueling call and response between the two guitars.
2:27	Verse 3 ("Well I know it wasn't you . . .")	Solo voice supported by background harmonized "oohs"; lead guitar fills on 2nd and 4th lines more melodic than rhythmic; last half of verse harmonized.
2:53	Chorus	Last line repeats first line (rather than "woo hoo hoo").
3:20	Coda	Extension of chorus, modulate to C; stop time chords (like intro) on the hook; repetition of hook with gradual fade over dueling lead guitars.

Riding on the success of *On the Border*, the Eagles recorded and released their best-selling album to that point, *One of These Nights*, in 1975. Convinced that the band was drifting more to a rock style, rather than country rock, Leadon left to pursue a solo career and was replaced by ex-James Gang lead guitarist Joe Walsh. This created a formidable triple lead guitar format with Felder and Frey and turned the Eagles to a definitely more rock-oriented sound. The resulting album was the group's biggest selling album, *Hotel California* (1976), which remained at the top of the *Billboard* album charts for most of 1976 and 1977, as did the title cut by Felder. The song *Hotel California* is a kind of ghost story set to music and demonstrates an elaborate, multi-textured overlaying of musical parts.

Listening Timeline 8-15

HOTEL CALIFORNIA (1976)
THE EAGLES
from *Hotel California*
Strophic song form
Original progression in B minor
Asylum 103-2, 1976
6:28

0:00	Introduction	Solo acoustic 12-string guitar plays progression accompanied by single bass notes on chord roots.
0:26		2nd time through progression, 6-string acoustic guitar plays countermelody to 12-string; 2nd rhythm guitar added, as is cymbals and distorted keyboard for effect; two drum beats over sustained guitar chord leads to verse.
0:51	Verse 1 ("On a dark desert highway . . .")	Solo vocal (Henley), 12-string continues picking pattern; bass plays more active root/fifth bass line under chords; electric rhythm guitar plays muted rhythm pattern.
1:18	Verse 2 ("There she stood in the doorway . . .")	Electric lead guitar added on long, sustained notes; hard-edged scale pattern leads to chorus.
1:44	Chorus ("Welcome to the Hotel California . . .")	Harmonized lead vocal; second lead electric guitar added.

2:10	Verse 3 ("Her mind is Tiffany twisted . . .")	Two electric guitars harmonize sustained notes of verse 2.
2:36	Verse 4 ("So I called up the Captain . . .")	Third lead electric guitar plays fills at end of sung lines; third phrase of verse ("and still those voices") is harmonized by second voice; revert back to solo voice for last line.
3:02	Chorus	Lead guitar fills louder, more distorted (feedback); note change in lyric of last line compared to first chorus; band sustains final chord to lead into last verses.
3:28	Verse 5 ("Mirrors on the ceiling . . .")	Solo 12-string guitar picking pattern (like intro) accompanied by bass and cymbals; drums and congas fill lead into final verse.
3:54	Verse 6 ("Last thing I remember . . .")	Full band returns; final statement of the "nightman" is punctuated by the full band, leading into solo section coda.
4:20	Coda/Solo	Begins with lead guitar one over rest of the band.
4:46		Lead guitar two enters with new melody.
5:12		Dual lead guitars, sometimes in harmony, sometimes call and response.
5:38		Harmonized syncopated pattern, accented by bass and drums.
6:04		Repeat harmonized syncopated pattern, bass returns to root/fifth pattern, gradual fade out.

The Eagles were out of the public light for the next several months, returning to the public eye with their next album, *The Long Run* (1979). By this time, Meisner had left to pursue a solo career and was replaced by Timothy B. Schmidt (who had, coincidentally, replaced Meisner in Poco when Meisner left to join the Eagles). After the release of a double-live album, the Eagles called it quits, claiming that they would get back together when hell froze over. During the 1980s, the various group members had successful careers, particularly Henley, Frey, and Walsh. In 1994, they reunited for a successful *Hell Freezes Over* tour and album.

Linda Ronstadt

One of the most successful women performers of the 1970s, Linda Ronstadt was born and raised in Tucson, Arizona. She moved to Los Angeles in 1964 to begin a singing career, gradually becoming known in the folk rock circle in LA. She had a minor hit in 1967 with the song *Different Drum*, composed by ex-Monkee Mike Nesmith and recorded with her group the Stone Poneys. Ronstadt began her country rock career in earnest with the albums *Hand Sown . . . Home Grown* (1969) and *Silk Purse* (1970), and achieved some success with her self-titled album (1971) on which she was accompanied by the future Eagles. She hit cross over success with her 1974 album *Don't Cry Now*, which featured the country classic *Silver Threads and Golden Needles*.

Listening Timeline 8-16

SILVER THREADS AND GOLDEN NEEDLES
LINDA RONSTADT
from *Greatest Hits*
Strophic song form
Simple I, IV, V progression in E-flat
Asylum 106-2, 1976
2:22

0:00	Introduction	Band (bass, guitars, drums) play root/fifth drone under fiddle.
0:06	Verse 1 ("I don't want your lonely mansion . . .")	Solo lead vocal accompanied by country-style band; 2nd half of verse is harmonized by male vocalist.
0:35	Chorus ("Silver threads and golden needles . . .")	Lead vocal is harmonized; steel guitar enters; middle phrases are sung as solo with backing "oohs"; harmonized lead returns for hook.
1:04	Solo	Fiddle (Gib Gilbeau);
1:20		Steel guitar (Ed Black).
1:35	Chorus	Fiddle more active.
2:05	Coda	Repeats hook line for finish.

Ronstadt's big break into the rock arena came in 1975 with the release of her album *Heart Like a Wheel*, produced by ex-British beat singer Peter Asher (Peter and Gordon). The big hit from this album was the song *You're No Good*. In the late 1970s, Ronstadt continued her role as a dominant female rock artist with covers of various 1950s and 1960s rock 'n' roll songs, including *It's So Easy* and *That'll Be the Day* (both by Buddy Holly), *Back in the USA* (Chuck Berry), *Blue Bayou* (Roy Orbison), *Heatwave* (Martha and the Vandellas), and *Hurt So Bad* (Little Anthony and the Imperials). In the 1980s she teamed with composer/arranger Nelson Riddle for three albums of jazz/pop standards composed by George Gershwin, Rodgers and Hart, and Irving Berlin. She also appeared in stage and film productions of Gilbert and Sullivan's *Pirates of Penzance*. In the late 1980s and 1990s, Ronstadt returned to her country rock roots, recording an album with Emmylou Harris and Dolly Parton (1987), and she recorded an album of Mexican folk songs in tribute to her father (*Canciones de mi padre*, 1988). She also collaborated on recordings with soul artists James Ingram and Aaron Neville. She has been out of the public limelight since 1994.

Southern Rock

Southern rock is a style of rock music that began in the late 1960s and reached a peak in the mid 1970s. Southern rock bands exhibit characteristic traits that are found in blues, Memphis-based rock and roll (rockabilly), and country music:

Blues: Blues progressions (esp. 12-bar blues, but not limited to that)
Delta slide guitar style
Bent notes on guitar
Blues vocal inflections

Country: Two-beat country bass (root-fifth)
Country style drum beat
Country string bands: acoustic guitars, steel guitars, fiddles, banjos
Country singing styles (nasally vocal, accent)

Rock 'n' roll: Hard driving rhythms
Twangy or trebly guitar sound
Loud electric sound
Electronic distortion
Extremely fast tempos

Not every Southern rock band exhibits all of these characteristics all the time and in fact most bands exhibit their individual tendencies by incorporating some of these characteristics in varying degrees and mixtures.

Although each Southern band has its own individual sound and style, there are some general similarities that exist in the style as a whole:

+ Bands favor two and sometimes three lead guitarists.
+ All lead guitarists have virtuosic abilities (rock characteristic).
+ Lead guitarists favor playing syncopated licks in unison or harmony at extremely fast tempos:

Example 8-1

Southern rock guitar syncopated lick.
Guitar

+ Prominent Southern accent on vocals.
+ Vocal harmonies are in tight or close harmony in thirds (country and rockabilly trait).
+ Rhythm sections tend to be more country-oriented than rock-oriented.
+ Many songs are narratives, ballads (country and blues trait).
+ The music is strongly aggressive.
+ Often display attitudes of strong Southern (regional) pride and patriotism (national).

Again, these are general style characteristics and not every Southern band exhibits each of these qualities. But it is an organizational beginning to the style known as Southern rock music. The examples we are going to hear represent only a few of the better known Southern rock bands. Note that the examples span a spectrum of musical style from the bands that are most strongly blues-oriented to those that are most strongly country-oriented.

Allman Brothers Band

The Allman Brothers Band, begun by Duane and Gregg Allman in 1969, is considered by many to be the original Southern rock band. The band consisted of two lead guitars (Duane Allman and Dickey Betts), keyboards

(Gregg Allman), bass (Berry Oakley), and two drummers (Jaimoe Johanny Johanson and Butch Trucks). The use of both dual lead guitars and dual drummers created a full, thick-textured sound that was unique to the Allman Brothers Band. *Statesboro Blues*, originally released on the album *Live at the Fillmore East*, illustrates the Delta blues and soul background of the band. The song features some great and intricate guitar playing between Allman and Betts, trading solos and alternating phrases, that is similar to the type of guitar work Allman had recently recorded with Eric Clapton for the *Layla* sessions.

Listening Timeline 8-17

STATESBORO BLUES (1971)
THE ALLMAN BROTHERS BAND
from *Live at the Fillmore East*
Strophic song form
12-bar blues progression in D
Capricorn 314 531 260-2, 1971
4:17

0:07	Introduction	Call and response between full band and solo lead slide guitar (Duane); one run through the progression as Duane solos.
0:47	Verse 1 ("Wake up mama . . .")	Solo lead vocal (Gregg) with slide guitar fills.
1:10	Verse 2 ("I woke up this morning . . .")	
1:32	Solo	Slide guitar (Duane) plays twice through 12-bar progression; melodic range expands as solo progresses.
2:18	Verse 3 ("Well my mama died and left me . . .")	Departure from previous verse melodies, featuring stop time in the band for the first line of this verse, then blues structure resumes.
2:40	Solo	Electric guitar (Betts) plays twice through 12-bar progression; though melodic range expands as solo progresses, Betts makes much use of repeated notes.
3:26	Verse 4 ("Well I love that woman")	Vocal style turns to shout style singing.
3:48	Verse 1 repeated	Drums louder, more active; much use of syncopation in fills.

Shortly after *Live at the Fillmore* album was recorded, Duane Allman was killed in a motorcycle accident in Macon, Georgia. The band had already laid down some tracks for their next album, *Eat a Peach*, with Duane; this album was also a big seller for the group. Ironically, the following year after Duane's death, bassist Berry Oakley was also killed in a motorcycle accident in Macon. As the group recuperated from the loss of Duane and Berry, Gregg Allman switched over to sometimes lead guitar so as to keep the dual lead guitar sound the band had established for themselves on their first three albums. The band hired keyboardist Chuck Leavell and bassist Lamar Williams to round out the group. Guitarist Dickey Betts took on a more active role in the direction of the band and resulting in the songs *Ramblin' Man* and *Jessica* from the album *Brothers and Sisters* (1973).

The Allman Brothers Band went through a lot of changes in the rest of the decade; Gregg Allman went solo for a couple of albums, Betts

Folk and Related Styles **167**

formed a new group, Great Southern, and Leavell, Williams and Johanson formed the jazz rock group Sea Level. They have since reunited and broken apart several times, sometimes coming together for tours in the late 1990s.

ZZ Top

Texas rockers ZZ Top are a blues-based band with hard-driving rock sensibilities. The group was formed in Houston, Texas in the early 1970s by guitarist Billy Gibbons, bassist Dusty Hill, and drummer Frank Beard (Gibbons typically overdubbed extra guitar parts). The group's first three albums—*First Album* (1971), *Rio Grande Mud* (1972), and *Tres Hombres* (1973)—display ZZ Top's background in delta blues and east Texas blues. A good example of their blues rock style is the song *La Grange* from the album *Tres Hombres*. *La Grange*, which celebrates a well-known east Texas house of ill repute, is characterized by its rhythm and its harmonic structure. The rhythm, a fast-paced shuffle or boogie rhythm, is derived from the sound of blues singer John Lee Hooker, in particular Hooker's 1948 classic *Boogie Chillun*. The harmonic structure is based on a modal progression in A, however, the chords utilize only the roots and fifths of each chord: A and E, C and G, D and A. The chords are palm-muted to help emphasize the boogie rhythm.

Listening Timeline 8-18

LA GRANGE (1973)
ZZ TOP
from *Tres Hombres*
Strophic song form
Modal progression in A
Warner Bros. 3270-2, 1973
3:47

0:00	Introduction	Solo muted guitar with drummer keeping rhythm on rim of snare drum.
0:08	Verse 1 ("Rumors spreading 'round . . .")	Low bass solo vocal; Loud drum fill sets up first interlude.
0:35	Interlude 1	Increase in volume, guitar slightly distorted, bass enters.
0:46	Verse 2 ("Well I hear it's fine . . .")	Vocal becomes more shout-like; verse ends with drum fill.
1:11	Solo	Key modulates to C; original rhythm retained by rhythm guitar, bass, and drums under lead solo (Gibbons).
1:58	Interlude 2	Break away from the boogie rhythm; lead guitar plays syncopated descending chromatic riff over stop time chords;
2:11		Harmony modulates back to original A modality, and the sound returns to the feel of the intro.
2:23	Solo	Solo resumes in original A modal progression after drum fill; boogie rhythm continues under solo lead; gradually fades.

After the release of their albums *Fandango!* (1974), which had a huge radio hit with *Tush*, and *Tejas* (1976), ZZ Top took a break from touring and recording for three years. They returned full force in 1979 with the album *Deguello* and, changing their image and releasing two major videos

(*Legs* and *Sharp Dressed Man*) from the album *Eliminator* (1983). They were riding high throughout the 1980s, but have since dropped from view.

Lynyrd Skynyrd

Lynyrd Skynyrd formed in the early 1970s in Jacksonville, Florida. Skynyrd is an excellent representation of a Southern hard rocking bar band—they were discovered by producer Al Kooper playing in bars in the South and they never really lost that bar band edge in their sound. The band also featured three lead guitarists in Ed King, Gary Rossington, and Allen Collins as well as the distinctive voice of lead singer Ronnie Van Zant. Their first album, *Pronounced leh-nerd skin-nerd*, ended with *Free Bird* which the band had written in memory of Duane Allman. *Free Bird* is in two distinct sections: the first section is sung and a slow almost ballad-like delivery—the organ playing gives the song a kind of reverential attitude. The second section is an improvisatory coda that highlights the abilities of the three guitarists, sometimes playing in unison, sometimes in harmony, and sometimes trading licks between themselves. The energetic driving build up, propelled by the drums and the bass, reaches a climax before the final fade out of the track. This driving build up was incredibly effective in live shows to drive the audience to a wild frenzy, as can be heard on the album *One More From the Road* and it is for this reason that the band used it consistently as their closing number.

Listening Timeline 8-19

FREE BIRD (1974)
LYNYRD SKYNYRD
from (*pronounced leh-nerd skin-nerd*)
Strophic song form with extended coda
Original progression in G (verses) and G blues (coda)
MCA MCAD-11534, 1974
9:04

0:00	Introduction	Slow tempo, solo organ joined by piano and strummed acoustic guitar (bar 2), drums, bass, and electric guitar (bar 5).
0:35		Slide solo guitar enters bar 9.
1:09	Verse 1 ("If I leave here tomorrow . . .")	Solo vocal; slide guitar continues as countermelody; band becomes louder, more active at end of verse.
2:36	Instrumental interlude	Like second part of introduction.
3:10	Verse 2 ("Bye bye, it's been a sweet love . . .")	
3:41		Strings enter on second half of verse.
4:15	Coda	Begins with extension of last line of verse, band becomes gradually more active.
4:39		At the word "change" Van Zandt oscillates his vocal pitch, kicking the band into double-time.
4:56	Solos	Harmony changes to G blues (G, B-flat, C), repeated continuously under solos; lead guitar one (Collins) begins in high range, plays many repeated notes and syncopated riffs.
5:40		Joined by lead guitar two (Rossington) in a lower range.

Folk and Related Styles **169**

6:32	Both guitarists play fast, repetitive riffs in harmony as band plays chords in stop time.
6:58	Regular rhythm returns, lead guitars trade licks.
7:23	Drums, bass propel rhythm forward with repetitive, driving 16th-notes, joined by lead guitars.
8:13	Return of original coda rhythm as all instruments the climax of their parts.
8:26	Lead guitars continue to trade licks as sound gradually fades out.

After the deaths of singer Van Zant, guitarist Steve Gaines (who had replaced King), and backup singer Cassie Gaines in a 1977 plane crash, Skynyrd reformed as the Rossington-Collins Band with the relatively same sound as Skynyrd. Rossington and Collins eventually reformed Lynyrd Skynyrd and they re-recorded *Free Bird* without vocals. Skynyrd is also important for the Southern bands they inspired, such as Molly Hatchet and 38 Special. Skynyrd has had a run of bad luck with various members having substance abuse problems (which they have mostly cleared up); Collins died from respiratory failure in 1990. The band has continued to tour with Johnny Van Zant (Ronnie's younger brother and founder of the group 38 Special) as the front man; they have also recently recruited guitarist Rickey Medlocke (from Blackfoot) and Hughie Thomasson (from the Outlaws) as lead guitarists.

The Outlaws

The Outlaws is another representative Southern rock band with leanings toward more of a country feel while still possessing a hard-driving rock sound. The band at the high point of their career (mid-1970s) consisted of two lead guitarists in Hughie Thomasson and Billy Jones, with an occasional third lead guitar from vocalist Henry Paul. Thomasson in particular demonstrated a great deal of talent and facility on the standard country string instruments—acoustic guitar, banjo, and a very country-influenced electric guitar style. Their first album, *The Outlaws* (1975), did very well and contained two major hits for the band, *Green Grass and High Tides* and *There Goes Another Love Song*. Based on the popularity of these songs, the Outlaws began appearing as the warmup band for a variety of groups including the Who and the Rolling Stones as well as for fellow southern rockers Lynyrd Skynyrd, the Marshall Tucker Band, and the Charlie Daniels Band. By the time of the release of their third album, *Hurry Sundown* (1977), the Outlaws had become a headline act.

The title cut of the album, *Hurry Sundown*, is a narrative (story) song. The instrumental solos, and the introduction and coda, feature the harmonized guitars of Thomasson and Jones against a country-oriented rhythm section.

0:00	Introduction	Dual lead guitars supported by full band.

Listening Timeline 8-20

HURRY SUNDOWN (1977)
THE OUTLAWS
from *Best of the Outlaws*
Strophic song form
Original progression in E minor
Arista 07822-18936-2, 1977
4:02

Time	Section	Description
0:18	Verse 1 ("Gypsies danced around the campfire . . .")	Solo lead vocal, band is subdued in the background.
0:36	Interlude	Lead guitar two, leads into verse 2.
0:43	Verse 2 ("She had hair as black as darkness . . .")	
1:03	Chorus ("Ooh, ooh Hurry Sundown . . .")	3-part harmonized vocal over lead vocal; rhythm becomes more country-like in drums and bass.
1:19	Solo	Lead guitar one plays over accompaniment, smooth sound, not distorted, but with echo.
1:35		Lead guitar two plays next part of solo, sound is more distorted, overdriving amplifier, but no echo.
1:54	Chorus	
2:08	Verse 3 ("Silver devils in his holsters . . .")	2-part harmonized lead vocals.
2:27	Interlude	Lead guitar two.
2:34	Verse 1 repeated	Return of solo lead vocal.
2:54	Chorus	
3:11	Coda	Lead guitar one plays joined by lead guitar two; return of intro, ending on a sustained E major chord.

The Outlaws went through a number of personnel changes in the 1980s and 1990s though during this time they released several excellent and well-received albums, including *Ghost Riders* (1980) and *Diablo Canyon* (1994). The group disbanded in 1994 and guitarist Hughie Thomasson joined Lynyrd Skynyrd.

The Marshall Tucker Band

The Marshall Tucker Band began in 1972 in Spartanburg, South Carolina with brothers Toy and Tommy Caldwell and friends; they took their name from a blind piano tuner with whom they used to share rehearsal space.[7] Marshall Tucker is even more country-based than the Outlaws as can be heard on their first top forty single *Fire on the Mountain*. *Fire on the Mountain* is a narrative song, very ballad like in its presentation. The addition of Toy Caldwell's steel guitar and a guest fiddle give the song a distinct country flavor while the addition of the flute solo that arises from the steel guitar line is an interesting addition to both the country and rock sounds of the band.

Listening Timeline 8-21

FIRE ON THE MOUNTAIN (1975)
THE MARSHALL TUCKER BAND
from *Greatest Hits*
Strophic song form
Original progression in E minor (verse) and G (chorus)
AJK Music A 799-2, 1978
3:53

Time	Section	Description
0:00	Introduction	Sustained chords in acoustic guitar and rolls on cymbals accompany the steel guitar in a slow, free-metric style.
0:14		Acoustic guitar plays descending line, kicking the band into tempo; steel guitar continues solo.

Folk and Related Styles

0:35	Verse 1 ("Took my family from my Carolina home . . .")	Solo lead vocal, band subdued in the background.
0:54	Chorus ("Fire on the mountain . . .")	Lead vocal is harmonized.
1:02	Interlude	Like last part of the introduction.
1:12	Verse 2 ("We were digging and sifting . . .")	Solo lead vocal, steel guitar more prominent.
1:31	Chorus	
1:39	Interlude	
1:48	Solo	Steel guitar (Toy Caldwell) over chorus progression.
2:07		Flute (Jerry Eubanks) over verse progression.
2:26	Verse 3 ("Dance hall girls . . .")	
2:45	Chorus	
2:53	Interlude	
3:02	Verse 4 ("Now my widow . . .")	Band plays sustained chords on downbeats, steel and acoustic guitars play fills.
3:22	Chorus	Regular tempo returns; fiddle plays fill at end of chorus leading to repeat of chorus.
3:32	Repeat chorus	
3:41	Coda	Free meter with repetition of last line of chorus.

The Marshall Tucker Band was primarily a concert and album band rather than a hit single band; their only top forty singles in the 1970s were *Fire on the Mountain* and *Heard It in a Love Song* (1977) which actually fared much better on the country charts than on the popular music charts. In 1980, bassist Tommy Caldwell was seriously injured when his car overturned in Spartanburg; despite emergency surgery, he died six days later. The Marshall Tucker Band continued but could not regain the momentum they had in the late 1970s; they disbanded in 1984, though singer Doug Gray and woodwind player Jerry Eubanks bought the legal rights to the name Marshall Tucker Band and have continued performing and recording. Toy Caldwell took a brief hiatus from music then returned to performing and songwriting. He established a new band, the Toy Caldwell Band, in 1993 but just weeks before the band was going to begin a major tour, Toy Caldwell died of respiratory failure.

The Charlie Daniels Band

Of all the Southern rock bands discussed, the Charlie Daniels Band has the closest affinity to country music while still maintaining a relationship with rock and blues styles. Leader Daniels is a fascinatingly adept musician who is equally at home on fiddle, electric guitar, acoustic guitar, and slide guitar as well as vocals. He began his career playing in various blue grass bands in North Carolina before moving to Nashville in the mid 1960s to become a session player. As a session player, Daniels appears on various country albums as well as Bob Dylan's *Nashville Skyline* and *Self-Portrait*. *The South's Gonna Do It* is a good demonstration of Daniels' country-based sound coupled with a boogie blues beat. The song lyrics are some of the best examples of regional pride, with Daniels not only naming various Southern bands and the cities from which they hail, but also employing several southern musical styles (blues, boogie woogie, country, and honky tonk).

Listening Timeline 8-22

THE SOUTH'S GONNA DO IT (1975)
THE CHARLIE DANIELS BAND
from *Super Hits*
Strophic song form
12-bar blues progression in A
Epic EK 64182, 1994
3:57

Time	Section	Description
0:00	Introduction	Solo fiddle (Daniels) plays against band playing stop time chords.
0:12		Rhythm and meter kick in at measure 4 on IV chord.
0:23	Verse 1 ("Well the train to Grinderswitch . . .")	Lead vocal (Daniels) against boogie woogie accompaniment.
0:41	Chorus ("So gather 'round . . .")	
0:58	Interlude	Fiddle and lead guitar in unison lead to solo section.
1:04	Solos	Lead guitar (Barry Barnes) plays twice through progression.
1:34		Piano (Joel "Taz" diGregorio) plays twice through progression.
2:08	Verse 2 ("Elvin Bishop's sittin' on a bale of hay . . .")	
2:26	Chorus	
2:43	Solo	Fiddle (Daniels) plays twice through progression.
3:19	Coda	Riff pattern played by guitar and fiddle, twice through the progression—1st time in unison, 2nd time guitar harmonizes the fiddle part.
3:51		Concluding formula played by guitar and fiddle in unison.

The Charlie Daniels Band over the years have had several major hits in both the pop and the country charts. Daniels has remained a major force in southern music, rock and country, with his recordings and producing abilities. His Volunteer Jam is still a major annual event, drawing crowds from all over the world to Murfreesboro, Tennessee. He has also recorded gospel albums; his 1994 release *The Door* was given the Dove Award by the Gospel Music Association.

The bands discussed in this section have barely scratched the surface of the legacy of southern rock. Several bands that are considered some of the originators of southern rock, such as Grinderswitch, the Atlanta Rhythm Section, and Wet Willie, all have their place in the history of the style. Several band members of the groups discussed have also formed new outfits, such as Gov't Mule (Warren Haynes and Allen Woody from the Allman Brothers Band) and Great Southern (headed by Brother Dickie Betts). There are many new bands that are currently gaining popularity, including the Derek Trucks Band, OKB, and Widespread Panic. Southern rock is still alive and going strong.

Endnotes

1. Charles Brown, *The Art of Rock and Roll*, 3rd edition. Englewood Cliffs, NJ: Prentice-Hall, Inc., 1992, p. 150.
2. Robert Shelton, *No Direction Home: The Life and Music of Bob Dylan* (New York: Da Capo Press, 1986), pp. 49–50. Other sources that have been claimed for his name include his mother's maiden name (which was actually Stone) and that he was from a town called Dillon, Oklahoma. At the University of Minnesota, he was known as "Bob Dillon"; after he began to be known on the folk circuit in New York, he began spelling his name "Dylan."
3. Hammond was a particularly astute judge of musical talent. Some of his other discoveries for Columbia include Bessie Smith, Count Basie, Billie Holiday, Lester Young, Charlie Christian, Pete Seeger, Aretha Franklin, and Bruce Springsteen.
4. Nat Hentoff, notes for *The Freewheelin' Bob Dylan* (Columbia CK 8786, 1963), p. 5.
5. Bob Spitz, *Dylan: A Biography* (New York: W.W. Norton and Company, 1989), pp. 334–343.
6. Rob Bowman, liner notes for The Band, *Music from Big Pink*. Capitol 72435-25390-2-4, 2000, p. 11.
7. Scott Stanton, *The Tombstone Tourist: Musicians* (Portland, OR: 3T Publishing, 1998), p. 38.

9 The 1970s—Out with the Old—In with the New

Hard Rock

Blues Rock—Led Zeppelin: Dominators of the 1970s

Led Zeppelin was the definitive blues based hard rock band. It wasn't just their crushingly loud interpretation of the blues—it was how they incorporated mythology, mysticism, and a variety of other genres (most notably world music and British folk)—into their sound. Led Zeppelin had mystique. They rarely gave interviews, since the music press detested the band. Consequently, the only connection the audience had with the band was through the records and the concerts. More than any other band, Led Zeppelin established the concept of album-oriented rock, refusing to release popular songs from their albums as singles. In doing so, they established the dominant format for heavy metal, as well as the genre's actual sound.

Led Zeppelin formed out of the ashes of the Yardbirds. Jimmy Page had joined the band in its final days, playing a pivotal role on their final album, 1967's *Little Games*, which also featured string arrangements from John Paul Jones. During 1967, the Yardbirds were fairly inactive. While the Yardbirds decided their future, Page returned to session work in 1967. In the spring of 1968, he played on Jones' arrangement of Donovan's *Hurdy Gurdy Man*. During the sessions, Jones requested to be part of any future project Page would develop. Page would have to assemble a band sooner than he had planned. In the summer of 1968, the Yardbirds' Keith Relf and James McCarty left the band, leaving Page and bassist Chris Dreja with the rights to the name, as well as the obligation of fulfilling an upcoming fall tour. Page set out to find a replacement vocalist and drummer. Page contacted Robert Plant, who was singing with a band called Hobbstweedle.

After hearing him sing, Page asked Plant to join the band in August of 1968. John Paul Jones joined the group as its bassist. Plant recommended that Page hire John Bonham, the drummer for Plant's old band, the Band of Joy. By September, Bonham agreed to join the band. Performing under the name the New Yardbirds, the band fulfilled the Yardbirds' previously booked engagements in late September 1968. The following month, they recorded their debut album in just under 30 hours. Also in October, the group switched their name to Led Zeppelin. The band secured a contract with Atlantic Records in the United States before the end of the year.

That in itself is a stroke of music business genius. Atlantic Records had built a reputation as a predominantly black music record label, giving rise to such artists as Aretha Franklin. Atlantic Records expanded their reach in the music industry tremendously with Led Zeppelin in the fold. Certainly it was a bit of a business gamble, for who could know that Led Zeppelin would become the prime dominating force in rock music throughout the 1970s? This is in the same light as Sun Records selling Elvis Presley to RCA for forty thousand dollars just to see RCA see a return on their investment in the neighborhood of ten million records sold in just that first year that Elvis was with RCA. Atlantic records signing Led Zeppelin was probably one of the most daring and rewarding music business ventures of any record label in the whole history of rock music.

Early in 1969, Led Zeppelin set out on their first American tour, which helped set the stage for the January release of their eponymous debut album. Two months after its release, Led Zeppelin had climbed into the U.S. Top Ten. Throughout 1969, the band toured relentlessly, playing dates in America and England. While they were on the road, they recorded their second album, *Led Zeppelin II*, which was released in October of 1969. Like its predecessor, *Led Zeppelin II* was an immediate hit, topping the American charts two months after its release and spending seven weeks at number one.

The album helped establish Led Zeppelin as an international concert attraction, and for the next year, the group continued to tour relentlessly. Led Zeppelin's sound began to deepen with *Led Zeppelin III*. Released in October of 1970, the album featured an overt British folk influence. The group's infatuation with folk and mythology would reach a fruition on the group's untitled fourth album, which was released in November of 1971. *Led Zeppelin IV* was the band's most musically diverse effort to date, featuring everything from the crunching rock of *Black Dog* to the folk of *The Battle of Evermore*, as well as *Stairway to Heaven*, which found the bridge between the two genres.

Stairway to Heaven was an immediate radio hit, eventually becoming the most played song in the history of album-oriented radio; the song was never released as a single. Despite the fact that the album never reached number one in America, *Led Zeppelin IV* was their biggest album ever, selling well over 16 million copies over the next two and a half decades. Again, another stroke of genius in the music business. They knew they had a hit song with *Stairway*, and they knew that a single release of the song would take away from the album sales. So by not releasing the song as a single, album sales on *Led Zeppelin IV* remained brisk and lucrative, even so still today.

Led Zeppelin did tour to support both *Led Zeppelin III* and *Led Zeppelin IV*, but they played fewer shows than they did on their previous tours. Instead, they concentrated on only playing larger venues. After completing their 1972 tour, the band retreated from the spotlight and recorded their fifth album. Released in the spring of 1973, *Houses of the Holy* continued the band's musical experimentation, featuring touches of funk and reggae among their trademark heavy metal rock and folk.

The success of *Houses of the Holy* set the stage for a record-breaking American tour. Throughout their 1973 tour, Led Zeppelin broke box-office records—most of which were previously held by the Beatles—across America. The group's concert at Madison Square Garden in July was filmed for use in the feature film *The Song Remains the Same*, which was released three years later.

After their 1973 tour, Led Zeppelin spent a quiet year during 1974, releasing no new material and performing no concerts. They did, however, establish their own record label, Swan Song, which released all of Led Zeppelin's subsequent albums. *Physical Graffiti*, a double album released in February of 1975, was the band's first release on Swan Song. The album was an immediate success, topping the charts in both America and England. Led Zeppelin launched a large American tour in 1975, but it came to a halt when Robert Plant and his wife suffered a serious car crash while vacationing in Greece. The tour was cancelled, and Plant spent the rest of the year recuperating from the accident.

Led Zeppelin returned to action in the spring of 1976 with *Presence*. Although the album debuted at number one in both America and England, the reviews for the album were lukewarm, as was the reception to the live concert film *The Song Remains the Same*, which appeared in the fall of 1976. The band finally returned to tour America in the spring of 1977. A couple of months into the tour, Plant's six-year-old son Karac died of a stomach infection. Led Zeppelin immediately cancelled the tour and offered no word whether or not it would be rescheduled, causing not only widespread speculation about the band's future, but wild speculations about cult activity and their attraction to mysticism.

For a while, it did appear that Led Zeppelin was finished. Robert Plant spent the latter half of 1977 and the better part of 1978 in seclusion. But by then, the large venue rock scene was in full bloom, so rock fans barely noticed the absence, assuming that the band would certainly be back on stage sooner or later. Strangely enough though, other changes were brewing in music that would soon wipe the large, theatrical heavy metal sound and shows into the backdrop of the whole rock music landscape. Punk rock, a lashing out at the overly flamboyant arena rock environment, was gaining a strong foothold, and inner city break dancing hip hoppers and rappers were making their presence felt. As well, disco was merging with punk energy in the late 1970s, creating the first of the new wave bands like Blondie. The landscape of rock music was expanding faster than most people, even record industry executives, could keep track of. Bands that were on top of the world just a year or two earlier, were finding the musical shifts happening at a pace that few could keep up with. It seemed that every year there was a new style, new breed of rock musician, new venues and smaller halls, and shifts in all these elements as new people rushed to the scene. The late 1970s was probably one of the most uncertain and fast changing times in American music, and Led Zeppelin, as staunch and stable a rock band that ever was, was also feeling the shifts in society, culture, and fickle musical tastes.

The group didn't begin work on a new album until late in the summer of 1978, when they began recording at ABBA's Polar studios in Sweden. A year later, the band played a short European tour, performing in Switzerland, Germany, Holland, Belgium, and Austria. In August of 1979, Led Zeppelin played two large concerts at Knebworth; the shows would be their last English performances.

In Through the Out Door, the band's much-delayed eighth studio album, was finally released in September of 1979. But by then, the musical landscape was so utterly changed from just a couple of years earlier, Led Zeppelin was already seen as classic rock, a new category describing the arena and festival big show rock of the late 1960s and 1970s.

Led Zeppelin was, however, Led Zeppelin. The album entered the charts at number one in both America and England. In May of 1980, Led Zeppelin embarked on their final European tour. In September, Led Zeppelin began rehearsing at Jimmy Page's house in preparation for an American tour. On September 25, John Bonham was found dead in his bed—following an all-day drinking binge. In December of 1980, Led Zeppelin announced they were disbanding, since they could not continue without Bonham.

In 1994, Jimmy Page and Robert Plant reunited to record a segment for *MTV Unplugged*, which was released as *Unledded* in the fall of 1994. Although the album went platinum, the sales were disappointing considering the anticipation of a Zeppelin reunion. The following year, Page and Plant embarked on a successful international tour, which eventually led to an all new studio recording in 1998. The duo still perform and record, but have shunned the "Led Zeppelin" image and bombast. They have both evolved quite a bit musically right on up to today and continue to do so—Page working with numerous younger bands, and Plant exploring various aspects of world music.

Heavy Metal

Black Sabbath

Black Sabbath has been so influential in the development of heavy metal rock music as to be a defining force in the style.

Once Led Zeppelin kicked open the door to heavy metal, in came some of the most defining artists in the development of the genre as a driving force in popular music. No band defined the whole style, attitude, theatrics and musical vocabulary as Black Sabbath. Their influence is felt today in heavy metal, death metal, speed metal, and any other kind of metal more than any band to come out of the genre. They took the foundations that Hendrix and Led Zeppelin laid down, transformed it with theatrics with a "dark side" theme, and simply changed the entire landscape of the genre. All the bombastically dark heavy metal, as well as the varied offshoots we see today such as goth (oh those poor children . . . won't someone give them something to eat and tell them that living isn't so bad?), industrial, or any musical style and scene that plays up the whole tortured, dark hearted but tough, "we're gonna' eat your children" theatrics in their music can thank one band for opening that dark dungeon door.

The group took the blues-rock sound of late 1960s acts like Cream, Jimi Hendrix, Led Zeppelin, and the one-hit wonder Iron Butterfly to its logical conclusion, slowing the tempo, emphasizing the bass, and, most importantly for our musical discussion, shining the spotlight most dominantly on searing guitar solos and howled vocals full of lyrics expressing mental anguish and dark fantasies. If their predecessors clearly came out of an electrified blues tradition, Black Sabbath took that tradition, dressed it in theatrics based on a theme and guided the course of this genre right up to today.

The group was formed by four teenage friends from Aston, near Birmingham, England: Anthony "Tony" Iommi, guitar; William "Bill" Ward, drums; John "Ozzy" Osbourne, vocals; and Terence "Geezer" Butler, bass. They originally called their band Polka Tulk, later renaming themselves

Earth, and they played extensively in Europe. In early 1969, they decided to change their name again when they found that they were being mistaken for another group called Earth. Butler had written a song that took its title from a novel by occult writer Dennis Wheatley, *Black Sabbath*, and the group adopted it as their name as well. As they attracted attention for their live performances, record labels showed interest, and they were signed to Phillips Records in 1969. In January 1970, the Phillips subsidiary Fontana released their debut single, *Evil Woman (Don't Play Your Games With Me)*, a cover of a song that had just become a United States hit for Crow; it did not chart. The following month, a different Phillips subsidiary, Vertigo, released Black Sabbath's self-titled debut album, which reached the U.K. Top Ten. Though it was a less immediate success in the United States—where the band's recordings were licensed to Warner Bros. Records and appeared in May 1970—the LP broke into the American charts in August, reaching the Top 40, remaining in the charts over a year, and selling a million copies.

As exemplified by the diversity found in all the musical styles and sounds available by the time rock music finds itself at Woodstock, the 1960s proved without a doubt that many different aspects of popular music could be integrated into an eclectic style with broad appeal. The Beatles were as likely to perform an acoustic ballad as a hard rocker or R&B-influenced tune. The array of music styles and sounds at the Monterey Pop Festival or Woodstock was, beyond any doubt, a vastly rich gumbo of all the musical roots that went into rock music to that point. The audience had shown that it would accept any creative adaptation and interpretation.

Though the musical press at the time didn't put a whole lot of support behind an act like Black Sabbath, the band had discovered a new audience eager for its uncompromising approach. Black Sabbath quickly followed its debut album with a second album, *Paranoid*, in September 1970. This album is not only responsible for luring droves of teens to music stores to buy guitars and fuzz boxes, but drew in a young fan base seeking something new, fresh sounding, and certainly an irritant to parents, which is what a teenager wants to do anyway. Remember, this is the peak time of the generation gap, and a popular saying was "If your parents hate it, then it must be good." Black Sabbath, and particularly the *Paranoid* album, certainly gave parents something to hate, or at the very least worry about.

Master of Reality, their third album, followed in August 1971, reaching the Top Ten on both sides of the Atlantic and selling over a million copies. For *Sabbath Bloody Sabbath* (November 1973), the band brought in prog rocker and Yes keyboard player Rick Wakeman, signaling a slight change in musical direction; it was Black Sabbath's fifth straight Top Ten hit and million-seller. In July 1975, with their sixth album, *Sabotage*, they were welcomed back at home, but in the United States the musical climate had changed.

By the mid-1970s, the album oriented, big theatrical show bands were finding themselves the target of a new generation of musicians, tired of the extravagant environment of arena rock, but just as aggressive musically, if not more so—the punks. The mainstream pop market was going in a direction of less heavy, aggressive music, while the underground music world was driving into harder and darker, in-your-face political directions. Black Sabbath and the legions of new heavy metal bands who emulated them were caught in the middle of all this. Some adapted to the pop market, merging it with glam and giving rise to an army of pretty boy hair metal bands. Some went in the other direction, taking heavy metal into ever darker, slower, more aggressive death metal. Some took heavy metal in directions that had nothing to do with either selling out to the pop mainstream or singing low odes to darkness dirges—the speed metal bands. The notable aspect of what Black Sabbath started, and heavy metal as a genre, is that while heavy metal may have had its ups and downs, it's still there, and it's still branching off in different directions. It adapts and incorporates new styles—mostly from underground musical genres, such as punk and industrial or anything with an edge to it. It's real. And it evolves. So whether you are fan of heavy metal or not, there's no denying that there's an attraction to it when each new generation hits that rebellious youth phase of teenagedom.

Punk Rock

Iggy Pop—Birth of a True Punk

Iggy Pop was the first. Sure, there were other predecessors that had the punk sound, but Iggy Pop was the guy who put the anger and politics and attitude to it all that so many bands to follow would incorporate. Iggy was definitely an in-your-face sort of musician and songwriter. He defined what being "punk" was for just about every punk rocker to follow. Again, we have an individual whose influence can be easily seen and heard throughout the history of rock music. Since he presented his version of rock music to the world, his aggressive influence on style and attitude have guided each generation that follows.

There's a reason why many consider Iggy Pop the godfather of punk—every single punk band of the past and present has either knowingly or unknowingly borrowed a thing or two from Pop and his late 1960s/early 1970s band, the Stooges. Born on April 21, 1947, in Muskegon, Mich., James Newell Osterberg was intrigued by rock and roll. Osterberg began playing drums and formed his first band, the Iguanas, in the early 1960s. Via the Rolling Stones, Osterberg discovered the blues, forming a similarly styled outfit, called the Prime Movers, upon graduating from high school in 1965. When a brief stint at the University of Michigan didn't work out, Osterberg moved to Chicago, playing drums alongside bluesmen.

But his true love was still rock and roll, and shortly after returning to Ann Arbor, Osterberg decided to form a rock band, but this time, he would leave the drums behind and be the frontman (inspired by the Velvet Underground's Lou Reed and the Doors' Jim Morrison). He tried to find the right musicians who shared his same musical vision: to create a band whose music would be primordial, sexually charged, political, and aggressive. In 1967, he hooked up with an old acquaintance from his high school days, guitarist Ron Asheton, who also brought along his drummer brother Scott, and bassist Dave Alexander, forming the Psychedelic Stooges. Although it would take a while for their sound to gel—they experimented with such non-traditional instruments as empty oil drums, vacuums, and other objects before returning to their respective instruments—the group fit in perfectly with such other high-energy Detroit bands as the MC5, becoming a local attraction.

It was around this time that the group shortened their name to the Stooges, and Osterberg changed his stage name to Iggy Pop. With the name change, Pop became a man possessed on-stage—going into the crowd nightly to confront members of the audience and working himself into such a frenzy that he would be bleeding by the end of the night from various nicks and scratches. (Eventually, Iggy would take that aspect of his act to dangerous levels throughout the early 1970s, before recreating his image in the later 1970s to a more fit, healthy, even muscular Iggy and a music not quite so confrontational.)

Elektra Records signed the quartet in 1968, issuing their self-titled debut a year later, and a follow-up in 1970, *Funhouse*. Although both records sold poorly upon release, both have become rock classics and can be pointed to as the official beginning of what would become known as punk rock. The group was dropped from their record company in 1971 due to the public's disinterest and the group's growing addictions to hard drugs (and additionally in Pop's case, continuous death-defying acts like stage diving onto a bed of broken shards of glass), leading to the group's breakup the same year.

But Stooges fan and sky-rocketing rock star David Bowie tracked down Pop and convinced the newly clean and sober singer to restart his career. Pop enlisted guitarist James Williamson (who was briefly a second guitarist for the Stooges before their breakup), and after the pair signed to Bowie's Mainman management company and relocated to England, eventually reunited with the Asheton brothers (with Ron moving from the six-string to the bass).

Signed by major label Columbia Records and hoping to follow in Bowie's footsteps toward a major commercial breakthrough, the Stooges penned another punk classic—the brutally explosive *Raw Power*. Pop's plan for the Stooges' third release overall would be to create a record that would be so over the top sonically that it would actually hurt you when it poured out of the speakers. Although it may not have been that extreme, it came pretty close (with Bowie signed on as the producer), but yet again, the album sank without a trace in the mainstream. But the underground music scene, driven primarily by college radio, was in no way forgetting Iggy.

It was right about this time—the mid-1970s—that mainstream commercial rock radio was becoming so self-absorbed and disconnected from new trends that a new generation of rock fans were seeking something fresh, raw, and real. Commercial radio was something your older brother listened to, but college radio was hitting its most vital period. You could hear real, non-corporate rock there, and hear it commercial free all the time. Sure, you might have to put up with a Slovenian Hour or German Hour or some public service radio show every now and then, but for the most part, college radio programmers were the only vital and evolving force in rock music in the late 1970s and into the 1980s. That is, until CMJ came along (College Music Journal) as a means by which corporate record companies could tap into and exert control on the college radio music market. Just like after Woodstock, when the corporate music business world saw the numbers of people attending rock concerts and said to its collective self, "wow, look at that . . . market," the corporate music industry saw a market developing in underground college radio and the bands and audiences that fed it and rushed in to control it as best they could while attempting to maintain an image of "indie" there.

While FM album-oriented, commercial rock radio, along with their "zoo crews" and "work in the factory—party on the weekends" attitudes and format, were putting their older hippie siblings to sleep and giving them a soundtrack for their entrance into suburban life, this next generation—post Baby Boomer but pre-GenX, sometimes referred to as the "blank" generation because of that, had gravitated to the left end of the radio dial where all the college stations are. This was the realm of Iggy and the Stooges and countless other bands who could not find a place in the mainstream pop rock market no matter what the music industry marketers in New York City tried.

By 1974, Pop and most of the Stooges' star was fading fast before it even shined in the mainstream, the band called it quits for a second and final time. After a brief spell becoming very disassociated with the rock scene and more associated with hospitals and actual homelessness, Pop would soon rise again from his own ashes. During a hospital stay, an old friend came to visit him. David Bowie, whose career was still in high gear, offered to take Pop on the road with him during his tour in support of *Station to Station*. The pair got along so well that they both moved to Berlin in late 1976, during which time Bowie helped Pop secure a solo record deal with Virgin. Bowie was interested in European electronic rock (Kraftwerk, Can, etc.) and admitted later that he used Pop as a musical guinea pig on such releases as *The Idiot* and *Lust for Life* (both issued in 1977 and produced/co-written by Bowie). Both albums sold better than his previous efforts with the Stooges, but at the price of losing much of the edge that Iggy was known for in the underground music scene. Bowie also toured in support of these albums as Pop's keyboardist. Pop would vacillate between polished work with Bowie and raw punk music out on his own, but he would always maintain that essence of what it is to be punk. His influence was most strongly felt in the late 1980s and early 1990s with the emergence of neo punk and grunge bands such as Nirvana, Mudhoney, and Soundgarden.

Around the same time, a wide variety of bands covered Pop and/or Stooges tracks—Slayer, Duran Duran, Guns N' Roses, R.E.M., and even Tom Jones, while Pop issued another fine solo set, 1993's *American Caesar*. Pop enjoyed another hit when the nearly twenty-year-old title-track from *Lust for Life* was used prominently on the hit movie soundtrack *Trainspotting*, providing the punk legend with a fresh generation of fans. Iggy Pop almost single-handedly created an entire genre of music and remains one of rock's top live performers and all-time influential artists.

Glam Rock

New York Dolls

While Iggy Pop was mutilating himself and declaring to the world that he was here to "Search and Destroy," the New York Dolls created their own version of punk rock before there was a term for it. Building on the Rolling Stones' dirty rock and roll, Mick Jagger's androgyny, girl group pop, the glam rock of David Bowie and T. Rex, and the Stooges' anarchic noise, the New York Dolls created a new form of hard rock that presaged both punk rock and heavy metal. Their drug-fueled, theatrical performances and crossdressing attitude influenced a generation of musicians in New

York and London, who all went on to form punk bands. The most notable fan of the Dolls that went on to create their own version of what the Dolls were trying to do was Gene Simmons, who took what he saw of the New York Dolls performances and created Kiss. And although they self-destructed quickly, the band's two albums remain two of the most popular cult records in rock and roll history.

All of the members of the New York Dolls played in New York bands before they formed in late 1971. Guitarists Johnny Thunders and Rick Rivets, bassist Arthur Kane, and drummer Billy Murcia were joined by vocalist David Johansen. Early in 1972, Rivets was replaced by Syl Sylvian, and the group began playing regularly in lower Manhattan, particularly at the Mercer Arts Center. Within a few months, they had earned a dedicated cult following, but record companies were afraid of signing the band because of their cross-dressing and blatant vulgarity.

Late in 1972, the New York Dolls embarked on their first tour of England. During the tour, drummer Murcia died after mixing drugs and alcohol. He was replaced by Jerry Nolan. After Nolan joined the band, the Dolls finally secured a record contract with Mercury Records. Todd Rundgren—whose sophisticated pop seemed at odds with the band's crash-and-burn rock and roll—produced the band's eponymous debut, which appeared in the summer of 1973. The record received overwhelmingly positive reviews, but it didn't stir the interest of the general public; the album peaked at number 116 on the U.S. charts. The band's follow-up, *Too Much Too Soon*, was produced by the legendary girl group producer George "Shadow" Morton. Although the sound of the record was relatively streamlined, the album was another commercial failure, only reaching number 167 upon its early summer 1974 release.

Following the disappointing sales of their two albums, Mercury Records dropped the New York Dolls. No other record labels were interested in the band, so they decided to hire a new manager, the British Malcolm McLaren, who would soon become famous for managing the Sex Pistols. With the Dolls, McLaren began developing his skill for turning shock into invaluable publicity. Although he made it work for the Pistols just a year later, all of his strategies backfired for the Dolls. McLaren made the band dress completely in red leather and perform in front of the USSR's flag; all of which meant to symbolize the Dolls' alleged communist allegiance. The new approach only made record labels more reluctant to sign the band and members soon began leaving the group.

By the middle of 1975, Thunders and Nolan left the Dolls. The remaining members, Johansen and Sylvain, fired McLaren and assembled a new lineup of the band. For the next two years, the duo led a variety of different incarnations of the band to no success. In 1977, Johansen and Sylvain decided to break up the band permanently. Over the next two decades, various outtakes collections, live albums, and compilations were released by a variety of labels and the New York Dolls' two original studio albums never went out of print.

Upon the Dolls' break up, David Johansen began a solo career that would eventually metamorphose into his lounge-singing alter-ego Buster Poindexter in the mid-1980s. Syl Sylvain played with Johansen for two years before he left to pursue his own solo career. Johnny Thunders formed the Heartbreakers with Jerry Nolan after they left the group in 1975. Over the next decade, the Heartbreakers would perform sporadically and Thunders would record the occasional solo album. On April 23, 1991, Thunders—who was one of the more notorious drug abusers in rock and roll history—died of a heroin overdose. Nolan performed at a tribute concert for Thunders later in 1991; a few months later, he died of a stroke at the age of forty.

T-Rex

Initially a British folk-rock combo called Tyrannosaurus Rex, T. Rex was the primary force in glam rock, thanks to the creative direction of guitarist/vocalist Marc Bolan (born Marc Feld). Bolan created a deliberately trashy form of rock and roll that was proud of its own disposability. T. Rex's music borrowed the underlying sexuality of early rock and roll, adding dirty, simple grooves and fat distorted guitars, as well as an overarching folky/hippie spirituality that always came through the clearest on ballads. While most of his peers concentrated on making cohesive albums, Bolan kept the idea of a three-minute pop single alive in the early 1970s. In Britain, he became a superstar, sparking a period of "T. Rextacy" among the pop audience with a series of Top Ten hits, including four number one singles. Over in America, the group only had one major hit—the Top Ten *Bang a Gong (Get It On)*—before disappearing from the charts in 1973. T. Rex's popularity in the U.K. didn't begin to waver until 1975, yet they retained a devoted following until Marc Bolan's death in 1977. Over the next two decades, Bolan emerged as a cult figure and the music of T. Rex has proven quite influential on hard rock, punk, new wave, and alternative rock.

Following a career as a teenage model, Marc Bolan began performing music professionally in 1965, releasing his first single, *The Wizard*, on Decca Records. Bolan joined the psychedelic folk-rock combo John's Children in 1967, appearing on three unsuccessful singles before the group disbanded later that year. Following the breakup, he formed the folk duo Tyrannosaurus Rex with percussionist Steve Peregrine Took. The duo landed a record deal with a subsidiary of EMI in February 1968, recording their debut album with producer Tony Visconti. *Debora*, the group's first single, peaked at number thirty-four in May of that year, and their debut album, *My People Were Fair and Had Sky in Their Hair . . . But Now They're Content to Wear Stars on Their Brow*, reached number fifteen shortly afterward. The duo released their second album, *Prophets, Seers & Sages, the Angels of the Ages*, in November of 1968.

By this time, Tyrannosaurus Rex was building a sizable underground following, which helped Bolan's book of poetry, *The Warlock of Love*, enter the British best-seller charts. In the summer of 1969, the duo released their third album, *Unicorn*, as well as the single *King of the Rumbling Spires*, the first Tyrannosaurus Rex song to feature an electric guitar. Following an unsuccessful American tour that fall, Took left the band and was replaced by Mickey Finn. The new duo's first single did not chart, yet their first album, 1970's *A Beard of Stars*, reached number twenty-one.

The turning point in Bolan's career came in October of 1970, when he shortened the group's name to T. Rex and released *Ride a White Swan*, a fuzz-drenched single driven by a rolling backbeat. *Ride a White Swan* became a major hit in the U.K., climbing all the way to number two. The band's next album, T. Rex, peaked at number thirteen and stayed on the charts for six months. Encouraged by the results, Bolan expanded T. Rex to a full band, adding bassist Steve Currie and drummer Bill Legend (born Bill Fifield). The new lineup recorded *Hot Love*, which spent six weeks at number one in early 1971. That summer, T. Rex released *Get It On* (retitled *Bang a Gong (Get It On)* in the United States), which became their second straight U.K. number one; the single would go on to be their biggest international hit, reaching number ten in the United States in 1972. *Electric Warrior*, the first album recorded by the full band, was released in the fall of 1971; it was number one for six weeks in Britain and cracked America's Top Forty.

By now, "T. Rextacy" was in full swing in England, as the band had captured the imaginations of both teenagers and the media with its sequined, heavily made-up appearance; the image of Marc Bolan in a top hat, feather boa, and platform shoes, performing *Get It On* on the BBC became as famous as his music. At the beginning of 1972, T. Rex signed with EMI, setting up a distribution deal for Bolan's own T.Rex Wax Co. record label. *Telegram Sam*, the group's first EMI single, became their third number one single.

Metal Guru also hit number one, spending four weeks at the top of the chart. *The Slider*, released in the summer of 1972, shot to number one upon its release, allegedly selling 100,000 copies in four days; the album was also T. Rex's most successful American release, reaching number seventeen. Appearing in the spring of 1973, *Tanx* was another Top Five hit for T. Rex; the singles *20th Century Boy* and *The Groover* soon followed it to the upper ranks of the charts. However, those singles would prove to be the band's last two Top Ten hits. In the summer of 1973, rhythm guitarist Jack Green joined the band, as did three backup vocalists, including the American soul singer Gloria Jones; Jones would soon become Bolan's girlfriend. At the beginning of 1974, drummer Bill Legend left the group and was replaced by Davy Lutton, as Jones became the group's keyboardist.

In early 1974, the single *Teenage Dream* was the first record to be released under the name Marc Bolan and T. Rex. The following album, *Zinc Alloy and the Hidden Riders of Tomorrow*, was the last Bolan recorded with Tony Visconti. Throughout the year, T. Rex's popularity rapidly declined—by the time *Zip Gun Boogie* was released in November, it could only reach number forty-one. Finn and Green left the group at the end of the year, while keyboardist Dino Dins joined. The decline of T. Rex's popularity was confirmed when 1975's *Bolan's Zip Gun* failed to chart. Bolan took the rest of the year off, returning in the spring of 1976 with *Futuristic Dragon*, which peaked at number fifty. Released in the summer of 1976, *I Love to Boogie*, a disco-flavored three-chord thumper, became Bolan's last Top Twenty hit.

Bolan released *Dandy in the Underworld* in the spring of 1977; it was a modest hit, peaking at number twenty-six. While *The Soul of My Suit* reached number forty-two on the charts, T. Rex's next two singles failed to chart. Sensing it was time for a change of direction, Bolan began expanding his horizons in August. In addition to contributing a weekly column for Record Mirror, he hosted his own variety television show, *Marc*. Featuring guest appearances by artists like David Bowie and Generation X, *Marc* helped restore Bolan's hip image. Signing with RCA Records, the guitarist formed a new band with bassist Herbie Flowers and drummer Tony Newman, yet he never was able to record with the group. While driving home from a London club with Bolan, Gloria Jones lost control of her car, smashing into a tree. Marc Bolan, riding in the passenger's seat of the car, was killed instantly.

While T. Rex's music was intended to be disposable, it has proven surprisingly influential over the years. Hard rock and heavy metal bands borrowed the group's image, as well as the pounding insistence of their guitars. Punk bands may have discarded the high heels, feather boas, and top hats, yet they adhered to the simple three-chord structures and pop aesthetics that made the band popular.

David Bowie—The Man Who Fell to Earth

The cliché about David Bowie says he's a musical chameleon, adapting himself according to fashion and trends. While such a criticism is too glib, there's no denying that Bowie demonstrated remarkable skill for perceiving musical trends at his peak in the 1970s. After spending several years in the late 1960s as a mod and as an all-around music-hall entertainer, Bowie reinvented himself as a hippie singer/songwriter. Prior to his breakthrough in 1972, he recorded a proto-metal record and a pop/rock album, eventually redefining glam rock with his ambiguously sexy Ziggy Stardust persona. Ziggy made Bowie an international star, yet he wasn't content to continue to churn out glitter rock. By the mid-1970s, he developed an effete, sophisticated version of Philly soul that he dubbed "plastic soul," which eventually morphed into the eerie avant-pop of 1976's *Station to Station*. Shortly afterward, he relocated to Berlin, where he recorded three experimental electronic albums with Brian Eno. At the dawn of the 1980s, Bowie was still at the height of his powers, yet following his blockbuster dance-pop album *Let's Dance* in 1983, he slowly sank into mediocrity before salvaging his career in the early 1990s. Even when he was out of fashion in the 1980s and 1990s, it was clear that Bowie was one of the most influential musicians in rock, for better and for worse. Each one of his phases in the 1970s sparked a number of subgenres, including punk, new wave, goth rock, the new romantics, and electronica. Few rockers ever had such lasting impact.

David Jones began performing music when he was thirteen years old, learning the saxophone while he was at Bromley Technical High School; another pivotal event happened at the school, when his left pupil became permanently dilated in a schoolyard fight. Following his graduation at sixteen, he worked as a commercial artist while playing saxophone in a number of mod bands, including the King Bees, the Manish Boys (which also featured Jimmy Page as a session man), and Davey Jones & the Lower Third. All three of those bands released singles, which were generally ignored, yet he continued performing, changing his name to David Bowie in 1966 after the Monkees' Davy Jones became an international star. Over the course of 1966, he released three mod singles on Pye Records, which were all ignored. The following year, he signed with Deram, releasing the music hall, Anthony Newley-styled *David Bowie* that year. Upon completing the record, he spent several weeks in a Scottish Buddhist monastery. Once he left the monastery, he studied with Lindsay Kemp's mime troupe, forming his own mime company, the Feathers, in 1969. The Feathers were short-lived, and he formed the experimental art group Beckenham Arts Lab in 1969.

Bowie needed to finance the Arts Lab, so he signed with Mercury Records that year and released *Man of Words, Man of Music*, a trippy singer/songwriter album featuring *Space Oddity*. The song was released as a single and became a major hit in the U.K., convincing Bowie to concentrate on music. Hooking up with his old friend Marc Bolan, he began miming at some of Bolan's T. Rex concerts, eventually touring with Bolan, bassist/producer Tony Visconti, guitarist Mick Ronson, and drummer Cambridge as Hype. The band quickly fell apart, yet Bowie and Ronson remained close, working on the material that formed Bowie's next album, *The Man Who Sold the World*, as well as recruiting Michael "Woody" Woodmansey as their drummer. Produced by Tony Visconti, who also played bass, *The Man Who Sold the World* was a heavy guitar rock album that failed to gain much attention. Bowie followed the album in late 1971 with the pop/rock *Hunky Dory*, an album that featured Ronson and keyboardist Rick Wakeman.

Following the release of *Hunky Dory*, Bowie began to develop his most famous incarnation, Ziggy Stardust: an androgynous, bisexual rock star from another planet. Before he unveiled Ziggy, Bowie claimed in a January 1972 interview with the Melody Maker that he was gay, helping to stir interest in his forthcoming album. Taking cues from Bolan's stylish glam rock, Bowie dyed his hair orange and began wearing women's clothing. He began calling himself Ziggy Stardust, and his backing band—Ronson, Woodmansey, and bassist Trevor Bolder—were the Spiders from Mars. *The Rise & Fall of Ziggy Stardust and the Spiders from Mars* was released with much fanfare in England in late 1972. The album and its lavish, theatrical concerts became a sensation throughout England, and it helped him become the only glam rocker to carve out a niche in America. *Ziggy Stardust* became a word-of-mouth hit in the United States, and the re-released *Space Oddity*—which was now also the title of the re-released *Man of Words, Man of Music*—reached the American Top Twenty. Bowie quickly followed *Ziggy* with *Aladdin Sane* later in 1973. Not only did he record a new album that year, but he also produced Lou Reed's *Transformer*, the Stooges' *Raw Power*, and Mott the Hoople's comeback *All the Young Dudes*, for which he also wrote the title track.

Given the amount of work Bowie packed into 1972 and 1973, it wasn't surprising that his relentless schedule began to catch up with him. After recording the all-covers *Pin-Ups* with the Spiders from Mars, he unexpectedly announced the band's breakup, as well as his retirement from live performances, during the group's final show that year. He retreated from the spotlight to work on a musical adaptation of George Orwell's *1984*, but once he was denied the rights to the novel, he transformed the work into *Diamond Dogs*. The album was released to generally poor reviews in 1974, yet it generated the hit single *Rebel Rebel*, and he supported the album with an elaborate and expensive American tour. As the tour progressed, Bowie became fascinated with soul music, eventually redesigning the entire show to reflect his new "plastic soul." Hiring guitarist Carlos Alomar as the band's leader, Bowie refashioned his group into a Philly soul band and recostumed himself in sophisticated, stylish fashions. The change took fans by surprise, as did the double-album *David Live*, which featured material recorded on the 1974 tour.

Young Americans, released in 1975, was the culmination of Bowie's soul obsession, and it became his first major crossover hit, peaking in the

American Top Ten and generating his first U.S. number one hit in *Fame*, a song he co-wrote with John Lennon and Alomar. Bowie relocated to Los Angeles, where he earned his first movie role in Nicolas Roeg's *The Man Who Fell to Earth* (1976). While in L.A., he recorded *Station to Station*, which took the plastic soul of *Young Americans* into darker, avant-garde-tinged directions, yet was also a huge hit, generating the Top Ten single *Golden Years*. The album inaugurated Bowie's persona of the elegant *Thin White Duke*, and it reflected Bowie's growing cocaine-fueled paranoia. Soon, he decided Los Angeles was too boring and returned to England; shortly after arriving back in London, he gave the awaiting crowd a Nazi salute, a signal of his growing, drug-addled detachment from reality. The incident caused enormous controversy, and Bowie left the country to settle in Berlin, where he lived and worked with Brian Eno.

Once in Berlin, Bowie sobered up and began painting, as well as studying art. He also developed a fascination with German electronic music, which Eno helped him fulfill on their first album together, *Low*. Released early in 1977, *Low* was a startling mixture of electronics, pop, and avant-garde technique. While it was greeted with mixed reviews at the time, it proved to be one of the most influential albums of the late 1970s, as did its follow-up, *Heroes*, which followed that year. Not only did Bowie record two solo albums in 1977, but he also helmed Iggy Pop's comeback records *The Idiot* and *Lust for Life*, and toured anonymously as Pop's keyboardist. He resumed his acting career in 1977, appearing in *Just A Gigolo* with Marlene Dietrich and Kim Novak, as well as narrating Eugene Ormandy's version of *Peter and the Wolf*. Bowie returned to the stage in 1978, launching an international tour that was captured on the double-album *Stage*. During 1979, Bowie and Eno recorded *Lodger* in New York, Switzerland, and Berlin, releasing the album at the end of the year. *Lodger* was supported with several innovative videos, as was 1980's *Scary Monsters*, and these videos—*DJ*, *Fashion*, *Ashes to Ashes*—became staples on early MTV.

Scary Monsters was Bowie's last album for RCA, and it wrapped up his most innovative, productive period. Later in 1980, he performed the title role in stage production of The Elephant Man, including several shows on Broadway. Over the next two years, he took an extended break from recording, appearing in *Christine F* (1982) and the vampire movie *The Hunger* (1982), returning to the studio only for his 1981 collaboration with Queen, *Under Pressure*, and the theme for Paul Schrader's remake of *Cat People*. In 1983, he signed an expensive contract with EMI Records and released *Let's Dance*. Bowie had recruited Chic guitarist Nile Rodgers to produce the album, giving the record a sleek, funky foundation, and hired the unknown Stevie Ray Vaughan as lead guitarist. *Let's Dance* became his most successful record, thanks to stylish, innovative videos for *Let's Dance* and *China Girl*, which turned both songs into Top Ten hits. Bowie supported the record with the sold-out arena tour Serious Moonlight.

Greeted with massive success for the first time, Bowie wasn't quite sure how to react, and he eventually decided to replicate *Let's Dance* with 1984's *Tonight*. While the album sold well, producing the Top Ten hit *Blue Jean*, it received poor reviews and ultimately was a commercial disappointment. He stalled in 1985, recording a duet of Martha & the Vandellas' *Dancing in the Street* with Mick Jagger for Live Aid. He also spent more time jet-setting, appearing at celebrity events across the globe, and appeared in several movies—*Into the Night* (1985), *Absolute Beginners* (1986),

Labyrinth (1986)—that turned out to be bombs. Bowie returned to recording in 1987 with the widely panned *Never Let Me Down*, supporting the album with the Glass Spider tour, which also received poor reviews. In 1989, he remastered his RCA catalog with Rykodisc for CD release, kicking off the series with the three-disc box *Sound + Vision*. Bowie supported the discs with an accompanying tour of the same name, claiming that he was retiring all of his older characters from performance following the tour. *Sound + Vision* was successful, and *Ziggy Stardust* re-charted amidst the hoopla.

Sound + Vision may have been a success, but Bowie's next project was perhaps his most unsuccessful. Picking up on the abrasive, dissonant rock of Sonic Youth and the Pixies, Bowie formed his own guitar rock combo, Tin Machine, with guitarist Reeves Gabrels, bassist Hunt Sales, and his drummer brother Tony, who had previously worked on Iggy Pop's *Lust for Life* with Bowie. Tin Machine released an eponymous album to poor reviews that summer and supported it with a club tour, which was only moderately successful. Despite the poor reviews, Tin Machine released a second album, the appropriately titled *Tin Machine II*, in 1991, and it was completely ignored.

Bowie returned to a solo career in 1993 with the sophisticated, soulful *Black Tie White Noise*, recording the album with Nile Rodgers and his now-permanent collaborator, Reeves Gabrels. The album was released on Savage, a subsidiary of RCA and received positive reviews, but his new label went bankrupt shortly after its release, and the album disappeared. *Black Tie White Noise* was the first indication that Bowie was trying hard to resuscitate his career, as was the largely instrumental 1994 soundtrack *The Buddha of Suburbia*. In 1995, he reunited with Brian Eno for the wildly hyped, industrial rock-tinged *Outside*. Several critics hailed the album as a comeback, and Bowie supported it with a co-headlining tour with Nine Inch Nails in order to snag a younger, alternative audience, but his gambit failed; audiences left before Bowie's performance and *Outside* disappeared. He quickly returned to the studio in 1996, recording *Earthling*, an album heavily influenced by techno and drum'n'bass. Upon its early 1997 release, *Earthling* received generally positive reviews, yet the album failed to gain an audience, and many techno purists criticized Bowie for allegedly exploiting their subculture.

Alice Cooper

Originally, there was a band called Alice Cooper led by a singer named Vincent Damon Furnier. Under his direction, Alice Cooper pioneered a grandly theatrical and violent brand of heavy metal that was designed to shock. Drawing equally from horror movies, vaudeville, heavy metal, and garage rock, the group created a stage show that featured electric chairs, guillotines, fake blood, and huge boa constrictors, all coordinated by the heavily made-up Furnier. By that time, Furnier had adopted the name for his androgynous on-stage personality. While the visuals were extremely important to the group's impact, the band's music was nearly as distinctive. Driven by raw, simple riffs and melodies that derived from 1960s guitar pop as well as show tunes, it was rock and roll at its most basic and catchy, even when the band ventured into psychedelia and art rock. After the original group broke up and Furnier began a solo career as Alice

Cooper, his actual music lost most of its theatrical flourishes, becoming straightforward heavy metal, yet his stage show retained all of the trademark props that made him the king of shock rock.

Furnier formed his first group, the Earwigs, as an Arizona teenager in the early 1960s. Changing the band's name to the Spiders in 1965, the group was eventually called the Nazz (not to be confused with Todd Rundgren's band of the same name). The Spiders and the Nazz both released local singles that were moderately popular. In 1968, after discovering there was another band called with the same name, the group changed its name to Alice Cooper. According to band legend, the name came to Furnier during a ouija board session, where he was told he was the reincarnation of a 17th-century witch of the same name. Comprised of vocalist Furnier—who would soon begin calling himself Alice Cooper—guitarist Mike Bruce, guitarist Glen Buxton, bassist Dennis Dunaway, and drummer Neal Smith, the group moved to California in 1968. In California, the group met Shep Gordon, who became their manager, and Frank Zappa, who signed Alice Cooper to his Straight Records imprint.

Alice Cooper released their first album, *Pretties for You*, in 1969. *Easy Action* followed early in 1970, yet it failed to chart. The group's reputation in Los Angeles was slowly shrinking, so the band moved to Furnier's hometown of Detroit. For the next year, the group refined their bizarre stage show. Late in 1970, the group's contract was transferred to Straight's distributor Warner Bros., and they began recording their third album with producer Bob Ezrin.

With Ezrin's assistance, Alice Cooper developed their classic heavy metal crunch on 1971's *Love It to Death*, which featured the number twenty-one hit single *Eighteen*; the album peaked at number thirty-five and went gold. The success enabled the group to develop a more impressive, elaborate live show, which made them highly popular concert attractions across the United States and eventually the U.K. *Killer*, released late in 1971, was another gold album. Released in the summer of 1972, *School's Out* was Alice Cooper's breakthrough record, peaking at number two and selling over a million copies. The title song became a Top Ten hit in the United States and a number one single in the U.K. *Billion Dollar Babies*, released the following year, was the group's biggest hit, reaching number one in both America and Britain; the album's first single, *No More Mr. Nice Guy*, became a Top Ten hit in Britain, peaking at number twenty-five in the United States. *Muscle of Love* appeared late in 1973, yet it failed to capitalize on the success of *Billion Dollar Babies*. After *Muscle of Love*, Furnier and the rest of Alice Cooper parted ways to pursue other projects. Having officially changed his name to Alice Cooper, Furnier embarked on a similarly theatrical solo career; the rest of the band released one unsuccessful album under the name *Billion Dollar Babies*, while Mike Bruce and Neal Smith both recorded solo albums that were never issued. In the fall of 1974, a compilation of Alice Cooper's five Warner albums, entitled *Alice Cooper's Greatest Hits*, became a Top Ten hit.

For his first solo album, Cooper hired Lou Reed's backing band from *Rock 'N' Roll Animal*—guitarists Dick Wagner and Steve Hunter, bassist Prakash John, keyboardist Joseph Chrowski, and drummer Penti Glan—as his supporting group. *Welcome to My Nightmare*, Alice Cooper's first solo album, was released in the spring of 1975. The record wasn't a great departure from his previous work, and it became a Top Ten hit in America, launching the hit acoustic ballad *Only Women Bleed*; its success put an end to any idea of reconvening Alice Cooper the band. Its follow-up, 1976's *Alice Cooper Goes to Hell*, was another hit, going gold in the United States. After *Alice Cooper Goes to Hell*, Cooper's career began to slip, partially due to changing trends and partially due to his alcoholism. Cooper entered rehabilitation in 1978, writing an album about his treatment called *From the Inside* (1978) with Bernie Taupin, Elton John's lyricist. During the early 1980s, Cooper continued to release albums and tour, yet he was no longer as popular as he was during his early-1970s heyday.

Cooper made a successful comeback in the late 1980s, sparked by his appearances in horror films and a series of pop-metal bands that paid musical homage to his classic early records and concerts. *Constrictor*, released in 1986, began his comeback, but it was 1989's *Trash* that returned Cooper to the spotlight. Produced by the proven hitmaker Desmond Child, *Trash* featured guest appearances by Jon Bon Jovi, Richie Sambora, and most of Aerosmith; the record became a Top Ten hit in Britain and peaked at number twenty in the United States, going platinum. *Poison*, a mid-tempo rocker featured on the album, became Cooper's first Top Ten single since 1977. After the release of *Trash*, he continued to star in the occasional film, tour, and record, although he wasn't able to retain the audience recaptured with *Trash*. Still, 1991's *Hey Stoopid* and 1994's *The Last Temptation* were generally solid, professional efforts that helped Cooper settle into a comfortable cult status without damaging the critical goodwill surrounding his 1970s output. After a live album, 1997's *Fistful of Alice*, Cooper returned on the smaller Spitfire label in 2000 with *Brutal Planet*.

Rebel Rock

Allman Brothers

The story of the Allman Brothers Band is one of triumph, tragedy, redemption, dissolution, and a new redemption. Over almost thirty years, they've gone from being America's single most influential band to a has-been group trading on past glories, to reach the 1990s as one of the most respected rock acts of their era.

For the first half of the 1970s, the Allman Brothers Band was the most influential rock group in America, redefining rock music and its boundaries. The band's mix of blues, country, jazz, and even classical influences, and their powerful, extended onstage jamming altered the standards of concert performance—other groups were known for their onstage jamming, but when the Allman Brothers stretched a song out for thirty or forty minutes, at their best they were exciting, never self-indulgent. They gave it all a distinctly Southern voice and, in the process, opened the way for a wave of 1970s rock acts from south of the Mason-Dixon Line, including the Marshall Tucker Band, Lynyrd Skynyrd, and Blackfoot, whose music, at least initially, celebrated their roots. And for a time, almost single-handedly, they also made Capricorn Records into a major independent label.

The group was founded in 1969 by Duane Allman on guitar; Gregg Allman on vocals and organ; Forrest Richard ("Dickey") Betts on guitar; Berry Oakley on bass; and Butch Trucks and Jaimoe Johnny Johanson on drums. Duane and Gregg Allman loved soul and R&B, although they listened to their share of rock and roll, especially as it sounded coming out of England in the mid-1960s. Their first group was a local Daytona Beach garage band called the Escorts, who sounded a lot like the early Beatles and Rolling Stones; they later became the Allman Joys and plunged into Cream-style British blues, and then the Hour Glass, a more soul-oriented outfit. The group landed a contract with Liberty Records with help from the Nitty Gritty Dirt Band, but the company wasted the opportunity on a pair of overproduced albums that failed to capture the Hour Glass's sound. The group split up after Liberty rejected a proposed third album steeped in blues and R&B.

Duane Allman began working as a session guitarist at Fame Studios in Muscle Shoals, Ala., and it was there, appearing on records by Wilson Pickett, Aretha Franklin, John Hammond, and King Curtis, among others, that he made his reputation. In 1969, at the coaxing of ex-Otis Redding manager Phil Walden, Allman gave up session work and began putting together a new band—Jaimoe (Johnny Lee Johnson) Johanson came aboard, and then Allman's longtime friend Butch Trucks, and another Allman friend, Berry Oakley, joined, along with Dickey Betts, with whom Oakley was playing in a group called Second Coming. A marathon jam session ensued, at the end of which Allman had his band, except for a singer—that came later when his brother Gregg agreed to join. They were duly signed to Walden's new Capricorn label.

The band didn't record their first album until after they'd worked their sound out on the road, playing heavily around Florida and Georgia. The self-titled debut album was a solid blues-rock album and one of the better showcases for guitar pyrotechnics in a year with more than its share, amid albums by the Cream, Blind Faith, the Jeff Beck Group, and Led Zeppelin. It didn't sell 50,000 copies on its initial release, but *The Allman Brothers Band* impressed everyone who heard it and nearly everyone who reviewed it. Coming out at the end of the 1960s, it could have passed as a follow-up to the kind of blues-rock coming out of England from acts like Cream, except that it had a sharper edge—the Allmans were American and Southern, and their understanding of blues (not to mention elements of jazz, mostly courtesy of Jaimoe) was as natural as breathing. The album also introduced one of the band's most popular concert numbers, *Whipping Post*.

Their debut album attracted good reviews and a cult following with its mix of assured dual lead guitars by Duane Allman and Dickey Betts, soulful singing by Gregg Allman, and a rhythm section that was nearly as busy as the lead instruments, between Oakley's rock-hard bass and the dual drumming of Trucks and Johanson. Their second album, 1970's *Idlewild South*, recorded at Capricorn's studios in Macon, Ga., was produced by Tom Dowd, who had previously recorded Cream. This was a magical combination—Dowd was completely attuned to the group's sound and goals, and *Idlewild South* broadened that sound, adding a softer acoustic texture to their music and introducing Dickey Betts as a composer (including the original studio version of "In Memory of Elizabeth Reed," an instrumental tribute to Miles Davis that would become a highlight of their shows, in many different forms, for the next thirty years). It also had a Gregg Allman number, *Midnight Rider*, which became one of the band's more widely covered originals and the composer's signature tune.

By this time, the band's concerts were becoming legendary for the extraordinarily complex yet coherent interplay between the two guitarists and

Gregg Allman's keyboards, sometimes in jams of forty minutes or more to a single song without wasting a note. And unlike the art rock bands of the era, they weren't interested in impressing anyone with how they played scales, how many different tunings they knew, or which classical riffs they could quote. Rather, the Allmans incorporated the techniques and structures of jazz and classical music into their playing. In March of 1971, the band played a series of shows at the Fillmore East that were recorded for posterity and subsequently transformed into their third album, *At Fillmore East*. This double album, issued in July of 1971, became an instant classic, rivaling the previous blues-rock touchstone cut at the Fillmore, Cream's *Wheels of Fire*. Duane Allman and his band were suddenly the new heroes to millions of mostly older teenage fans. Although it never cracked the Top Ten, *At Fillmore East* was certified as a gold record on October 15, 1971.

Fourteen days later, Duane Allman was killed in a motorcycle accident. The band had been midway through work on their next album, *Eat a Peach*, which they completed as a five-piece, with Dickey Betts playing all of the lead and slide guitar parts. Their second double album in a row became another instant classic, and their first album to reach the Top Ten, peaking at number five.

Despite having completed *Eat a Peach*, the group was intact in name only. Rather than try and replace Duane Allman as a guitarist, they contrived to add a second solo instrument in the form of a piano, played by Chuck Leavell. The group had already begun work on a long-delayed follow-up to *Eat a Peach*, when Oakley was killed in a motorcycle accident only a few blocks from Allman's accident site.

Lamar Williams (b. Jan. 15, 1949–d. Jan. 25, 1983) was recruited on bass, and the new lineup continued the group's concert activities, as well as eventually finishing their next album, *Brothers and Sisters*, which was released on August 1, 1973. During the extended gap in releases following *Eat a Peach*, Atco reissued *The Allman Brothers Band* and *Idlewild South* together as the double album *Beginnings*, which charted higher than either individual release.

Brothers and Sisters marked the beginning of a new era. The album had a more easygoing and freewheeling sound, less bluesy and more country-ish. This was partly a result of Capricorn's losing the services of Tom Dowd, who had produced their three previous albums. Additionally, Dickey Betts' full emergence as a songwriter and singer as well as the group's only guitarist, playing all of the lead and slide parts, altered the balance of the group's sound, pushing forth his distinct interest in country-rock. Betts also became the reluctant *de facto* leader of the band during this period, not from a desire for control as much as because he was the only one with the comparative stability and creative input to take on the responsibility.

The record occupied the number one spot for six weeks, spurred by the number two single *Ramblin' Man*, and became their most well-known album. It was an odd reversal of the usual order of success for a rock band—usually, it was the release of the album that drew the crowds to concerts, but in this case, the months of touring the band had done paved the way for the album. The fact that it kept getting pushed back only heightened the fans' interest.

Ironically, *Brothers and Sisters* was a less challenging record than the group's earlier releases, with a relatively laidback sound, relaxed compared to the groundbreaking work on the group's previous four albums. But all of this hardly mattered; based on the reputation they'd established with their first four albums, and the crowd-pleasing nature of *Ramblin' Man* and the Dickey Betts-composed instrumental *Jessica*, the group was playing larger halls and bigger crowds than ever.

An entire range of Southern-based rock acts had started to make serious inroads into the charts in the wake of the Allman Brothers. Labels such as MCA and even Island Records began looking for this same audience, signing acts like Lynyrd Skynyrd and Blackfoot, respectively, among others. For the first time since the mid-1950s, the heyday of the rockabilly era, a major part of the country was listening to rock and roll with a distinctly Southern twang.

The band began showing cracks in 1974, as Gregg Allman and Dickey Betts both began solo careers, recording albums separately from the group. Allman married Cher (twice), an event that set him up in a Hollywood-based lifestyle that created a schism with the rest of the band. They might have survived all of this, but for the increasing strain of the members' other personal habits—drugs and alcohol had always been a significant part of the lives of each of the members, except perhaps for Jaimoe, but as the strain and exhaustion of touring continued, coupled with the need to produce new music, these indulgences began to get out of control, and Betts' leadership of the group created a further strain for him.

The band's difficulties were showcased by their next album, the highly uneven *Win, Lose Or Draw*, which lacked the intensity and sharpness of their prior work. The whole band wasn't present for some of the album, and Gregg Allman's involvement with Cher, coupled with his serious drug problems, prevented him from participating with the rest of the group—his vocals were added separately, on the other side of the country.

The band finally came apart in 1976 when Allman found himself in the midst of a federal drug case against a supplier and agreed to testify against a friend and band employee. Leavall, Johanson, and Williams split to form Sea Level, which became a moderately successful band, cutting four albums for Capricorn over the next four years, while Betts pursued a solo career. All of them vowed never to work with Gregg Allman again.

Amid this split, Capricorn Records, reaching ever deeper into its vaults for anything that could generate income, issued two collections, a double-album live collection called *Wipe the Windows, Check the Oil, Dollar Gas*, showcasing the *Brothers and Sisters*-era band at various concerts, and a double-album best-of package, *And the Road Goes On Forever*. *Wipe the Windows* was a modest seller, appearing as it did when the group's sales had already fallen off, and it was compared unfavorably with the legendary work on *At Fillmore East*. The studio compilation passed with barely a ripple, however, because most fans already had the stuff on the original albums.

They were all back together by 1978, however, and over the next four years the group issued a somewhat uneven series of albums. *Enlightened Rogues* (1979) somewhat redeemed their reputations—produced by Tom Dowd, who had always managed to get the very best work out of the group, it had more energy than any record they'd issued in at least six years. It also restored the two-guitar lineup, courtesy of Dan Toler (from Dickey Betts' solo band), who was brought in when Chuck Leavell (along with Lamar Williams) refused to return to the Allmans. By that time, however, the

Allmans were fighting against time and musical trends. Disco, punk, and power-pop had pretty much stolen a march on the arena acts epitomized by the Allmans; whatever interest they attracted was a matter of nostalgia for their earlier releases. The group was in danger of becoming arena rock's third big oldies act (after the Moody Blues and Paul McCartney's Wings).

Additionally, their business affairs were in a shambles, owing to the bankruptcy of Capricorn Records in late 1979. When the fallout from the Capricorn collapse settled, PolyGram Records, the company's biggest creditor, took over the label's library, and the Allman Brothers were cut loose from their contract.

Their signing to Arista enabled the group to resume recording. What they released, however, was safe, unambitious, routinely commercial pop-rock, closer in spirit to the Doobie Brothers than their own classic work, and a shadow of that work, without any of the invention and daring upon which they'd built their reputations. The group's fortunes hit a further downturn when Jaimoe was fired, breaking up one of the best rhythm sections in rock. For most of the 1980s, the group was on hiatus, while the individual members sorted out their personal and professional situations. During those years, only Dickey Betts seemed to be in a position to do much with his music, and most of that wasn't selling.

In 1989, the band was reactivated again, partly owing to the PolyGram's decision to issue the four-CD box set retrospective *Dreams*. That set, coupled with the reissue of their entire Capricorn catalog on compact disc in the years leading up to the box's release, reminded millions of older listeners of the band's greatness, and introduced the group to millions of people too young to have been around for Watkins Glen, much less the Fillmore shows.

They reunited and also restored the band's original double-lead-guitar configuration, adding Warren Haynes on lead guitar alongside Dickey Betts, with Allen Woody playing bass; Chuck Leavell was gone, however, having agreed to join the Rolling Stones on tour as their resident keyboard player, and Lamar Williams had succumbed to cancer in 1983.

The new lineup reinvigorated the band, which signed with Epic Records and surprised everyone with their first release, *Seven Turns*. Issued in 1990, it got some of the best reviews and healthiest sales they'd had in more than a decade. Their subsequent studio albums failed to attract as much enthusiasm, and their two live albums, *An Evening With the Allman Brothers Band* and *2nd Set*, released in 1992 and 1995, respectively, were steady but not massive sellers. Much of this isn't the fault of the material so much as a natural result of the passage of time, which has left the Allmans competing with two decades' worth of successors and rivals.

The group has stayed together since 1989, overcoming continuing health and drug problems, which have occasionally battered their efforts at new music. They remain a top concert attraction more than twenty-five years after their last historically important album, easily drawing more than 20,000 fans at a time to outdoor venues, or booking 2,000-seat theaters for three weeks at a time. Their back catalog, especially the first five albums, remain consistent sellers on compact disc and recently returned to the reconstituted Capricorn label (still a home for Southern rockers, including the latter-day Lynyrd Skynyrd, as well as reissues of Elmore James and other classic bluesmen), under a 1997 licensing agreement that has resulted in their third round of digital remastering.

Apart from their Arista releases, the Allman Brothers Band has remained remarkably consistent, altering their music only gradually over thirty years. They sound more country than they did in their early days, and they're a bit more varied in the vocal department, but the band still soars at their concerts and on most of their records for the last ten years.

Lynyrd Skynyrd

Lynyrd Skynyrd was the definitive Southern rock band, fusing the overdriven power of blues-rock with a rebellious, Southern image and a hard rock swagger. Skynyrd never relied on the jazzy improvisations of the Allman Brothers. Instead, they were a hard-living, hard-driving rock and roll band—they may have jammed endlessly on stage, but their music remained firmly entrenched in blues, rock, and country. For many, Lynyrd Skynyrd's redneck image tended to obscure the songwriting skills of its leader, Ronnie VanZant. Throughout the band's early records, VanZant demonstrated a knack for lyrical detail and a down-to-earth honesty that had more in common with country than rock and roll. During the height of Skynyrd's popularity in the mid-1970s, however, VanZant's talents were overshadowed by the group's gritty, greasy blues-rock. Sadly, it wasn't until he was killed in a tragic plane crash in 1977 along with two other band members that many listeners began to realize his talents. Skynyrd split up after the plane crash, but they reunited a decade later, becoming a popular concert act during the early 1990s.

While in high school in Jacksonville, Fla., Ronnie VanZant (vocals), Allen Collins (guitar), and Gary Rossington (guitar) formed My Backyard. Within a few months, the group added bassist Leon Wilkeson and keyboardist Billy Powell, and changed their name to Lynyrd Skynyrd, a mocking tribute to their gym teacher Leonard Skinner, who was notorious for punishing students with long hair. With drummer Bob Burns, Lynyrd Skynyrd began playing throughout the South. For the first few years, the group had little success, but producer Al Kooper signed the band to MCA after seeing them play at an Atlanta club called Funocchio's in 1972. Kooper produced the group's 1973 debut, *Pronounced Leh-Nerd Skin-Nerd*, which was recorded after former Strawberry Alarm Clock guitarist Ed King joined the band. The group became notorious for their triple guitar attack, which was showcased on *Free Bird*, a tribute to the recently deceased Duane Allman. *Free Bird* earned Lynyrd Skynyrd their first national exposure and it became one of the staples of album-rock radio, still receiving airplay nearly twenty-five years after its release.

Free Bird and an opening slot on the Who's 1973 *Quadrophenia* tour gave Lynyrd Skynyrd a devoted following, which helped its second album, 1974's *Second Helping*, become its breakthrough hit. Featuring the hit single *Sweet Home Alabama*—a response to Neil Young's *Southern Man*—*Second Helping* reached number twelve and went multi-platinum. At the end of the year, Artimus Pyle replaced drummer Burns and King left the band shortly afterward. The new sextet released *Nuthin' Fancy* in 1975, and it became the band's first Top Ten hit. The record was followed by the Tom Dowd-produced *Gimme Back My Bullets* in 1976, which failed to match the success of its two predecessors. However, the band retained its following through its constant touring, which was documented on the double-live album *One More from the Road*. Released in late 1976, the album featured the band's new guitarist Steve Gaines and a trio of female backup singers, and it became Skynyrd's second Top Ten album.

Lynyrd Skynyrd released its sixth album, *Street Survivors*, on October 17, 1977. Three days later, a privately chartered plane carrying the band between shows in Greenville, S.C., and Baton Rouge, La., crashed outside of Gillsburg, Miss. Ronnie VanZant, Steve Gaines, and his sister Cassie, one of the group's backing vocalists, died in the crash; the remaining members were injured. (The cause of the crash was either fuel shortage or a fault with the plane's mechanics.) The cover for *Street Survivors* had pictured the band surrounded in flames; after the crash, the cover was changed. In the wake of the tragedy, the album became one of the band's biggest hits. Lynyrd Skynyrd broke up after the crash, releasing a collection of early demos called *Skynyrd's First And . . . Last* in 1978; it had been scheduled for release before the crash. The double album compilation *Gold and Platinum* was released in 1980.

Later in 1980, Rossington and Collins formed a new band, which featured four surviving members. Two years later, Pyle formed the Artimus Pyle Band. Collins suffered a car crash in 1986, which killed his girlfriend and left him paralyzed; four years later, he died of respiratory failure. In 1987, Rossington, Powell, King, and Wilkeson reunited Lynyrd Skynyrd, adding vocalist Johnny VanZant and guitarist Randall Hall. The band embarked on a reunion tour, which was captured on the 1988 double-live album, *Southern by the Grace of God/Lynyrd Skynyrd Tribute Tour—1987*. The re-formed Skynyrd began recording in 1991, and for the remainder of the decade, the band toured frequently, putting out albums occasionally. The reunited Skynyrd frequently switched drummers, but it had little effect on their sound.

During the 1990s, Lynyrd Skynyrd were made honorary colonels in the Alabama State Militia, due to their classic-rock staple *Sweet Home Alabama*. During the mid-1990s, VanZant, Rossington, Wilkeson, and Powell regrouped by adding two Southern rock veterans to Skynyrd's guitar stable: former Blackfoot frontman Rickey Medlocke and ex-Outlaw Hughie Thomasson. With ex-Damn Yankee Michael Cartellone bringing stability to the drum chair, the reconstituted band signed to CMC International for the 1997 album *Twenty*. This lineup went on to release *Lyve from Steeltown* in 1998, followed a year later by *Edge of Forever*. The seasonal effort *Christmas Time Again* was released in fall 2000.

The bigger picture, however, in the whole discussion of Southern, or Rebel rock, and, in fact, the whole topic of American grassroots music in general, is the grassroots nature of it. The way the guitars are played, reflecting the delta blues slide styles, the many tips of the musical hat to earlier pioneers in music, and the often down home lyric content reflects images straight out of our earlier discussions of American delta, blues, gospel, and hillbilly music. The threads that trace right back to those ideas, and the people they came from are easily defined. A prime example is within the Lynyrd Skynyrd song *Sweet Home Alabama*. We've already discussed the importance of Muscle Shoals, Alabama, and the Fame Recording Studio being the hotbed of activity by names such as Booker T and the MGs, Otis Redding, Wilson Pickett, and Aretha Franklin—artists that represent the very core of soul music. In *Sweet Home Alabama*, the roots of Skynyrd's music is exposed when Ronnie sings, *"Now Muscle Shoals they got the swamp licks, and they been known to pick a song or two. Lord, they get me off so much. Pick me up when I'm feeling blue . . . now how about you?"*

The current of understanding the American heritage runs like a river through time, held together by and flowing with the diversity of all the stories and all the music of the many characters who make it up. There are so many branches to the river, but they all trace back to a central river. And all musicians who become a part of that find their way by understanding what it means to dig their fingers into the mud of the delta and tributaries of that river.

Or view the whole discussion very much like a tree. A musical tree called American music. And each individual, like the many that we've discussed, and many more we haven't—who they learned from, comes along and grafts a little piece of themselves onto that tree, and a new flower grows. To not study, appreciate, and understand intimately the diversity of culture of American roots music, from the lone bluesman wandering the Mississippi delta, to the hippies at Woodstock, is to deny us all our heritage. The experiment called America can never be more fully appreciated than by viewing it through its authentic grassroots music.

"Music is not an option."

Sam Phillips (1923–2003)

10 Heavy Metal

"Heavy metal" is a term for music that developed from the psychedelic rock of the 1960s. This music is also referred to as "hard rock," and from it developed such substyles as "speed metal," "thrash," and "death metal." Other rock styles, such as punk, new wave, and grunge, are closely related to heavy metal and exhibit noticeable style characteristics that stem from heavy metal rock. There are so many bands that fit in this category that it is impossible to mention them all, much less discuss them all. We must content ourselves with first defining the general characteristics of the style and then acquainting ourselves with representative examples of the style.

The term "heavy metal" has been traced back to the nineteenth century when it referred to large guns on warships. By the end of the century the term was also used to describe a man of heavy power or influence or a person of great ability or power (bodily or mentally). The term has always been synonymous with power. In music, "heavy metal" denotes concepts, images, and experiences of power and/or intensity. The names chosen by heavy metal bands exhibit images of power or intensity:

Electrical, mechanical power: Tesla, AC/DC, Motörhead
Dangerous or unpleasant animals: Scorpions, Ratt
Dangerous or unpleasant people: Twisted Sister, Quiet Riot, Mötley Crüe
Blasphemy or mysticism: Judas Priest, Blue Öyster Cult, Black Sabbath
Death or the terror of death: Anthrax, Poison, Slayer, Megadeth

Several bands add umlauts to give their names an archaic or gothic look: Motörhead, Mötley Crüe, Queensrÿche; these bands also use gothic-looking typefaces on their album covers which adds to the mysticism of the music. Other bands may drop letters from conventional words as part of their name or spell words phonetically, also giving an archaic (rather than illiterate) look: Led Zeppelin, Def Leppard.

The term "heavy metal" in a song lyric first appears in the second verse of the song *Born To Be Wild* (1968) by Steppenwolf and is actually referring to a motorcycle. The loud volume of a big-engined motorcycle is synonymous with the loud volume of the music. Many sources indicate or claim that Steppenwolf lifted the term from William S. Burroughs's novel *The Naked Lunch* (1962), about a beat junkie's fantasies and confessions of drugs, sleaze, and violent sex. However, the term is not contained in *The Naked Lunch*, though Burroughs uses a character called "The Heavy Metal Kid" and refers to "the Heavy Metal People of Uranus" in a later book, *Nova Express* (1964). But remember that the term has been around for at least two centuries as an expression of power.

As stated earlier, there are many heavy metal bands, each with an individual style. Yet each of these bands exhibit general style characteristics that can be categorized in this way:

Sound: Loud volumes; lead guitar-oriented bands; use of electronic distortion; thick sound in which all instruments are combined equally; vocals are generally mixed into the texture rather than being the dominant sound.

Form: Mostly riff-based songs; some are based on blues structures, some on standard AABA song structures, others are original forms based on the form of the text.

Harmony: Generally simple chord progressions based on what is practical to play on the guitar; usually chord progressions of three to five chords; the bass generally plays a simple ostinato riff that is the harmonic foundation of the songs.

Time: Tempos are generally very fast, although there are some groups who record slow ballads; typically in simple duple meter; drums often provide a heavy accent on the backbeat (beats 2 and 4); the bass ostinato is also the metric foundation of the songs.

Melody: The vocals are generally of limited range, sometimes shouted in a monotone; guitar solos, however, are more sweeping in range, covering the entire fingerboard to demonstrate the facility of the lead guitarist.

Other: Most bands are album-oriented, though there are a few that had top twenty singles; with some groups (the so-called "occult rock" bands), the lyrics relate more negative images such as witchcraft, black magic, death, and suicide. Other lyrics deal with sex, drugs, and party attitudes in general.

Of great importance the style of heavy metal music is the use of the **power chord**. The power chord is a full-barred chord played without the thirds of that chord, emphasizing the intervals of perfect fourths and perfect fifths (the basis of natural acoustic phenomenon, the overtone series) and negating any modal characteristics by eliminating the third of the chord. In performance, one guitarist typically plays the lower three strings of the instrument as bar chords while the bass is playing the root of the chords an octave lower. The lead guitar typically plays double-stops of roots and fifths of the chords in a higher range. The chord is heavily amplified and distorted on the electric guitar and is made up of tones and overtones that are constantly renewed and energized by electronic feedback. It can be percussive and rhythmic or sustained indefinitely, used to suspend or to express time: it is the musical articulation of power. A typical example of a power chord riff is the basic riff of Deep Purple's *Smoke on the Water*.

The following examples are just a few of the bands that were responsible for the development of heavy metal rock. Most of these examples are from the late 1960s to the early 1970s when the style was just emerging. There are many other groups and songs that are as worthy of study as these, but due to time limitations we will hold with these examples.

Steppenwolf

This American group formed in 1967 under the leadership of guitarist John Kay. The name of the group is taken from the title of a novel by Hermann Hesse. The band went through several personnel changes, especially going through bass players. The basic instrumentation of the group is: lead vocals, lead guitar, rhythm guitar, bass, drums, and organ. Some writers consider Steppenwolf to be a precursor to the heavy metal style, labeling them a "proto-metal band." But their style clearly exhibits many of the characteristics of heavy metal: Loud volumes, thick textures, lead guitar-oriented, riff-based songs, simple harmonic progressions, medium to fast tempos. However, the band is also related to psychedelic rock, particularly in terms of subject matter of their songs: *Magic Carpet Ride*, *Don't Step On the Grass, Sam*, and *The Pusher* are all based on drug experiences. However, the best example of their heavy metal style is their first single, *Born To Be Wild*.

Listening Timeline 10-1

BORN TO BE WILD (1968)
STEPPENWOLF
from *16 Greatest Hits* (1973)
Strophic form
Modal riff in E minor
MCA MCAD-37049, 1985
3:27

0:00	Introduction	Single drum beat announces the guitar, bass, and drums on the basic riff of the song.
0:15	Verse 1	Solo male vocal (Kay) against the band riff; organ enters.
0:41	Verse 2	
1:07	Refrain	Full band emphasizes all four beats of the measure, driving the pulse to raise excitement level.
1:21	Hook	Single chords play on the downbeats, leading to the solo.
1:34	Solo	Organ (Goldie McJohn) plays over the basic riff from the guitar, bass, and drums;
2:00		lead guitar ends the solo section playing the melody derived from the sung hook, followed by a solo drum fill.
2:10	Verse 1 repeated	

The group recorded six albums between 1967 and 1973 when they disbanded. Their most notable songs include *Born To Be Wild* (1968), *The Pusher* (1967), *Magic Carpet Ride* (1968), and the politically charged *Monster* (1969). Kay tried unsuccessfully to re-form the group twice, first in 1974 and later in 1987, but the band could never recapture the style or excitement of the period from 1967–1969.

Black Sabbath

Black Sabbath is a British band that formed in 1969 and went through several personnel changes between then and the present. They began as a blues-based band called Earth in Birmingham, England and in late 1969 they changed their name to Black Sabbath and recorded their first, self-titled album. This album established them as an occult-oriented band with somewhat evil overtones. The original line-up included Ozzy Osbourne (vocals), Tony Iommi (guitar), Terry "Geezer" Butler (bass), and Bill Ward (drums). Black Sabbath's international fame came with the release of their second album, *Paranoid*, in 1970. This was followed by a string of hard rock albums such as *Masters of Reality* (1971), *Black Sabbath 4* (1972), *Sabbath, Bloody Sabbath* (1973), *Sabotage* (1975). The sound of Black Sabbath, which influenced an entire generation of heavy metal bands, can be heard clearly in the title cut from their second album, *Paranoid*.

Listening Timeline 10-2

PARANOID (1970)
BLACK SABBATH
from *Paranoid*
Strophic form
Modal power chord riff on E
Warner Brothers 3104-2, 1970
2:45

0:00	Introduction	Solo distorted guitar plays an introductory modal E riff; bass and drums join in the riff, setting tempo and key.
0:12	Verse 1 "Finished with my woman . . ."	Solo male vocal (Osbourne) with echo distortion sings over the basic riff.
0:24	Interlude	Instrumental, shifts power chords E, C, D, E twice.
0:36	Verse 2 "All day long I think of things . . ."	
0:47	Interpolation "Can you help me . . ."	Alternating shift between E and D power chords; too brief and innocuous to be considered a bridge. This is the only time in the song this phrase is sung. Followed by the basic riff played twice.
1:11	Verse 3 "I need someone to show me . . ."	
1:23	Solo	Lead guitar (Iommi), played with heavy fuzz distortion over the basic riff.
1:46		Riff played twice.
1:58	Verse 4 "Make a joke and I will sigh . . ."	
2:10	Interlude	
2:22	Verse 5 "And so as you hear these words . . ."	
2:33	Coda	Riff played twice; full final cadence on the last note of the riff.

As with a great many heavy metal groups, Black Sabbath underwent several personnel changes, most prominently with the vocalists: Osbourne left in 1978, came back, and then left again in 1979 to form his own band, Ozzy Osbourne's Blizzard of Oz. Osbourne was replaced by singer Ronnie James Dio, formerly of Ritchie Blackmore's Rainbow. Dio left and was replaced by Ian Gillan, formerly of Deep Purple. And Gillan left to be replaced by Dave Donate. The mainstay of Black Sabbath through their many personnel changes has been guitarist Tony Iommi.

Deep Purple

This British group originally formed in 1968 as a pop-oriented outfit with line-up of Rod Evans (vocals), Ritchie Blackmore (guitar), Jon Lord (keyboards), Nick Simper (bass), and Ian Paice (drums); this line-up released the single *Hush* later that year, which reached the number four position on the U.S. sales charts. In 1970, Evan and Simper were replaced by Ian Gillan and Roger Glover, respectively. From this point, the band began to establish themselves as one of the most influential and successful bands of the early 1970s. Some of their hits include *Hush, Smoke on the Water, Woman from Tokyo, Space Truckin'*, and *Highway Star*. A good example of Deep Purple from the early 1970s is the hit *Smoke on the Water*, from the album *Machine Head* (1972).

Listening Timeline 10-3

SMOKE ON THE WATER (1972)
DEEP PURPLE
from *Deepest Purple: The Very Best of Deep Purple*
Strophic form
Power chord riff in G
Warner Brothers 3486-2, 1970
5:36

0:00	Introduction	Single, distorted guitar (Blackmore) plays riff twice.
0:17		Drums, second guitar enter on riff.
0:34		Bass enters on riff.
0:51	Verse 1 "We all came out to Montreaux . . ."	Solo male vocal (Gillan) over an essentially static G power chord riff in the full band; organ is added.
1:25	Chorus "Smoke on the water . . ."	Vocals are harmonized; the riff progression changes to power chords on C, G-flat, and G.
1:38	Interlude	Full band plays the riff twice.
1:55	Verse 2 "They burned down the gambling house . . ."	
2:28	Chorus	
2:41	Interlude	
2:57	Solo	Lead guitar (Blackmore) solos over the power chord riff; drums play a double-time riff and the bass becomes more active. The solo leads into the chorus progression and ends as the rest of the band plays the riff interlude twice.
3:56	Verse 3 "We ended up at . . ."	
4:29	Chorus	
4:42	Interlude	
4:58	Coda	Riff continues, guitar and organ solo as the song fades out.

Big ego problems began to surface in 1972. In 1973, Gillan left to form his own band (which did very well; Gillan also sang the lead in the London production of *Jesus Christ, Superstar*) and was replaced by the then unknown David Coverdale. Glover also left and went into record production; he was replaced by bassist Glenn Hughes. In 1975, Blackmore left to form his own group, Rainbow (which had several successful releases), and was replaced by American guitarist Tommy Bolin (formerly with the

James Gang). In 1976, Deep Purple disbanded and Coverdale, Lord, and Paice organized the group Whitesnake; Hughes became a session player; and Bolin died of a heart attack in Miami.

In 1984 Gillan, Lord, Paice, Blackmore, and Glover reformed Deep Purple and recorded the album *Perfect Strangers*, which went platinum in the U.S. They are currently playing together, although Gillan has left the group, being replaced by vocalist Joe Lynne Turner.

Led Zeppelin

Led Zeppelin was one of the major proponents of the hard rock style between 1968 and 1980. The band is definitely blues-based in its background, yet many writers refer to the band as a "heavy metal band." There are certainly characteristics within the music of Led Zeppelin that point towards a heavy metal label; yet there are also elements of blues in their music as well as some incidents of psychedelic characteristics in their music. There are also shades of British and Celtic folk music from the third album on, as well as lyrical ideas that were inspired by Celtic mythology. So, as with other groups, labeling does not necessarily fit the subject.

BACKGROUND

In the early 1960s, guitarist Jimmy Page played with several groups in and around London. While with these groups, Page attracted a large following of fans. Page's influences were primarily the 1950s rock and roll guitarists such as Chuck Berry, James Burton, and Scotty Moore. Page has also cited blues guitarists such as Muddy Waters and Elmore James as influences on his guitar style. In 1962 Page was playing lead guitar for a London group known as Neil Christian and the Crusaders; he had developed a reputation as a great guitarist. In 1963, Page had to quit the band because of health problems.

From 1963, Page began earning his living as a session guitarist in London. He quickly developed a reputation among record producers as a talented guitarist who worked well with others and had an almost chameleon-like ability to make his guitar sound like any guitarist. In the mid 1960s Page performed on recordings by the Rolling Stones *(Heart of Stone)*, the Who *(I Can't Explain)*, the Kinks *(You Really Got Me,* supposedly*)*, Van Morrison and Them *(Here Comes the Night)*, and on pop recordings by Tom Jones *(It's Not Unusual)* and Petula Clark *(I Know a Place)*, among several others.

When Eric Clapton left the Yardbirds in 1965 (see Chapter 16), Page was originally approached and offered the lead guitar spot. But he declined because Clapton was his friend and Page did not want to create any professional or personal tensions between Clapton and himself. Page recommended his old school friend, Jeff Beck, and Page remained in London as a session player. From 1965, Page not only had a great reputation as a studio guitarist, but also as a record producer. Producing records for others gave Page the chance to learn record production, which would later come into great use with Led Zeppelin.

In the course of his studio work, Page frequently worked with a talented musician named John Baldwin who played piano, organ, bass, and guitar, and who was also a talented music arranger. Baldwin later changed his name to John Paul Jones. Page and Jones worked together on several recordings, probably most notably with Donovan on his songs *Hurdy Gurdy Man* and *Sunshine Superman*. Jones was also the arranger of the Rolling Stones' *She's a Rainbow* from *Their Satanic Majesties Request* album.

The Yardbirds

After Eric Clapton had quit the Yardbirds, the group was at a dilemma regarding what they should do for a lead guitarist. They at first approached Jimmy Page, who by this time (1965) had a very solid career going as a session guitarist and producer. Page declined the lead guitar spot, citing the possibility of professional conflict with Clapton, and instead recommended an old art school friend of his—Jeff Beck. Beck had played lead in a local London band, Trident, that did not attract any attention, so he was eager to play in an established group. With Beck on guitar, the Yardbirds recorded some of their most familiar songs including *I'm a Man* (a cover of Bo Diddley's 1956 hit), *Train Kept A-Rollin'*, *Shapes of Things*, and *Heart Full of Soul*. During this time that Beck was with the Yardbirds, he began introducing feedback and electronic distortion effects into their music, becoming one of the first rock guitarists to use distortion extensively.

In 1966 the Yardbirds' bass player quit the band and Page was again asked to join the band, this time on bass guitar, which he accepted. By late 1966, Beck began to have some problems with the band (both medical and personal problems), and Page was asked to take over the lead guitar spot in the middle of the 1967 American tour. Beck came back to the band and the Yardbirds played some concert dates with the dual lead guitars of Beck and Page; although not many songs were recorded by the Yardbirds featuring their dynamic twin-lead guitar line-up, two songs were recorded and released as a single at the end of 1966: *Happenings Ten Years Time Ago* and the flip side *Psycho Daisies*. Both songs are soaked in the new psychedelic sound that was just starting to appear in San Francisco, New York City, and London. The A-side of the single, *Happenings Ten Years Time Ago* also featured John Paul Jones on bass in his first recording as a Yardbird.

Listening Timeline 10-4

HAPPENINGS TEN YEARS TIME AGO (1966)
THE YARDBIRDS
from *Roger the Engineer*
Strophic form
Modal riff on E minor and D
Warner Brothers 45734-2, 1996
2:54

0:00	Introduction	Lead guitars (Page and Beck) play melody of chorus over bass and drums, leading into the rhythm riff of the song.
0:15	Verse 1	Solo male vocal (Relf) distorted with sings over the band riff.
0:30	Chorus	Voice is doubled by a second higher voice, also distorted.
0:49	Interlude	Riff played twice by the band.
0:53	Verse 2	
1:12	Interlude	
1:16	Verse 3	
1:31	Interlude	Sustained chords and distortion, lead guitar plays a line similar to the sound of an English siren.

1:46	Solo	Lead guitars trade licks back and forth while voices speak in the background.
2:12	Interlude	
2:17	Verse 4	
2:35	Coda	Based on the interlude, with solo guitars as the song fades out.

Beck eventually quit the band to do his own music, but the career of the Yardbirds was rapidly descending. Some of the few songs that the Yardbirds recorded with Page as lead guitarist were *Ha Ha Said the Clown* (1967) and *Little Games*, which was never released.

By 1967, the original members of the Yardbirds that were still with the band (Relf, Dreja, McCarty) decided to call it quits, leaving Page with the legal rights to the name of the group, and also with the legal responsibility of several already booked concerts in Scandinavia. Page recruited his old session buddy Jones and the two of them hired two relatively unknown performers to complete the group: singer Robert Plant and drummer John Bonham. With this lineup, and calling themselves the New Yardbirds, the group completed the concert obligations of the Yardbirds. On their return to England, the group booked some studio time to record a demo tape for them to take around to various companies for a recording contract.

With the personnel established, the band began looking for a new name, trying for example the Mad Dogs and The Whoopee Cushion, among others. They eventually settled on a name which had been coined either by Keith Moon or John Entwistle (of the Who) in reference to the continued popularity of the group. They called themselves Led Zeppelin, the misspelling intentional so as to avoid mispronunciations.

Led Zeppelin

Led Zeppelin's sound is characterized by the use of speed (i.e., fast tempos and guitar licks) and power, unusual rhythmic patterns, the wailing vocals of Robert Plant, the heavy distortion of Jimmy Page's guitar, and the heavy drum sound of John Bonham. In general, their songs are built around catchy guitar riffs. In their lyrics can be found a partiality toward the occult, the supernatural, and Celtic legend and their melodies often display an influence of Eastern modalities.

The first album by the group begins where the New Yardbirds left off. Some of the songs of this first album are in a very hard-rocking style, such as *Good Times, Bad Times* and *Communication Breakdown*. Others are very strongly blues influenced, such as the cover of Otis Rush's *I Can't Quit You, Baby*.

In general, the songs on the first Led Zeppelin album are characterized as blues-oriented hard rock. The songs are mostly in fast tempos but interspersed with slower tempo songs to create resting points between the faster numbers. The fast songs are characterized by repetitive riffs which serve as the foundations of the songs. A good example of the hard rock style on the first album is *Communication Breakdown*. The song is played at a rapid tempo and is based on a riff. It is an alteration of 16-bar verses and 8-bar choruses and a guitar solo by Page after the second chorus. The solo is fairly typical of Page's hard rock style: very fast, very loud, played primarily in the high register of the guitar, rhythmically strict with even note divisions, and the use of insistent repetitive figures. The fast tempo, the repeated figures, and the steady ascent in pitch all work together to drive the listener to a fever-pitch of excitement.

The second album by the group did much better on the sales charts than did the first album. It opens with what may be considered one of the classic hard rock anthems, *Whole Lotta Love*. The song is based on a blues song written by Willie Dixon and recorded by Muddy Waters in 1963, *You Need Love*, but was not credited as such on the Led Zeppelin album. The Led Zeppelin version is based on a repeated riff and is in ternary form (ABA) with an introduction and a coda. Based on a power chord riff, *Whole Lotta Love* demonstrates the hard rock sound of Led Zeppelin.

Listening Timeline 10-5

WHOLE LOTTA LOVE (1969)
LED ZEPPELIN
from *Led Zeppelin II*
Ternary ABA form
Power chord riff in E
Atlantic 19127-2, 1969
5:30

0:00	Introduction	Electric guitars (Page, overdubbed) lay down the basic riff;
0:06		Bass (Jones) joins in with the riff the second time.
0:11	**A:** Verse 1	Solo male voice (Plant) over the riff.
0:32		Drums (Bonham) enter after singer sings "I'm gonna give you my love . . .", leading to the chorus.
0:35	Chorus	Repeated four times, with multiple voices, while one guitar plays a descending slide after each statement of the phrase.
0:46	Verse 2	
1:09	Chorus	
1:18	**B: Instrumental section.**	An ametric section based on a regular pulse of the high-hat cymbals; not in duple, triple, or quadruple time, just a regular pulse. Bonham plays various accented beats on the ride cymbals, and other rhythms on the tom-toms.
1:43	Distortion is panned through the stereo channels.	
2:05	Plant's voice, distorted, is also panned.	
2:24	Various guitar distortions.	
2:44	Plant yells.	
3:02	Drum beats.	
3:06	Solo guitar plays fills.	
3:20	Return to the riff.	
3:21	**A':** Verse 3	
3:49	Chorus	
3:58	Coda	Pause on sustained chord; Plant sings with various echo responses ("Way down inside . . ."); there is no tempo or meter.
4:16		Two power chords; Plant screams "love" with a long, sustained descent.
4:26		Drum beats.

4:29	Return of the basic riff, various screams, and lyrics from Plant as the song is extended over the riff. The song eventually begins to fade out slowly.

Other songs on the album reflect the strong influence of the blues on the group such as *What Is and What Should Never Be*, *The Lemon Song*, derived from Robert Johnson's *Traveling Riverside Blues*, and a cover of Sonny Boy Williamson's *Bring It On Home*. There are also some hard driving rock songs, such as *Living Loving Maid* and *Heartbreaker*.

The group's third album *Led Zeppelin III* (1970) also showed some similar crossings between the blues and hard rock. Especially noteworthy on the album are the top twenty single *The Immigrant Song* and the blues-based *Since I've Been Loving You*. Also on this album, the band turns to more acoustic, folk-oriented songs such as *Gallows Pole* and *Bron-Yr-Aur Stomp*. This folk music influence was somewhat hinted at on the first album with *Black Mountain Side* and on the second album with *Thank You*. It is taken to a higher level on the next album, *Led Zeppelin IV* (1971). This album, variously referred to as *Zoso* and the *Runes* album, is a continuation of the musical direction of the third album. The entire album is considered to be the group's best effort, and the song *Stairway to Heaven* is considered a masterpiece of rock music. The album opens with two songs of incredibly high-powered rock, *Black Dog* and *Rock and Roll*.

Other songs on the album reflect the band's growing interest in folklore and Celtic mythology. The song *The Battle of Evermore* was inspired by J.R.R. Tolkien's *Lord of the Rings* trilogy and the classic *Stairway to Heaven* was inspired by several readings in Celtic mythology including Edmund Spenser's *The Faerie Queene*. An especially important influence on *Stairway to Heaven* was the work of British mythologist Lewis Spence and his writings about various Celtic goddesses such as the Lady of the Lake, Morgen le Fay, and Rhiannon.

Stairway to Heaven is a well-constructed song that adds layers of sound to the texture as the song progresses. The lyrics are about a woman searching for spiritual perfection. There have also been some who have linked different background stories to the song, for instance that the song is in code and relates the story of largest drug bust in British history. There are also several stories that insist that there are satanic messages mixed backwards into the song. However that may be, the song is still an impressive recording in the rock genre.

The form of the song is not the typical verse/chorus structure of the rock song, but there is a recurring line that could be considered a chorus of sorts. Since the music remains mostly the same while the lyrics change, and since the recurring sections are more than choruses, the form of the song may be better understood by labeling sections as A, B, C, etc., than by trying to impose a verse/chorus labeling that does not quite fit.

Listening Chart 8

STAIRWAY TO HEAVEN
LED ZEPPELIN
from *Led Zeppelin IV*
Atlantic 19129-2, 1971.

Robert Plant, vocal; Jimmy Page, 6-string and 12-string acoustic guitars, electric rhythm guitars, and electric lead guitar; John Paul Jones, bass guitar, synthesized bass, and harmonium; John Bonham, drums.

Sound: The song is built of layers of instrumental sounds from solo six-string guitar plucking an arpeggiated chord pattern to the heavy electric band of the final section. The aesthetic perception, and therefore the longevity of the song's popularity, lies in the careful structuring and layering of these sounds.

Form: On a large level, the song is in two parts: a slow, mostly acoustic opening section and a fast, intensely electric closing section. The slow section breaks down further into three separate stanzas: "A", two stanzas based on the introductory progression ("There's a lady who's sure . . ."); "B", a new chord progression ("Ooh, it makes me wonder . . ."); and "C", a chord progression based on the second phrase of the introduction ("There's a feeling I get . . ."). The complete form for the first section is **Introduction Al A2 B Cl B C2 B C3 B C4**.

The last C stanza (C4) is followed by a transition in which electric instruments are used, and during which there is a tempo modulation. This leads to Page's guitar solo over a repeated descending ostinato, and a final stanza, "D" ("And as we wind on down the road . . ."), sung by Plant. The song gradually slows in the coda, an extension of the D section chord progression, leading to a free-metered statement by Plant to end the song.

Harmony: The song uses original chord progressions in A minor and C major; the four sections are further unified by the similarities of the progressions.

Introduction and Stanza A: The first part is in A minor with a chromatic, descending bass line: Am, Am9/G-sharp (second note refers to bass note), C/G, D/F-sharp, F major7, G/B, Am (twice); the second part is in C: C, D, F major7. Am, C, G, D4-3 (twice). Stanza B is in A minor: Am7, D4-3, Am7, Em, F-sharp m, Em, F-sharp m (played twice). Stanza C is in C/A minor: C, G, Am, C, G, F, Am (played twice). Stanza D is a descending minor progression in A minor: Am, G, F major7, G, Am (repeated several times).

Rhythm: The whole song is in a quadruple meter. The basic pulse for the first section (A, B, and C) is between 80 and 84 beats per minute. The basic pulse for the second section is between 100 and 104 beats per minute.

Melody: The vocal melody is in a high vocal range, but the note range of the melody is relatively narrow. The guitar solo spreads throughout the range of the instrument. The vocal melody is mostly in a diatonic minor mode; the guitar solo is built entirely from the A minor pentatonic scale. The guitar solo also features some interesting and unique traits of Led Zeppelin: call and response between Plant's voice and Page's guitar; repetitive licks in Page's solo; and a gradual ascent in the solo from the lower range to the highest.

Text: The text, completely composed by Plant, describes a woman on a spiritual journey, trying to reach, ultimately, heaven. His sources include mythological writings by noted British mythologist Edward Spence (Spence wrote many books on Egyptian mythology as well as several books on Celtic mythology and the goddesses of Celtic lore, such as The Lady of the Lake and Rhiannon, among others), the *Lord of the Rings* trilogy by J.R.R. Tolkien, and Elizabethan poet Edmund Spenser's epic poem, *The Faerie Queene.*

Other: Fundamentalist Christian accusations that the recording contains subliminal satanic messages hidden in the recorded grooves and mixed into the recording via "'backwards masking" are completely unfounded. According to recording engineer Eddie Kramer, who worked frequently with Led Zeppelin: "Why would they want to spend so much studio time doing something so dumb?" He also adds "there is no such thing as backwards masking and Led Zeppelin never recorded any hidden messages in their songs."[1]

One of the reasons for the success of *Stairway to Heaven*, and of Led Zeppelin in general, lies in the production talents of Page. He has stated in interviews that every song the group recorded was orchestrated and planned out before recording even began. This is a very different approach to recording than The Beatles or Hendrix, who often used the recording studio as a part of the compositional process.

Led Zeppelin continued to release material throughout the 1970s. Although their musical style really did not change very much, their songs were mostly of very high quality and the group continued to do well in record sales and concert sales. In 1976, they began their own record label, Swan Song Records, and their double album set *Physical Graffiti* was the first release on the new label. Unfortunately, there were several tragic incidents that affected the group as well: Robert Plant was nearly killed in a car accident in 1975 and Plant's son died of a virus infection in 1977. They did not travel for two years because of Plant's incapacity, but they released the album *Presence* (1976) and the film and soundtrack album *The Song Remains the Same* (1976).

Led Zeppelin recorded their ninth album, *In Through the Out Door* (1979), in Sweden near the end of 1978. They hit the charts with the song *In the Evening* from this album.

Listening Timeline 10-6

IN THE EVENING (1979)
LED ZEPPELIN
from *In Through the Out Door*
Strophic form
Modal mixolydian riff on E
Swan Song 92443-2, 1979
6:45

0:00	Introduction	Free form electronic Middle Eastern sounds in guitars, bass, and synthesizers.
0:52		Plant intones title phrase in free meter with distortion, leading to a mixolydian riff in tempo.
0:58	Verse 1	
1:34	Chorus	Change in key and new riff alternating G and D, A and E.
1:52	Verse 2	
2:31	Chorus	
2:47	Verse 3	
3:26	Chorus	
3:44	Solo	Solo guitar (Page) on the verse riff.
4:21	Interlude	A change in key and texture, based on a descending progression (C, Bm, Am, G). The solo guitar continues over this new progression.
4:55		A sustained "oooh" by Plant segues into next verse.

4:57	Verse 4	Return of the original mixolydian riff.
5:33	Chorus	Lead guitar is more prominent.
5:51	Coda	Mixolydian riff with Plant improvising vocals over it; Page improvises and the song gradually fades out.

In 1980, drummer John Bonham died of a heart attack brought on by excessive drinking and partying and the rest of the band called it quits. Each remaining member has gone on to other projects: Baldwin has produced recordings for other groups, recorded some of his own material, and composed some film soundtracks. Page also has turned to production and film soundtracks, as well as recording his own albums; in 1985, Page joined forces with ex-Bad Company singer Paul Rodgers to create the band The Firm, which released two albums. Robert Plant has had a great deal of success with various musicians on his solo albums *Pictures at Eleven* (1982), *The Principle of Moments* (1983), *Shaken and Stirred* (1985), *Now and Zen* (1988), and *Manic Nirvana* (1990), as well as the 1985 collaboration with Page and Jeff Beck for *The Honeydrippers*. In 1994 and 1995, Page and Plant reunited for several concert tours, which resulted (in part) in the album *No Quarter*.

Metal Bands in the Late '70s–Early '80s

In the late 1970s and early 1980s there was a increase of metal bands, especially from England, but also many coming from the United States as well as other countries around the world. The British groups in particular, another sort of "British Invasion" that was dubbed by the media with the unwieldy acronym NWOBHM (the New Wave Of British Heavy Metal), featured such bands in the mid-1970s as Diamond Head, Motörhead, and Judas Priest. These groups, along with Australian head bangers AC/DC, German metalists the Scorpions and UFO, and the American Van Halen took metal rock to an interesting and exciting new level of experience. The British bands that followed in their wake became some of the most popular bands in the 1980s, including Def Leppard, Iron Maiden, and Saxon. The bands at the end of the 1970s, strongly influenced by the music of the originators of metal like Black Sabbath and Deep Purple, were still somewhat indebted to the blues as a source of inspiration; the bands of the 1980s would change all of that.

AC/DC

AC/DC is an Australian group that formed in 1974. It is centered around brothers Malcolm and Angus Young, who play rhythm and lead guitar, respectively. Other band members include Phil Rudd (drums), Mark Evans (bass), and Bon Scott (vocals). Scott died from alcohol abuse in 1980 and was replaced with singer Brian Johnson for the album *Back In Black*, and eventually drummer Rudd and bassist Evans were also replaced.

The style of the band is a hard-driving, steady rock beat, songs based on catchy riffs, especially in introductions and endings, and lyrics that are concerned with sex, violence, and drinking. There are many good examples of their style just on the album *Back In Black*: one of my favorites is the riff-based *You Shook Me All Night Long*.

Listening Timeline 10-7

YOU SHOOK ME ALL NIGHT LONG (1980)
AC/DC
from *Back In Black*
Strophic form
Power chord riff in G
Atco 92418-2, 1980
3:29

Time	Section	Description
0:00	Introduction	Lead and rhythm guitars (Angus and Malcolm Young) play the opening phrases, leading to the verse riff in
0:16		time with a drum kick; the riff is played twice.
0:30	Verse 1	Solo male vocal (Johnson) over the power riff. Bass enters at the end of the verse.
1:01	Chorus	Harmonized vocals, phrase is sung twice.
1:16	Verse 2	
1:47	Chorus	Sung four times.
2:20	Solo	Lead guitar (Angus) based on the chorus progression.
2:50	Chorus	Sung four times.
3:18	Coda	Extension of the chorus, the phrase "yeah you shook me" is repeated; the song ends with a final cadence on the dominant chord.

AC/DC has remained active recording and touring over the years. Although they have undergone several personnel changes (besides the death of Bon Scott) in the rhythm section, AC/DC has remained a hard-working band and are one of the most popular bands in the world.

Van Halen

Van Halen is a U.S. group formed in 1974 around brothers Eddie (guitar) and Alex (drums) Van Halen. Other original group members were vocalist David Lee Roth and bassist Michael Anthony. In 1985, Roth left to pursue his own career and was replaced by singer/guitarist Sammy Hagar. Hagar left the band to return to a solo career in 1998.

The Van Halen brothers (born in the Netherlands) were trained in classical music by their father, who wanted them to pursue a concert career. Eddie's classical training surfaces in the keyboard tracks and synthesizer programs that he played on some of the later albums. Eddie's classical training has also manifested itself in his guitar solos, in which he often plays well-thought out, lyrical melodic lines, and in some of the unusual (for rock music) harmonies that occur in some songs. Eddie also makes use of classical guitar technique in his playing, using natural and artificial guitar harmonics to create solid melodic lines. He has in fact worked out a performance method in which both hands pluck and hammer the guitar strings on the guitar neck, instead of just plucking or strumming the strings, resulting in sound effects that were new to rock guitar. This style of playing has come to be known as "tapping" or "tap technique" and has been adapted by many guitarists as part of their own style.

The group has released several albums with some very good material, for example their cover version of the Kinks' *You Really Got Me* and their original song *Runnin' with the Devil*, both from the first album (1978). *Runnin' with the Devil* opens with a steady bass pulse that remains constant throughout the song; this turns out to be a major contributor to the overall affective power of the song. The lyrics are not about literally worshipping the Devil (as many critics of heavy metal insist), but are rather emphasizing the freedom of social ties: freedom from love, law, responsibility, and the power that this freedom engenders, according to music historian Rob Walser. In most heavy metal songs there is an extended, virtuosic guitar solo—this is, after all, one of the main characteristics of the style. In *Runnin' with the Devil*, there is no extended solo; instead, Van Halen plays a four-bar instrumental section that is too short to be considered a solo and is more like an instrumental transition (this appears twice, after the second verse and after that verse is repeated).[2]

The cut that follows *Runnin' with the Devil* is an extended *cadenza*, or improvised solo section, for unaccompanied guitar called *Eruption*. *Eruption* begins with an initial power chord that establishes the tonal center and displays Van Halen's guitar technique.

Listening Timeline 10-8

ERUPTION (1978)
VAN HALEN
from *Van Halen*
Through-composed form
Melodic figures based in A
Warner Brothers 3075-2, 1978
1:42

Time	Section	Description
0:00	Introduction	Three drum beats and a cymbal crash signal the lead guitar (Eddie) to enter on sustained notes bent with the tremolo bar to a full A power chord.
0:04		Free-form ascent on rapid pitches with a slower descent to low notes bent with the tremolo bar and sustained, with vibrato.
0:18		Four chords ascend, leading to a rapid figure in the high range that descends slightly, ending with tremolo bends.
0:31		"Classical" lick is double-picked (this lick is based on a violin study by 19th century composer Rudolph Kreutzer); the line ascends and then descends to a low note bent lower with the tremolo bar and sustained with distortion.
0:47		A rapidly-picked figure ascends in pitch.
0:57		A rapid triplet/sextuplet tapped figure ascends and descends.
1:24		A final sustained note, bent lower with the tremolo bar, slightly touched with feedback; the note is bent lower again and sustained as the recording fades out.

Currently, with all the in-fighting and back-stabbing between former members and the Van Halen brothers, it is a mystery as to what has become of Van Halen. Both David Lee Roth and Sammy Haggar have toured extensively with their new groups, and in fact were rumored to possibly headline a tour together. In the meanwhile, nothing has been heard (as of this writing) from either Eddie or Alex.

Judas Priest

One of the most influential British metal bands of the 1970s was the Birmingham-based group Judas Priest. The group was formed in 1970 by guitarist K.K. Downing and bassist Ian Hill. They went through several personnel changes before hitting the classic line up that included second lead guitarist Glenn Tipton, vocalist Rob Halford, and drummer Dave Holland, which was in place by 1979's *British Steel* album.

Judas Priest began forming their sound with the release of *Rocka Rolla* in 1974. Their next album, *Sad Wings of Destiny* (1975), is considered by many to be one of the most influential albums on the 1980s generation of metal bands, including Iron Maiden, Motörhead, Megadeth, and Metallica.

Their 1978 album *Stained Class* in particular became a favorite with future thrash metal rockers. The dark sound of *Better By You, Better Than Me* illustrates what Judas Priest was all about—a darker, heavier sound than the punk, new wave, and disco that was hitting the airwaves at the same time.

 **Listening Timeline 10-9**

BETTER BY YOU, BETTER THAN ME (1978)
JUDAS PRIEST
from *Stained Class*
Standard song form
Verse: Riff based on A/A minor
Bridge: Progression on D minor, B-flat, and A
Interlude: Riff based on G
Columbia CK 35296, 1978
3:16

Time	Section	Description
0:00	Introduction	Solo rhythm guitar with distortion plays basic riff;
0:08		Drums and bass enter;
0:10		Lead guitar plays a brief solo over the riff.
0:20	Verse A1	Solo male vocal (Halford) over the basic riff. The title phrase hook is sung as the band pauses, followed by a return of the riff.
0:46	Verse A2	The second part of the verse ("tell her now . . .") is harmonized by a second voice, leading to a return of the hook sung solo, followed by the riff.
1:14	Interlude	Key change to G, the vocal is distorted with echo; the phrase is sung twice.
1:24	Bridge B	Full sustained chords, the key changes to D minor; vocal distortion is deleted.
1:46	Verse A3	Return to the riff in A; second half of the verse ("guess I'll learn . . .") is harmonized.
2:13	Interlude	
2:23	Bridge B	Repeated with a gradual fade out.

Judas Priest followed up the energy of *Stained Class* with the release of *Hell Bent for Leather* also in 1978. By this time, the dark, steady riff sound of Priest was being surpassed by their own fans in the NWOBHM, like Iron Maiden, and the American progeny like Metallica, Megadeth, and Anthrax. Judas Priest remained active through the 1980s and 1990s, touring and releasing albums. In the 1980s they scored respectable hits with the albums *British Steel* (1980), with the single *Living After Midnight*, and *Screaming for Vengeance* (1982), with its popular single and video *You've Got Another Thing Coming*. After the release of *Painkiller* in 1990, singer Halford left to pursue his own career. The band was inactive until 1997 when they released the album *Jugulator*, considered a major flop. Halford had organized his own groups Fight and later Halford (named for himself) in the 1990s, but neither group were successful. As of this writing, Judas Priest and Rob Halford are on inactive status.

Around 1983 another wave of metal bands came out of Los Angeles—Mötley Crüe, Slayer, Quiet Riot, and Dokken, for example. As Los Angeles became the center of heavy metal, bands from around the country (such as Poison and Guns 'n' Roses) moved to L.A. with the hopes of getting a recording contract. In 1984, metal bands from around the world joined in the boom: Loudness (Japan) and Europe (Sweden), for example. Heavy metal fan magazines sprang up all over the world as well.

The metal bands of the 1980s began to abandon the blues roots of their forebears. The harmonies these groups began to explore were chord progressions that suggested themselves from the strings of the guitar, practical chords (especially power chord patterns) that fit comfortably under the hand. The musical characteristics of hard rock began to be transformed in heavy metal, helping to create a variety of metal styles:

+ Almost no use of 12-bar blues progressions.
+ Chord progressions move by whole step (two frets) or half steps (one fret), creating a more disjunct, angular type of chord progression.
+ More dependence melodically (in solos) on diatonic scale patterns rather than blues scales.
+ Extremely fast tempos.
+ Rapidly played scale passages (thrashing) came into common use.
+ Tapping became a common practice.
+ Blues guitar techniques (slide, bends, etc.) are completely abandoned.

Among the most studious practitioners of the new style of playing metal music was the California band Metallica.

Metallica

Metallica originated in 1982 as the brainchild of drummer Lars Ulrich (b. 1963) and guitarist James Hetfield (b. 1963). Ulrich, born in Copenhagen, Denmark, moved with his family in 1972 to Los Angeles. Growing up with exposure to jazz and rock music gave Ulrich an open mind in regards to musical influences. Reaching his teen years in Los Angeles in the mid and late 1970s, however, was not conducive to the music that he particularly enjoyed: the British heavy metal bands that followed in the wake of the metal originators, such as Judas Priest, Diamond Head, Motörhead, and Saxon. In meeting Hetfield at a Los Angeles metal concert, Ulrich realized he had found a kindred spirit. At least as far as musical taste was concerned.

The music of Los Angeles of the early 1980s was mostly underground punk like X and Black Flag, which did not necessarily do anything for these metal heads. Playing in local clubs that usually catered to punk audiences, the variety of music in the LA clubs gradually widened to include the new up and coming metal bands like Metallica and Slayer. After arranging to provide a song on a compilation album of metal music in 1982 called *Metal Massacre*, Ulrich and Hetfield realized that they would need to put together an official band in a hurry. Advertising for players, they turned up lead guitarist Dave Mustaine.

Mustaine, also a fan of the British metal groups that Ulrich and Hetfield were into, provided Metallica with a harsh, driving lead guitar sound that fit perfectly under the dark rhythm chords of Hetfield. They also tried a variety of bass players, most of whom did not really work out very well for the band.

Hired to play a gig in San Francisco, the band went to hear various local bands at the San Francisco clubs. Watching one band called Trauma, Ulrich and Hetfield went nuts over the very talented bass player, Cliff Burton (1962–1986); Ulrich and Hetfield set their sights on recruiting Burton for Metallica. Burton at first demurred, stating that he wanted to stay in San Francisco and remain in community college. When they realized that they could not get Burton to go down with them to Los Angeles,

Metallica pulled up stakes and moved to San Francisco. With this move, they successfully recruited Burton to join the band.

After a number of low level successes in recording and live performances, Metallica hooked up with an east coast manager, a record store manager named Jon Zazula. Under Zazula's guidance and help, Metallica gradually became a known quantity in the music world. Before they could begin touring and recording, the band needed to readjust the personnel of the group; guitarist Mustaine was becoming more and more undependable because of his drinking and drug habits, so the band fired him and replaced him with lead player Kirk Hammett (b. 1962). With this line up now in place, Metallica was ready to take the metal world by storm. Mustaine went on to form the very successful band Megadeth.

The band released the albums *Kill 'Em All* (1983) and *Ride the Lightning* (1984) on the independent label Megaforce. The success of these albums in the metal underground brought Metallica to the attention of Elektra Records, who offered them a deal for their next records. The first album that Metallica turned out for Elektra turned out to be a mega-hit for them, particularly the title cut, *Master of Puppets*. The song lyrics "tell the story of drug addiction as a parable of power."[3]

Listening Timeline 10-10

MASTER OF PUPPETS (1986)
METALLICA
from *Master of Puppets*
Strophic form
Verse: Power riff in E
Chorus: Power riff in G
Interlude: Original progression: Em, D, C A5, B5
Elektra 9 60439-2, 1986
8:31

Time	Section	Description
0:00	Introduction	Sustained, distorted descending power chord pattern;
0:04		Power chord pattern is played in time, becomes the verse riff.
0:12		Bass and drums accent the chords.
0:22		Solo guitar plays the riff, accented by the bass and drums.
0:31		Bass and drums set the groove.
0:55	Transition	The riff is played four times.
1:01	Verse 1	Solo male vocal (Hetfield) screams the lyric.
1:29	Chorus	"Faster" is echoed by a second voice; key change to G.
2:10	Transition	Original riff played four times.
2:20	Verse 2	
2:47	Chorus	
3:31	Extension	The band cuts out; "master" is repeated by various distorted voices.
3:34	Interlude	The tempo slows down greatly; a new chord progression in E minor is played in arpeggios on electric guitar;
4:10	Solo	Melodic guitar solo (Hetfield) is played based on the new progression.
4:48		Gradual increase in force and tempo.
5:11		Key change to F-sharp power chords.
5:20		Sung by multiple voices.
5:38	Transition	The tempo kicks up to the original speed and the original riff returns.

5:43	Solo	Fast guitar solo (Hammett) based on the basic riff.
6:40	Transition	Riff from the introduction leads back to the verse.
6:49	Verse 3	Based on the riff.
7:16	Chorus	
7:58	Coda	Riff is repeated with guitar solo (Hammett)
8:18		Song ends with laughter over a sustained chord that fades out.

Master of Puppets became a strong seller for Elektra and made Metallica a well-known name in heavy metal. After its release, the group embarked on a world tour to promote the album. While touring Sweden in September 1986, after playing a show in Stockholm, the tour bus in which the band was riding hit a patch of ice late in the night. The bus skidded out of control and flipped over several times. Bassist Cliff Burton, sleeping in one of the overhead beds, was thrown out of the window and crushed by the bus as it rolled over him.

The death of Burton traumatized Metallica for some time, but eventually they regrouped and continued to tour and play. Burton's replacement was Jason Newstead who came on and helped to rejuvenate the band and their fans after the tragedy. Metallica continued to release a number of quality recordings into the 1990s including *Metallica* (1991; best known as *The Black Album*) and *Load* (1996). In 2001, bassist Newstead announced his retirement from Metallica; the band released the album *St. Anger* in 2003.

The popularity of heavy metal increased throughout the 1980s and 1990s. This was attributed in large part to the fact that metal had broadened its audience base; according to *Billboard* magazine metal was "no longer the exclusive domain of male teenagers. The metal audience has become older (college-aged), younger (pre-teen), and more female." MTV also joined in the heavy metal frenzy by programming more videos into their regular video shows and in 1986 introducing a late-night show that would prove to be tremendously popular (1.3 million viewers each week): the *Headbangers' Ball.*

Robert Walser notes in his book *Running with the Devil* that the

> *expansion of the metal scene in the 1980s was accompanied by its fragmentations. Genres proliferated: magazine writers and record marketers began referring to thrash metal, commercial metal, lite metal, power metal, American metal, black (satanic) metal, white (Christian) metal, death metal, speed metal, glam metal—each of which bears a particular relationship to that older, vaguer, more prestigious term "heavy metal."*[4]

Heavy metal in the 1980s exerted an influence on other kinds of popular music, including funk (Michael Jackson's *Beat It* featuring a guitar solo by Eddie Van Halen) and rap (Run-D.M.C.'s version of Aerosmith's *Walk This Way*). By the middle of the decade, the sound of metal began appearing in advertising. The groups particularly in Los Angeles were taking on heavy makeup as part of their image. This resulted in the so-called "hair bands," groups that featured neatly coifed and excessively made-up males who may or may not have been able to play their instruments well, so long as they looked good. Groups in the 1990s and 2000s have begun to fuse many different types of music into their metal sound, resulting in a variety of groups like Korn and Limp Bizkit, both influenced by rap and hip hop, and Wilco, with an interesting mix of country and metal.

Endnotes

1. Stephen Davis, *Hammer of the Gods* (New York: Ballantine Books, 1985), pp. 309–310.
2. Robert Walser, *Running with the Devil: Power, Gender, and Madness in Heavy Metal Music* (Hanover, NH and London: Wesleyan University Press, 1993), p. 54. Walser gives some interesting insights into the songs *Runnin' with the Devil* (pp. 46–54) and *Eruption* (pp. 68–76).
3. Chris Crocker, *Metallica: The Frayed Ends of Metal* (New York: St. Martin's Griffin, 1993), p. 77.
4. Walser, *Running with the Devil*, p. 13.

11 Fusions

Introduction

By the end of the 1960s, various musical styles had merged with rock to create new styles in rock music: in 1965 folk/protest music had merged with rock to create folk rock, which then merged with country and western around 1968 to create country rock in southern California. Jazz, which had always exerted some influence on the development of rock, was actively combined with rock in the mid-1960s, creating jazz rock. Also in the mid-to-late-1960s, elements of classical music were merged with rock, resulting in what was referred to in the 1970s as progressive rock (in Europe) or art rock (in the U.S.). Because their creators successfully fused elements of these styles—folk, country, jazz, and classical—with rock to create new rock styles, the new hybrids can be referred to as fusions. It should be remarked that for most musicians and rock historians, "fusion" actually refers to the hybrid musical style created through the merging of jazz with rock and is more often considered a jazz style rather than a rock style. However, all of these rock hybrids are created by combining elements of unique musical styles with rock. In other words, the fusing of elements from one established musical style with those of rock, there is a justification in the use of the term "fusion" as a general label for these hybrid rock styles.

Jazz Rock

Since the beginnings of rock 'n' roll in the 1950s, jazz has played an interesting and influential role in the development of rock. Many of the jump groups and rhythm and blues outfits were originally jazz groups, such as Louis Jordan's Tympany Five. It has also been shown that some of the earliest rock 'n' roll performers were influenced by jazz—Bill Haley's Comets were originally a western swing band (combining elements of country and big band swing), and his guitarists (Danny Cedrone and Frank Beecher) were originally jazz performers heavily influenced by jazz guitarist Charlie Christian. Chuck Berry cited the influence of jazz tenor saxophonist Illinois Jacquet on his own approach to melodic soloing. Many of the psychedelic guitarists, such as Jerry Garcia, were influenced by jazz saxophonist John Coltrane. And in England, trad jazz had been an important musical scene in the early and mid-1960s at the same time that the beat groups were starting to make an impact on rock music. The whole blues scene in England was entwined with the jazz traditionalists: Alexis Korner's Blues Incorporated was a jazz/blues group that featured besides guitarist Korner bassist Jack Bruce (later in Cream), and drummer Charlie Watts and singer Mick Jagger before they became the Rolling Stones. Other British beat groups, such as Manfred Mann, the Who, and the Spencer Davis Group, had likewise begun their careers playing jazz styles that they later combined with rock.

As with folk rock and country rock, the rock elements that are present in jazz rock include:

+ Electric instruments.
+ Distortion devices
+ The rock rhythm section (drums, electric rhythm guitar, and electric bass).
+ Loud volumes.
+ Rock singing styles and techniques, such as screamed vocals.
+ Strong dependence on the guitar as a solo instrument.
+ Rock guitar techniques, such as bent notes and feedback.

The musical elements contributed to the hybrid style from jazz include:

+ Extensive improvisation.
+ Extended chord structures.
+ Extended harmonies, such as 9th and 11th chords.
+ Jazz-influenced rhythmic intricacies, syncopations, and changing meters.

The first groups to successfully (that is, commercially) combine jazz and rock into a new musical style emerged in the United States in the mid 1960s. One of the first was called The Electric Flag, a group created in 1967 by blues guitarist Mike Bloomfield (ex-Paul Butterfield Blues Band), singer Nick Gravenites (later to join briefly Big Brother and the Holding Company backing Janis Joplin), and drummer Buddy Miles (later with Jimi Hendrix's Band of Gypsys). The Electric Flag was centered around the blues styles of Bloomfield and Gravenites, but in the background was a horn section of saxophones, trumpets, and trombone that played musical arrangements inspired by the black jazz combos of the 1940s—not rhythm and blues horn sections, but rather the jump horn sections epitomized by Count Basic's small groups. While the horns were still used to punctuate background riffs, in the manner of rhythm and blues and soul horn sections, the horn section of the Flag also provided some jazz-influenced counterpoint behind the core blues rock rhythm section. These jazz-influenced arrangements would become the basis of the jazz rock style, heavily influential on such groups as Blood, Sweat, & Tears, Chicago, Chase, The Ides of March, and others.

Blood, Sweat & Tears

Formed in 1968 by session multi-instrumentalist Al Kooper and New York studio musicians Randy Brecker (trumpet) and Bobby Colomby (drums), BS&T recorded their first album *Child Is Father to the Man* which was received with very little acclaim by critics and the listening public. Kooper was soon hired by Columbia Records as a producer and was replaced by vocalist David Clayton-Thomas. Brecker also quit, returning to the New

York studio scene where he later joined such jazz fusion groups as White Elephant and later formed an exceptional fusion group with his tenor sax-playing brother Michael, the Brecker Brothers Band. Colomby remained with BS&T as drummer and arranger until 1974.

With the addition of Clayton-Thomas, BS&T began recording more pop-oriented material and released their second album, *Blood, Sweat & Tears*, in 1969. This album included the hit single *Spinning Wheel*, written by Clayton-Thomas, and also included covers of Billie Holiday's *God Bless the Child* and Laura Nyro's *And When I Die*. The album opens and ends with arrangements of 20th-century French composer Erik Satie's piano work *Gymnopedie*, thereby incorporating not only jazz elements with rock, but also classical elements.

A good example of the sound and style of BS&T is Clayton-Thomas's song *Lucretia MacEvil* from the 1970 album *Blood, Sweat & Tears 3*. The song opens with a percussive horn riff, joined by rhythm section, that will become the hook between verses. It is AABA form with extended coda *(Lucretia's Reprise)*. The saxophone fills of first verse are scored for the full horn section in subsequent verses. Note the interesting rhythmic syncopations in the drums, not the typical rock style of drumming. The bridge features a very dissonant horn arrangement and the coda *(Lucretia's Reprise)* features more horn improvisation than is usual for BS&T, particularly featuring trumpeter Lew Soloff.

Listening Timeline 11-1

LUCRETIA MacEVIL and *LUCRETIA'S REPRISE (1970)*
BLOOD, SWEAT & TEARS
from *Blood, Sweat & Tears 3*
Standard song form with extended coda/reprise
Original progression in E
Columbia CD 30090, 1970
5:39

Time	Section	Description
0:00	Introduction	Brass and saxes blast the opening figure that will become the basic riff for transitions and solos; rhythm section enters the second time.
0:08	Verse A1	Solo male vocal (Clayton-Thomas), with fills from the saxophones.
0:38	Transition	Brass lick from the introduction is played twice.
0:46	Verse A2	Full horn section plays fills and bops.
1:16	Interlude	Bass, drums, and piano lead into the bridge.
1:21	Bridge B	Dissonant horn bops and organ lines; ends with a ritardando, a sustained note on "due" then solo vocal phrase "what you goin' to do" sets the tempo up again.
1:50	Verse A3	Saxophone fills.
2:20	Coda (spoken)	Piano plays riff;
2:25		brief guitar solo;
2:32		horn riffs over the guitar solo;
2:56		unison brass riff.
3:04 (0:00)	Lucretia's Reprise	Solo piano plays the riff;
3:14 (0:10)		Clayton-Thomas speaks over the riff;
3:31 (0:27)		horn punches played over the riff;
3:56 (0:52)	Solo	Trumpet solo (Lew Soloff) plays over the repeated horn riff. The riff gradually fades, then the solo also begins to fade.

Blood, Sweat & Tears remained active throughout the 1970s, releasing their last album, *Nuclear Blues*, in 1980. Clayton-Thomas is still performing and often forms a touring group to play concerts.

Chicago

Chicago was originally formed in 1966 by guitarist/vocalist Terry Kath and woodwind player Walter Parazaider (saxophones and flute). Teaming with Parazaider's fellow music students from DePaul University James Pankow (trombone), Lee Loughnane (trumpet), Danny Seraphine (drums), and Robert Lamm (keyboards and vocals), the group was originally called The Missing Links, though they soon changed their name to The Big Thing in 1967. Discovered by Columbia Records producer James William Guercio (an old school friend of Parazaider) in 1967, the band moved to Los Angeles where they were joined by bassist/vocalist Peter Cetera. Guercio changed the band's name to Chicago Transit Authority, under which they recorded their first self-titled album. *Chicago Transit Authority* (1969) featured many sounds that would come to typify Chicago:

- Hard-edged rock guitar with distortion *(Free Form Guitar)*.
- Tightly-structured horn arrangements *(Beginnings, Does Anybody Really Know What Time It Is?)*.
- Extended improvisations *(I'm a Man, Beginnings)*.
- Ensemble harmony vocals *(Does Anybody Really Know What Time It Is?, Beginnings)*.

After threatened with a lawsuit by Chicago Mayor Richard Daley, the band shortened its name to Chicago.[1] With the release of their second album, *Chicago II* in 1971, Chicago demonstrated a clear rock-based style with jazz overtones. Several songs on the second album were popular sellers, such as *Colour My World* and *25 or 6 to 4*. There was also a strong antiwar feeling on the album with the extended ending song, *It Better End Soon*. A good example of their early style (as opposed to their later pop-oriented style) is the Terry Kath song *25 or 6 to 4* from *Chicago II*. The song also links Chicago with the then fading psychedelic movement: the narrator of the song has ingested some kind of substance that has made him lose track of time and he is wondering while "sitting cross-legged on the floor" whether it is 25 or 26 minutes before 4:00 in the morning.

Listening Timeline 11-2

25 OR 6 TO 4 (1971)
CHICAGO
from *Chicago II*
Strophic form
Verse: descending minor progression in A minor
Refrain: original IV, I, V progression in C major
Columbia CRD-3002, 1971
4:48

Time	Section	Description
0:00	Introduction	Electric guitar and bass play the verse progression twice;
0:07		drums enter the second time; horn riff played the
0:13		third and fourth times.
0:26	Verse 1	Solo male voice (Lamm) over the descending minor chord progression; horn section plays fills.
0:53	Refrain 1	Harmonized vocals (add Cetera and Kath); guitar plays fills.
1:06	Interlude	Horn section plays riffs while the guitar plays a brief solo.

1:19	Verse 2	Solo voice, horns and guitar play fills.
1:45	Refrain 2	Harmony vocals.
1:58	Solo	Guitar solo (Kath) over the verse progression;
2:52		Add wah wah pedal distortion.
3:15	Interlude	Rhythm guitar, bass, and drums play the riff figure while the guitar continues to play the solo.
3:28		Horn riff from the introduction is played twice.
3:42	Verse 3	Solo vocal, guitar continues solo; horns play fills.
4:08	Refrain 3	Harmony vocals.
4:20	Interlude	Riff is played twice and guitar solos more.
4:33	Coda	Horns play sustained chords over the verse progression and the tempo ritards ending the song with a sustained tonic 13th chord.

As their career continued, their music became gradually more pop-oriented with jazz accents and rock accouterments. They have remained extremely popular over the years and have placed several singles high in the *Billboard* pop music charts, including *Colour My World* (1970), *Dialogue* (1972), *Feelin' Stronger Everyday* (1973), *If You Leave Me Now* (1976), *Hard To Say I'm Sorry* (1984), and *You're the Inspiration* (1986). Although having a very successful career, Chicago has endured several upsets including a rift with manager-producer Guercio in 1977 and Terry Kath's accidental death from a self-inflicted gunshot in 1978. Cetera left the band for a successful solo career in 1985 and Seraphine left in 1988.

Tower of Power

Tower of Power was formed in 1968 in Oakland, California. Strongly based in jazz and rhythm and blues, Tower of Power is seen by some as an alternative to the psychedelic rock of the Bay area. However, the band is more properly an amalgam of the soul, jazz, blues, rock, and Latin styles of other San Francisco area groups like Sly and the Family Stone and Santana. Because of the strong influence of soul and rhythm and blues, Tower of Power is also linked to the 1970s funk bands and is especially compared with Earth, Wind & Fire. The multi-ethnic makeup of the band also contributes to their fusion style.

By 1973, Tower of Power had grown to a 12-piece band with lead singer Lennie Williams backed by a tightly organized rhythm section of Francis Rocco Prestia (bass) and David Garibaldi (drums); like the funk bands, Prestia's bass lines set up the rhythmic direction for their tunes while working closely with and against the rhythmic patterns supplied by Garibaldi's drums. Other members of the rhythm section include jazz/soul-based organist and vocalist Chester Thompson, jazz/rock-based guitarist Bruce Conte, Latin percussionist Brent Byars. The horn section, sometimes sounding like a percussive soul/funk horn group and sometimes like a jazz-based big band wind group, consists of Lenny Pickett (tenor sax, flute, clarinet), Emilio Castillo (tenor sax), Stephen Kupka (baritone sax, oboe), Mic Gillette (trumpet, trombone, fluegelhorn), and Greg

Adams (trumpet, fluegelhorn). *What Is Hip*, the opener from their third album, *Tower of Power* (1973), demonstrates the multiple sources of their style as well as the extraordinary musicianship of the group.

Listening Timeline 11-3

WHAT IS HIP? (1973)
TOWER OF POWER
from *Tower of Power*
Strophic form
Verse: Funk vamp on E
Chorus: Original progression in E
Warner Brothers 2681-2, 1973
5:02

Time	Section	Description
0:00	Introduction	Drum kick into the bass riff and guitar solo (Conte), with horn bops.
0:19	Verse 1	Solo male vocal (Williams) over the funk groove of the band; horn fills.
0:37	Chorus 1	Multiple voices call and solo voice responds ("tell me");
0:47		Ends with a solo distorted trumpet solo (Gillette).
1:01	Interlude	Band plays the funk groove while the guitar solos above.
1:10	Verse 2	
1:28	Chorus 1	Ends again with the distorted trumpet solo.
1:52	Chorus 2	Multiple voices call, solo voice responds; horns play hard bop figures to accentuate the sung phrases.
2:12	Interlude	Guitar solo featured.
2:21	Verse 3	
2:39	Chorus 1	
3:03	Extension	Distorted trumpet solo from the end of the chorus continues;
3:22	Solo/Chorus 1	Organ solo (Thompson) over the sung chorus;
3:49		Horns play descending harmony figure over the band groove, solo, and chorus.
4:44		Horn bops with percussion end on a sustained note.

Steely Dan

Steely Dan was formed in New York in 1972 by jazz aficionados Walter Becker (bass, vocals) and Donald Fagen (keyboards, vocals) and named after a steam-powered dildo in William S. Burroughs's novel *The Naked Lunch*. Originally a recording and touring group consisting of guitarists Denny Dias and Jeff "Skunk" Baxter, drummer Jim Hodder, and lead vocalist David Palmer, by 1976 Steely Dan had become a duet with Becker and Fagen supported by the best east coast and west coast studio musicians.

The group's first two albums, *Can't Buy a Thrill* (1972) and *Countdown to Ecstasy* (1973) were mostly rock sounds that exhibited a strong influence from jazz. Dias left the band in 1974 before their next album, *Pretzel Logic* (1974), which began to incorporate more studio personnel. Palmer was replaced by lead vocalist Michael McDonald for the album *Katy Lied* (1975). By this time, Hodder and Baxter had left the band, Baxter becoming one of the lead guitarists for the Doobie Brothers; after the release of *Katy Lied*, McDonald also left to join the Doobie Brothers. By the time they released *The Royal Scam* (1976), Steely Dan had become a strictly studio band. The 1977 album *Aja* demonstrated more fully than the previous albums the strong influence that jazz had on Becker and Fagen. Backed by such strong session players as drummers Steve Gadd, Paul Humphries, Bernard Purdie, and Jim Keltner, bassist Chuck Rainey, guitarists Larry Carlton, Steve Kahn, and Lee Ritenour, and saxophonists Tom Scott, Wayne Shorter, and Peter Christlieb, four of the seven songs on *Aja* reached the top forty: *Aja, Deacon Blues, Peg,* and *Josie*. While any of these four songs demonstrates the studio style of Steely Dan, *Peg* represents a more clearly distinguished fusion of rock and jazz elements. The verse is based on a Gospel-sounding progression, that is, a focus on subdominant to tonic chord relationships (C and G; F and C; G and D in this song). Saxophonist Tom Scott, one of the premier studio saxophone players of the time, is playing a synthesized saxophone-like instrument called a lyricon. The chorus also features the unique harmony vocals of Michael McDonald.

Listening Timeline 11-4

PEG (1977)
STEELY DAN
from *Aja*
Strophic form
Verse: Gospel I, IV, V progression in G
Chorus: Original progression in E minor
MCA MCAD-37214, 1984
3:51

Time	Section	Description
0:00	Introduction	Keyboard, drum, bass and lyricon play a descending major chord progression leading to the gospel progression of the verse.
0:16	Verse 1	Solo male vocal (Fagan) over the gospel progression.
0:40	Verse 2	Fills played by the lyricon (Scott).
1:06	Chorus	Multiple harmony vocals on "Peg," solo vocal on the rest of the phrase; multiple voices harmonize the next two lines; solo voice sings the last line ("it's your favorite . . .").
1:30	Interlude	Material from the introduction.
1:47	Solo	Guitar solo (Jay Graydon) over the verse progression.
2:11	Verse 2 repeated	
2:36	Chorus, sung twice	
3:09	Coda	Extension of the chorus and guitar solo; gradual fade out during the solo.

Steely Dan released one more album *(Gaucho)* after *Aja* and then went on an extended hiatus. They returned to recording in 2000 with the release of the album *Two Against Nature*, which was received with great critical acclaim and won four Grammy awards that year. Their next release, *Everything Must Go* (2003), won the Grammy for Album of the Year.

Art Rock

Another style that developed in the 1970s is one that combines elements of classical music with elements of rock, variously referred to as **art rock**, **classical-rock**, **eclectic rock**, and **progressive rock**. (Eclectic: composed of material gathered from various sources.) For some, the terms are perceived as critical and even derisive-snobbish, pretentious, self-important, and "lame affectations of cultured sensibilities" are all terms and phrases that have been applied to art rock. For others, the terms are often considered in a more positive light as being experimental, expanding the style in more artistic directions, using the musical language of rock to create important works of art, rather than being limited to the 2-1/2 minute, 3-chord song, and therefore comparable to works of art in the classical tradition.

Art rock musicians do not limit themselves to borrowings from the western European art music tradition. Some groups and individuals are influenced by and make use of musical material from the art music of other cultures, such as India, the Middle East, Latin America, and so on. There is a wide spectrum of combining art music traditions with rock music styles, on one end incorporating instruments from art music (violins, cellos, full orchestras) or ethnic instruments such as sitars and tablas and on the other end those artists who create large, multi-movement works for rock ensembles that are based on art music forms and genres such as symphonies, concertos, and operas. Within these wide boundaries, almost any rock song that has used traditional art music instruments may be considered an art rock song. That leaves a wide number of songs and artists in this style, including Elvis Presley, Buddy Holly, The Beach Boys, The Beatles, The Rolling Stones, Jimi Hendrix, Led Zeppelin, Bob Dylan, and so on. Yet the groups that most writers, critics, and rock fans are referring to when they use the term art rock are groups like Yes, Emerson, Lake, and Palmer, The Moody Blues, Genesis, King Crimson, and Pink Floyd, among others. So what is it about these latter groups that make their music **art rock**?

General Style Characteristics of Art Rock

(Not all of these style characteristics will appear in each and every art rock performance)

I. Sound
   A. Traditional art music instruments—violins, violas, cellos, flutes, etc. and full string orchestras
   B. Ethnic instruments—sitar, tabla, etc.
   C. Several keyboards including organs, electric and acoustic pianos, synthesizers
   D. Thick, polyphonic textures (i.e., many musical lines playing simultaneously)

II. Form
   A. More than the standard strophic type of rock song:
      1. Ternary forms (A B A)
      2. Sonata form borrowed from classical symphonies
      3. Rondo form borrowed from classical sonatas
      4. Opera
      5. Song cycles
   B. Concept albums—entire albums based on a single idea, songs are related by this idea (Beatles, *Sgt. Pepper*; Moody Blues, *Days of Future Passed*; Jethro Tull, *Thick As A Brick*)
   C. Forms or genres based on classical forms—concerto, suite (Deep Purple, *Concerto for Group and Orchestra*; The Nice, *Five Bridges Suite*; Yes, *Close to the Edge*)
   D. Rock interpretations of actual large-scale classical works (Emerson, Lake, and Palmer, *Pictures at an Exhibition*)

III. Harmony
  A. Extended harmonic progressions (i.e., beyond the standard blues progression)
  B. Extended chords (9ths, 11ths, 13ths)
  C. Unusual chord progressions adapted from classical works or inspired by classical composers

IV. Rhythm
  A. Use of odd meters—7/8, 5/4, 7/4, etc.—rather than standard 4/4 meter
  B. Unusual surface rhythms based on the accentuations of the text
  C. Often incorporate intricate polyrhythmic lines

V. Melody
  A. Long, lyrical melodies (as opposed to brief, motivic melodies)
  B. Some melodies are taken from preexisting classical works (ELP, *Knife Edge* adapted from Janacek, *Sinfonietta*)
  C. Melodies are usually woven into the song texture, not the most prominent part of the song
  D. There may be some thematic development
  E. Often based on modes, especially Middle Eastern modes, rather than major/minor scales

VI. Text
  A. Texts are often very poetic, usually of high quality
  B. Texts may deal with philosophical, social, or political issues

VII. Other
  A. Musicians are usually trained in classical music
  B. Generally have a high level of proficiency on their instruments
  C. Most art rock groups are from England

Practically every rock source states that the Beatles' *Sgt. Pepper's Lonely Hearts Club Band* album (1967) is the first significant album in the art rock vein because the group designed the album in a conceptual framework—i.e., it is usually considered to be the first concept album. It also includes the London Symphony Orchestra, besides other classical influences, and in this sense points toward the art rock groups of the 1970s. However, the first band to consistently experiment with classical elements and in essence embody the art rock style was the **Moody Blues**.

The Moody Blues

The Moody Blues began as a British beat group (formed in 1964) that copied American rhythm and blues and 1950s rock and roll. One of the original members of the group was singer/guitarist Denny Laine, who left the Moodys in 1966 and later became a member of Paul McCartney's band Wings. With Laine, the Moody Blues had a number one hit in England (number ten in the U.S.) with a cover of a rhythm and blues ballad, *Go Now* in 1964. After Laine left, the Moody Blues reassessed themselves and their music.

Laine was replaced by Justin Hayward and original bassist Clint Warwick was replaced by John Lodge in 1967; the rest of the band was already in place: Ray Thomas, flute, vocals; Mike Pinder, keyboards, vocals; and Graeme Edge, percussion, vocals. This line-up worked with the London Festival Orchestra in 1967 to create the album *Days of Future Passed* (1967).

The album is a suite of movements based on the single concept of time. It opens with an instrumental overture that is based on the various principal themes of each song on the album.

On the entire album, there is not a real blending of the band with the orchestra or a real blending of styles. Other than the "overture" and a few spots where the orchestra is used to emphasize a musical passage, the orchestra provides transitional material between the songs by the band. The orchestral style (and this is true of most art rock orchestral music) is patterned after that of the mid-19th century, resulting in a curious blend of a modern rock style and an outdated classical style. Perhaps the best-known song from the album is *Nights in White Satin*, which reached the number 2 spot on the sales charts when it was re-released in 1972.

Listening Timeline 11-5

NIGHTS IN WHITE SATIN (1967)
THE MOODY BLUES
from *Days of Future Passed*
Strophic form
Original progression in E minor
Deram 820 006-2, 1967
7:20

Time	Section	Description
0:00	Introduction	Flutes play melody from the song *Time to Get Away* earlier on the album, accompanied by strings and harp.
0:12		Solo acoustic guitar and drums begin chord progression and the 6/8 meter of *Nights*; bass enters also.
0:23	Verse 1	Solo male voice (Hayward) over the guitar, bass, and drums.
0:42	Verse 2	Strings play fills and background.
1:00	Chorus	Orchestra becomes louder, harmony voices sing in the background.
1:20	Verse 3	Softer sound in the strings.
1:39	Verse 4	
1:56	Chorus	
2:19	Solo	Solo flute (Thomas) accompanied by picked acoustic guitar and bass; strings and drums enter lightly on the third phrase.
3:13	Verse 1 repeated	
3:31	Verse 2 repeated	More strings plus oboe plays fills.
3:47	Chorus	Chorus repeated
4:10	Chorus/Coda	Sustained chord, orchestral sweep for the final cadence;
4:57		orchestra plays the verse melody softly, sustains chords, and crescendos to a
5:33		final cadence.
5:38		Bells, flutes, and harp.
5:54		Poem spoken over sustained string chords;
6:41		final orchestral flourish;

6:58	sustained chord;
7:06	gongbeat with fade.

The Moody Blues continued on into the 1970s producing several interesting albums including *In Search of the Lost Chord* (1968), *On the Threshold of a Dream* (1969), *Every Good Boy Deserves Favour* (1971), and their best selling album to that point, *Seventh Sojourn* (1972). After *Seventh Sojourn*, the band did not record any new material for six years though various band members released solo albums. In 1981, keyboardist Pinder was replaced by Patrick Moraz, who had replaced and then was himself replaced by Rick Wakeman in Yes. They released the album *Long Distance Voyager*, which included the song *Gemini Dream*. The album hit number one in the U.S. and *Gemini Dream* hit number fourteen. A 1986 release, *The Other Side of Life*, included the top twenty hit *Your Wildest Dreams*. The Moody Blues are still performing occasionally.

Emerson, Lake and Palmer

This group was formed in England in 1970 from the ashes of different bands. In the 1960s, keyboardist Keith Emerson was a member of the group **Nice**. This group arranged and recorded several pieces by classical composers for a rock quartet (keyboards, bass, guitar, and drums). Some of these pieces include the *Intermezzo* from Sibelius's *Karelia Suite*, the 3rd movement from Tchaikovsky's *Symphony 6* (the *Pathetique*), and a version of *America* by Leonard Bernstein from *West Side Story*. The Nice's version of *America* is played at an incredibly fast tempo and is interspersed with themes from the 4th movement of Czech composer Antonin Dvorak's *Symphony 9 in E Minor (From the New World)*. On their stage shows, the Nice used to burn an American flag behind them while playing this song as a protest to U.S. involvement in Vietnam. For this reason, composer Bernstein would never allow the group to play the song on their American tours.

At the time that Emerson was performing with the Nice, guitarist/bassist/singer Greg Lake was working with **King Crimson**, which included Robert Fripp on guitar and Ian McDonald on keyboards. Before Lake left to become one-third of Emerson, Lake, and Palmer, King Crimson recorded the album *In the Court of the Crimson King* (1969). Drummer Carl Palmer had lately been playing with Chris Farlowe, Atomic Rooster, and The Crazy World of Arthur Brown. The trio was formed in 1970 and debuted at the August 1970 Isle of Wight Festival. In 1971, they released their first album, Emerson, Lake, and Palmer which contained the single *Lucky Man*. The song *Knife Edge* is based on the opening theme of *Sinfonietta* by the Czech composer Leos Janacek.

Their first album was followed by the release of *Tarkus* (1971), which contained a suite of a futuristic nature, and a live rock version of Russian composer Modeste Mussorgsky's *Pictures at an Exhibition* (1971). By this time, fans were beginning to be disenchanted with the group, hearing a sameness in all three releases. What had been novel once was no longer novel after three albums, no matter how good the playing was. They then released the album *Trilogy* in 1972, followed by the release of *Brain Salad Surgery* (1973). It is on *Brain Salad Surgery* that Emerson, Lake, and Palmer achieve their best work, particularly on the three-part work *Karn Evil 9*.

The First Impression is in two parts, each consisting of several musical segments. Part I has three verses with an introduction, instrumental interludes, and a short codetta (closing an internal section), each verse is in two segments of verse and chorus, the chorus ("I'll be there") is announced by a descending bass pattern. The second interlude (after verse 2) is interrupted by a solo section.

The second part of the First Impression is of a completely different mood, more like a carnival sideshow. Part II opens with a fast introduction in 7/4 time followed by a short section of changing meters. This part consists of seven verses of an AAB form: two 4-bar phrases followed by a 4-bar refrain ("See the show"), which is announced by a 2-bar segment ("Roll up!"), similar to what occurred in Part I. There is an instrumental break after the third verse followed by a return to the sung verses. But verse 4 is a shortened version of the verse (AA) and is followed by a new section of music and text (CCD) rather than the expected "Roll up!" refrain. Verse five is even shorter (A) and followed by the new section in an abbreviated form (CD), and an instrumental break. Verse 6 follows the break with a return to the original form (AAB), and finally verse 7 presents two phrases (AA) followed by a coda with new music and words ("Come and see the show"). The instrumental section of the coda contains material from the introduction, and ends with a final series of chords leading to the final cadence of the movement.

Listening Timeline 11-6

KARN EVIL 9 1ST IMPRESSION
EMERSON, LAKE, AND PALMER
from *Brain Salad Surgery*
Two-part sectional form
Original progression in A-flat major
Victory 383 480 020-2, 1973
13:21

Part I

0:00	Introduction	Solo organ in relatively free time;
0:16		bass and drums enter and set the rhythm.
0:26	Verse A1	Solo male vocal (Emerson) against percussion rhythms and chromatic piano line in the bass range; organ, bass guitar, guitar, and drums fill between the sung phrases.
0:54	Chorus 1	Band accents the words of the chorus.
0:59	Interlude 1	Organ, bass guitar, guitar, and synthesizers play the figure from the introduction; brief solo by the organ (Emerson).
1:37	Verse A2	Vocal is accompanied by synthesizers; fills as before.
2:06	Chorus 1	
2:10	Interlude 1	
2:19	Solo	Synthesizer solo (Emerson), the tempo increases slightly, and there is a lighter texture in the bass and drums.
2:44	Interlude 1	
2:56	Verse A3	Vocal accompanied by drums, bass guitar, synthesizer, and organ.
3:17	Chorus 1a	
3:25	Transition	Tempo slows a bit; organ, bass, and drums play;
3:37		sustained chords with gong introduce Part II

Part II

3:42	Introduction	Organ, synthesizer, bass guitar, and drums play introductory figure in 7/4 meter.
4:32	Interlude 2	Descending scale patterns in bass guitar and keyboards;
4:52		Change to 4/4 time, quick pulse is established leading to new verse, with synthesizer solos and organ fills.
5:22	Verse B1	Solo vocal over a carnival-like atmosphere.
5:41	Chorus 2	
5:55	Verse B2	
6:14	Chorus 2	
6:28	Verse B3	
6:47	Chorus 2	
6:59	Interlude 3	Featuring guitar solo (Lake) over an active keyboard and drum riff;
7:32		lyrical guitar melody;
8:01		descending scale patterns on guitar
8:14		lyrical guitar melody in a minor key;
8:35		add synthesizer and tambourine.
8:42	Verse B4	
8:57	Verse C1	Organ becomes more prominent; drums and
9:05		bass enter.
9:12	Chorus 3	
9:20	Verse B5	
9:28	Verse C1 repeated	
9:35	Chorus 3 repeated	
9:43	Interlude 4	Guitar and cowbell set the rhythm; organ solo;
10:37	Interlude 3	lyrical guitar scale patterns;
10:59		descending guitar scale patterns;
11:12		lyrical guitar melody in a minor key;
11:33		drums play fill
11:39	Verse B6	Sung over intricate drum rhythms; drum pattern slows and keyboards enter for second part of the verse.
11:56	Chorus 2	
12:08	Verse B7	
12:23	Coda	
12:51		Return of interlude 3; gradual ritardando
13:11		"See the show" ends the movement on a final, conclusive cadence.

Fusions **231**

ELP released a triple live set in 1974, *Welcome Back My Friends to the Show That Never Ends*, based on the *Brain Salad Surgery* album. For the next three years, the group did not have any releases. They released the double album *Works, Volume I* in 1977, followed by *Works, Volume II* (1978) and *Love Beach* (1978), both of which were very disappointing. After releasing a live album and a greatest hits album, the group virtually disappeared as each member followed their own interests. In 1986, Emerson and Lake regrouped with drummer Cozy Powell (ex-Jeff Beck Group and ex-Ritchie Blackmore's Rainbow). Powell was replaced in 1988 by drummer Robert Berry for the album *The Power of Three* which did not sell very well at all. In 1992, original drummer Palmer was back for the release of *Black Moon* (1992).

Yes

Yes is a British group that formed in 1968 consisting of **Jon Anderson** (vocals), **Chris Squire** (bass), **Bill Bruford** (drums), **Peter Banks** (guitar), and **Tony Kaye** (organ). With this line-up, the band released their first two albums, *Yes* (1969) and *Time and a Word* (1970). The album *Yes* is described as a collection of Beatles and Byrds covers expanded to "almost unrecognizable extravaganzas," a sound that was influenced by Emerson and the Nice. *Time and a Word* was followed by *The Yes Album* (1971), which contained the songs *Yours Is No Disgrace*, *Starship Trooper*, and *I've Seen All Good People*. For *The Yes Album*, Banks had been replaced by guitarist Steve Howe. Also, keyboardist Tony Kaye added synthesizers and all the material on the album was original songs.

In 1971, after the release of *The Yes Album*, Kaye was replaced by keyboardist Rick Wakeman who brought with him an incredible array of keyboard instruments including acoustic piano, electric piano, organ, mellotron, clavinet, harpsichord, and various synthesizers. Wakeman had been a classically trained musician, and he will be discussed at greater length momentarily when we consider his solo career. At this point, Wakeman's classical training coincided perfectly with the direction that the other band members wanted to explore. With Wakeman in the line-up, Yes released the critically acclaimed album *Fragile* (1972), which reached the number four position on the album charts and had a successful top-twenty single in the song *Roundabout* (number 13, 1972).

The song opens with a backward tape of sound that breaks into harmonics on the guitar, in free time. At the end of the intro, the guitar plays a descending melody that establishes the tempo. The bass and drums play an 8-bar riff that becomes the basis of the verses, solo, and instrumental sections of the song.

Listening Timeline 11-7

ROUNDABOUT (1972)
YES
from *Fragile*
Strophic form
Original progression in E minor
Atlantic A2 19132, 1972
8:28

Time	Section	Description
0:00	Introduction	Single tone, mixed backwards so tone crescendos rather than decays;
0:08		Acoustic nylon-string guitar (Howe) plays harmonics and a slow melodic figure twice;
0:23		backwards tone and acoustic guitar material played again;
0:40		descending figure on the acoustic guitar leads to the basic riff of the verse.

0:58	Verse 1	Solo male vocal (Anderson) over guitars, bass, and drum riff in E minor; organ enters on last line.
1:18	Transition	Full band plays the E minor riff.
1:25	Verse 2	High harmony vocals added on lines 2 and 3.
1:45	Chorus	Harmonized vocals; electric guitar is more prominent; organ plays fills; drums and bass added.
2:15	Transition	E minor riff with organ fills.
2:29	Verse 3	
2:49	Chorus	
3:25	Interlude 1	Minor riff by guitar and bass;
3:40		dual vocals; gradually adds keyboards (synthesizers and organ) and guitars;
4:36		First line of verse 1 is repeated twice.
4:57	Introduction returns	
5:33	Chorus	Abridged to use only the first, second, and last lines.
5:50	Interlude 2	Hard rock sound with organ solo and electric guitar solo.
7:05	Verse 1	Second voice harmonizes entire verse.
7:24	Chorus	Entire chorus is sung.
7:55	Coda	Multiple voices ("da da da . . .") in harmony; other voices ("doot doot . . .") are added counter to other voices in a syncopated rhythm over a steady drum feel.
8:20		Song ends with acoustic and electric guitars playing the descending figure of the introduction to end on a sustained E major chord.

This line-up of Yes also recorded and released the album *Close to the Edge* (1972) before drummer Bruford left to play with King Crimson. Bruford was replaced by Alan White, who had played a bit with the Plastic Ono Band. With White on drums, the group released the triple live album *Yessongs* (1973) and the double album *Tales from Topographic Oceans* (1973) before Wakeman left to pursue his own career.

Wakeman was replaced in 1974 by keyboardist **Patrick Moraz** for the albums *Relayer* (1974) and *Yesterdays* (1975). Wakeman returned to the group for the albums *Going for the One* (1977) and *Tormato* (1978), neither of which sold very well. Wakeman finally left and returned to his own solo projects. After 1978, Yes went through various personnel changes, primarily on keyboards. Singer Anderson left after *Tormato* to do some solo projects, but returned in 1983 for the album *90125*, which featured the group's best selling single, *Owner of a Lonely Heart*, which reached number one on the *Billboard* sales charts. This line-up consisted of Anderson, Squire, White, Kaye, and guitarist Trevor Rabin. In 1991, the band was re-formed with Anderson, Wakeman, Squire, Kaye, White, and Howe; this line-up released the album *The New Union* (1991).

Rick Wakeman

When Rick Wakeman left Yes in 1974, he embarked on a very successful solo career. Wakeman was from a very musical family—his father was a professional pianist and Rick had been classically trained from the age of four. When he finished his public schooling, Wakeman attended the Royal College of Music and began making a name for himself as a session musician. He eventually gave up his studies in favor of a recording career. As a studio musician, Wakeman has appeared on recordings by David Bowie, T. Rex, Al Stewart, and Cat Stevens. In 1970, Wakeman was persuaded to join a newly formed group called The Strawbs, where he remained for the next 16 months until he replaced Tony Kaye in Yes. While with Yes, Wakeman quickly became a keyboard star and began to record solo projects. The first solo album he released was *The Six Wives of Henry VIII* (1973), while still a member of Yes. Bassist Squire and drummer Bruford from Yes also performed on this album, but it is primarily a showcase for Wakeman's multi-keyboard set-up.

Wakeman continued to record his own projects in the 1970s and 1980s and also took a turn with composing music for films. Some of his most remarkable work is *Journey to the Center of the Earth* (1974), *The Myths and Legends of King Arthur and the Knights of the Round Table* (1975), and *Rick Wakeman's Criminal Record* (1977). The *Criminal Record* is a concept album dealing with crimes and criminals, such as *Crime of Passion*, *The Birdman of Alcatraz*, etc. One of the most fascinating pieces on this album is *Chamber of Horrors*, a somewhat programmatic expression of the famous exhibit at Madame Tussaud's Wax Works in London. *Chamber of Horrors* is composed in a classical structure known as sonata form. In sonata form, there are three distinct sections (A B A) in which the A section features three main ideas or themes (primary theme, secondary theme, closing theme), the B section expands on or develops these themes, and the final A section presents the main themes of the first section again. In addition, *Chamber of Horrors* begins with a slow introduction and ends with a somewhat lengthy coda. These are the same structural elements found in the piano compositions and orchestral works of Mozart and Beethoven, among others.

Listening Timeline 11-8

CHAMBER OF HORRORS (1977)
RICK WAKEMAN
from *Rick Wakeman's Criminal Record*
A B A' quasi sonata form
Original progression in E minor
A & M SP-4660, 1977
6:43

Time	Section	Description
0:00	Introduction	Slow tempo introduction with piano, synthesizers, organ, drums, and bass; the meter alternates
0:33		between 4/4 and 6/4; the primary theme is introduced on a synthesizer;
0:51		the full band plays the main theme.
1:21		Synthesizer, bass, and vibraphone play a new, light melodic theme in a major key over chords in the piano; this new theme will return later as an important theme in the work.
1:45	Exposition (A)	An abrupt shift in tempo moves this section faster as the primary theme in E minor played by the synthesizer, bass, and drums.

2:14	Transition	Harmonically unstable, the transition leads to a modulation in a new key and a new thematic idea.
2:50		Third new theme, acting as a closing idea, in a new key (F major); the synthesizers have a distorted, calliope-like sound; this section cadences in the new key.
3:31	Development (B)	Returns to the original E minor key. The primary theme is developed using augmentation (doubling the time value of notes), diminution (halving the time value of notes) and is treated like a fugue, with the melody played several times like a round (imitation).
4:17		The secondary theme from the introduction (light, major key) recurs in the synthesizers, accompanied by piano and bass;
4:39	Retransition	Sets up the dominant chord for a return of the original melodic ideas in the tonic key.
4:59	Recapitulation (A')	The primary theme returns in the original key with countermelodies in various keyboards;
5:27		Second theme returns in E major (tonic major).
5:56	Coda	Primary theme comes back in the organ and the bass;
6:32		Sudden stop, woman screams, and a final sustained chord in E major.

Wakeman has had a fairly successful career on his own, though he has frequently returned to tour and record with Yes.

Pink Floyd

This British band was formed in 1966 from the remains of several other bands. The Pink Floyd Sound, as the band was originally known, consisted of **Syd Barrett** (guitar, vocals), **Bob Close** (guitar), **Roger Waters** (bass), **Nick Mason** (drums), and **Rick Wright** (keyboards); this band played blues and rhythm and blues covers. As Barrett gradually became more involved with psychedelic drugs (i.e., LSD), the music tended to expand in length, to include long, detailed improvisations, and to also incorporate more electronic effects. As they progressed to more psychedelic music, guitarist Close was eliminated from the band and Pink Floyd became a four-piece outfit.

The band released some singles in early 1967—*Arnold Layne* and *See Emily Play*—that reached the top twenty in England. Both singles were composed by Barrett. These singles and their backing sides were in the psychedelic style: much electronic distortion, image-laden lyrics, a generally distorted, fuzzy recording quality, the use of feedback, free improvisation, and some drug references in the lyrics. The song *Candy and a Currant Bun*, the flip side of *Arnold Layne*, clearly demonstrates the psychedelic sound of Pink Floyd.

Listening Timeline 11-9

CANDY AND A CURRANT BUN (1967)
PINK FLOYD
from *Pink Floyd 1967/The First 3 Singles*
Strophic form
Simple alternation of A and G
EMI 7243 9 59895, 1977

Time	Section	Description
0:00	Introduction	Sustained fuzz and distorted guitar.
0:08	Verse 1	Solo male vocal (Barrett), heavily distorted against distorted guitar and bass; high harmony vocal in the back; key is mostly in A.
0:23	Refrain	Whispered vocal; key is mostly in G;' ends with A, B, C, G, A chords that will be used later to end the song.
0:38	Verse 2	
0:54	Refrain	
1:09	Instrumental interlude	Distorted guitars (Barrett) and keyboards (Wright) solo on A.
1:49	Refrain	
2:05	Verse 1 repeated	
2:19	Coda	Instrumental based on the refrain; ends with A, B, C, G, A chords ending on a heavily distorted sustained chord.

In the summer of 1967, Pink Floyd released their first album, *Piper at the Gates of Dawn*, which clearly demonstrates the dominance of Syd Barrett. Out of 10 songs, two were instrumental collaborations by the whole band and one was penned by Waters; the rest were all by Barrett. Barrett's songs in general are full of childlike images that combine an impression of innocence with that of anxiety or danger. Barrett's guitar work is described as highly innovative, expressive, and unpredictable. At some points, lyrical melodic solos turn into harsh dissonant sections to almost jazz-like improvisations. His guitar work is a very good complement to Wright's keyboard style. A good example of the band's sound can be found in the song *Astronomy Domine*, the opening cut of the album.

The Piper at the Gates of Dawn, which was recorded at EMI Records' Abbey Road studios, shows a definite influence of the Beatles, who were recording *Sgt. Pepper* at the same time and place; the Beatles album also demonstrates a reciprocal influence from the Floyd album. Floyd's album was in fact recorded by the same recording engineer who had worked with George Martin and the Beatles on every album up through *Rubber Soul*.

In early 1968, Barrett began to behave more erratic, possibly a side effect of his many hallucinogenic trips. At some performances it was said that Barrett just froze on stage and played nothing. In February 1968, guitarist **David Gilmour** was brought in to replace Barrett, who finally left the band in April. Barrett contributed two songs to the Floyd's next album, *A Saucerful of Secrets*; the remaining pieces were by Waters and Wright. This album continued the practice of extended improvisations and electronic effects and the group soon attracted the attention of various film directors and producers who wanted to use Pink Floyd's music in their soundtracks.

The title track of the album, *A Saucerful of Secrets*, is the only cut on the album credited to all the band members (except Barrett). It is a long instrumental suite, that is a collection of several songs connected together. Gilmour describes the piece as the "aural equivalent of a war. The first part is tension, a build up . . . and the middle part, with all the crashing and banging—that's the war going on. The aftermath is a sort of a requiem."[2]

Gilmour goes on to add that the title track is "the first clue to our direction forwards . . . If you take *Saucerful of Secrets*, the track *Atom Heart Mother*, then the track *Echoes*—all lead quite logically towards *Dark Side of the Moon* and what comes after it."³

Listening Timeline 11-10

A SAUCERFUL OF SECRETS (1968)
PINK FLOYD
from *A Saucerful of Secrets*
Ternary A B C form
Atonal soundscape
Capitol CDP 7 46383, 1968
11:53

0:00	**The Buildup (A):**	A soft, gradual entry of keyboards and percussion; the strings inside the piano are strummed; there is a gradual crescendo and the harmony becomes increasingly discordant; several sounds are gradually mixed in. A sudden stop signals that the war is about to begin.
4:01	**The War (B):**	The drums gradually enter with a militaristic beat; piano and other keyboards also enter and synthesized sounds are used; there is a gradual crescendo as a distorted guitar enters; the sound becomes more and more discordant; everything increases in volume and distortion. This section ends with a rumbling bass sound, simulating a huge explosion.
7:16	**Requiem (C):**	The church organ sound gradually emerges from the rumbling explosion that ended the second section; various percussion and synthesized sounds add to the solemn feeling of this section. The entire section sounds very funereal, as if it is a Requiem Mass for all mankind. Vocal "ahs" at the end intone solemn sounding chords against the organ and bass synthesizer. Sweeping synthesized strings bring the piece to a close on a major chord, possibly suggesting that some hope still exists.

After leaving Pink Floyd, Barrett began a solo recording career and released the album *The Madcap Laughs* in 1969 and *Barrett* in 1970. Both albums are similar in structure and content to the work he did on the early Pink Floyd albums, but the music itself often sounds awkward and without purpose. As one of Barrett's friends stated, the music was "all going on in his head, but only little bits of it manage to come out of his mouth."⁴ As the 1970s wore on, Barrett became more reclusive and stayed away from the public spotlight.

After a period of touring and releasing live concert albums, Pink Floyd released the album *Atom Heart Mother* (1970), which reached the top of the British charts that year. The title track, which is a suite of six movements, is a collaborative effort by the whole band and electronic music composer Ron Geesin. The principal theme was derived from a chord sequence that Gilmour had written and called *Theme from an Imaginary Western*. Waters concluded that the theme had a "heroic, plodding quality . . . like some very heavy movie score."⁵ Waters and Wright were inspired to add other themes to the one Gilmour had written, and the piece, which had been retitled *The Amazing Pudding*, began to take shape. Geesin was hired to score brass fanfares and choral parts for the suite.

The end result is a massive, sweeping expression that is surprisingly conventional from one of England's most progressive rock bands. The final title was suggested by a news story about a pregnant woman with an atomic-powered pacemaker, headlined "Atom Heart Mother." In retrospect, Gilmour describes Atom Heart Mother as a "load of rubbish" because they really didn't know what they were doing. Waters is also of this opinion. However, the album was hugely successful in England and was Floyd's first number one album. It is in step with other art rock examples of the time, such as Emerson, Lake and Palmer's releases and Yes' releases. And, as drummer Mason points out, it enabled the group to think on the scale of the song *Echoes*, from *Meddle*, and subsequent concept albums.

The album *Meddle* (1971) was the first post-Barrett Pink Floyd album to really define the sound of the group. The masterpiece of the *Meddle* album was the full-side song *Echoes*, another collaboration by the entire band. *Echoes* is full of slow 4/4 tempos that gradually build to dramatic crescendos and then veer off into unexpected musical directions. It is described by Waters as an "epic sound poem." Supposedly, *Echoes* was made up of bits of material taped by the individual band members who went into the recording studio individually and recorded whatever ideas occurred to them at the moment. There was no concern for any general plan, key, chord progression, or any other kind of unifying device. Organization came later when the tapes were put together for the album.

After *Meddle*, Floyd released the soundtrack album to the film *La Vallée*, entitled *Obscured by Clouds* (1972). The album which has proven to be the most successful Pink Floyd album, and in fact one of the most successful rock albums ever, was their next release, *Dark Side of the Moon* (1973). *Dark Side of the Moon* is a skillful blend of sound effects and speech fragments with music and studio technology. It begins with a gradual fade in of a human heart beat interspersed with various spoken lines: "I've been mad for fucking years," "I've always been mad, I *know* I've been mad." These break into a steady ticking of a clock and synchronized cash registers, until the rising tension finds release in the first chords of the album. There is an underlying tone of pessimism in Waters' songs, perhaps the opposite of the romantic idealism of Barrett's earlier songs. It is this album that is the culmination of all of the preceding albums. The album contains the band's first American top twenty hit, *Money*, and is the longest-charting album in history, staying on *Billboard's* album charts for over thirteen years, dropping off the chart in 1988. It is the fourth best-selling album of all time, after Michael Jackson's *Thriller*, the soundtrack to *Saturday Night Fever*, and Fleetwood Mac's *Rumours*.

The songs on *Dark Side of the Moon* are studies in the side of human nature that is usually kept hidden. *Time* discusses the dangers of procrastination and wasting time; *Money* is a song about greed and how money is the root of all humanity's evils. The last two songs, *Brain Damage* and *Eclipse*, deal with the question of insanity and the fear that material things can be lost with a sudden change of fortune, respectively. Ultimately, Waters states, everything good can be suddenly and inexplicably overshadowed by bad.

Listening Timeline 11-11a

BRAIN DAMAGE (1973)
PINK FLOYD
from *Dark Side of the Moon*
Strophic form
Verse: Original progression in D
Refrain: Original progression in G
Capitol CDP 7 46001 2, 1973
3:50

Time	Section	Description
0:00	Introduction	Emerges out of the preceding song *Any Colour You Like*. Electric guitar picks the chord pattern using first position D chord, accompanied by bass and drums.
0:15	Verse 1	Guitar picking pattern continues; solo male vocal.
0:44	Verse 2	
1:16	Refrain	Add organ and drums, with backing vocals; the lead part is harmonized with two voices.
1:48	Verse 3	Solo voice, but it is harmonized on the last two lines of the verse; "mad" sounding laughter (Syd?) appears.
2:17		The second half of the verse is repeated with new words.
2:35	Refrain	Add women's vocals as backup.
3:07	Interlude	Synthesizers, guitars, bass, and drums play the verse progression; spoken words are heard under the music with some laughing. The song segues immediately into *Eclipse*.

Listening Timeline 11-11b

ECLIPSE (1973)
PINK FLOYD
from *Dark Side of the Moon*
Through-composed list song
Original descending progression in D (D, D/C, B-flat, A)
Capitol CDP 7 46001 2, 1973
1:54

Time	Section	Description
0:00	Introduction	Solo organ (Wright), guitars, drums, and bass emerge from the last chord of *Brain Damage*. The song is a series of lists that are stated in four-bar phrases.
0:11		
0:21		
0:32		
0:42		
0:53		Solo woman's voice enters in the background.
1:03		
1:14	Tag ending	Song ends with a sustained note and a stop. The last sound on the recording is the heart beat that began the album.

The next album, *Wish You Were Here* (1975), is a tribute to Syd Barrett. Though unable to top the masterpiece *Dark Side of the Moon*, the album sold relatively well. They toured throughout 1976 and recorded the album *Animals* which was released in January 1977. The various band members worked on individual projects for the next couple of years as fans began to speculate that the group had disbanded. In 1979, Pink Floyd released *The Wall*, an album that reveals further the pessimistic psyche of Roger Waters. A film version was released in 1982 which starred Boomtown Rats vocalist Bob Geldoff as the unhappy protagonist Pink Floyd. Several of Pink's illusions and delusions were portrayed with psychedelic animated sequences.

Listening Timeline 11-12

COMFORTABLY NUMB
(1979)
PINK FLOYD
from *The Wall*
Strophic form
Verse: Descending minor
Progression in B minor
Chorus: I–V progression in D
Columbia C2K 68519, 1997
6:19

Time	Section	Description
0:00	Introduction	Bass, drums, and guitar play a sustained B minor chord.
0:07	Verse 1	solo male voice (Waters) over the descending progression of the band.
0:54	Chorus	Key change to D major; more synthesizers are used.
2:05	Solo 1	Lead guitar (Gilmour) plays on the chorus progression; the last line of the chorus ("I have become . . .") is restated.
2:35		
2:47	Verse 2	B minor progression.
3:17	Chorus	D major progression.
4:33	Solo 2	Lead guitar solos over the verse progression. The solo gradually builds in intensity, reaching its highest point, then fades.

The last release by the complete band was *The Final Cut* (1983), which emphasized Waters' dominance of the group with more bleak interpretations of modern society. Shortly after the release of *The Final Cut*, Mason left to pursue a career in auto racing while the other band members carried on with various solo projects. In 1987, Wright, Gilmour and Mason began touring and recording again as Pink Floyd. Their stage shows, which featured many of the props that had been used earlier such as the flying pig, and the use of the name Pink Floyd caused ex-band member Waters to sue the others because he felt that he was the main creative force behind the band. Waters lost and Pink Floyd (Wright, Gilmour, and Mason) released *A Momentary Lapse of Reason* (1987) and *The Delicate Sound of Thunder* (1988). In the summer of 1995, Gilmour, Wright, and Mason reunited to record a new Pink Floyd album and for an international tour.

Endnotes

1. Joe Stuessy and Scott Lipscomb, *Rock and Roll: Its History and Stylistic Development*, third edition (Upper Saddle River, NJ: Prentice Hall, 1999), p. 264.
2. Nicholas Schaffner, *A Saucerful of Secrets* (New York: Delta, 1991), p. 133.
3. ibid., pp. 134–135.
4. ibid., p. 116.
5. ibid., p. 151.